Mercedes-Benz 190 Owners Workshop Manual

John S Mead

Models covered
Mercedes-Benz 190 & 190 E
1997 cc petrol engine

Does not cover Diesel engine, 190 E 2.3-16 or 190 E 2.6 models

THE BOOK ®

(928-4S1)

ABCDE FGHIJ K

Haynes Publishing Group
Sparkford Nr Yeovil
Somerset BA22 7JJ England

Haynes Publications, Inc
861 Lawrence Drive
Newbury Park
California 91320 USA

Acknowledgements

Thanks are due to the Champion Sparking Plug Company Limited, who supplied the illustrations showing the spark plug conditions, and to Duckhams Oils, who provided lubrication data. Certain illustrations are the copyright of Mercedes-Benz (United Kingdom) Limited, and are used with their permission. Thanks are also due to Sykes-Pickavant Limited who provided some of the workshop tools, and to all those people at Sparkford who helped in the production of this manual.

© **Haynes Publishing Group 1991**

A Book in the **Haynes Owners Workshop Manual Series**

Printed by J. H. Haynes & Co. Ltd., Sparkford, Nr Yeovil Somerset BA22 7JJ, England

ISBN 0 85696 928 1

British Library Cataloguing in Publication Data
Mead, John S. *1950-*
    Mercedes-Benz 190 owners workshop manual.
    1. Cars. Maintenance & repair – Amateurs'
    manuals
    I. Title   II. Series
    629.28'722
    ISBN 0-85696-928-1

Restoring and Preserving our Motoring Heritage

Few people can have had the luck to realise their dreams to quite the same extent and in such a remarkable fashion as John Haynes, Founder and Chairman of the Haynes Publishing Group.

Since 1965 his unique approach to workshop manual publishing has proved so successful that millions of Haynes Manuals are now sold every year throughout the world, covering literally thousands of different makes and models of cars, vans and motorcycles.

A continuing passion for cars and motoring led to the founding in 1985 of a Charitable Trust dedicated to the restoration and preservation of our motoring heritage. To inaugurate the new Museum, John Haynes donated virtually his entire private collection of 52 cars.

Now with an unrivalled international collection of over 210 veteran, vintage and classic cars and motorcycles, the Haynes Motor Museum in Somerset is well on the way to becoming one of the most interesting Motor Museums in the world.

A 70 seat video cinema, a cafe and an extensive motoring bookshop, together with a specially constructed one kilometre motor circuit, make a visit to the Haynes Motor Museum a truly unforgettable experience.

Every vehicle in the museum is preserved in as near as possible mint condition and each car is run every six months on the motor circuit.

Enjoy the picnic area set amongst the rolling Somerset hills. Peer through the William Morris workshop windows at cars being restored, and browse through the extensive displays of fascinating motoring memorabilia.

From the 1903 Oldsmobile through such classics as an MG Midget to the mighty 'E' Type Jaguar, Lamborghini, Ferrari Berlinetta Boxer, and Graham Hill's Lola Cosworth, there is something for everyone, young and old alike, at this Somerset Museum.

Haynes Motor Museum

Situated mid-way between London and Penzance, the Haynes Motor Museum is located just off the A303 at Sparkford, Somerset (home of the Haynes Manual) and is open to the public 7 days a week all year round, except Christmas Day and Boxing Day.

Contents

4

Mercedes-Benz 190

About this manual

Its aim

The aim of this manual is to help you get the best value from your vehicle. It can do so in several ways. It can help you decide what work must be done (even should you choose to get it done by a garage), provide information on routine maintenance and servicing, and give a logical course of action and diagnosis when random faults occur. However, it is hoped that you will use the manual by tackling the work yourself. On simpler jobs it may even be quicker than booking the car into a garage and going there twice, to leave and collect it. Perhaps most important, a lot of money can be saved by avoiding the costs a garage must charge to cover its labour and overheads.

The manual has drawings and descriptions to show the function of the various components so that their layout can be understood. Then the tasks are described and photographed in a step-by-step sequence so that even a novice can do the work.

Its arrangement

The manual is divided into twelve Chapters, each covering a logical sub-division of the vehicle. The Chapters are each divided into Sections, numbered with single figures, eg 5; and the Sections into paragraphs (or sub-sections), with decimal numbers following on from the Section they are in, eg 5.1, 5.2, 5.3 etc.

It is freely illustrated, especially in those parts where there is a detailed sequence of operations·to be carried out. There are two forms of illustration: figures and photographs. The figures are numbered in sequence with decimal numbers, according to their position in the Chapter – eg Fig. 6.4 is the fourth drawing/illustration in Chapter 6. Photographs carry the same number (either individually or in related groups) as the Section or sub-section to which they relate.

There is an alphabetical index at the back of the manual as well as a contents list at the front. Each Chapter is also preceded by its own individual contents list.

References to the 'left' or 'right' of the vehicle are in the sense of a person in the driver's seat facing forwards.

Unless otherwise stated, nuts and bolts are removed by turning anti-clockwise, and tightened by turning clockwise.

Vehicle manufacturers continually make changes to specifications and recommendations, and these, when notified, are incorporated into our manuals at the earliest opportunity.

Whilst every care is taken to ensure that the information in this manual is correct, no liability can be accepted by the authors or publishers for loss, damage or injury caused by any errors in, or omissions from, the information given.

Project vehicles

The main project vehicle used in the preparation of this manual, and appearing in many of the photographic sequences was a 1985 Mercedes-Benz 190. Additional work was carried out and photographed on Mercedes-Benz 190 E models with both manual and automatic transmission.

Introduction to the Mercedes-Benz 190

The Mercedes-Benz 190 was launched in Europe at the end of 1982, and introduced into the UK in September of the following year. The innovative new model heralded a departure from traditional Mercedes thinking, and marked the first venture into the medium-sized saloon market by one of the world's most respected manufacturers of large quality cars.

All cars feature traditional, solid, practical Mercedes design and engineering, with new advances in automotive technology, foremost amongst these being the meticulous attention to ride quality and handling. This has been achieved by further refining the proven MacPherson strut front suspension arrangement, used extensively by other manufacturers but not previously by Mercedes, and combining this with a new multi-link independent rear suspension.

The model range is not extensive, offering just one body style, but with a choice of engines and options to enhance the package. The cars covered by this manual are all four door saloons powered by a 1997 cc four cylinder overhead camshaft engine, with carburettor induction on 190 models, or electronic fuel injection on 190 E models. The engine is mounted longitudinally, and drives the rear wheels through a five-speed manual gearbox, or four-speed automatic transmission.

Full instrumentation is provided, together with power steering and central locking, and additional options which include electric windows, electric sunroof and air conditioning.

General dimensions, weights and capacities

Dimensions
Overall length	4420 mm (174.1 in)
Overall width	1678 mm (66.1 in)
Overall height	1390 mm (54.8 in)
Wheelbase	2665 mm (105.0 in)
Front track	1437 mm (56.6 in)
Rear track	1418 mm (55.9 in)

Weights
Kerb weight:	
190	1130 kg (2491.7 lb)
190 E	1140 kg (2513.7 lb)
Gross vehicle weight:	
190	1630 kg (3594.2 lb)
190 E	1640 kg (3616.2 lb)
Maximum roof rack load	100 kg (200.5 lb)
Maximum luggage compartment load	100 kg (220.5 lb)
Maximum trailer load:	
Unbraked trailer	600 kg (1323.0 lb)
Braked trailer	1200 kg (2646.0 lb)
Maximum loading on trailer drawbar	75 kg (165.4 lb)

Capacities
Engine oil:	
Engine codes 102.921 and 102.961 KE:	
Total capacity	5.0 litres (8.8 Imp pints)
Refill with filter change	4.5 litres (7.9 Imp pints)
Engine codes 102.924 and 102.962 KE:	
Total capacity	5.5 litres (9.7 Imp pints)
Refill with filter change	5.0 litres (8.8 Imp pints)
Cooling system (including heater)	8.5 litres (15.0 Imp pints)
Fuel tank	55 litres (12.1 Imp gal)
Manual gearbox	1.5 litres (2.6 Imp pints)
Automatic transmission:	
Total capacity	6.6 litres (11.6 Imp pints)
Drain and refill	5.5 litres (9.7 Imp pints)
Final drive differential	0.7 litres (1.2 Imp pints)
Power steering reservoir	0.6 litres (1.1 Imp pints)

Jacking, towing and wheel changing

Jacking and wheel changing

To change a roadwheel, first remove the spare wheel and jack, which are located under the luggage compartment floor. If the wheel is being changed at the roadside, remove the hazard warning triangle from the boot lid and set this up on the road to face the oncoming traffic. Firmly apply the handbrake and engage 1st gear, or move the selector lever to 'P' if automatic transmisson is fitted. Chock the wheel diagonally opposite the one to be changed.

Using both hands, pull off the wheel trim (where fitted) or carefully release it using a screwdriver if tight (photo). Loosen the wheel bolts with the tool provided, but do not remove them at this stage.

Withdraw the protective cap out of the jack engagement point on the sill, which is located just in front of the rear wheels or just behind the front wheels. Insert the jack fully into the hole, and position it so that it is vertical, as viewed from the side. Raise the car until the wheel is clear of the ground but still just dragging. Undo the wheel bolts and remove the wheel. Reposition the jack if necessary so that the spare wheel can be slipped on without having to lift it, then fit the wheel. Insert the wheel bolts and lightly tighten them. Lower the car, refit the protective cap, then tighten the wheel bolts evenly and in a diagonal sequence. Refit the wheel trim then stow the tools and the wheel in the luggage compartment. Don't forget to retrieve the warning triangle.

When jacking up the car with a trolley jack, position the jack beneath a sturdy part of the vehicle underbody, such as the reinforced chassis sections behind the front wheels, and in front of the rear wheels, or the crossmember under the engine. Do not jack up the car by means of the sump, or any of the suspension or steering components. Supplement the jack using axle stands or sturdy blocks. Never work under, around, or near a raised car unless it is adequately supported in at least two places.

Towing

Towing eyes are fitted to the front and rear of the vehicle for attachment of a tow-rope. The rear towing eye is below the bumper on the right-hand side, and the front towing eye is behind a detachable flap under the bumper on the right-hand side also. Always unlock the steering if the vehicle is being towed, and remember that the brake servo is inoperative if the engine is not running.

If automatic transmission is fitted, the selector lever must be in the 'N' position when being towed. With the rear wheels on the ground, the maximum towing distance should not exceed 74 miles (120 km), and the towing speed must be kept down to a maximum of 30 mph (50 kph). Whenever possible, a trailer should be used for transporting automatic transmission models, particularly if transmission damage is suspected.

Remove the wheel trim using both hands

Vehicle jack inserted in one of the front lifting holes

Using a screwdriver to remove the wheel trim

Pull out the flap for access to the front towing eye

Buying spare parts and vehicle identification numbers

Buying spare parts

Spare parts are available from many sources, Mercedes-Benz have many dealers throughout the country and other dealers, accessory stores and motors factors will also stock Mercedes-Benz spare parts. Our advice regarding spare parts sources is as follows.

Officially appointed vehicle main dealers: This is the best source of parts which are peculiar to your vehicle and are otherwise not generally available (eg, complete cylinder heads, internal transmission components, badges, interior trim etc). It is also the only place at which you should buy parts if your vehicle is still under warranty. To be sure of obtaining the correct parts it will always be necessary to give the storeman your vehicle's engine and chassis number, and if possible to take the 'old' part along for positive identification. Remember that many parts are available on a factory exchange scheme – any parts returned should always be clean! It obviously makes good sense to go straight to the specialists on your vehicle for this type of part for they are best equipped to supply you.

Other dealers and auto accessory shops – These are often very good places to buy materials and components needed for the maintenance of your car (eg, oil filters, spark plugs, bulbs, fan belts, oil and greases, touch-up paint, filler paste etc). They also sell general accessories, usually have convenient opening hours, charge lower prices and can

often be found not far from home.

Motor factors – Good factors will stock all of the more important components which wear out relatively quickly (eg, clutch components, pistons, valves, exhaust systems, brake cylinders/pipes/hoses/seals/shoes and pads etc). Motor factors will often provide new or reconditioned components on a part exhange basis – this can save a considerable amount of money.

Vehicle identification numbers

Modifications are a continuing and unpublicised process in vehicle manufacture. Spare parts manuals and lists are compiled on a numerical basis, the individual vehicle numbers being essential for correct identification of the component required.

The vehicle identification plate is located on the front body panel, just to the right of the radiator.

The chassis number is stamped on the engine compartment inner bulkhead on the right-hand side.

The body and paint code numbers are located on the left of the front body panel.

The engine number is stamped on the cylinder block below the inlet manifold.

Vehicle identification number locations

| 1 | Vehicle identification plate | 2 | Chassis number | 3 | Body and paint code numbers | 4 | Engine number |

General repair procedures

Whenever servicing, repair or overhaul work is carried out on the car or its components, it is necessary to observe the following procedures and instructions. This will assist in carrying out the operation efficiently and to a professional standard of workmanship.

Joint mating faces and gaskets

Where a gasket is used between the mating faces of two components, ensure that it is renewed on reassembly, and fit it dry unless otherwise stated in the repair procedure. Make sure that the mating faces are clean and dry with all traces of old gasket removed. When cleaning a joint face, use a tool which is not likely to score or damage the face, and remove any burrs or nicks with an oilstone or fine file.

Make sure that tapped holes are cleaned with a pipe cleaner, and keep them free of jointing compound if this is being used unless specifically instructed otherwise.

Ensure that all orifices, channels or pipes are clear and blow through them, preferably using compressed air.

Oil seals

Whenever an oil seal is removed from its working location, either individually or as part of an assembly, it should be renewed.

The very fine sealing lip of the seal is easily damaged and will not seal if the surface it contacts is not completely clean and free from scratches, nicks or grooves. If the original sealing surface of the component cannot be restored, the component should be renewed.

Protect the lips of the seal from any surface which may damage them in the course of fitting. Use tape or a conical sleeve where possible. Lubricate the seal lips with oil before fitting and, on dual lipped seals, fill the space between the lips with grease.

Unless otherwise stated, oil seals must be fitted with their sealing lips toward the lubricant to be sealed.

Use a tubular drift or block of wood of the appropriate size to install the seal and, if the seal housing is shouldered, drive the seal down to the shoulder. If the seal housing is unshouldered, the seal should be fitted with its face flush with the housing top face.

Screw threads and fastenings

Always ensure that a blind tapped hole is completely free from oil, grease, water or other fluid before installing the bolt or stud. Failure to do this could cause the housing to crack due to the hydraulic action of the bolt or stud as it is screwed in.

When tightening a castellated nut to accept a split pin, tighten the nut to the specified torque, where applicable, and then tighten further to the next split pin hole. Never slacken the nut to align a split pin hole unless stated in the repair procedure.

When checking or retightening a nut or bolt to a specified torque setting, slacken the nut or bolt by a quarter of a turn, and then retighten to the specified setting.

Locknuts, locktabs and washers

Any fastening which will rotate against a component or housing in the course of tightening should always have a washer between it and the relevant component or housing.

Spring or split washers should always be renewed when they are used to lock a critical component such as a big-end bearing retaining nut or bolt.

Locktabs which are folded over to retain a nut or bolt should always be renewed.

Self-locking nuts can be reused in non-critical areas, providing resistance can be felt when the locking portion passes over the bolt or stud thread.

Split pins must always be replaced with new ones of the correct size for the hole.

Special tools

Some repair procedures in this manual entail the use of special tools such as a press, two or three-legged pullers, spring compressors etc. Wherever possible, suitable readily available alternatives to the manufacturer's special tools are described, and are shown in use. In some instances, where no alternative is possible, it has been necessary to resort to the use of a manufacturer's tool and this has been done for reasons of safety as well as the efficient completion of the repair operation. Unless you are highly skilled and have a thorough understanding of the procedure described, never attempt to bypass the use of any special tool when the procedure described specifies its use. Not only is there a very great risk of personal injury, but expensive damage could be caused to the components involved.

Tools and working facilities

Introduction

A selection of good tools is a fundamental requirement for anyone contemplating the maintenance and repair of a motor vehicle. For the owner who does not possess any, their purchase will prove a considerable expense, offsetting some of the savings made by doing-it-yourself. However, provided that the tools purchased meet the relevant national safety standards and are of good quality, they will last for many years and prove an extremely worthwhile investment.

To help the average owner to decide which tools are needed to carry out the various tasks detailed in this manual, we have compiled three lists of tools under the following headings: *Maintenance and minor repair*, *Repair and overhaul*, and *Special*. The newcomer to practical mechanics should start off with the *Maintenance and minor repair* tool kit and confine himself to the simpler jobs around the vehicle. Then, as his confidence and experience grow, he can undertake more difficult tasks, buying extra tools as, and when, they are needed. In this way, a *Maintenance and minor repair* tool kit can be built-up into a *Repair and overhaul* tool kit over a considerable period of time without any major cash outlays. The experienced do-it-yourselfer will have a tool kit good enough for most repair and overhaul procedures and will add tools from the *Special* category when he feels the expense is justified by the amount of use to which these tools will be put.

It is obviously not possible to cover the subject of tools fully here. For those who wish to learn more about tools and their use there is a book entitled *How to Choose and Use Car Tools* available from the publishers of this manual.

Maintenance and minor repair tool kit

The tools given in this list should be considered as a minimum requirement if routine maintenance, servicing and minor repair operations are to be undertaken. We recommend the purchase of combination spanners (ring one end, open-ended the other); although more expensive than open-ended ones, they do give the advantages of both types of spanner.

Combination spanners - 10, 11, 12, 13, 14 & 17 mm
Adjustable spanner - 9 inch
Engine sump/gearbox/rear axle drain plug key
Spark plug spanner (with rubber insert)
Spark plug gap adjustment tool
Set of feeler gauges
Brake bleed nipple spanner
Screwdriver - 4 in long x $^1/4$ in dia (flat blade)
Screwdriver - 4 in long x $^1/4$ in dia (cross blade)
Combination pliers - 6 inch
Hacksaw (junior)
Tyre pump
Tyre pressure gauge
Oil can
Fine emery cloth (1 sheet)
Wire brush (small)
Funnel (medium size)

Repair and overhaul tool kit

These tools are virtually essential for anyone undertaking any major repairs to a motor vehicle, and are additional to those given in the *Maintenance and minor repair* list. Included in this list is a comprehensive set of sockets. Although these are expensive they will be found invaluable as they are so versatile - particularly if various drives are included in the set. We recommend the ½ in square-drive type, as this can be used with most proprietary torque wrenches. If you cannot afford a socket set, even bought piecemeal, then inexpensive tubular box spanners are a useful alternative.

The tools in this list will occasionally need to be supplemented by tools from the *Special* list.

Sockets (or box spanners) to cover range in previous list
Reversible ratchet drive (for use with sockets)
Extension piece, 10 inch (for use with sockets)
Universal joint (for use with sockets)
Torque wrench (for use with sockets)
'Mole' wrench - 8 inch
Ball pein hammer
Soft-faced hammer, plastic or rubber
Screwdriver - 6 in long x $^5/16$ in dia (flat blade)
Screwdriver - 2 in long x $^5/16$ in square (flat blade)
Screwdriver - 1$^1/2$ in long x $^1/4$ in dia (cross blade)
Screwdriver - 3 in long x $^1/8$ in dia (electricians)
Pliers - electricians side cutters
Pliers - needle nosed
Pliers - circlip (internal and external)
Cold chisel - $^1/2$ inch
Scriber
Scraper
Centre punch
Pin punch
Hacksaw
Valve grinding tool
Steel rule/straight-edge
Allen keys (inc. splined/Torx type if necessary)
Selection of files
Wire brush (large)
Axle-stands
Jack (strong trolley or hydraulic type)

Special tools

The tools in this list are those which are not used regularly, are expensive to buy, or which need to be used in accordance with their manufacturers' instructions. Unless relatively difficult mechanical jobs are undertaken frequently, it will not be economic to buy many of these tools. Where this is the case, you could consider clubbing together with friends (or joining a motorists' club) to make a joint purchase, or borrowing the tools against a deposit from a local garage or tool hire specialist.

The following list contains only those tools and instruments freely available to the public, and not those special tools produced by the vehicle manufacturer specifically for its dealer network. You will find occasional references to these manufacturers' special tools in the text of this manual. Generally, an alternative method of doing the job without the vehicle manufacturers' special tool is given. However, sometimes, there is no alternative to using them. Where this is the case and the relevant tool cannot be bought or borrowed, you will have to entrust the work to a franchised garage.

> Valve spring compressor (where applicable)
> Piston ring compressor
> Balljoint separator
> Universal hub/bearing puller
> Impact screwdriver
> Micrometer and/or vernier gauge
> Dial gauge
> Stroboscopic timing light
> Dwell angle meter/tachometer
> Universal electrical multi-meter
> Cylinder compression gauge
> Lifting tackle
> Trolley jack
> Light with extension lead

Buying tools

For practically all tools, a tool factor is the best source since he will have a very comprehensive range compared with the average garage or accessory shop. Having said that, accessory shops often offer excellent quality tools at discount prices, so it pays to shop around.

There are plenty of good tools around at reasonable prices, but always aim to purchase items which meet the relevant national safety standards. If in doubt, ask the proprietor or manager of the shop for advice before making a purchase.

Care and maintenance of tools

Having purchased a reasonable tool kit, it is necessary to keep the tools in a clean serviceable condition. After use, always wipe off any dirt, grease and metal particles using a clean, dry cloth, before putting the tools away. Never leave them lying around after they have been used. A simple tool rack on the garage or workshop wall, for items such as screwdrivers and pliers is a good idea. Store all normal wrenches and sockets in a metal box. Any measuring instruments, gauges, meters, etc, must be carefully stored where they cannot be damaged or become rusty.

Take a little care when tools are used. Hammer heads inevitably become marked and screwdrivers lose the keen edge on their blades from time to time. A little timely attention with emery cloth or a file will soon restore items like this to a good serviceable finish.

Working facilities

Not to be forgotten when discussing tools, is the workshop itself. If anything more than routine maintenance is to be carried out, some form of suitable working area becomes essential.

It is appreciated that many an owner mechanic is forced by circumstances to remove an engine or similar item, without the benefit of a garage or workshop. Having done this, any repairs should always be done under the cover of a roof.

Wherever possible, any dismantling should be done on a clean, flat workbench or table at a suitable working height.

Any workbench needs a vice: one with a jaw opening of 4 in (100 mm) is suitable for most jobs. As mentioned previously, some clean dry storage space is also required for tools, as well as for lubricants, cleaning fluids, touch-up paints and so on, which become necessary.

Another item which may be required, and which has a much more general usage, is an electric drill with a chuck capacity of at least 5/16 in (8 mm). This, together with a good range of twist drills, is virtually essential for fitting accessories such as mirrors and reversing lights.

Last, but not least, always keep a supply of old newspapers and clean, lint-free rags available, and try to keep any working area as clean as possible.

Spanner jaw gap comparison table

Jaw gap (in)	Spanner size
0.250	1/4 in AF
0.276	7 mm
0.313	5/16 in AF
0.315	8 mm
0.344	11/32 in AF; 1/8 in Whitworth
0.354	9 mm
0.375	3/8 in AF
0.394	10 mm
0.433	11 mm
0.438	7/16 in AF
0.445	3/16 in Whitworth; 1/4 in BSF
0.472	12 mm
0.500	1/2 in AF
0.512	13 mm
0.525	1/4 in Whitworth; 5/16 in BSF
0.551	14 mm
0.563	9/16 in AF
0.591	15 mm
0.600	5/16 in Whitworth; 3/8 in BSF
0.625	5/8 in AF
0.630	16 mm
0.669	17 mm
0.686	11/16 in AF
0.709	18 mm
0.710	3/8 in Whitworth; 7/16 in BSF
0.748	19 mm
0.750	3/4 in AF
0.813	13/16 in AF
0.820	7/16 in Whitworth; 1/2 in BSF
0.866	22 mm
0.875	7/8 in AF
0.920	1/2 in Whitworth; 9/16 in BSF
0.938	15/16 in AF
0.945	24 mm
1.000	1 in AF
1.010	9/16 in Whitworth; 5/8 in BSF
1.024	26 mm
1.063	11/16 in AF; 27 mm
1.100	5/8 in Whitworth; 11/16 in BSF
1.125	11/8 in AF
1.181	30 mm
1.200	11/16 in Whitworth; 3/4 in BSF
1.250	11/4 in AF
1.260	32 mm
1.300	3/4 in Whitworth; 7/8 in BSF
1.313	15/16 in AF
1.390	13/16 in Whitworth; 15/16 in BSF
1.417	36 mm
1.438	17/16 in AF
1.480	7/8 in Whitworth; 1 in BSF
1.500	11/2 in AF
1.575	40 mm; 15/16 in Whitworth
1.614	41 mm
1.625	15/8 in AF
1.670	1 in Whitworth; 11/8 in BSF
1.688	111/16 in AF
1.811	46 mm
1.813	113/16 in AF
1.860	11/8 in Whitworth; 11/4 in BSF
1.875	17/8 in AF
1.969	50 mm
2.000	2 in AF
2.050	11/4 in Whitworth; 13/8 in BSF
2.165	55 mm
2.362	60 mm

Safety first!

Professional motor mechanics are trained in safe working procedures. However enthusiastic you may be about getting on with the job in hand, do take the time to ensure that your safety is not put at risk. A moment's lack of attention can result in an accident, as can failure to observe certain elementary precautions.

There will always be new ways of having accidents, and the following points do not pretend to be a comprehensive list of all dangers; they are intended rather to make you aware of the risks and to encourage a safety-conscious approach to all work you carry out on your vehicle.

Essential DOs and DON'Ts

DON'T rely on a single jack when working underneath the vehicle. Always use reliable additional means of support, such as axle stands, securely placed under a part of the vehicle that you know will not give way.

DON'T attempt to loosen or tighten high-torque nuts (e.g. wheel hub nuts) while the vehicle is on a jack; it may be pulled off.

DON'T start the engine without first ascertaining that the transmission is in neutral (or 'Park' where applicable) and the parking brake applied.

DON'T suddenly remove the filler cap from a hot cooling system – cover it with a cloth and release the pressure gradually first, or you may get scalded by escaping coolant.

DON'T attempt to drain oil until you are sure it has cooled sufficiently to avoid scalding you.

DON'T grasp any part of the engine, exhaust or catalytic converter without first ascertaining that it is sufficiently cool to avoid burning you.

DON'T allow brake fluid or antifreeze to contact vehicle paintwork.

DON'T syphon toxic liquids such as fuel, brake fluid or antifreeze by mouth, or allow them to remain on your skin.

DON'T inhale dust – it may be injurious to health (see *Asbestos* below).

DON'T allow any spilt oil or grease to remain on the floor – wipe it up straight away, before someone slips on it.

DON'T use ill-fitting spanners or other tools which may slip and cause injury.

DON'T attempt to lift a heavy component which may be beyond your capability – get assistance.

DON'T rush to finish a job, or take unverified short cuts.

DON'T allow children or animals in or around an unattended vehicle.

DO wear eye protection when using power tools such as drill, sander, bench grinder etc, and when working under the vehicle.

DO use a barrier cream on your hands prior to undertaking dirty jobs – it will protect your skin from infection as well as making the dirt easier to remove afterwards; but make sure your hands aren't left slippery. Note that long-term contact with used engine oil can be a health hazard.

DO keep loose clothing (cuffs, tie etc) and long hair well out of the way of moving mechanical parts.

DO remove rings, wristwatch etc, before working on the vehicle – especially the electrical system.

DO ensure that any lifting tackle used has a safe working load rating adequate for the job.

DO keep your work area tidy – it is only too easy to fall over articles left lying around.

DO get someone to check periodically that all is well, when working alone on the vehicle.

DO carry out work in a logical sequence and check that everything is correctly assembled and tightened afterwards.

DO remember that your vehicle's safety affects that of yourself and others. If in doubt on any point, get specialist advice.

IF, in spite of following these precautions, you are unfortunate enough to injure yourself, seek medical attention as soon as possible.

Asbestos

Certain friction, insulating, sealing, and other products – such as brake linings, brake bands, clutch linings, torque converters, gaskets, etc – contain asbestos. *Extreme care must be taken to avoid inhalation of dust from such products since it is hazardous to health.* If in doubt, assume that they *do* contain asbestos.

Fire

Remember at all times that petrol (gasoline) is highly flammable. Never smoke, or have any kind of naked flame around, when working on the vehicle. But the risk does not end there – a spark caused by an electrical short-circuit, by two metal surfaces contacting each other, by careless use of tools, or even by static electricity built up in your body under certain conditions, can ignite petrol vapour, which in a confined space is highly explosive.

Always disconnect the battery earth (ground) terminal before working on any part of the fuel or electrical system, and never risk spilling fuel on to a hot engine or exhaust.

It is recommended that a fire extinguisher of a type suitable for fuel and electrical fires is kept handy in the garage or workplace at all times. Never try to extinguish a fuel or electrical fire with water.

Note: *Any reference to a 'torch' appearing in this manual should always be taken to mean a hand-held battery-operated electric lamp or flashlight. It does NOT mean a welding/gas torch or blowlamp.*

Fumes

Certain fumes are highly toxic and can quickly cause unconsciousness and even death if inhaled to any extent. Petrol (gasoline) vapour comes into this category, as do the vapours from certain solvents such as trichloroethylene. Any draining or pouring of such volatile fluids should be done in a well ventilated area.

When using cleaning fluids and solvents, read the instructions carefully. Never use materials from unmarked containers – they may give off poisonous vapours.

Never run the engine of a motor vehicle in an enclosed space such as a garage. Exhaust fumes contain carbon monoxide which is extremely poisonous; if you need to run the engine, always do so in the open air or at least have the rear of the vehicle outside the workplace.

If you are fortunate enough to have the use of an inspection pit, never drain or pour petrol, and never run the engine, while the vehicle is standing over it; the fumes, being heavier than air, will concentrate in the pit with possibly lethal results.

The battery

Never cause a spark, or allow a naked light, near the vehicle's battery. It will normally be giving off a certain amount of hydrogen gas, which is highly explosive.

Always disconnect the battery earth (ground) terminal before working on the fuel or electrical systems.

If possible, loosen the filler plugs or cover when charging the battery from an external source. Do not charge at an excessive rate or the battery may burst.

Take care when topping up and when carrying the battery. The acid electrolyte, even when diluted, is very corrosive and should not be allowed to contact the eyes or skin.

If you ever need to prepare electrolyte yourself, always add the acid slowly to the water, and never the other way round. Protect against splashes by wearing rubber gloves and goggles.

When jump starting a car using a booster battery, for negative earth (ground) vehicles, connect the jump leads in the following sequence: First connect one jump lead between the positive (+) terminals of the two batteries. Then connect the other jump lead first to the negative (–) terminal of the booster battery, and then to a good earthing (ground) point on the vehicle to be started, at least 18 in (45 cm) from the battery if possible. Ensure that hands and jump leads are clear of any moving parts, and that the two vehicles do not touch. Disconnect the leads in the reverse order.

Mains electricity and electrical equipment

When using an electric power tool, inspection light etc, always ensure that the appliance is correctly connected to its plug and that, where necessary, it is properly earthed (grounded). Do not use such appliances in damp conditions and, again, beware of creating a spark or applying excessive heat in the vicinity of fuel or fuel vapour. Also ensure that the appliances meet the relevant national safety standards.

Ignition HT voltage

A severe electric shock can result from touching certain parts of the ignition system, such as the HT leads, when the engine is running or being cranked, particularly if components are damp or the insulation is defective. Where an electronic ignition system is fitted, the HT voltage is much higher and could prove fatal.

Routine maintenance

Maintenance is essential for ensuring safety, and desirable for the purpose of getting the best in terms of performance and economy from your car. Over the years the need for periodic lubrication has been greatly reduced if not totally eliminated. This has unfortunately tended to lead some owners to think that because no such action is required, the items either no longer exist, or will last forever. This is certainly not the case; it is essential to carry out regular visual examination as comprehensively as possible in order to spot any possible defects at an early stage before they develop into major expensive repairs.

The following service schedules are a list of the maintenance requirements and the intervals at which they should be carried out, as recommended by the manufacturers. Where applicable these procedures are covered in greater detail throughout this Manual, near the beginning of each Chapter.

Engine and under-bonnet component location on a 1985 190 model (air cleaner removed for clarity)

1 Windscreen washer water level indicator sensor
2 Washer reservoir filler cap
3 Engine oil dipstick
4 Coolant expansion tank filler cap
5 Front suspension strut upper mounting
6 Brake fluid reservoir filler cap
7 Additional relay holder
8 Central electrics unit (fusebox)
9 Oil filter
10 Carburettor piston damper fluid filler plug
11 Battery filler caps
12 Battery negative terminal
13 Ignition system electronic switching unit
14 Fuel pump
15 Ignition coil
16 Power steering fluid reservoir filler cap
17 Radiator
18 Distributor
19 Vehicle identification plate
20 Thermostat housing
21 Alternator
22 Oil filler cap

14

Front underbody view of a
1985 190 model

1 Water drain tube
2 Exhaust downpipes
3 Steering track rod
4 Front wishbone
5 Anti-roll bar
6 Alternator
7 Drag link
8 Steering damper
9 Gearbox drain plug
10 Gearbox crossmember
11 Speedometer cable
12 Steering idler arm assembly
13 Engine oil drain plug
14 Power steering pump

**Rear underbody view of a
1985 190 model**

1 Rear subframe mounting
2 Spring support arm
3 Anti-roll bar
4 Pulling strut
5 Pushing strut
6 Water drain tube
7 Handbrake cable
8 Propeller shaft flexible
   rubber coupling
9 Intermediate silencer
10 Track rod
11 Fuel lines
12 Final drive differential
13 Driveshaft constant velocity
    joint

Every 250 miles (400 km) or weekly

Engine, cooling system, suspension and brakes
Check the engine oil level and top up if necessary
Check the coolant level and top up if necessary
Check the fluid level in the power steering reservoir, and top up
if necessary
Check the brake fluid level in the master cylinder reservoir, and
top up if necessary

Lights and wipers
Check the operation of the horn, all the lights and the wipers
and washers – adjust washer aim if necessary
Check and if necessary top up the washer reservoir

Tyres
Check the tyre pressures, including the spare, and correct if
necessary
Visually examine the tyres for tread depth, and wear or damage

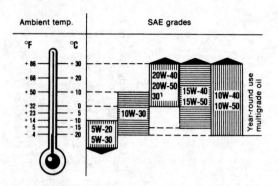

[1] SAE 40 may be used if ambient temperatures constantly exceed
+30° C/+86° F.

Engine oil viscosity chart

Every 6 000 miles (10 000 km) or 6 months – whichever comes first

Engine (Chapter 1)
Renew the engine oil and filter

Fuel and exhaust systems (Chapter 3)
Check the operation of the accelerator cable and linkage, and
lubricate the pivot and contact areas

Manual gearbox (Chapter 6)
Check and if necessary top up the gearbox oil level

Final drive and driveshafts (Chapter 8)
Check and if necessary top up the final drive differential oil level

Every 12 000 miles (20 000 km) or 12 months – whichever comes first

In addition to the items in the weekly and 6000 mile (10 000
km) services, carry out the following:

Engine (Chapter 1)
Check and if necessary adjust the valve clearances (where
applicable)
Visually check the engine for oil leaks, and for the security and
condition of all related components and attachments

Cooling system (Chapter 2)
Check the hoses, hose clips and visible joint gaskets for leaks,
and any signs of corrosion or deterioration

Fuel and exhaust systems (Chapter 3)
Visually check the fuel pipes and hoses for security, chafing,
leaks and corrosion
Check and if necessary top up the carburettor piston damper oil
level
Check and if necessary adjust the engine idle speed and mixture
settings
Check the exhaust system for corrosion, leaks and security and
the tightness of the flange attachments

Ignition system (Chapter 4)
Renew the spark plugs
Clean and check the condition of the distributor cap, HT leads,
and ignition-related leads and wiring
Check and if necessary adjust the ignition timing

Clutch (Chapter 5)
Check the operation of the clutch and clutch pedal

Manual gearbox (Chapter 6)
Visually check for oil leaks around the joint faces and oil seals
Drain and refill the gearbox with fresh fluid

Automatic transmission (Chapter 6)
Check and if necessary top up the transmission fluid
Visually check for oil leaks around the joint faces and oil seals,
and check the condition and security of the fluid cooler hoses
and unions

Propeller shaft (Chapter 7)
Check the condition of the propeller shaft flexible rubber
couplings, centre support bearing and universal joint

Final drive and driveshafts (Chapter 8)
Drain and refill the final drive differential with fresh oil
Check the final drive oil seals and joint faces for oil leaks
Check the condition of the driveshaft constant velocity joints

Braking system (Chapter 9)
Check the disc pads for wear, and the discs for condition
Drain the brake hydraulic system and refill with fresh fluid
Check visually all brake pipes, hoses and unions for corrosion,
leakage and security
Check the operation of the handbrake, and lubricate the
exposed cables and linkages. Adjust if required

Suspension and steering (Chapter 10)
Adjust the front hub bearings
Check and if necessary adjust, or renew, the power steering
pump drivebelt
Check the front suspension struts and rear shock absorbers for
fluid leakage and efficiency of operation
Check the condition and security of all suspension and steering
joints, linkages and mountings
Inspect the roadwheels for damage, and check the tightness of
the wheel bolts

Bodywork (Chapter 11)
Lubricate the locks and hinges (except the steering lock)
Check and if necessary adjust, or renew, the air conditioning
refrigerant compressor drivebelt (where fitted)

Electrical system (Chapter 12)
Check and if necessary top up the battery
Check and if necessary adjust, or renew, the alternator drivebelt
Check the condition and security of all accessible wiring
connectors, harnesses, retaining clips, washer hoses and
connections
Check the operation of all electrical equipment and accessories
Check the condition of the wiper blades and renew if necessary
Clean the battery terminals and smear with petroleum jelly

Every 36 000 miles (60 000 km) or three years – whichever comes first

In addition to the items listed in the previous services, carry out the following:

Cooling system (Chapter 2)
Drain and flush the cooling system, and fill with fresh coolant

Fuel and exhaust systems (Chapter 3)
Renew the air cleaner element
Renew the fuel filter (fuel injection engines)

Clutch (Chapter 5)
Check the clutch driven plate for wear

Automatic transmission (Chapter 6)
Drain and refill the transmission with fresh fluid, and fit a new fluid filter screen

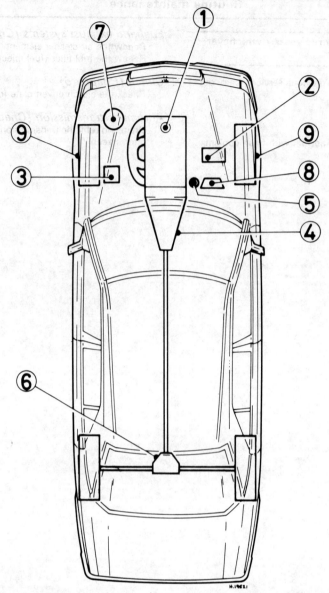

Recommended lubricants and fluids

Component or system	Lubricant type/specification	Duckhams recommendation
Engine (1)	Multigrade engine oil, viscosity SAE 10W/40 or 15W/50	Duckhams QXR, Hypergrade, or 10W/40 Motor Oil
Cooling system (2)	Mercedes-Benz approved antifreeze	Duckhams Universal Antifreeze and Summer Coolant
Carburettor piston damper (3)	Mercedes-Benz approved ATF	Duckhams MB-Matic
Manual gearbox (4)	Mercedes-Benz approved ATF	Duckhams Fleetmatic A
Automatic transmission (5)	Mercedes-Benz approved ATF	Duckhams MB-Matic
Final drive differential (6)	Hypoid gear oil, viscosity SAE 90EP	Duckhams Hypoid 90S
Power steering pump reservoir (7)	Mercedes-Benz approved ATF	Duckhams Fleetmatic A
Brake and clutch fluid (8)	Universal brake and clutch fluid to FMVSS 116 DOT 3 or DOT 4	Duckhams Universal Brake and Clutch Fluid
Front hub bearings (9)	Mercedes-Benz high temperature bearing grease	Duckhams LB 10

Conversion factors

Length (distance)

Inches (in)	X	25.4	= Millimetres (mm)	X	0.0394	= Inches (in)
Feet (ft)	X	0.305	= Metres (m)	X	3.281	= Feet (ft)
Miles	X	1.609	= Kilometres (km)	X	0.621	= Miles

Volume (capacity)

Cubic inches (cu in; in³)	X	16.387	= Cubic centimetres (cc; cm³)	X	0.061	= Cubic inches (cu in; in³)
Imperial pints (Imp pt)	X	0.568	= Litres (l)	X	1.76	= Imperial pints (Imp pt)
Imperial quarts (Imp qt)	X	1.137	= Litres (l)	X	0.88	= Imperial quarts (Imp qt)
Imperial quarts (Imp qt)	X	1.201	= US quarts (US qt)	X	0.833	= Imperial quarts (Imp qt)
US quarts (US qt)	X	0.946	= Litres (l)	X	1.057	= US quarts (US qt)
Imperial gallons (Imp gal)	X	4.546	= Litres (l)	X	0.22	= Imperial gallons (Imp gal)
Imperial gallons (Imp gal)	X	1.201	= US gallons (US gal)	X	0.833	= Imperial gallons (Imp gal)
US gallons (US gal)	X	3.785	= Litres (l)	X	0.264	= US gallons (US gal)

Mass (weight)

Ounces (oz)	X	28.35	= Grams (g)	X	0.035	= Ounces (oz)
Pounds (lb)	X	0.454	= Kilograms (kg)	X	2.205	= Pounds (lb)

Force

Ounces-force (ozf; oz)	X	0.278	= Newtons (N)	X	3.6	= Ounces-force (ozf; oz)
Pounds-force (lbf; lb)	X	4.448	= Newtons (N)	X	0.225	= Pounds-force (lbf; lb)
Newtons (N)	X	0.1	= Kilograms-force (kgf; kg)	X	9.81	= Newtons (N)

Pressure

Pounds-force per square inch (psi; lbf/in²; lb/in²)	X	0.070	= Kilograms-force per square centimetre (kgf/cm²; kg/cm²)	X	14.223	= Pounds-force per square inch (psi; lbf/in²; lb/in²)
Pounds-force per square inch (psi; lbf/in²; lb/in²)	X	0.068	= Atmospheres (atm)	X	14.696	= Pounds-force per square inch (psi; lbf/in²; lb/in²)
Pounds-force per square inch (psi; lbf/in²; lb/in²)	X	0.069	= Bars	X	14.5	= Pounds-force per square inch (psi; lbf/in²; lb/in²)
Pounds-force per square inch (psi; lbf/in²; lb/in²)	X	6.895	= Kilopascals (kPa)	X	0.145	= Pounds-force per square inch (psi; lbf/in²; lb/in²)
Kilopascals (kPa)	X	0.01	= Kilograms-force per square centimetre (kgf/cm²; kg/cm²)	X	98.1	= Kilopascals (kPa)
Millibar (mbar)	X	100	= Pascals (Pa)	X	0.01	= Millibar (mbar)
Millibar (mbar)	X	0.0145	= Pounds-force per square inch (psi; lbf/in²; lb/in²)	X	68.947	= Millibar (mbar)
Millibar (mbar)	X	0.75	= Millimetres of mercury (mmHg)	X	1.333	= Millibar (mbar)
Millibar (mbar)	X	0.401	= Inches of water (inH₂O)	X	2.491	= Millibar (mbar)
Millimetres of mercury (mmHg)	X	0.535	= Inches of water (inH₂O)	X	1.868	= Millimetres of mercury (mmHg)
Inches of water (inH₂O)	X	0.036	= Pounds-force per square inch (psi; lbf/in²; lb/in²)	X	27.68	= Inches of water (inH₂O)

Torque (moment of force)

Pounds-force inches (lbf in; lb in)	X	1.152	= Kilograms-force centimetre (kgf cm; kg cm)	X	0.868	= Pounds-force inches (lbf in; lb in)
Pounds-force inches (lbf in; lb in)	X	0.113	= Newton metres (Nm)	X	8.85	= Pounds-force inches (lbf in; lb in)
Pounds-force inches (lbf in; lb in)	X	0.083	= Pounds-force feet (lbf ft; lb ft)	X	12	= Pounds-force inches (lbf in; lb in)
Pounds-force feet (lbf ft; lb ft)	X	0.138	= Kilograms-force metres (kgf m; kg m)	X	7.233	= Pounds-force feet (lbf ft; lb ft)
Pounds-force feet (lbf ft; lb ft)	X	1.356	= Newton metres (Nm)	X	0.738	= Pounds-force feet (lbf ft; lb ft)
Newton metres (Nm)	X	0.102	= Kilograms-force metres (kgf m; kg m)	X	9.804	= Newton metres (Nm)

Power

Horsepower (hp)	X	745.7	= Watts (W)	X	0.0013	= Horsepower (hp)

Velocity (speed)

Miles per hour (miles/hr; mph)	X	1.609	= Kilometres per hour (km/hr; kph)	X	0.621	= Miles per hour (miles/hr; mph)

Fuel consumption*

Miles per gallon, Imperial (mpg)	X	0.354	= Kilometres per litre (km/l)	X	2.825	= Miles per gallon, Imperial (mpg)
Miles per gallon, US (mpg)	X	0.425	= Kilometres per litre (km/l)	X	2.352	= Miles per gallon, US (mpg)

Temperature

Degrees Fahrenheit = (°C x 1.8) + 32   Degrees Celsius (Degrees Centigrade; °C) = (°F - 32) x 0.56

*It is common practice to convert from miles per gallon (mpg) to litres/100 kilometres (l/100km), where mpg (Imperial) x l/100 km = 282 and mpg (US) x l/100 km = 235

Fault diagnosis

Introduction

The vehicle owner who does his or her own maintenance according to the recommended schedules should not have to use this section of the manual very often. Modern component reliability is such that, provided those items subject to wear or deterioration are inspected or renewed at the specified intervals, sudden failure is comparatively rare. Faults do not usually just happen as a result of sudden failure, but develop over a period of time. Major mechanical failures in particular are usually preceded by characteristic symptoms over hundreds or even thousands of miles. Those components which do occasionally fail without warning are often small and easily carried in the vehicle.

With any fault finding, the first step is to decide where to begin investigations. Sometimes this is obvious, but on other occasions a little detective work will be necessary. The owner who makes half a dozen haphazard adjustments or replacements may be successful in curing a fault (or its symptoms), but he will be none the wiser if the fault recurs and he may well have spent more time and money than was necessary. A calm and logical approach will be found to be more satisfactory in the long run. Always take into account any warning signs or abnormalities that may have been noticed in the period preceding the fault – power loss, high or low gauge readings, unusual noises or smells, etc – and remember that failure of components such as fuses or spark plugs may only be pointers to some underlying fault.

The pages which follow here are intended to help in cases of failure to start or breakdown on the road. There is also a Fault Diagnosis Section at the end of each Chapter which should be consulted if the preliminary checks prove unfruitful. Whatever the fault, certain basic principles apply. These are as follows:

Verify the fault. This is simply a matter of being sure that you know what the symptoms are before starting work. This is particularly important if you are investigating a fault for someone else who may not have described it very accurately.

Don't overlook the obvious. For example, if the vehicle won't start, is there petrol in the tank? (Don't take anyone else's word on this particular point, and don't trust the fuel gauge either!) If an electrical fault is indicated, look for loose or broken wires before digging out the test gear.

Cure the disease, not the symptom. Substituting a flat battery with a fully charged one will get you off the hard shoulder, but if the underlying cause is not attended to, the new battery will go the same way. Similarly, changing oil-fouled spark plugs for a new set will get you moving again, but remember that the reason for the fouling (if it wasn't simply an incorrect grade of plug) will have to be established and corrected.

Don't take anything for granted. Particularly, don't forget that a 'new' component may itself be defective (especially if it's been rattling round in the boot for months), and don't leave components out of a fault diagnosis sequence just because they are new or recently fitted. When you do finally diagnose a difficult fault, you'll probably realise that all the evidence was there from the start.

Electrical faults

Electrical faults can be more puzzling than straightforward mechanical failures, but they are no less susceptible to logical analysis if the basic principles of operation are understood. Vehicle electrical wiring exists in extremely unfavourable conditions – heat, vibration and chemical attack – and the first things to look for are loose or corroded connections and broken or chafed wires, especially where the wires pass through holes in the bodywork or are subject to vibration.

All metal-bodied vehicles in current production have one pole of the battery 'earthed', ie connected to the vehicle bodywork, and in nearly all modern vehicles it is the negative (–) terminal. The various electrical components – motors, bulb holders etc – are also connected to earth, either by means of a lead or directly by their mountings. Electric current flows through the component and then back to the battery via the bodywork. If the component mounting is loose or corroded, or if a good path back to the battery is not available, the circuit will be incomplete and malfunction will result. The engine and/or gearbox are also earthed by means of flexible metal straps to the body or subframe; if these straps are loose or missing, starter motor, generator and ignition trouble may result.

Assuming the earth return to be satisfactory, electrical faults will be due either to component malfunction or to defects in the current supply. Individual components are dealt with in Chapter 12. If supply wires are broken or cracked internally this results in an open-circuit, and the easiest way to check for this is to bypass the suspect wire temporarily with a length of wire having a crocodile clip or suitable connector at each end. Alternatively, a 12V test lamp can be used to verify the presence of supply voltage at various points along the wire and the break can be thus isolated.

If a bare portion of a live wire touches the bodywork or other earthed metal part, the electricity will take the low-resistance path thus formed back to the battery: this is known as a short-circuit. Hopefully a short-circuit will blow a fuse, but otherwise it may cause burning of the insulation (and possibly further short-circuits) or even a fire. This is why it is inadvisable to bypass persistently blowing fuses with silver foil or wire.

Spares and tool kit

Most vehicles are supplied only with sufficient tools for wheel changing; the *Maintenance and minor repair* tool kit detailed in *Tools and working facilities*, with the addition of a hammer, is probably sufficient for those repairs that most motorists would consider attempting at the roadside. In addition a few items which can be fitted without too much trouble in the event of a breakdown should be carried. Experience and available space will modify the list below, but the following may save having to call on professional assistance:

Spark plugs, clean and correctly gapped
HT lead and plug cap – long enough to reach the plug furthest from the distributor
Distributor rotor
Drivebelt(s) – emergency type may suffice
Spare fuses
Set of principal light bulbs
Tin of radiator sealer and hose bandage
Exhaust bandage
Roll of insulating tape
Length of soft iron wire
Length of electrical flex
Torch or inspection lamp (can double as test lamp)
Battery jump leads
Tow-rope
Ignition water dispersant aerosol
Litre of engine oil
Sealed can of hydraulic fluid
Emergency windscreen
Worm drive clips

If spare fuel is carried, a can designed for the purpose should be used to minimise risks of leakage and collision damage.

When touring abroad it may be advisable to carry additional spares which, even if you cannot fit them yourself, could save having to wait

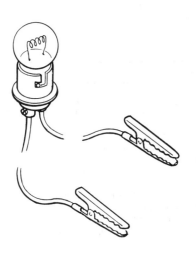

A simple test lamp is useful for tracing electrical faults

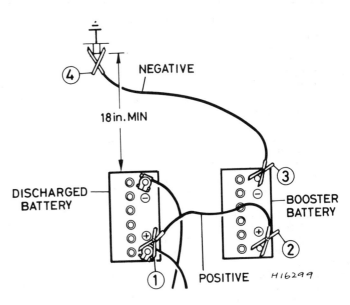

NEGATIVE

18 in. MIN

DISCHARGED BATTERY

BOOSTER BATTERY

POSITIVE

H16299

Jump start lead connections for negative earth vehicles – connect leads in order shown

Carrying a few spares can save you a long walk

while parts are obtained. The items below may be worth considering:

Clutch and throttle cables
Cylinder head gasket
Alternator brushes
Fuel pump repair kit
Tyre valve core

One of the motoring organisations will be able to advise on availability of fuel etc in foreign countries.

Engine will not start

Engine fails to turn when starter operated
Flat battery (recharge, use jump leads, or push start)
Battery terminals loose or corroded
Battery earth to body defective
Engine earth strap loose or broken
Starter motor (or solenoid) wiring loose or broken
Automatic transmission selector in wrong position, or inhibitor switch faulty
Ignition/starter switch faulty
Major mechanical failure (seizure)
Starter or solenoid internal fault (see Chapter 12)

Starter motor turns engine slowly
Partially discharged battery (recharge, use jump leads, or push start)
Battery terminals loose or corroded
Battery earth to body defective
Engine earth strap loose
Starter motor (or solenoid) wiring loose
Starter motor internal fault (see Chapter 12)

Starter motor spins without turning engine
Flat battery
Starter motor pinion sticking on sleeve
Flywheel gear teeth damaged or worn
Starter motor mounting bolts loose

Engine turns normally but fails to start
Damp or dirty HT leads and distributor cap (crank engine and check for spark)
No fuel in tank
Excessive choke (hot engine) or insufficient choke (cold engine)
Fouled or incorrectly gapped spark plugs (remove, clean and regap)
Other ignition system fault (see Chapter 4)
Other fuel system fault (see Chapter 3)
Poor compression (see Chapter 1)
Major mechanical failure (eg camshaft drive)

Engine fires but will not run
Insufficient choke (cold engine)
Air leaks at carburettor or inlet manifold
Fuel starvation (see Chapter 3)
Other ignition fault (see Chapter 4)

Engine cuts out and will not restart

Engine cuts out suddenly – ignition fault
Loose or disconnected LT wires
Wet HT leads or distributor cap (after traversing water splash)
Coil or condenser failure (check for spark)
Other ignition fault (see Chapter 4)

Engine misfires before cutting out – fuel fault
Fuel tank empty
Fuel pump defective or filter blocked (check for delivery)
Fuel tank filler vent blocked (suction will be evident on releasing cap)
Carburettor needle valve sticking (where applicable)
Carburettor jets blocked (fuel contaminated) – where applicable
Other fuel system fault (see Chapter 4)

Engine cuts out – other causes
Serious overheating
Major mechanical failure (eg camshaft drive)

Engine overheats

Ignition (no-charge) warning light illuminated
Slack or broken drivebelt – retension or renew (Chapter 12)

Ignition warning light not illuminated
Coolant loss due to internal or external leakage (see Chapter 12)
Thermostat defective
Low oil level
Brakes binding
Radiator clogged externally or internally
Cooling fan not operating correctly
Engine waterways clogged
Ignition timing incorrect or automatic advance malfunctioning
Mixture too weak

Note: *Do not add cold water to an overheated engine or damage may result*

Low engine oil pressure

Gauge reads low or warning light illuminated with engine running
Oil level low or incorrect grade
Defective gauge or sender unit
Wire to sender unit earthed
Engine overheating
Oil filter clogged or bypass valve defective
Oil pressure relief valve defective
Oil pick-up strainer clogged
Oil pump worn or mountings loose
Worn main or big-end bearings

Note: *Low oil pressure in a high-mileage engine at tickover is not necessarily a cause for concern. Sudden pressure loss at speed is far more significant. In any event, check the gauge or warning light sender before condemning the engine.*

Engine noises

Pre-ignition (pinking) on acceleration
Incorrect grade of fuel
Ignition timing incorrect
Distributor faulty or worn
Worn or maladjusted carburettor (where applicable)
Excessive carbon build-up in engine

Whistling or wheezing noises
Leaking vacuum hose
Leaking carburettor or manifold gasket
Blowing head gasket

Tapping or rattling
Incorrect valve clearances
Worn valve gear
Worn timing chain or belt
Broken piston ring (ticking noise)

Knocking or thumping
Unintentional mechanical contact
Worn drivebelt
Peripheral component fault (generator, water pump etc)
Worn big-end bearings (regular heavy knocking, perhaps less under load)
Worn main bearings (rumbling and knocking, perhaps worsening under load)
Piston slap (most noticeable when cold)

Chapter 1 Engine

Contents

Specifications

General

Engine type .... Four cylinder in-line, overhead camshaft
Engine code:
   Carburettor engines:
      Pre-October 1984 .... 102.921
      October 1984 onwards 102.924
   Fuel injection engines:
      Pre-October 1984 .... 102.961 KE
      October 1984 onwards .... 102.962 KE
Capacity .... 1997 cc
Bore .... 89.00 mm (3.51 in)
Stroke .... 80.25 mm (3.16 in)
Compression ratio:
   Engine code 102.921 .... 9.0:1
   Engine code 102.924 .... 9.1:1
   Engine codes 102.961 KE and 102.962 KE 9.1:1
Compression pressures (all engines) .... 10.0 to 12.0 bar (145.0 to 174 lbf/in²)
Minimum acceptable compression pressure .... 8.5 bar (123.25 lbf/in²)
Maximum compression difference between cylinders .... 1.5 bar (21.75 lbf/in²)
Firing order .... 1–3–4–2 (No 1 at timing cover end)
Direction of crankshaft rotation .... Anti-clockwise

Cylinder block

Material .... Cast iron
Number of main bearings 5
Cylinder bore diameter:
   Standard .... 88.998 to 89.028 mm (3.507 to 3.508 in)
   1st oversize (0.5 mm) .... 89.498 to 89.528 mm (3.526 to 3.527 in)
   2nd oversize (1.0 mm) .... 89.998 to 90.028 mm (3.546 to 3.547 in)
Maximum acceptable cylinder bore ovality .... 0.10 mm (0.0039 in)
Maximum acceptable cylinder bore taper .... 0.05 mm (0.0019 in)
Cylinder block height .... 292.45 to 292.55 mm (11.523 to 11.526 in)
Minimum acceptable height after machining .... 292.35 mm (11.519 in)
Maximum acceptable gasket face distortion:
   At cylinder head face .... 0.03 mm (0.0012 in)
   At sump face .... 0.04 mm (0.0016 in)

Crankshaft

Main bearing journal diameter:
   Standard .... 57.935 to 57.965 mm (2.283 to 2.284 in) in six grades
   1st undersize (0.25 mm) .... 57.705 to 57.715 mm (2.2736 to 2.2740 in)
   2nd undersize (0.50 mm) .... 57.455 to 57.465 mm (2.2637 to 2.2641 in)
   3rd undersize (0.75 mm) .... 57.205 to 57.215 mm (2.2539 to 2.2543 in)

4th undersize (1.0 mm)	56.955 to 56.965 mm (2.2440 to 2.2444 in)
Main bearing running clearance	0.025 to 0.070 mm (0.0010 to 0.0028 in)
Big-end bearing journal diameter:	
Standard	47.955 to 47.965 mm (1.889 to 1.890 in)
1st undersize (0.25 mm)	47.705 to 47.715 mm (1.8796 to 1.8800 in)
2nd undersize (0.50 mm)	47.455 to 47.465 mm (1.8697 to 1.8701 in)
3rd undersize (0.75 mm)	47.205 to 47.215 mm (1.8599 to 1.8603 in)
4th undersize (1.0 mm)	46.955 to 46.965 mm (1.8500 to 1.8504 in)
Big-end bearing running clearance	0.030 to 0.070 mm (0.0012 to 0.0028 in)
Crankshaft endfloat	0.12 to 0.30 mm (0.005 to 0.012 in)
Crankshaft thrustwasher thicknesses	2.15, 2.20, 2.25, 2.35 and 2.40 mm (0.085, 0.087, 0.089, 0.093 and 0.095 in)

Minimum acceptable diameter of big-end cap studs or bolts:

Caps retained by studs and nuts	8.0 mm (0.315 in) at stud stepped down portion
Caps retained by bolts	7.1 mm (0.280 in) at bolt stepped down portion

Flywheel and torque converter driveplate

Minimum acceptable diameter of retaining stretch bolts	8.0 mm (0.315 in) at bolt stepped down portion
Maximum acceptable length of retaining stretch bolts	22.5 mm (0.887 in)

Pistons and piston rings

Piston diameter:	
Standard	88.968 to 89.002 mm (3.5053 to 3.5067 in) in three classes
1st oversize (0.5 mm)	89.468 to 89.502 mm (3.5250 to 3.5264 in) in three classes
2nd oversize (1.0 mm)	89.968 to 90.002 mm (3.5447 to 3.5461 in) in three classes
Piston to bore clearance	0.016 to 0.040 mm (0.0006 to 0.0016 in)
Piston ring to groove clearance:	
Top ring	0.050 to 0.15 mm (0.0020 to 0.0059 in)
Second ring	0.010 to 0.10 mm (0.0004 to 0.0039 in)
Oil control ring	0.010 to 0.10 mm (0.0004 to 0.0039 in)
Piston ring end gaps (fitted gap in bore):	
Top ring	0.30 to 1.0 mm (0.0118 to 0.0394 in)
Second ring	0.25 to 0.8 mm (0.0099 to 0.0315 in)
Oil control ring	0.25 to 0.8 mm (0.0099 to 0.0315 in)
Gudgeon pin clearance in piston at 21° (70°F)	0.002 to 0.012 mm (0.0001 to 0.0005 in)
Gudgeon pin fit in connecting rod:	
Pre-January 1984 engines	0.007 to 0.018 mm (0.0003 to 0.0007 in) clearance at 21°C (70°F)
Post-January 1984 engines	Interference fit at 21°C (70°F)

Camshaft

Number of bearings	5
Bearing journal diameter:	
Standard	31.934 to 31.950 mm (1.2582 to 1.2588 in)
Oversize	32.434 to 32.450 mm (1.2779 to 1.2785 in)
Camshaft bearing running clearance	0.050 to 0.11 mm (0.0020 to 0.0043 in)
Camshaft endfloat	0.07 to 0.18 mm (0.0028 to 0.0071 in)

Cylinder head

Material	Aluminium alloy
Cylinder head height	98.4 to 98.5 mm (3.877 to 3.881 in)
Minimum acceptable height after machining	97.8 mm (3.853 in)
Maximum acceptable longitudinal distortion	0.15 mm (0.006 in)
Maximum acceptable transverse distortion	0.05 mm (0.002 in)
Camshaft bearing bore diameter:	
Standard	32.025 to 32.050 mm (1.2608 to 1.2618 in)
Oversize	32.500 to 32.525 mm (1.2805 to 1.2815 in)
Maximum acceptable camshaft bore ovality	0.012 mm (0.0005 in)
Valve seat angle	45°
Valve seat width:	
Inlet	1.8 to 2.5 mm (0.07 to 0.10 in)
Exhaust	1.5 to 2.5 mm (0.06 to 0.10 in)
Seat cutter correction angle:	
Upper	15°
Lower	60°
Valve guide length:	
Inlet	46.0 mm (1.81 in)
Exhaust	51.0 mm (2.01 in)
Valve guide internal diameter:	
Inlet	8.000 to 8.015 mm (0.3152 to 0.3158 in)
Exhaust	9.000 to 9.015 mm (0.3546 to 0.3552 in)
Maximum acceptable cylinder head stretch bolt length	122.0 mm (4.807 in)

Valves – general

Operation	Camshaft and rocker arms
Type:	
Inlet valve	Solid

Exhaust valve	Hollow, sodium filled
Valve clearances:	
Engine codes 102.921 and 102.961 KE:	
Inlet (cold)	0.15 mm (0.006 in)
Exhaust (cold)	0.30 mm (0.012 in)
Inlet (hot)	0.20 mm (0.008 in)
Exhaust (hot)	0.35 mm (0.014 in)
Engine codes 102.924 and 102.962 KE	Self-adjusting
Valve timing @ at 2.0 mm (0.08 in) valve lift:	
Engine code 102.921:	
Inlet valve opens	7° ATDC
Inlet valve closes	10° ABDC
Exhaust valve opens	42° BBDC
Exhaust valve closes	23.5° BTDC
Engine code 102.961 KE:	
Inlet valve opens	11° ATDC
Inlet valve closes	21° ABDC
Exhaust valve opens	31.5° BBDC
Exhaust valve closes	13° BTDC
Engine codes 102.924 and 102.962 KE:	
Inlet valve opens	11° ATDC
Inlet valve closes	17° ABDC
Exhaust valve opens	32° BBDC
Exhaust valve closes	13° BTDC
Valve spring free length	48.5 mm (1.91 in)

Inlet valve

Length	114.70 to 115.10 mm (4.519 to 4.535 in)
Head diameter:	
Engine code 102.921	39.90 to 40.10 mm (1.572 to 1.580 in)
Engine codes 102.924, 102.961 KE and 102.962 KE	42.90 to 43.10 mm (1.690 to 1.698 in)
Stem diameter	7.955 to 7.970 mm (0.3134 to 0.3140 in)
Valve stem to guide clearance	0.03 to 0.045 mm (0.0012 to 0.0018 in)
Valve seat angle	45°

Exhaust valve

Length	115.60 to 116.00 mm (4.555 to 4.570 in)
Head diameter:	
Engine code 102.921	35.90 to 36.10 mm (1.414 to 1.422 in)
Engine codes 102.924, 102.961 KE and 102.962 KE	38.90 to 39.10 mm (1.533 to 1.541 in)
Stem diameter	8.938 to 8.960 mm (0.352 to 0.353 in)
Valve stem to guide clearance	0.040 to 0.055 mm (0.0016 to 0.0022 in)
Valve seat angle	45°

Lubrication

Oil pump type	Gear type, driven by crankshaft
Relief valve opening pressure	4.5 bar (65.2 lbf/in²)
Lubricant type	Multigrade engine oil, viscosity SAE 10W/40 or 15W/50 (Duckhams QXR, Hypergrade, or 10W/40 Motor Oil)
Lubricant capacity:	
Engine codes 102.921 and 102.961 KE:	
Total capacity	5.0 litres (8.8 Imp pints)
Refill with filter change	4.5 litres (7.9 Imp pints)
Engine codes 102.924 and 102.962 KE:	
Total capacity	5.5 litres (9.7 Imp pints)
Refill with filter change , ...	5.0 litres (8.8 Imp pints)

Torque wrench settings

	Nm	lbf ft
Rocker cover bolts	15	11
Camshaft bearing bracket bolts	21	15
Camshaft sprocket bolt	80	59
Timing chain tensioner retaining nut	70	52
Cylinder head retaining bolts (M12):		
Stage 1	70	52
Stage 2	Tighten further by 90°	Tighten further by 90°
Stage 3	Tighten further by 90°	Tighten further by 90°
Cylinder head front bolts (M8)	25	18
Crankshaft pulley and vibration damper retaining bolt	300	221
Timing cover retaining bolts	23	17
Sump retaining bolts	10	7
Sump drain plug	30	22
Oil pump cover bolts	10	7
Oil pick-up tube to pump cover	10	7
Oil pick-up tube to main bearing cap	10	7
Intermediate shaft retaining plate bolt	5	4
Oil pressure relief valve plug	30	22

Torque wrench settings

	Nm	lbf ft
Big-end bearing retaining nuts:		
Stage 1	40 to 50	30 to 37
Stage 2	Tighten further by 90° to 100°	Tighten further by 90° to 100°
Big-end bearing cap retaining bolts:		
Stage 1	30	22
Stage 2	Tighten further by 90° to 100°	Tighten further by 90° to 100°
Main bearing cap bolts	90	66
Crankshaft rear oil seal carrier	10	7
Flywheel or torque converter driveplate bolts:		
Stage 1	30 to 40	22 to 30
Stage 2	Tighten further by 90° to 100°	Tighten further by 90° to 100°
Engine mounting bracket to mounting	50	37
Engine mounting to crossmember	40	30

1 General description

The engine is of four-cylinder in-line overhead camshaft type, of 1997 cc displacement, and mounted conventionally at the front of the car.

The crankshaft is supported in five main bearings within the cast iron cylinder block. Crankshaft endfloat is controlled by thrust washers, fitted on either side of the centre main bearing.

The forged steel connecting rods are attached to the crankshaft by horizontally split big-end bearings, and to the pistons by fully floating gudgeon pins on early models, or by interference-fit gudgeon pins from early 1984 onwards. The aluminium alloy pistons are fitted with three piston rings; two compression and one oil control.

The camshaft is driven by a single-row chain from the crankshaft sprocket. The chain also drives the intermediate shaft, which is used to drive the distributor and also the fuel pump on carburettor models.

The camshaft is supported in five bearings in the aluminium alloy cylinder head, and actuates the valves via rocker arms. The rocker arms fitted to early engines incorporate conventional adjusting screws and locknuts for valve clearance (tappet) adjustment, but from October 1984 onwards, a compact, self-adjusting hydraulic tappet assembly is fitted to each rocker arm at the valve stem end.

The engine has a full-flow lubrication system from a gear-type oil pump, located in the timing cover and driven directly by the crankshaft. The oil filter is of the cartridge type on early models, or canister type on later models, and is located on the left-hand side of the engine at the rear.

2 Maintenance and inspection

1 At the intervals given in Routine Maintenance at the beginning of this manual, carry out the following maintenance operations on the engine.

2 Visually inspect the engine joint faces, gaskets and seals for any sign of water or oil leaks. Pay particular attention to the areas around the rocker cover, cylinder head, timing cover and sump joint faces. Rectify any leaks by referring to the appropriate Sections of this Chapter.

3 Place a suitable container beneath the oil drain plug on the left-hand side of the sump.

4 Unscrew the plug using a spanner or socket and allow the oil to drain. Inspect the condition of the drain plug sealing washer and renew it, if necessary. Refit and tighten the plug after draining.

5 Move the container to the rear of the engine beneath the oil filter.

6 On early models with a cartridge type filter, unscrew the central retaining bolt and remove the bolt and filter housing cover.

7 Lift out and discard the old filter and remove any oil remaining in the housing using a syringe such as a poultry baster.

8 Wipe clean the inside of the housing and insert the new filter cartridge.

9 Renew the sealing rings on the housing cover and central retaining bolt. Place the cover in position, refit the bolt and tighten to the specified torque.

10 On later models with a canister type filter, slacken the filter using a strap wrench or filter removal tool, then unscrew it from the engine and discard.

Fig. 1.1 Oil drain plug location on the left-hand side of the sump (Sec 2)

Fig. 1.2 Removing the cartridge type oil filter as fitted to early models (Sec 2)

11 Wipe the face of the filter housing flange with a rag, then lubricate the seal on the new filter with clean engine oil.
12 Screw the filter into position and tighten it firmly by hand only, do not use any tools.
13 Remove the filler cap on the rocker cover and fill the engine, using the correct grade of oil, until the level is up to the upper mark on the dipstick (photo). Refit the cap.
14 Start the engine and run it for a few minutes while checking for leaks around the filter. Switch off and re-check the level on the dipstick, topping-up if required.
15 On pre-October 1984 models, check the valve clearances as described in Section 5.

3 Major operations possible with the engine in the car

The following work can be carried out without having to remove the engine:

(a) Valve clearances – adjustment
(b) Camshaft – removal and refitting
(c) Cylinder head – removal and refitting, dismantling and reassembly
(d) Timing chain – renewal
(e) Engine mountings – removal and refitting
(f) Oil filter and filter housing – removal and refitting

4 Major operations requiring engine removal

The following work can only be carried out after removal of the engine from the car:

(a) Sump – removal and refitting
(b) Timing cover – removal and refitting
(c) Timing chain components and intermediate shaft – removal and refitting
(d) Oil pump – dismantling and reassembly
(e) Flywheel or torque converter driveplate – removal and refitting (alternatively after removing gearbox or transmission)
(f) Connecting rod and piston assemblies – removal and refitting
(g) Crankshaft – removal and refitting

5 Valve clearances – adjustment

Note: Valve clearance adjustment is only necessary on engines without hydraulic tappets, manufactured up to October 1984. Checking and adjustment may be carried out with the engine cold or warm.
1 Remove the air cleaner as described in Chapter 3.
2 Pull off the HT leads at the spark plugs, and release the two distributor cap retaining clamps using a screwdriver.
3 On fuel injection models, disconnect the idle speed air distributor hose on the side of the rocker cover.
4 Undo the retaining bolts and remove the rocker cover, complete with HT leads and distributor cap. On cars with air conditioning, unscrew the refrigerant suction line bracket on the front of the cylinder head, and move the suction line slightly to allow the distributor cap to be pulled through.
5 Disconnect the LT wiring plug at the ignition system electronic switching unit (refer to Chapter 4, Section 3).
6 Using a 27 mm socket or spanner, turn the engine by means of the pulley bolt and in the normal direction of rotation, until the cam lobes for No 1 cylinder inlet and exhaust valves are pointing downwards away from the rocker arms.
7 Using a feeler blade of thickness equal to the specified valve clearance, check that the blade is a tight sliding fit between the valve stem and rocker arm. Note that the inlet valves are on the carburettor or fuel injection system side of the cylinder head, the exhaust valves are on the exhaust manifold side, and the clearances are different for both.
8 If adjustment is required, slacken the locknut, turn the rocker arm adjusting screw until the correct clearance is obtained, then tighten the locknut while holding the adjusting screw.

Fig. 1.3 On cars with a cartridge type oil filter, renew the sealing ring on the housing cover (1) and retaining bolt (2) (Sec 2)

Fig. 1.4 Oil filler cap and dipstick locations (Sec 2)

2.13 Fill the engine with oil through the rocker cover

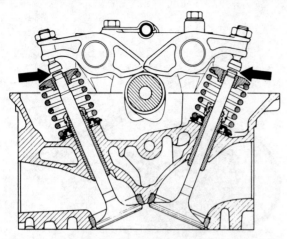

Fig. 1.5 Check the valve clearances between the valve stems and rockers with the cam lobes pointing downwards (Sec 5)

9 When both the valves for No 1 cylinder have been adjusted, turn the crankshaft until the cam lobes for the next pair of valves (No 2 cylinder) are pointing downwards, and adjust these valves in the same way. Repeat the procedure for cylinders 3 and 4.

10 On completion, refit the rocker cover using a new gasket if the original shows any sign of deterioration. Tighten the rocker cover retaining bolts to the specified torque. Reconnect the air hose on fuel injection models.

11 Reconnect the HT leads in the correct sequence and refit the distributor cap. Secure the refrigerant suction line bracket where applicable.

12 Refit the LT wiring plug to the switching unit, then refit the air cleaner as described in Chapter 3.

---

6 Hydraulic tappets – description, removal and refitting

1 On engines manufactured from October 1984 onwards, hydraulic tappet elements incorporated in each rocker arm were fitted, to reduce valve train noise and eliminate the need for periodic valve clearance adjustment. The elements operate as follows.

2 When the engine is stopped and the tappet element is under load from the cam lobe, oil is displaced from the operating chamber through the clearance between the plunger and guide sleeve walls and into the supply chamber via the return bores. This allows the element to completely retract.

3 When the engine is started and the cam lobe moves past the rocker arm, the load on the plunger is removed, and the compression spring pushes the plunger upward until the rocker arm again contacts the cam lobe. As this happens, a vacuum is created in the operating chamber which draws the ball valve off its seat and allows oil from the supply chamber to fill the operating chamber. As the cam lobe starts to move the rocker arm, the ball valve closes, the plunger is placed under load and the oil in the operating chamber creates a hydraulic lock within the element. The element, now in a solid condition, opens the valve as the cam lobe rotates, and actuates the rocker arm.

4 The oil supply for the hydraulic element is supplied from the main oil gallery and into a drilling in the rocker arm. From here it passes to the supply chamber through slots in the upper retaining washer.

5 To remove the hydraulic tappet elements, first remove the relevant camshaft bearing bracket complete with rocker arms (Section 7).

6 Remove the element from the rocker arm by pushing it down from above with a suitable mandrel. Withdraw the element and upper retaining washer from the underside of the rocker arm.

7 Prior to refitting, the unit must be filled with engine oil. To do this, hold the element vertically and fill the supply chamber with oil. Using a thin piece of wire inserted down through the supply chamber, push the ball valve off its seat so that oil can enter the operating chamber. At the same time, push the plunger upwards to its stop. Repeat this two or three times until no more oil can be added.

8 Still holding the element in a vertical position, insert the upper retaining washer into the rocker arm, with the oil slots toward the

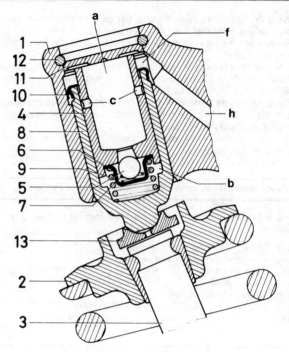

Fig. 1.6 Sectional view of the hydraulic tappet elements (Sec 6)

1	*Rocker arm*	*10*	*Closing cap*
2	*Valve spring cap*	*11*	*Upper retaining washer*
3	*Valve*	*12*	*Snap-ring*
4	*Plunger*	*13*	*Tappet contact seat*
5	*Ball valve*	*a*	*Supply chamber*
6	*Ball guide*	*b*	*Operating chamber*
7	*Ball valve spring*	*c*	*Return bores*
8	*Guide sleeve*	*f*	*Annular duct*
9	*Compression spring*	*h*	*Oil duct*

element, then insert the element. Push it up into contact with the snap ring. The camshaft bearing bracket can now be refitted to the car.

9 The design and construction of the hydraulic tappet element is such that the amount of free play, or clearance, that it can cope with is limited. This is mainly due to the small, compact size of the unit. To keep this clearance to a minimum and to within the operating tolerances of the unit, the upper retaining washer is available in a number of thicknesses.

10 Under normal operating conditions, the hydraulic tappet element will automatically adjust to take up the clearance between the rocker arm and valve stem, and no problems will occur.

11 If, however, after renewal of the camshaft, rocker arms, valves, or any of the hydraulic elements themselves, the valve train becomes noisy in operation, it is possible that the operating clearance has now become more than the element can cope with. In this case, it will be necessary to change the upper retaining washer for one of a different thickness.

12 To determine the required thickness of washer requires the use of a Mercedes-Benz special clamping fixture and dial gauge, and the work should be entrusted to a dealer if problems of this nature are experienced.

---

7 Camshaft – removal and refitting

1 Remove the air cleaner as described in Chapter 3, and the alternator as described in Chapter 12.

2 Pull off the HT leads at the spark plugs, and release the two distributor cap retaining clamps using a screwdriver.

3 On fuel injection models, disconnect the idle speed air distributor hose on the side of the rocker cover.

4 Undo the retaining bolts and remove the rocker cover, complete with HT leads and distributor cap. On cars with air conditioning,

unscrew the refrigerant suction line bracket on the front of the cylinder head, and move the suction line slightly to allow the distributor cap to be pulled through.

5 Disconnect the LT wiring plug at the ignition system electronic switching unit (refer to Chapter 4, Section 3).

6 Using a 27 mm socket or spanner, turn the engine by means of the pulley bolt and in the normal direction of rotation until the following conditions are obtained: the pointer on the timing cover aligns with the TDC (∅T) mark on the crankshaft pulley vibration damper scale, the distributor rotor arm points towards the notch in the rim of the distributor body and, more importantly, the mark on the camshaft flange aligns with the edge of the cylinder head (photo). The engine is now positioned with No 1 piston at top dead centre (TDC) on compression.

7 Using quick-drying white paint, make a reference mark on the camshaft sprocket and an adjacent link on the timing chain to aid refitting.

8 Unscrew the timing chain tensioner retaining nut on the right-hand side of the cylinder block (photo), and remove the spring and sealing ring (photo). **Note**: *The nut is under considerable tension from the spring, so be prepared for it to fly off when it reaches the end of the threads.*

9 Undo and remove the bolt and thrust washer securing the sprocket to the camshaft (photo). The camshaft can be held with a 24 mm open-ended spanner on the two flats at the rear, to prevent it turning as the bolt is undone (photo).

10 Withdraw the sprocket from the camshaft and remove it from the chain (photo).

11 Check that the rocker arm and camshaft bearing brackets are each numbered on their right-hand side according to their respective cylinder (photo) ie from front to rear, 1 to 4 respectively. A corresponding mark is cast in the cylinder head beneath the camshaft. If any of the brackets are not marked, suitably do so using a small file or punch marks. The brackets must not be mixed up after removal.

12 On early engines having valve clearance adjusting screws in the rocker arms, slacken the locknuts and unscrew the adjusting nuts as far as possible.

13 Undo the rocker arm and camshaft bearing bracket retaining bolts, noting the location of the oil spray pipe retaining clips.

14 Withdraw the oil spray pipe, then remove the four bearing bracket assemblies (photos). If they are stuck, lightly tap them free with a plastic mallet.

15 On engines with hydraulic tappets, remove the tappet contact seat from the top of each valve stem (photo), and keep them strictly in order in a compartment box marked for each valve, ie inlet 1, 2, 3, 4, and the same for the exhaust valves.

16 Lift the camshaft upwards and out of its bearings in the cylinder head.

17 Carry out a careful inspection of the components as described in Section 25.

18 Lubricate the camshaft and its bearings with engine oil (photo) and place the camshaft in the cylinder head. Turn the camshaft so that the mark on the flange is aligned with the edge of the cylinder head as was done prior to removal (photo).

19 On engines with hydraulic tappets, place each tappet contact seat in position on its respective valve stem.

20 Refit each bearing bracket in the correct numbered order so that the identification numbers are on the right-hand (exhaust manifold) side, and the mounting surface for the oil spray pipe is towards the rear.

21 Locate the oil spray pipe over the bearing brackets, ensuring that the oil pick-up holes are over the oil holes in the bearing brackets.

22 Refit the bearing bracket (and oil spray pipe) retaining bolts, and tighten the bolts progressively and in a diagonal sequence to the specified torque (photo).

23 Check that the engine and camshaft are still positioned at TDC as previously described, then engage the camshaft sprocket with the timing chain so that the reference marks made prior to removal are aligned.

24 Fit the sprocket to the camshaft, followed by the retaining bolt and thrust washer. Hold the camshaft at the rear machined flats, and tighten the sprocket bolt to the specified torque (photo).

25 Refit the chain tensioner spring, sealing ring and nut, then tighten the nut to the specified torque.

7.6 Camshaft TDC mark (arrowed) aligned with the edge of the cylinder head

7.8A Unscrew the timing chain cover tensioner retaining nut ...

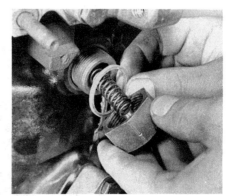
7.8B ... and remove the spring and sealing ring

7.9A Undo and remove the camshaft sprocket bolt and thrust washer ...

7.9B ... while holding the camshaft flats at the rear with a spanner

7.10 Remove the sprocket from the camshaft and chain

7.11 Camshaft bearing bracket identification numbers (arrowed)

7.14A Withdraw the oil spray pipe ...

7.14B ... and remove the bearing brackets

7.15 Removing the tappet contact seat

7.18A Lubricate the camshaft thoroughly ...

7.18B ... and position the camshaft notch at TDC (arrowed)

7.22 Tighten the bearing bracket bolts to the specified torque

7.24 Tighten the sprocket bolt to the specified torque

26 Turn the engine through two complete revolutions of the crankshaft, return it to the TDC position, and make sure the mark on the camshaft flange is aligned with the edge of the cylinder head. If not, it is likely that the sprocket has been fitted one tooth out in relation to the chain position. If so, remove the sprocket, re-position it and check the marks again.

27 On engines without hydraulic tappets, refer to Section 5 and adjust the valve clearances.

28 Refit the rocker cover, using a new gasket if necessary, and tighten the retaining bolts to the specified torque. Reconnect the air hose on fuel injection engines.

29 Refit the HT leads to the spark plugs and refit the distributor cap.

30 Connect the LT wiring plug to the ignition switching unit.

31 Refit the air cleaner as described in Chapter 3, and the alternator as described in Chapter 12.

8 Cylinder head (carburettor engines) – removal and refitting

Note: *The cylinder head must only be removed when the engine is cold.*

1 Disconnect the battery negative terminal.

2 Raise the bonnet to its vertical position by pressing the catch on the left-hand hinge, and releasing the safety spring on the support strut (photos). Push the bonnet up until the hinge locking catch engages.

3 Remove the air cleaner as described in Chapter 3.

4 Drain the cooling system as described in Chapter 2.

5 Disconnect the coolant hoses at the front and rear of the cylinder head (photos).

6 Undo the brake servo vacuum hose banjo union on the inlet

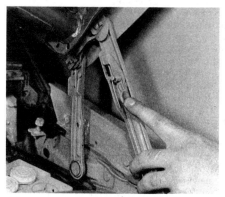

8.2A Raise the bonnet to the vertical position by pressing the hinge catch ...

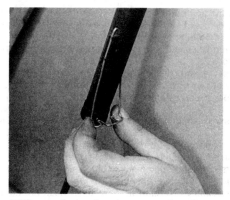

8.2B ... and releasing the strut spring

8.5A Disconnect the coolant hose at the front pipe junction (arrowed) ...

8.5B ... and at the rear of the cylinder head

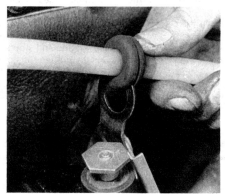

8.6 Release the servo vacuum hose at the support bracket

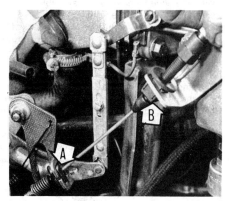

8.7 Disconnect the accelerator cable at the guide lever (A) and support bracket (B)

manifold, and recover the two sealing washers. Release the vacuum hose from the support bracket at the rear of the cylinder head (photo).
7   Disconnect the accelerator cable end from the linkage guide lever by releasing the square retainer and slipping the cable out of the lever slot. Compress the legs of the outer cable retainer and pull the cable up and out of the support bracket (photo).
8   On automatic transmission models, disconnect the control pressure cable from the guide lever ball socket and from the support bracket.
9   Disconnect the linkage return spring at the guide lever and fuel pump clip.
10 Disconnect the fuel supply hose from the fuel pump at the carburettor float chamber. Plug the hose with a bolt or dowel rod after removal.
11 Disconnect the vacuum hose at the inlet manifold adjacent to the throttle linkage bracket.
12 Disconnect the wiring plugs at the coolant temperature sensor, and at the thermal switches and connectors on the cylinder head (photos).

13 Disconnect the wiring plugs at the carburettor solenoid, choke housing, thermotime delay valve and fuel shut-off valve.
14 Disconnect the wiring plug at the pre-heater on the underside of the inlet manifold.
15 Undo the nut and bolt, and remove the wiring harness support bracket from the mounting bracket adjacent to the oil filter housing (photo).
16 Undo the bolt at the inlet manifold and engine mounting bracket (photo) securing the manifold support strut. Release the cable and hose clips, and remove the strut.
17 On cars with air conditioning, undo the refrigerant suction line support attachments at the front of the cylinder head, and any other support bracket mountings likely to impede removal of the cylinder head.
18 Undo the nut securing the engine oil dipstick tube clip to the adjacent manifold and release the clip. Pull out the dipstick and plug the dipstick tube.

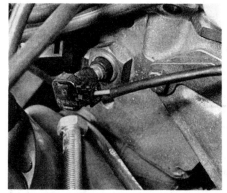

8.12A Disconnect the wiring at the coolant temperature sensor ...

8.12B ... and at the thermal switches and connectors (arrowed)

8.15 Release the wiring harness support bracket

19 On automatic transmission models, unscrew the bolt securing the transmission dipstick tube to the rear of the cylinder head.
20 Undo the exhaust downpipe-to-manifold retaining nuts or bolts.
21 Remove the thermostat housing as described in Chapter 2.
22 Remove the alternator as described in Chapter 12.
23 Pull off the spark plug HT leads at the spark plugs, and release the two distributor cap retaining clamps using a screwdriver.
24 Undo the retaining bolts, and remove the rocker cover complete with HT leads and distributor cap.
25 Refer to Section 7 and carry out the operations in paragraphs 5 to 10 inclusive.
26 It is now necessary to pull out the two bearing bolts in the front of the cylinder head which support the timing chain slide rail (Fig. 1.7). The Mercedes-Benz tool for doing this consists of a slide hammer which screws into the centre of the bearing bolt. The bolt is then impacted out under the action of the slide hammer. A similar arrangement can be adopted using an M6 bolt and washer screwed into the bearing bolt, and then using a three-legged puller with slide hammer attached (photo). Alternatively strike the puller body with a mallet if a slide hammer is not available. Be prepared however for the bearing bolt to be quite tight.
27 Once the two bearing bolts are released, remove them from the cylinder head and take out the slide rail (photos).
28 Check that all wiring, hoses, cable and hose clips and attachments likely to impede removal have been disconnected and moved well clear.
29 Using a multi-toothed socket bit, undo the cylinder head retaining bolts in the reverse sequence to that shown in Fig. 1.8 (photo). Also undo the four additional bolts securing the cylinder head to the timing cover and cylinder block at the front (photo).
30 The cylinder head, complete with manifolds, can now be removed from the cylinder block. If it is stuck, tap it up using a mallet in contact with a sturdy part of the casting, or use the manifolds for additional leverage. Do not attempt to lever between the head and the block, as this may damage the mating faces. Due to the considerable weight of the cylinder head with the manifolds attached, the help of an assistant will be necessary to lift it off. Alternatively, attach chains or ropes to the lifting brackets, and use a crane or hoist if one is available.
31 Remove the cylinder head gasket.
32 Remove the timing chain tensioner plunger in a forward direction from the tensioner body (Fig. 1.9).
33 Before refitting the cylinder head, measure the length of the retaining bolts with reference to Fig. 1.10. If the dimension exceeds the maximum permissible length, the bolts must be renewed.
34 Thoroughly clean the mating surfaces of the cylinder head and block, ensuring that all the bolt holes are free of dirt, water or oil.
35 Place a new cylinder head gasket on the block, then locate the cylinder head on the gasket.
36 Screw in the cylinder head bolts and tighten them initially finger-tight.
37 Tighten the cylinder head bolts in the sequence shown in Fig. 1.8 in three stages as follows. First tighten them to the torque setting given in the Specifications. Secondly, using a socket extension bar, not a torque wrench, tighten each bolt in the correct sequence by 90°. This can be judged by starting with the socket bar lengthwise in relation to the engine and stopping when it is crosswise in relation to the engine. Finally tighten the bolts by a further 90°, again in the correct sequence.
38 Refit the four additional bolts at the front of the cylinder head and tighten to the specified torque.
39 Locate the slide rail over the timing chain so that the open side is towards the cylinder head and the angled end is at the top. Move the slide rail into position, and hold it there temporarily with a screwdriver inserted through the upper bearing bolt hole.
40 Apply sealing compound to the lower bearing bolt, insert it

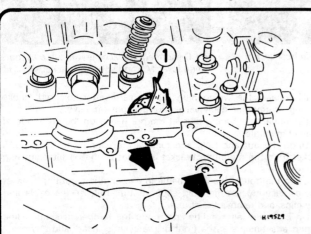

Fig. 1.7 Timing chain slide rail (1) and retaining bearing bolts (arrowed) (Sec 8)

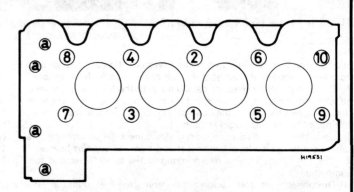

Fig. 1.8 Cylinder head bolt tightening sequence (Sec 8)

a Additional retaining bolts not part of sequence

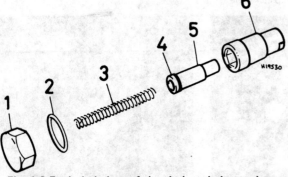

Fig. 1.9 Exploded view of the timing chain tensioner (Sec 8)

1 Retaining nut	3 Spring	5 Tensioner plunger
2 Sealing ring	4 Detent ring	6 Tensioner body

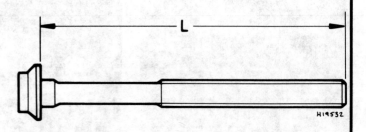

Fig. 1.10 Cylinder head bolt length measuring point (Sec 8)

L Maximum acceptable length = 122.0 mm (4.807 in)

Are your plugs trying to tell you something?

Normal.
Grey-brown deposits, lightly coated core nose. Plugs ideally suited to engine, and engine in good condition.

Heavy Deposits.
A build up of crusty deposits, light-grey sandy colour in appearance.
Fault: Often caused by worn valve guides, excessive use of upper cylinder lubricant, or idling for long periods.

Lead Glazing.
Plug insulator firing tip appears yellow or green/yellow and shiny in appearance.
Fault: Often caused by incorrect carburation, excessive idling followed by sharp acceleration. Also check ignition timing.

Carbon fouling.
Dry, black, sooty deposits.
Fault: over-rich fuel mixture.
Check: carburettor mixture settings, float level, choke operation, air filter.

Oil fouling.
Wet, oily deposits. Fault: worn bores/piston rings or valve guides; sometimes occurs (temporarily) during running-in period.

Overheating.
Electrodes have glazed appearance, core nose very white – few deposits. Fault: plug overheating. Check: plug value, ignition timing, fuel octane rating (too low) and fuel mixture (too weak).

Electrode damage.
Electrodes burned away; core nose has burned, glazed appearance. Fault: pre-ignition. Check: for correct heat range and as for 'overheating'.

Split core nose.
(May appear initially as a crack). Fault: detonation or wrong gap-setting technique. Check: ignition timing, cooling system, fuel mixture (too weak).

WHY DOUBLE COPPER IS BETTER FOR YOUR ENGINE.

Unique Trapezoidal Copper Cored Earth Electrode — 50% Larger Spark Area — Copper Cored Centre Electrode

Champion Double Copper plugs are the first in the world to have copper core in both centre <u>and</u> earth electrode. This innovative design means that they run cooler by up to 100°C – giving greater efficiency and longer life. These double copper cores transfer heat away from the tip of the plug faster and more efficiently. Therefore, Double Copper runs at cooler temperatures than conventional plugs giving improved acceleration response and high speed performance with no fear of pre-ignition.

TRAPEZOIDAL COPPER CORED EARTH ELECTRODE

NEW TRAPEZOIDAL COPPER CORED EARTH ELECTRODE / CONVENTIONAL SOLID NICKEL ALLOY EARTH ELECTRODE

50% INCREASE IN SPARK AREA

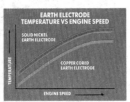

EARTH ELECTRODE TEMPERATURE VS ENGINE SPEED

SOLID NICKEL EARTH ELECTRODE

COPPER CORED EARTH ELECTRODE

TEMPERATURE / ENGINE SPEED

Champion Double Copper plugs also feature a unique trapezoidal earth electrode giving a 50% increase in spark area. This, together with the double copper cores, offers greatly reduced electrode wear, so the spark stays stronger for longer.

 FASTER COLD STARTING

 FOR UNLEADED OR LEADED FUEL

 ELECTRODES UP TO 100°C COOLER

 BETTER ACCELERATION RESPONSE

 LOWER EMISSIONS

 50% BIGGER SPARK AREA

 THE LONGER LIFE PLUG

Plug Tips/Hot and Cold.
Spark plugs must operate within well-defined temperature limits to avoid cold fouling at one extreme and overheating at the other.
Champion and the car manufacturers work out the best plugs for an engine to give optimum performance under all conditions, from freezing cold starts to sustained high speed motorway cruising.
Plugs are often referred to as hot or cold. With Champion, the higher the number on its body, the hotter the plug, and the lower the number the cooler the plug.

Plug Cleaning
Modern plug design and materials mean that Champion no longer recommends periodic plug cleaning. Certainly don't clean your plugs with a wire brush as this can cause metal conductive paths across the nose of the insulator so impairing its performance and resulting in loss of acceleration and reduced m.p.g.
However, if plugs are removed, always carefully clean the area where the plug seats in the cylinder head as grit and dirt can sometimes cause gas leakage.
Also wipe any traces of oil or grease from plug leads as this may lead to arcing.

CHAMPION

DOUBLE **CC** COPPER

This photographic sequence shows the steps taken to repair the dent and paintwork damage shown above. In general, the procedure for repairing a hole will be similar; where there are substantial differences, the procedure is clearly described and shown in a separate photograph.

First remove any trim around the dent, then hammer out the dent where access is possible. This will minimise filling. Here, after the large dent has been hammered out, the damaged area is being made slightly concave.

Next, remove all paint from the damaged area by rubbing with coarse abrasive paper or using a power drill fitted with a wire brush or abrasive pad. 'Feather' the edge of the boundary with good paintwork using a finer grade of abrasive paper.

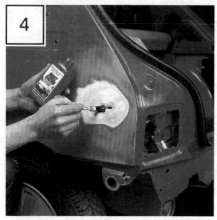

Where there are holes or other damage, the sheet metal should be cut away before proceeding further. The damaged area and any signs of rust should be treated with Turtle Wax Hi-Tech Rust Eater, which will also inhibit further rust formation.

For a large dent or hole mix Holts Body Plus Resin and Hardener according to the manufacturer's instructions and apply around the edge of the repair. Press Glass Fibre Matting over the repair area and leave for 20-30 minutes to harden. Then ...

... brush more Holts Body Plus Resin and Hardener onto the matting and leave to harden. Repeat the sequence with two or three layers of matting, checking that the final layer is lower than the surrounding area. Apply Holts Body Plus Filler Paste as shown in Step 5B.

For a medium dent, mix Holts Body Plus Filler Paste and Hardener according to the manufacturer's instructions and apply it with a flexible applicator. Apply thin layers of filler at 20-minute intervals, until the filler surface is slightly proud of the surrounding bodywork.

For small dents and scratches use Holts No Mix Filler Paste straight from the tube. Apply it according to the instructions in thin layers, using the spatula provided. It will harden in minutes if applied outdoors and may then be used as its own knifing putty.

Use a plane or file for initial shaping. Then, using progressively finer grades of wet-and-dry paper, wrapped round a sanding block, and copious amounts of clean water, rub down the filler until glass smooth. 'Feather' the edges of adjoining paintwork.

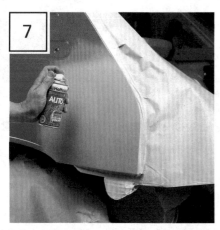

Protect adjoining areas before spraying the whole repair area and at least one inch of the surrounding sound paintwork with Holts Dupli-Color primer.

Fill any imperfections in the filler surface with a small amount of Holts Body Plus Knifing Putty. Using plenty of clean water, rub down the surface with a fine grade wet-and-dry paper – 400 grade is recommended – until it is really smooth.

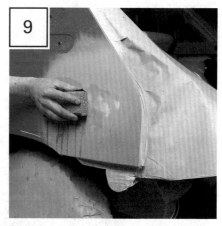

Carefully fill any remaining imperfections with knifing putty before applying the last coat of primer. Then rub down the surface with Holts Body Plus Rubbing Compound to ensure a really smooth surface.

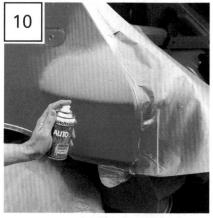

Protect surrounding areas from overspray before applying the topcoat in several thin layers. Agitate Holts Dupli-Color aerosol thoroughly. Start at the repair centre, spraying outwards with a side-to-side motion.

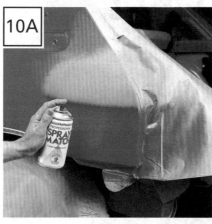

If the exact colour is not available off the shelf, local Holts Professional Spraymatch Centres will custom fill an aerosol to match perfectly.

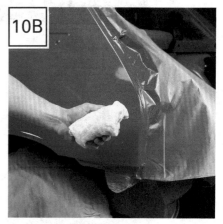

To identify whether a lacquer finish is required, rub a painted unrepaired part of the body with wax and a clean cloth.

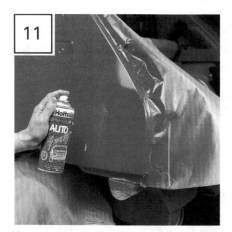

If *no* traces of paint appear on the cloth, spray Holts Dupli-Color clear lacquer over the repaired area to achieve the correct gloss level.

The paint will take about two weeks to harden fully. After this time it can be 'cut' with a mild cutting compound such as Turtle Wax Minute Cut prior to polishing with a final coating of Turtle Wax Extra.

When carrying out bodywork repairs, remember that the quality of the finished job is proportional to the time and effort expended.

HAYNES No1 for DIY

Haynes publish a wide variety of books besides the world famous range of *Haynes Owners Workshop Manuals*. They cover all sorts of DIY jobs. Specialist books such as the *Improve and Modify* series and the *Purchase and DIY Restoration Guides* give you all the information you require to carry out everything from minor modifications to complete restoration on a number of popular cars. In addition there are the publications dealing with specific tasks, such as the *Car Bodywork Repair Manual* and the *In-Car Entertainment Manual*. The *Household DIY* series gives clear step-by-step instructions on how to repair everyday household objects ranging from toasters to washing machines.

Whether it is under the bonnet or around the home there is a Haynes Manual that can help you save money. Available from motor accessory stores and bookshops or direct from the publisher.

8.16 Undo the manifold support bracket bolt (arrowed)

8.26 Using a puller and slide hammer arrangement to release the bearing bolts

8.27A Remove the bearing bolts ...

8.27B ... and take out the slide rail

8.29A Undo the main cylinder head retaining bolts ...

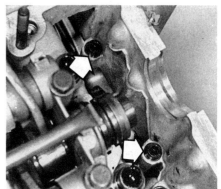

8.29B ... and the four additional front bolts (two centre bolts arrowed)

through the slide rail, and tap it fully into place. Fit the upper bearing bolt in the same way.
41 Insert the timing chain tensioner plunger into the tensioner body up to detent 'A' (Fig. 1.11).
42 Refit the camshaft sprocket, chain and tensioner as described in Section 7, paragraphs 23 to 28 inclusive.
43 The remainder of the refitting operations are a direct reversal of the removal procedures, bearing in mind the following points:

(a) Check the accelerator cable adjustment as described in Chapter 3
(b) On automatic transmission models, check the control pressure cable adjustment as described in Chapter 6
(c) Refill the cooling system as described in Chapter 2

9 Cylinder head (fuel injection engines) – removal and refitting

Note: *The cylinder head must only be removed when the engine is cold*
1 Disconnect the battery negative terminal.
2 Raise the bonnet to its vertical position by pressing the catch on the left-hand hinge and releasing the safety spring on the support strut. Push the bonnet up until the hinge locking catch engages.
3 Remove the air cleaner as described in Chapter 3.
4 Drain the cooling system as described in Chapter 2.
5 Disconnect the coolant hoses at the front and rear of the cylinder head.
6 Undo the brake servo vacuum hose union nut on the inlet manifold and move the hose clear. Note the location of the support bracket on the air cleaner mounting block.
7 Disconnect the accelerator cable end from the linkage guide lever by releasing the square retainer and slipping the cable out of the lever slot. Compress the legs of the outer cable retainer, and pull the cable up and out of the support bracket (photo).

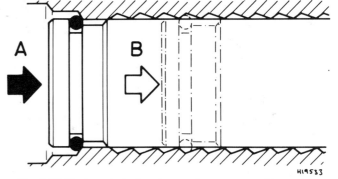

Fig. 1.11 Timing chain tensioner plunger assembly positions (Sec 8)

A Initial detent when fitting plunger
B Direction of plunger removal from tensioner body

8 On automatic transmission models, disconnect the control pressure cable from the guide lever, using the procedure described in Chapter 6.
9 Disconnect the linkage return spring at the guide lever.
10 Disconnect the fuel hoses at the fuel distributor and fuel pressure regulator (photo). Place rags around the union nuts to catch the escaping fuel as the union is slackened.
11 Disconnect the wiring multi-plugs at the cold start valve, electromagnetic pressure actuator on the side of the fuel distributor, airflow sensor, throttle valve housing, auxiliary air device, coolant temperature sensor, and at the thermal switches and wiring connectors on the cylinder head. Identify each connector with a label, or make notes to aid refitting.
12 Disconnect the wires at the main earth connection on the inlet manifold bracket (photo).
13 Detach the idle air distributor hose from the side of the rocker cover.

9.7 Accelerator cable attachments at the guide lever and support bracket (arrowed)

9.10 Fuel hose connections at the fuel distributor and fuel pressure regulator (arrowed)

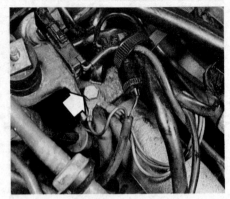

9.12 Inlet manifold earth connection

14 Disconnect any remaining wiring or vacuum hose connections likely to impede cylinder head removal, release the clips and ties, and move the wiring harness clear.

15 Undo the bolts and remove the inlet manifold support strut.

16 The remainder of the removal and refitting procedure is the same as for carburettor engines, described in Section 8, paragraphs 17 to 43 inclusive.

10 Cylinder head – dismantling and reassembly

1 With the cylinder head on the bench, begin dismantling by removing the inlet and exhaust manifolds as described in Chapter 3. Leave all the components attached to the manifold in place, disconnect their hose or electrical connections at the cylinder head, and remove them with the manifold.

2 Remove the camshaft from the cylinder head as described in Section 7.

3 Have ready a board with eight holes punched in it, into which each valve can be inserted as it is removed, or have a set of labelled containers, so that each valve and its associated parts can be identified and kept separate. Number the board or containers No 1 inlet, No 1 exhaust, No 2 inlet, No 2 exhaust, etc, noting that No 1 cylinder is at the timing chain end of the engine, and the exhaust valves are on the spark plug side of the cylinder head.

4 Using a valve spring compressor, compress each valve spring in turn until the collets can be removed (photo). Take out the collets (photo), release the spring compressor and remove it.

5 Remove the spring cap, valve spring (or springs on certain models), followed by the valve (photos).

6 Prise off the valve stem oil seal then remove the spring seat (photos).

7 Carry out a careful inspection of the components as described in

10.4A Compress the valve spring ...

10.4B ... and remove the collets

10.5A Remove the spring cap ...

10.5B ... valve spring ...

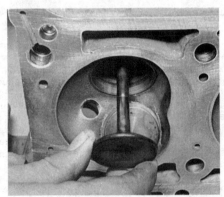

10.5C ... and the valve

10.6A Remove the valve stem oil seal ...

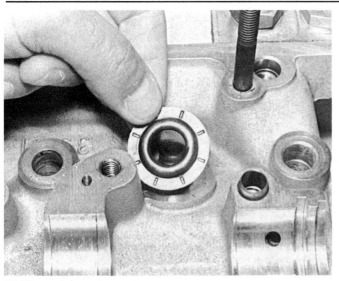

10.6B ... and the spring seat

10.9 Exhaust valve stem oil seal (left) and inlet stem seal (right)

Section 25, and decarbonise the cylinder head and valves as described in Section 26.
8   Begin reassembly by placing the spring seat for the first valve over the guide, so that the raised centre portion of the spring seat is uppermost.
9   Place the appropriate new valve stem oil seal over the valve guide, and push it fully into place. Note that the exhaust valve stem oil seal is identified by its bright wire ring, while the inlet seal has a black ring (photo). Ensure that the correct seal is fitted to its respective inlet or exhaust valve guide.
10   Liberally lubricate the valve stem and oil seal, then carefully insert the valve, taking care not to damage the oil seal as it is pushed through.
11   Place the spring over the valve, followed by the spring cap. On engines with double valve springs, the close coils must be towards the cylinder head.
12   Compress the spring and insert the collets, ensuring that they locate correctly in the valve stem groove.
13   Release and remove the compressor, then tap the top of the valve stem sharply with a soft-faced mallet to seat the components.
14   Refit the remaining valves in the same way, then refit the camshaft as described in Section 7 and the manifolds as described in Chapter 3.

11 Timing chain – renewal

Note: The timing chain itself can be renewed with the engine in the car, but removal and refitting of the timing cover, slide rails or tensioning rail can only be carried out with the engine removed. Renewal of the timing chain using the following procedure entails the use of a portable electric grinder to cut through one of the chain links. Ensure that such a tool is available, as well as a new chain and new connecting link before proceeding.
1   Disconnect the battery negative terminal.
2   Remove the air cleaner as described in Chapter 3.
3   Pull off the HT leads at the spark plugs, and release the two distributor cap retaining clamps using a screwdriver.
4   On fuel injection models, disconnect the idle speed air distributor hose on the side of the rocker cover.
5   Undo the retaining bolts and remove the rocker cover, complete with HT leads and distributor cap. On cars with air conditioning, unscrew the refrigerant suction line bracket on the front of the cylinder head, and move the suction line slightly to allow the distributor cap to be pulled through.
6   Remove the spark plugs.
7   Disconnect the LT wiring plug at the ignition system electronic switching unit (refer to Chapter 4, Section 3).
8   Remove the alternator as described in Chapter 12.
9   Unscrew the timing chain tensioner retaining nut on the right-hand side of the cylinder block, and remove the spring and sealing ring.

Note: The nut is under considerable tension from the spring, so be prepared for it to fly off when it reaches the end of the threads.
10   Using a large Allen key or hexagonal socket bit, unscrew the chain tensioner body and remove it from the cylinder block.
11   Remove the plunger from the tensioner body.
12   Cover the camshaft and the chain opening in the timing cover with rags, but keep the rags clear of the camshaft sprocket upper part.
13   Using the grinder, grind off the protruding legs of one of the chain links on the top of the sprocket. Remove the link plate, then push the link out of the chain toward the rear (Fig. 1.12).
14   Using the new link, connect one end of the new timing chain to the tail end of the old chain, in such a way that as the engine is turned, the new chain will be drawn down, around the sprockets and guides, then up the other side. Ensure that the new chain is connected so that the link heads are toward the rear, and the peened over ends of the link legs are towards the front.

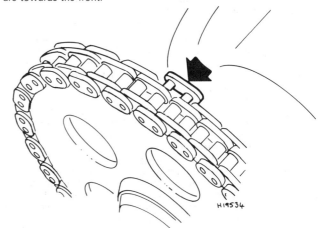

Fig. 1.12 Removing a timing chain link (arrowed) in a rearward direction (Sec 11)

15   Using a 27 mm socket on the crankshaft pulley bolt, slowly rotate the crankshaft in the normal direction of rotation. Keep the links of the new chain engaged with the camshaft sprocket as it is pulled through, otherwise the timing will be lost, and pull up on the old chain to stop it dropping off the crankshaft sprocket, or jamming in the guides.
16   When the end of the new chain appears, remove the link and disconnect it from the old chain. Place the new chain on the camshaft sprocket and join the two ends with the connecting link, inserted from the rear.
17   Fit the link plate and lock the link, using the two small circlips supplied, by inserting them into the link leg grooves.
18   Set the engine at the TDC position for No 1 piston, and check that

all the timing marks align as described in Section 7, paragraph 6. It is likely that the timing may have slipped by one tooth on the camshaft sprocket during this operation. If it has, it can be corrected by re-positioning the sprocket and camshaft one or more teeth either way as necessary in relation to the chain. This is also described in Section 7.
19 With everything correct, insert the timing chain tension plunger into the tensioner body up to detent 'A' as shown in Fig. 1.11.
20 Refit the tensioner body to the cylinder block and tighten it securely.
21 Refit the tensioner spring, sealing ring and retaining nut, and tighten the nut to the specified torque.
22 Refit the rocker cover, using a new gasket if necessary, and secure with the retaining bolts tightened to the specified torque.
23 Refit the spark plugs, HT leads and distributor cap.
24 Reconnect the idle speed air distributor hose and the refrigerant suction line bracket as applicable.
25 Refit the alternator as described in Chapter 12, and the air cleaner as described in Chapter 3.
26 Reconnect the battery negative terminal.

12 Engine mountings – removal and refitting

1   Jack up the front of the car and support it on axle stands.
2   Support the engine under the sump using a suitable jack and block of wood.
3   From above, undo the central bolt securing the mounting to the cylinder bolt bracket. If working on the right-hand mounting, remove the protective shield.
4   Raise the engine slightly until the cylinder block bracket is clear of the mounting.
5   Working through the access hole in the crossmember from below, undo the socket-headed bolt securing the mounting to the crossmember, and remove the mounting.
6   The mountings are not interchangeable from side to side, and are therefore colour-coded by means of a coloured dot on the mounting body. The left-hand mounting is identified by its red dot, and the right-hand mounting by its green dot.
7   Refitting is the reverse sequence to removal, but ensure that the lug on the mounting engages with the slot on the cylinder block bracket when fitting.

13 Lubrication system – description

The oil pump draws oil from the sump through a pick-up tube, and then supplies pressurised oil through a feed duct through the cylinder block to the oil filter at the rear of the engine. Should the pressure exceed a predetermined value, the oil pressure relief valve in the timing cover is opened against spring pressure, and some of the oil is diverted back to the suction side of the pump.
The full-flow oil filter is of cartridge type on early models, and throw-away canister type on later models. Contained within the filter housing are non-return valves, which prevent the oil draining back to the sump when the engine is stopped.
Filtered oil passes out of the housing and into the oil gallery in the block, where one branch diverts it to the main bearings in the crankcase. Oil at the main bearings enters drillings in the crankshaft, which supply the big end bearings, and pistons via squirt holes in the connecting rods. Another branch from the oil gallery supplies oil to operate the plunger in the timing chain tensioner.
Oil supplied to the cylinder head passes through the hollow camshaft to lubricate the bearing journals, and also through drillings in the rocker shafts and rocker arms to spray onto the cam lobes. Additional spray lubrication of the camshaft is provided by the longitudinal oil pipe over the camshaft and rocker arms.
From the cylinder head, oil flows through galleries to the front of the engine to lubricate the intermediate shaft and distributor shaft, the chain and gears. Passages in the cylinder head and block allow the oil to return under gravity to the sump.

14 Oil filter housing – removal and refitting

1   Drain the engine oil and remove the oil filter as described in Section 2.

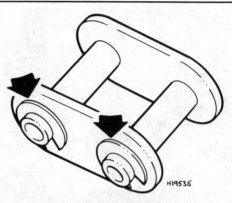

Fig. 1.13 Retaining circlips (arrowed) used to secure new link (Sec 11)

2   Disconnect the wiring at the oil pressure switch.
3   Using an Allen key, unscrew the socket-headed retaining bolts and remove the filter housing and gasket (photos).
4   Clean the housing and cylinder block mating faces thoroughly, and refit the housing using the reverse sequence to removal.
5   Fit a new filter and refill the engine with oil as described in Section 2.

14.3A Unscrew the oil filter housing bolts using an Allen key

14.3B Removing the filter housing gasket

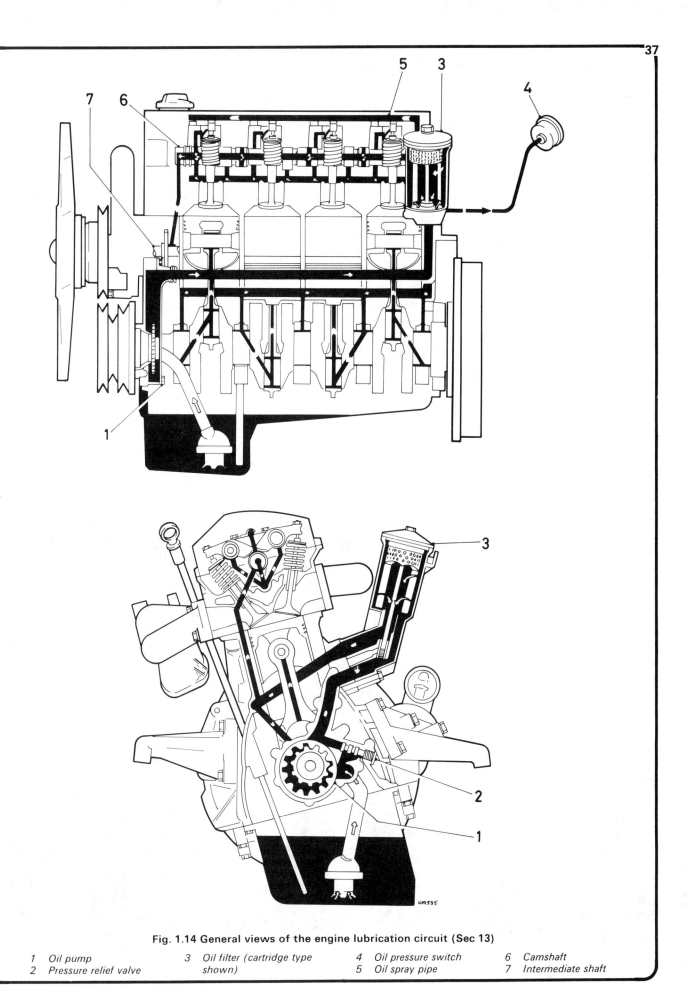

Fig. 1.14 General views of the engine lubrication circuit (Sec 13)

| 1 | Oil pump | 3 | Oil filter (cartridge type shown) | 4 | Oil pressure switch | 6 | Camshaft |
| 2 | Pressure relief valve | | | 5 | Oil spray pipe | 7 | Intermediate shaft |

15 Engine – method of removal

The engine must be removed complete with gearbox or automatic transmission, and is lifted upwards and out of the engine compartment from above.

16 Engine – removal and refitting

1   Disconnect the battery negative terminal.
2   Raise the bonnet to its vertical position by pressing the catch on the left-hand hinge and releasing the safety wire spring on the support strut. Push the bonnet up until the hinge locking catch engages.
3   Remove the air cleaner as described in Chapter 3.
4   Drain the cooling system and remove the radiator as described in Chapter 2.
5   On cars equipped with air conditioning, remove the refrigerant compressor drivebelt as described in Chapter 11 on models having multiple drivebelts, or Chapter 12, Section 6 on models with a single drivebelt arrangement. Having removed the drivebelt, unbolt the refrigerant compressor itself and move it clear of the engine, but without disconnecting any of the hoses. It may be necessary to remove other components to allow the hoses to clear depending on model, options fitted, and type of system used.
6   Unscrew the filler cap on the power steering pump reservoir and draw off the fluid, using a large syringe such as a poultry baster. Refit the filler cap when the reservoir has been emptied.
7   Disconnect the accelerator cable end from the linkage guide lever by releasing the square retainer and slipping the cable out of the lever slot. Compress the legs of the outer cable retainer and pull the cable up and out of the support bracket.
8   Undo the brake servo vacuum hose banjo bolt or union nut on the inlet manifold. Recover the two sealing washers where a banjo union is used.

9   Release the servo vacuum hose from the support bracket at the rear of the cylinder head.
10   Disconnect the radiator top hose at the coolant pump and the expansion tank hose at the thermostat housing.
11   Disconnect the right-hand heater hose at the coolant pump outlet, and the left-hand hose at the rear of the cylinder head.
12   Disconnect the vacuum supply hose at the inlet manifold.
13   On carburettor engines, disconnect the fuel supply hose at the fuel pump and the return hose at the carburettor. Plug the hoses after removal.
14   On fuel injection engines, disconnect the fuel hoses at the fuel distributor and fuel pressure regulator. Place rags around the union nuts to catch the escaping fuel as the union is slackened. Cover the unions after removal.
15   Make a careful note of all the wiring connections that affect engine removal, or preferably attach labels to the wires, then disconnect them. These will include the connectors and multi-plugs at the following components.

Carburettor engines: *Carburettor solenoid, choke housing, thermo-time delay valve, fuel shut-off valve, inlet manifold pre-heater, coolant temperature sensor and cylinder head thermal switches, sump oil level sensor, alternator, starter motor, oil pressure switch, distributor cap HT lead (photos).*
Fuel injection engines: *Cold start valve, electromagnetic pressure actuator, airflow sensor, throttle valve housing, auxiliary air device, coolant temperature sensor and cylinder head thermal switches, sump oil level sensor, alternator, starter motor, oil pressure switch, distributor cap HT lead.*

16   Disconnect the two wiring plugs at the ignition system electronic switching unit.
17   Undo the screws securing the diagnostic socket to the inner wing panel and disconnect the wiring plug from the rear of the socket (photo).
18   Undo the bolt securing the wiring harness support bracket to the mounting bracket on the inlet manifold adjacent to the oil filter.

16.15A Disconnect the wiring at the manifold pre-heater terminal (arrowed) ...

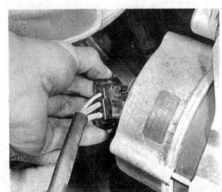

16.15B ... alternator ...

16.15C ... starter motor solenoid terminal (arrowed) ...

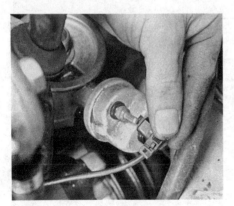

16.15D ... and oil pressure switch

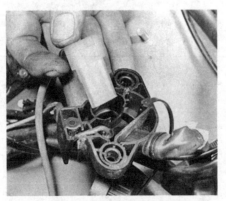

16.17 Disconnect the wiring plug at the rear of the diagnostic socket

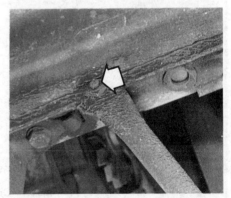

16.21A Undo the undertray front support (arrowed) ...

19 Release the wiring and cables from the various ties and cable clips and move all the disconnected wiring clear of the engine.

20 Suitably raise and support the car to provide adequate working clearance under the engine and transmission.

21 On cars fitted with an engine undertray, undo the front support strut nuts and bolts and the rear flange nuts and bolts and remove the undertray (photos).

22 On early models, undo the mountings and remove the engine front shock absorber.

23 Undo the flange nuts or bolts and separate the exhaust downpipes at the manifold.

24 Slacken the hose clip and undo the union nut to release the power steering hoses at the connections on the lower right-hand side of the engine (photo). Plug the hoses and pipe unions after removal.

25 Undo the nut and bolt and remove the engine earth strap at the bellhousing (photo).

26 On manual gearbox models, refer to Chapter 6, Section 3, and carry out the operations listed in paragraphs 4 to 19 inclusive.

27 On automatic transmission models, refer to Section 6, Section 23 and carry out the operations listed in paragraphs 10 to 26 inclusive.

28 Undo the bolts securing the engine mounting brackets to the mountings. Remove the shield on the right-hand mounting.

29 Attach a suitable crane or hoist by means of chains to the engine lifting brackets at the front and rear of the cylinder head. Position the chains so that the engine and transmission will adopt a 45° angle as they are removed.

30 Make a final check that all wiring, pipes, hoses and attachments likely to impede engine removal are disconnected and positioned well clear.

31 Raise the lifting gear to just take the weight of the engine, then remove the jack under the gearbox or transmission.

32 Slowly and carefully raise the unit and when sufficient clearance exists, swing it over the front body panel and out of the engine compartment (photo).

33 Lower the engine and transmission to the ground, or position them on a bench ready for separation.

34 Refitting is a direct reversal of the removal procedure, bearing in mind the following points.

   (a) Ensure that the lugs on the engine mountings engage with the slot on the mounting brackets as the engine is lowered into place

   (b) Attach the gearbox or automatic transmission, the propeller shaft, and the adjacent components, using the procedures described in Chapter 6

   (c) On manual gearbox models, bleed the clutch hydraulic system as described in Chapter 5

   (d) On automatic transmission models, fill the transmission with fluid and adjust the control pressure cable as described in Chapter 6

   (e) On cars equipped with air conditioning, refit the refrigerant compressor drivebelt as described in Chapter 11 or 12 as applicable, after refitting the compressor

   (f) Refill the power steering pump reservoir with the specified fluid as described in Chapter 10

   (g) Fill the cooling system as described in Chapter 2

17 Engine – separation from and attachment to transmission

Manual gearbox models

1 With the engine and gearbox removed from the car, undo the retaining bolts and remove the starter motor (photo).

2 Undo the two bolts and withdraw the clutch slave cylinder from the bellhousing (photo).

3 Undo all the bolts securing the gearbox bellhousing to the engine, noting the location of any cable support brackets, and also the engine earth strap if this was removed with the engine and gearbox.

4 Pull the gearbox squarely off the engine dowels, keeping it level until the input shaft is clear of the clutch assembly (photo).

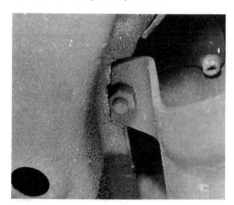
16.21B ... and rear flange attachment ...

16.21C ... then remove the undertray

16.24 Disconnect the power steering hoses at the lower right-hand connections

16.25 Disconnect the engine earth strap (arrowed)

16.32 Removing the engine and gearbox

17.1 Remove the starter motor ...

5 Attachment is the reverse of separation, but lubricate the input shaft splines with molybdenum disulphide grease prior to fitting.

Automatic transmission models
6 With the engine and transmission removed from the car, position the units to provide access to the underside of the converter housing.
7 Remove the rubber grommet from the front face of the converter housing under the engine sump.
8 Turn the engine crankshaft until each pair of torque converter retaining bolts (from a total of six) become accessible through the converter housing opening. Undo and remove the first two bolts, then repeat the procedure for the remaining bolts.
9 Disconnect the transmission fluid dipstick tube at the rear of the cylinder head, and where applicable at the rocker cover.
10 Disconnect the fluid cooler pipe support clips along their entire length, so that the pipes can be removed with the transmission.
11 Undo the retaining bolts and remove the starter motor.
12 Undo all the bolts securing the converter housing to the engine, noting the location of any cable support brackets, and also the engine earth strap if this was removed with the engine and transmission.
13 Pull the transmission squarely off the engine dowels, ensuring that the torque converter stays on the transmission as it is removed.
14 Attachment is the reverse of separation, but lightly lubricate the torque converter stub shaft and tighten the retaining bolts to the specified torque (see Chapter 6).

18 Sump – removal and refitting

1 Remove the engine from the car as described in Section 16.
2 Unscrew the sump drain plug, drain the oil into a suitable container, then refit the drain plug. Use a new sealing washer on the drain plug if the original is in any way damaged.
3 Undo the power steering pipe support bracket bolts and move the pipes clear (photo).

4 Undo the bolts securing the sump to the crankcase, timing cover and bellhousing (if the gearbox or automatic transmission are still attached).
5 Withdraw the sump from its location, tapping it lightly with a plastic mallet if it is stuck. Remove the gasket.
6 Scrape away all traces of old gasket from the mating faces, and clean the sump thoroughly inside and out with paraffin or a suitable solvent. Dry with a lint-free rag.
7 Smear gasket sealant on both sides of the new gasket, place the gasket in position, and refit the sump (photos).
8 Refit the sump bolts and tighten them progressively to the specified torque.
9 Refit the power steering pipe bracket, then refit the engine to the car as described in Section 16.

19 Timing cover – removal and refitting

1 Remove the engine from the car as described in Section 16.
2 Remove the coolant pump as described in Chapter 2, the distributor as described in Chapter 4, and the power steering pump as described in Chapter 10.
3 Remove the cylinder head as described in Sections 8 or 9, and the sump as described in Section 18.
4 On pre-October 1984 models, undo the bolts securing the power steering pump mounting bracket to the side of the cylinder head and remove the bracket.
5 On models manufactured from October 1984 onwards, undo the five bolts securing the power steering pump mounting bracket and drivebelt tensioner assembly to the cylinder block, and the three bolts and nuts securing it to the timing cover (photos). If a shock absorber for the tensioner is also fitted as part of this assembly, undo the additional mountings and brackets and remove the shock absorber and the mounting bracket/tensioner together.

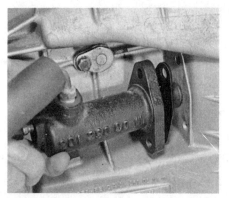
17.2 ... and the clutch slave cylinder

17.4 Withdraw the gearbox squarely from the engine

18.3 Power steering pipe support bracket attachment at the sump

18.7A Fitting a new sump gasket ...

18.7B ... followed by the sump

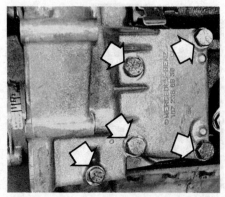
19.5A Power steering pump mounting bracket bolts on the side of the cylinder block (arrowed) ...

6 Remove any other ancillary component brackets which are attached to, or impeding removal of, the timing cover.
7 Lock the crankshaft either by means of an angle-iron strip or similar alternative between the flywheel teeth and the side of the cylinder block (photo), or by placing a block of wood between one of the crankshaft webs and the crankcase side.
8 With the crankshaft locked and an assistant supporting the engine, undo the crankshaft pulley retaining bolt using a 27 mm socket, socket bar and long extension. This bolt is extremely tight, and considerable effort will be needed to release it.
9 Remove the bolt and the spring cups behind the bolt head, then withdraw the vibration damper or hub, and the pulley as an assembly (photos).
10 Remove the Woodruff key from the front of the crankshaft (photo).
11 Undo the two bolts securing the oil pick-up tube support bracket to the main bearing cap (photo).

12 Undo the bolts securing the timing cover to the engine, withdraw the cover from its dowels and remove it complete with oil pick-up tube, and the spacing ring on the front of the crankshaft. It may be necessary to use a little judicious levering if the spacing ring is tight on the crankshaft.
13 The crankshaft front oil seal in the timing cover should be renewed as a matter of course. Prise out the old seal using a screwdriver, then place the new seal in position and tap it in using a hammer, block of wood and the old seal (photos).
14 Remove all traces of old gasket from the cylinder block and timing cover mating faces. Note that during manufacture, the timing cover is assembled using a jointing compound and a gasket is not used. Gaskets are supplied for repairs in service, but it is acceptable to use an RTV jointing compound as an alternative.
15 Place the new gaskets in position or apply jointing compound to the mating faces (photo).

19.5B ... and on the timing cover (arrowed)

19.7 Using a strip of angle-iron to lock the ring gear teeth

19.9A Remove the crankshaft pulley and vibration damper bolt and spring cups ...

19.9B ... then withdraw the pulley and damper assembly

19.10 Remove the crankshaft Woodruff key

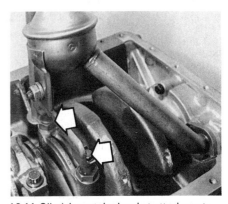
19.11 Oil pick-up tube bracket attachments to the main bearing cap bolts (arrowed)

19.13A Prise out the old front oil seal ...

19.13B ... fit a new seal ...

19.13C ... and tap it squarely into the timing cover

19.15 Applying jointing compound to the timing cover mating face on the cylinder block

19.16A Lubricate the oil supply line O-ring ...

19.16B ... and fit the timing cover

19.20 Refit the crankshaft spacing ring

19.23 Tighten the pulley and damper assembly retaining bolt to the specified torque

16 Lubricate the oil supply line O-ring on the inside of the timing cover, then place the timing cover in position (photos).
17 Identify the timing cover retaining bolts which are not used to secure any other components, and tighten them finger-tight only at this stage.
18 Fit the two bolts securing the oil pick-up tube to the main bearing cap, and tighten to the specified torque.
19 Refit the coolant pump (Chapter 2), alternator (Chapter 12), power steering pump bracket, and any other brackets, clips, or attachments which are also retained by the timing cover bolts. Now tighten the bolts in a diagonal sequence progressively to the specified torque.
20 Refit the spacing ring to the crankshaft (photo), then locate the Woodruff key in its groove.
21 Clean the oil seal bearing surface on the crankshaft pulley, then lubricate this surface thoroughly with engine oil.
22 Refit the pulley assembly, spring cups and retaining bolt, noting that the raised side of all three spring cups face the bolt head.
23 Lock the crankshaft using the same procedure as for removal, and tighten the retaining bolt to the specified torque (photo).
24 Refit the sump as described in Section 18 and the cylinder head as described in Sections 8 or 9 as applicable.
25 Refit the distributor as described in Chapter 4, and the power steering pump as described in Chapter 10.
26 Refit the engine to the car as described in Section 16.

20 Timing chain components and intermediate shaft – removal and refitting

1 Remove the timing cover as described in Section 19.

2 Withdraw the oil pump drive collar from the end of the crankshaft (photo).
3 Lift out the tensioning rail, followed by the slide rail (photos).
4 Using an Allen key, undo the intermediate shaft retaining plate bolt, inserting the Allen key through one of the sprocket holes (photo).
5 Remove the bolt and withdraw the retaining plate (photos).
6 Lift the intermediate shaft out of its bearing, slip off the chain and remove the shaft (photo).
7 Using a large Allen key or hexagonal adaptor, unscrew the timing chain tensioner body from its location (photo).
8 If required, the timing chain sprocket on the crankshaft can be removed using two screwdrivers positioned either side as levers. Remove the Woodruff key after removing the sprocket.
9 Carry out a careful inspection of the components as described in Section 25, and obtain new parts as necessary.
10 If removed, refit the Woodruff key and the sprocket to the crankshaft.
11 Lubricate the intermediate shaft bearing with engine oil, place the timing chain over the intermediate shaft sprocket and place the shaft in its bearing (photo).
12 Refit the intermediate shaft retaining plate and secure with the bolt.
13 Engage the timing chain over the crankshaft sprocket, then place the tensioning rail and slide rail over their locating pegs. Note that the angled end of the slide rail is towards the intermediate shaft.
14 Push out the timing chain tensioner plunger from the tensioner body and, with reference to Fig. 1.11 insert the plunger up to detent 'A'.
15 Refit the tensioner body and tighten securely.
16 Refit the oil pump drive collar to the crankshaft.
17 Pull the timing chain up so that it roughly adopts its normal running position, and keep it in this position during the engine reassembly procedure.
18 Refit the timing cover as described in Section 19.

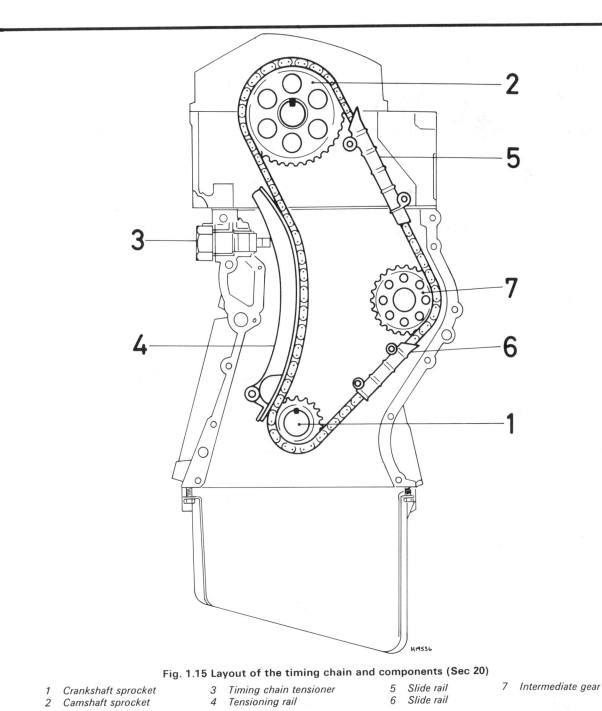

Fig. 1.15 Layout of the timing chain and components (Sec 20)

1 Crankshaft sprocket	3 Timing chain tensioner	5 Slide rail	7 Intermediate gear
2 Camshaft sprocket	4 Tensioning rail	6 Slide rail	

20.2 Withdraw the oil pump drive collar

20.3A Lift out the tensioning rail ...

20.3B ... followed by the slide rail

20.4 Undo the intermediate shaft retaining plate bolt

20.5A Remove the bolt ...

20.5B ... and the retaining plate

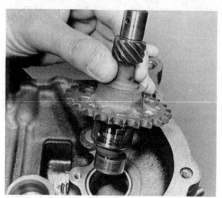
20.6 Removing the intermediate shaft

20.7 Unscrew the timing chain tensioner body

20.11 Refit the intermediate shaft with timing chain engaged

21 Oil pump – dismantling and reassembly

1 Remove the timing cover as described in Section 19.
2 Undo the bolts securing the oil pick-up tube to the oil pump cover, and remove the tube and gasket (photo).
3 Undo the bolts and lift off the oil pump cover (photo).
4 Withdraw the pump inner and outer rotors (photos).
5 Unscrew the oil pressure relief valve plug on the side of the timing cover and withdraw the tension spring, valve and sealing ring (photos).
6 Carry out a careful inspection of the pump components as described in Section 25, and obtain new parts as necessary.
7 Ensure that the timing cover, oil pump components and mating faces are thoroughly clean and dry.
8 Refit the pump inner and outer rotors, then fill the spaces between the rotor teeth with engine oil (photo).
9 Refit the pump cover and secure with the retaining bolts tightened to the specified torque.
10 Place a new pick-up tube gasket on the pump cover so that the rounded offset edge of the gasket is towards the top of the timing cover (photo).
11 Fit the pick-up tube and secure with the two bolts tightened to the specified torque.
12 Renew the O-ring on the oil gallery supply line outlet (photo).
13 Refit the pressure relief valve into its bore after lubricating it thoroughly, then fit the tension spring and valve plug. Tighten the plug to the specified torque.
14 Refit the timing cover as described in Section 19.

22 Flywheel or torque converter driveplate – removal and refitting

1 Remove the engine as described in Section 16, then separate the

gearbox or automatic transmission as described in Section 17. Alternatively, the work can be carried out with the engine in the car, but with the gearbox or automatic transmission removed as described in Chapter 6.
2 On manual gearbox models, remove the clutch assembly as described in Chapter 5.
3 Working in a diagonal sequence, one at a time, slacken the bolts securing the flywheel or driveplate to the crankshaft (photo). The crankshaft can be prevented from turning as the bolts are slackened using a strip of angle-iron or something similar between the ring gear teeth and the side of the cylinder block. Alternatively, hold the crankshaft pulley bolt using a 27 mm socket and extension bar.
4 With all the bolts slack, unscrew them completely and remove the flywheel or driveplate and spacers (where fitted).
5 Carry out a careful component inspection as described in Section 25.
6 Before refitting, the length of the stretch-type retaining bolts and the diameter of the stepped down portion must be measured and the dimensions compared with those given in the Specifications. Renew the bolts if the dimensions are outside the tolerance range.
7 Place the flywheel or driveplate on the crankshaft with the unused hole in each aligned. Where spacers are fitted, these must be positioned one on each side of the driveplate.
8 Refit the bolts and tighten them progressively and in a diagonal sequence to the specified 1st stage torque setting, while holding the crankshaft as before (photo).
9 Tighten each retaining bolt using a socket bar, not a torque wrench, by a further 90°.
10 On manual gearbox models, refit the clutch assembly as described in Chapter 5.
11 Reconnect and refit the engine and gearbox or automatic transmission as described in Sections 17 and 16 respectively, or refit the gearbox or transmission as described in Chapter 6, as applicable.

21.2 Remove the oil pick-up tube

21.3 Lift off the oil pump cover

21.4A Withdraw the oil pump inner rotor ...

21.4B ... and outer rotor

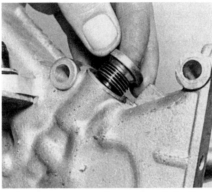

21.5A Unscrew the oil pressure relief valve plug ...

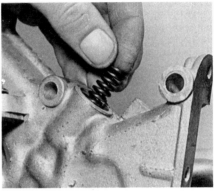

21.5B ... and withdraw the tension spring ...

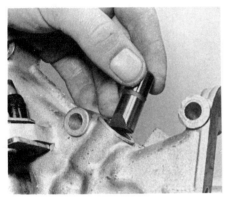

21.5C ... and pressure relief valve

21.8 Thoroughly lubricate the oil pump with engine oil

21.10 Position the pick-up tube gasket with the rounded offset edge towards the top of the timing cover

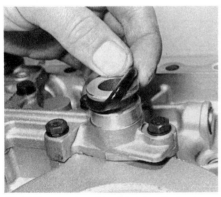

21.12 Renew the oil supply pipe O-ring

22.3 Flywheel retaining bolts

22.8 Tighten the bolts initially to the specified stage 1 torque setting

23 Connecting rod and piston assemblies – removal and refitting

1   Remove the engine from the car as described in Section 16, then remove the cylinder head and the sump as described in Sections 8 or 9 and 18 respectively.
2   Turn the crankshaft so that No 1 piston is at the bottom of its bore. While turning the crankshaft, keep tension on the timing chain so that it does not jam in the slide rails or become disengaged from the crankshaft sprocket.
3   Check that marks or numbers identifying each connecting rod and big-end cap in relation to its cylinder are visible on the side of the rod and cap (photo). If no form of identification can be seen, suitably mark each rod and cap with a centre punch accordingly.
4   Undo the big-end cap retaining nuts (or bolts on later models) and remove the cap and bearing shell (photo). Tap the cap from side to side if necessary to free it from the connecting rod.
5   Using the handle of a hammer, push the piston and connecting rod out of the top of the cylinder. Keep the bearing shells in position in the connecting rod and cap, and loosely refit the cap to the rod.
6   Repeat these operations to remove the remaining piston and connecting rod assemblies.
7   Removal of the pistons and piston rings, and inspection of the components, is covered in Section 25.
8   Starting with the assembly for No 1 cylinder, space the piston ring gaps so that they are all at 120° to each other, then thoroughly lubricate the piston, rings and cylinder bore with engine oil.
9   Turn the crankshaft so that No 1 journal is in its lowest position. Remove the big-end bearing cap from the connecting rod if still in place.
10 Fit a piston ring compressor over the rings and tighten it securely.
11 Introduce the assembly into the cylinder bore, with the arrow or triangular mark pointing towards the timing chain end of the engine (photos).
12 Tap the piston down into its bore until it is fully inserted in the cylinder (photo), then remove the piston ring compressor.
13 Guide the connecting rod, with big-end shell in place, onto the crankshaft journal while still tapping the piston down.
14 Lubricate the bearing journal thoroughly (photo), then fit the cap to the rod. The bearing shell locating notches on the connecting rod and big-end cap must be on the same side of the crankshaft journal when the cap is fitted.
15 Refit the cap retaining nuts or bolts. Tighten them initially to the stage 1 torque setting, then to the stage 2 torque angle, as given in the Specifications (photos). Use a socket bar, not a torque wrench, for the torque angle tightening.
16 Repeat these operations to refit the remaining piston and connecting rod assemblies.
17 On completion, refit the sump and cylinder head as described in Sections 18 and 8 or 9, then refit the engine to the car as described in Section 16.

24 Crankshaft – removal and refitting

1   Remove the engine from the car, separate it from the gearbox or transmission, then remove the cylinder head, sump, timing cover and chain components, flywheel or torque converter driveplate, and the connecting rod and piston assemblies as previously described.
2   Undo the seven bolts and remove the crankshaft rear oil seal carrier and seal from the rear of the block (photo).
3   Check that the main bearing caps are numbered 1 to 5 from the timing chain end, and if not, file some small notches on the edge of each cap to identify it accordingly.
4   Undo the bolts securing each main bearing cap to the crankcase (photo), and remove the caps complete with the lower main bearing shell. Remove the two thrust washers at the centre main bearing.
5   When all the bearing caps have been removed, lift out the crankshaft.
6   Remove the upper main bearing shells from the crankcase, together

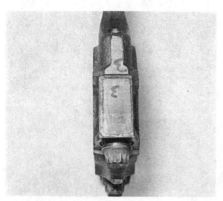

23.3 Identification numbers on the connecting rod and cap sides

23.4 Remove the big-end cap and bearing shell

23.11A With a piston ring compressor in place, introduce the piston and connecting rod into its bore ...

23.11B ... so that the directional mark points towards the timing chain end of the engine

23.12 Carefully tap the piston down into the bore

23.14 Lubricate the bearing journal before fitting the big-end cap

23.15A Tighten the nuts or bolts initially with a torque wrench ...

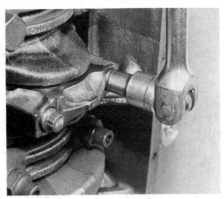

23.15B ... then to the torque angle specified using a socket bar

24.2 Crankshaft rear oil seal carrier bolts (arrowed)

with the two upper thrust washers, and place the bearings with their respective caps.

7   Carry out a careful inspection of the crankshaft, bearings and cylinder block, as described in Section 25.

8   Begin refitting by placing the bearing shell upper halves in their respective locations.

9   Stick the thrust washer upper halves to each side of the centre bearing, using a little grease, and so that the oil grooves are facing outwards (towards the crankshaft – photo). The thrust washer upper halves are the ones without the locating tags.

10   Thoroughly lubricate the bearing shells and crankshaft journals, then lower the crankshaft into position (photo).

11   Fit the lower bearing shell and the two remaining thrust washers to the centre main bearing cap, so that the tags on the thrust washers engage with the cap notches, and the oil grooves are facing outwards (photo).

12   Fit the cap to the centre bearing journal, so that the bearing shell locating notches in the cap and crankcase are on the same side of the bearing journal. The cap is slightly offset to one side, so it should be impossible to fit it the wrong way round.

13   Fit the remaining bolts and tighten them to the specified torque (photo).

14   Using a dial gauge, or alternatively feeler gauges between the thrust washers and the side of the crankshaft, check the crankshaft endfloat (photo). If new standard size thrust washers have been fitted, the endfloat should be within the tolerance range given in the Specifications. If the endfloat is excessive, oversize thrust washers are available.

15   Refit the remaining bearing shells and caps in the same way, noting that the special threaded bolts used to secure the oil pump pick-up tube are fitted to No 2 bearing cap (photo).

16   Renew the crankshaft rear oil seal by prising it out of the carrier

24.4 Undo the main bearing cap retaining bolts (arrowed)

24.9 Fitting the upper thrust washers with the oil grooves outwards

24.10 Lower the crankshaft into place

24.11 Lower thrust washers engaged with the bearing cap notches

24.13 Tighten the bearing cap bolts to the specified torque

24.14 Checking crankshaft endfloat

24.15 The special internally-threaded bolts are fitted to No 2 main bearing cap

24.17 Refit the rear oil seal carrier

using a screwdriver, then carefully tapping in a new seal using a hammer and large block of wood.

17 Lubricate the oil seal lips with multi-purpose grease, and apply RTV jointing compound to the carrier mating face (photo).

18 Carefully enter the seal over the crankshaft, then fit and tighten the carrier retaining bolts.

19 Refit all the components described in paragraph 1 with reference to the relevant Sections of this Chapter.

25 Examination and renovation

1 Clean all components using paraffin or a water-soluble solvent, then dry them with a lint-free rag.

2 Carefully examine each part as described in the following paragraphs, and with reference to the Specifications for dimensions, clearances, and tolerances etc. Renew any parts that are worn, damaged, or in any way suspect. Renew main and big-end bearing shells as a matter of course, unless you know that they have had little wear and are in perfect condition.

Crankshaft, main and big-end bearings

3 Examine the bearing surfaces of the crankshaft for scoring or grooving and, using a micrometer, check each main and big-end journal for ovality (photo). If the journals are scored, or if their size is outside the specified limits, the crankshaft will have to be reground and undersize bearing shells fitted.

4 Crankshaft regrinding should be carried out by a suitable engineering works, who will normally supply the matching main and big-end bearing shells.

5 If the crankshaft is in a satisfactory condition, new bearing shells and thrust washers should be obtained as a matter of course.

Cylinder block and crankcase

6 The cylinder bores must be examined for taper, ovality, scoring and scratches. Start by examining the top of the bores. If these are worn, a slight ridge will be found which marks the top of the piston ring travel. If the wear is excessive, the engine will have had a high oil consumption rate, accompanied by blue smoke from the exhaust.

7 Using an internal micrometer, measure the bore diameter just below the ridge, then halfway down the bore, then at the bottom of the bore, which is not subject to wear. Take these measurements in a longitudinal direction, ie in line with the crankshaft, then in a transverse direction. Compare the measurements with the figures in the Specifications for bore diameter, taper and ovality. If the wear is excessive, it will be necessary to have the cylinder rebored and oversize pistons fitted. If, however, only moderate wear has taken place, special oil control piston rings can be fitted to reduce oil consumption and restore compression.

25.3 Checking the main bearing journal size

8 If new pistons are being fitted to old bores, it is essential to roughen the bore walls slightly, using fine-grade emery cloth, to enable the new piston rings to bed in properly.

9 Thoroughly examine the crankcase and cylinder block for cracks and damage, and use a piece of wire to probe all oilways and waterways to ensure they are unobstructed.

10 The diameter of the main bearing bores with the bearing shells in place should be measured, so that the main bearing journal running clearances can be determined.

11 Fit the bearing shells to the crankcase and bearing caps, fit the caps in their correct positions, then fit and fully tighten the retaining bolts. Measure the internal diameter of each bearing, then measure the diameters of the respective journals on the crankshaft. Subtract the journal diameter from the bearing diameters to give the running clearance. If it is excessive, new bearing shells are required.

Piston and connecting rod assemblies

12 On cars manufactured prior to October 1984, the pistons are retained by fully floating gudgeon pins, which are retained by circlips. These can be easily removed, as described below, should it be necessary to renew the pistons or connecting rods. On later models, however, the gudgeon pins are an interference fit in the connecting rods. If the pistons or connecting rods on these engines are to be

renewed, it will be necessary to have this work carried out by a Mercedes-Benz dealer or suitable engineering works, who will have the necessary special tools required for removal and refitting.

13 To remove the fully floating gudgeon pins, extract the circlips in the piston grooves, support the piston and gently tap out the gudgeon pin using a soft metal drift. Before separating the piston and connecting rod, make a note of which side the bearing locating notch in the connecting rod is positioned on, in relation to the direction of travel arrow on the piston crown. This relationship must be maintained on reassembly.

14 To remove the piston rings, expand them carefully, starting with the top ring, and slide them up and off. The use of two or three old feeler blades will be helpful in preventing the rings dropping into empty grooves.

15 Ensure that the ring grooves in the piston are free of carbon by cleaning them using an old ring, break the ring in half to do this. Carefully remove the carbon from the piston crown using a scraper.

16 Check the piston for signs of excessive scuffing on the skirt or other signs of wear. Measure the piston diameter using a micrometer, and compare the figure with that given in the Specifications. The standard cylinder bore and piston sizes are divided into three classes which are identified 0, 1 and 2. This identification number is stamped on the cylinder lock face adjacent to the cylinder, and should also appear on the piston crown. A similar three-class size arrangement is also used for the oversize reboring dimensions. To maintain the correct piston-to-bore clearances the piston and its respective cylinder bore must always be of the same class.

17 Check the piston ring grooves in the piston for wear by placing the edge of the ring in the groove and viewing it end-on. Wear will be obvious if the ring can be moved up and down, but a more accurate check can be made using a feeler blade between the ring and the top face of the groove. Also check for wear ridges in the rings themselves.

18 Check the connecting rods for any signs of obvious distortion, and check the fit of the fully floating gudgeon pin in the small end bush.

19 The diameter of the big-end bearing bores should also be checked to determine the bearing running clearances, and is carried out in the same way as for the main bearings described in paragraphs 10 and 11.

20 Finally measure the width of the studs or bolts, used to secure the big-end cap, at the stepped down portion in the centre of the stud or bolt. If this dimension is less than shown in the Specifications, then the studs or bolts have stretched excessively and must be renewed.

21 Fit the pistons to the connecting rods so that the bearing notch in the rod is on the correct side in relation to the piston arrow, as noted during removal. As a double check, the offset of the oil hole in the top of the rod must be towards the timing chain end of the engine.

22 Push in the gudgeon pin by hand and secure with new circlips, located fully in the piston grooves.

23 Carefully fit the new rings to the pistons, starting with the oil control ring and using old feeler blades as for removal. The words TOP on the rings must be towards the top of the piston. When all the rings are in place, space out their ends at 120° to each other.

Timing cover, gears, chain and intermediate shaft

24 Examine all the teeth on the camshaft, crankshaft and intermediate shaft sprockets. If these teeth are 'hooked' in appearance, renew the sprockets.

25 Examine the timing chain for wear ridges on the rollers, or looseness of the rivets or side plates. If it has been in operation for a considerable time, or if when held horizontally (rollers vertical) it takes on a deeply bowed appearance, renew the chain.

26 Check the slide rails, tensioning rail and tensioner for obvious signs of wear or damage, and renew as necessary.

27 Check the distributor drivegear and fuel pump lobe (carburettor engines) on the intermediate shaft, and check the fit of the shaft in its bushes. Renew the intermediate shaft if worn. If the shaft bushes require renewal, this work will have to be carried out by a Mercedes-Benz dealer.

28 Check the timing cover for cracks or damage, and renew as necessary.

Oil pump

29 Check for scoring or wear ridges on the pump inner and outer rotors, rotor teeth, pump cover and the pump casing formed in the timing cover. If the rotors are worn, these can be renewed as a rotor set. If the pump casing or pump cover are worn, it will be necessary to obtain a new timing cover.

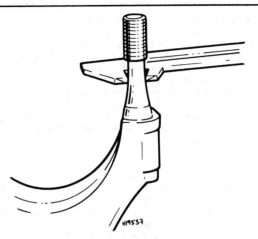

Fig. 1.16 Checking connecting rod stud width (Sec 25)

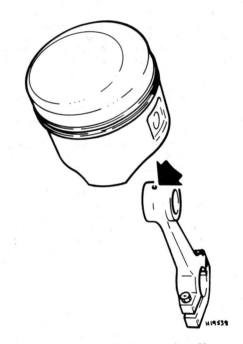

Fig. 1.17 Connecting rod oil hole must be offset towards the timing chain end of the engine when fitting piston (Sec 25)

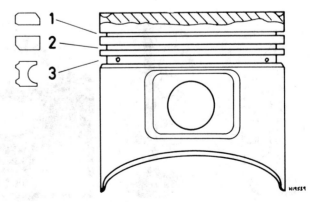

Fig. 1.18 Piston ring identification (Sec 25)

1 Top compression ring   3 Oil control ring
2 Second compression ring

Flywheel or torque converter driveplate

30 Examine the flywheel for scoring or grooving of the clutch face, and for wear or chipping of the ring gear teeth. If the clutch face is scored, the flywheel should be renewed. If the ring gear is worn or damaged it may be renewed separately, but this is a job best left to a Mercedes-Benz dealer or engineering works. The temperature to which the ring gear must be heated for installation is critical, and if not done accurately, the hardness of the teeth will be destroyed.

31 Check the torque converter driveplate carefully for signs of distortion, or any hairline cracks around the bolt holes or radiating outwards from the centre.

Cylinder head and valves

32 Before carrying out any examination, the cylinder head and valves should be completely decarbonised as described in Section 26.

33 Check each valve carefully for any obvious signs of wear or damage. If the valve appears initially satisfactory, measure the stem diameter at several points using a micrometer (photo). If the diameter is less than specified, renew the valve. Check the valve head for excessive pitting, or a concave appearance of the valve seat. Minor pitting can be removed when grinding in the valve but if the pitting is deep or the seat is concave then the valve should be machined to restore the seat condition, or if severe, renewed.

34 Check the condition of the valve seat in the cylinder head in the same way as for the valve. Light pitting can be removed by grinding-in, but if the seat condition is poor, it should be recut using valve seat cutting tools. If the seat is severely damaged beyond reclamation, the seat insert can be removed and a new one fitted. This work and any major seat reconditioning should be entrusted to a Mercedes-Benz dealer, or suitably equipped engineering works.

35 Place each valve in turn in its guide so that approximately one-third of its length enters. Rock the valve from side to side. If there is any more than a very slight movement, the valve guides are worn and will have to be renewed by a dealer.

36 Measure the valve spring length and renew the springs if the length is less than specified. It is advisable to renew the springs as a matter of course if major reconditioning work is being carried out on the cylinder head.

37 Check the condition of the cylinder head itself, paying particular attention to the camshaft bearing journals and the head mating face. If the journals are scored, or if the mating face has been damaged by corrosion to a serious level, reconditioning by machining operations can be carried out, but the advice of a dealer should be sought.

38 Measure the length of the cylinder head bolts as shown in Fig. 1.10. These stretch-type bolts must be renewed if their length exceeds the dimension shown.

Camshaft and rocker arms

39 Examine the camshaft bearings and the cam lobes for any sign of scoring, wear grooves or pitting and if apparent renew the camshaft. Any damage of this nature may be attributable to a blocked oil passage either in the cylinder head, rocker assemblies or the oil spray pipe, and carefully examination should be carried out to determine the cause. If the camshaft is renewed, all the rocker arms must be renewed at the same time.

40 With the camshaft bearing brackets removed, the rocker arms can be removed from the brackets after drawing out the short rocker shaft. Ideally the manufacturer's tool, which is a slide hammer that screws into the end of the shaft, should be used. An alternative method is to screw in a suitable long bolt and washer, then strike the washer with a hammer away from the bearing bracket to force out the shaft. The rocker can now be withdrawn.

41 Check for wear of the rocker arm to camshaft contact pad, check the fit of the rocker on its shaft, and check the condition of the adjusting screw end on engines without hydraulic tappets. Renew any of these components that show signs of wear.

42 When refitting the rocker arms and rocker shafts, ensure that the shaft is positioned with the groove for the retaining bolt aligned with the bolt hole in the bearing bracket.

Oil seals and gaskets

43 Renew the oil seals in the timing cover and crankshaft rear oil seal carrier, whenever these components are removed, as a matter of course. The seals are removed by prising them out with a screwdriver and tapping in the new seal squarely using a hammer and block of wood. The seals must be fitted so that their open side is towards the engine. Lubricate the oil seal lips with multi-purpose grease prior to refitting the oil seal carrier or timing cover.

44 Renew all gaskets either individually, or in a top or bottom overhaul set, if major repair work is being undertaken. Also renew any O-rings unless their condition is perfect after inspection.

45 When fitting a new rocker cover gasket, ensure that it locates in the rocker cover recess around the cover edge (photo). On later engines, a half-round projection engages with the opening on the cylinder head, and is incorporated in the gasket (photo). On earlier engines, there was a corresponding half-round opening in the rocker cover, and the resulting hole was sealed by a separate circular rubber sealing disc. This disc should be inspected and renewed at the same time as the rocker cover gasket on engines so equipped.

26 Cylinder head and pistons – decarbonising

1 With the cylinder head removed as described in Section 8 or 9, the carbon deposits should be removed from the combustion surfaces using a blunt scraper. Take great care as the head is of light alloy construction and avoid the use of a rotary (power-driven) wire brush.

2 Where a more thorough job is to be carried out, the cylinder head should be dismantled, as described in Section 10, so that the valves may be ground in, and the ports and combustion spaces cleaned and blown out after the manifolds have been removed.

3 Before grinding-in a valve, remove the carbon and deposits completely from its head and stem. With an inlet valve this is usually quite easy, simply a case of scraping off the soft carbon with a blunt knife and finishing with a wire brush. With an exhaust valve, the deposits are very much harder and those on the valve head may need a rub on coarse emery cloth to remove them. An old woodworking chisel as a useful tool to remove the worst of the valve head deposits.

4 Make sure that the valve heads are really clean, otherwise the

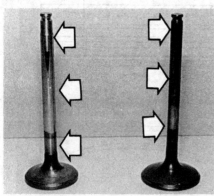
25.33 Measure the exhaust valve (left) and inlet valve (right) stem diameters at the points arrowed

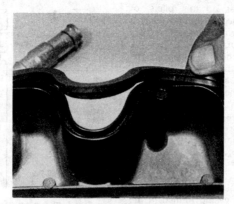
25.45A Ensure that the rocker cover gasket engages in the cover recess ...

25.4B ... and the half-round projection engages with the cylinder head opening

rubber suction cup grinding tool will not stick during the grinding-in operations.

5   Before starting to grind in a valve, support the cylinder head so that there is sufficient clearance under it for the valve stem to project fully without being obstructed, otherwise the valve will not seat properly during grinding.

6   Take the first valve and apply a little coarse grinding paste to the bevelled edge of the valve head. Insert the valve into its guide and apply the suction grinding tool to its head. Rotate the tool between the palms of the hands in a back-and-forth rotary movement until the gritty action of the grinding-in process disappears. Repeat the operation with fine paste and then wipe away all trace of grinding paste and examine the seat and bevelled edge of the valve. A matt silver mating band should be observed on both components, without any sign of black spots. If some spots do remain, repeat the grinding-in process until they have disappeared. A drop or two or paraffin, if applied to the contact surfaces, will speed the grinding process, but do not allow any paste to run down into the valve guide. On completion, wipe away

every trace of grinding paste using a paraffin-moistened cloth.

7   Repeat the operations on the remaining valves, taking care not to mix up their originally fitted sequence.

8   An important part of the decarbonising operation is to remove the carbon deposits from the piston crowns. To do this (engine in vehicle), turn the crankshaft so that two pistons are at the top of their stroke and press some grease between the pistons and the cylinder walls. This will prevent carbon particles falling down into the piston ring grooves. Plug the other two bores with rag.

9   Cover the oilways and coolant passages with masking tape and then, using a blunt scraper, remove all the carbon from the piston crowns. Take great care not to score the soft alloy of the crown or the surface of the cylinder bore.

10 Rotate the crankshaft to bring the other two pistons to tdc and repeat the operations.

11 Wipe away the circles of grease and carbon from the cylinder bores.

12 Clean the top surface of the cylinder block by careful scraping.

27 Fault diagnosis – engine

Symptom	Reason(s)
Engine fails to turn over when starter operated	Discharged or defective battery Dirty or loose battery leads Defective starter solenoid or switch Engine earth strap disconnected Defective starter motor
Engine turns over but will not start	HT leads disconnected LT leads at electronic switching unit disconnected Electronic ignition system fault (see Chapter 4) Fuel tank empty Fuel pump faulty Other fuel system fault (see Chapter 3)
Engine idles erratically	Incorrect carburettor or fuel injection system adjustments Inlet manifold air leak Leaking cylinder head gasket Worn camshaft lobes Incorrect valve clearances or faulty hydraulic tappet element Disconnected vacuum or air hoses Incorrect valve timing Incorrect ignition timing Uneven cylinder compressions Other fault or ignition system fault (Chapters 3 or 4)
Engine misfires	Incorrect spark plug gaps or faulty plug Faulty electronic ignition system component Distributor cap cracked or tracking Uneven cylinder compressions Leaking cylinder head gasket Incorrect valve clearances or faulty hydraulic tappet element Incorrect carburettor or fuel injection system adjustments Other fuel or ignition system fault (Chapters 3 or 4)
Excessive oil consumption	Worn pistons and cylinder bores Valve guides or valve stem oil seals worn Oil leakage from gaskets or oil seals
Engine backfires	Incorrect carburettor or fuel injection system adjustments Ignition timing incorrect Valve timing incorrect Inlet manifold air leak Sticking valve Other fuel or ignition system fault (Chapters 3 or 4)
Engine lacks power	Ignition timing incorrect Valve timing incorrect Low cylinder compression Excessive carbon build-up in engine Valve clearances incorrect or faulty hydraulic tappet element

Symptoms	Reason(s)
Unusual noises from engine	Worn valve gear or incorrect adjustment (noisy tapping from rocker cover)
	Worn timing chain, tensioner or slide rails (rattling from timing cover)
	Worn big-end bearings (regular metallic knocking)
	Worn main bearings (harsh rumbling and vibration on overrun)
	Worn or incorrectly adjusted drivebelt(s) (screeching or whine from front of engine)

Chapter 2 Cooling system

Contents

Specifications

System type	Pressurised pump-assisted thermo-syphon, with front-mounted radiator and electromagnetic cooling fan

Thermostat
Type .... Twin valve, wax operated
Opening temperature .... 85 to 89°C (185 to 192°F)

Expansion tank pressure cap
Pressure cap code number 120
Release pressure .... 1.2 bar (17.4 lbf/in²)

System capacity (including heater) .... 8.5 litres (15.0 Imp pints)

Antifreeze
Type .... Mercedes-Benz approved antifreeze (Duckhams Universal Antifreeze and Summer Coolant)

Mixing quantities of antifreeze and water for protection to:	**Antifreeze**	**Water**
−30°C (−22°F)	3.75 litre (6.6 Imp pint)	4.75 litre (8.4 Imp pint)
−40°C (−40°F)	4.50 litre (7.9 Imp pint)	4.0 litre (7.0 Imp pint)

Electromagnetic cooling fan
Operating temperature .... 100°C (212°F)

Torque wrench settings	Nm	lbf ft
Coolant pump to timing cover	10	7
Cooling fan to pump spindle	25	18
Fan pulley to pump spindle	10	7
Electromagnetic fan coupling body retaining bolts	10	7
Thermostat housing cover bolts	10	7
Alternator mounting bracket bolts	45	33
Cylinder block drain plug	30	22
Automatic transmission fluid cooler unions	20	15

1 General description

The cooling system is of the pressurised, pump-assisted thermo-syphon type, comprising a radiator, coolant pump, thermostat, electro-magnetic cooling fan, expansion tank and associated hoses.

Two types of radiator are used according to model. On cars fitted with air conditioning, the radiator is a light alloy crossflow type with plastic coolant compartments at each side. On cars without air conditioning, the radiator is a light alloy gravity flow type with plastic coolant compartments at the top and bottom. On cars also equipped with automatic transmission, a transmission fluid cooler is incorporated in either the right-hand side or bottom coolant compartment accordingly.

The thermostat is of the twin-valve type incorporating a main valve, which opens at a predetermined temperature to allow coolant flow to the radiator, and a bypass valve, which is open when the main valve is closed to allow coolant circulation through the engine and heater.

The impeller-type coolant pump is located on the front of the engine and is belt-driven from the crankshaft pulley.

The electromagnetic cooling fan is mounted on the coolant pump spindle, and operates in conjunction with a temperature-sensitive switch located in the cylinder head. When the engine coolant reaches a predetermined temperature, the electromagnetic coupling is energized and the fan is rigidly locked to the pump pulley. At lower temperatures, the coupling is released and the fan is allowed to freewheel, turning only under the influence of bearing friction or the inrush of air when the car is moving forwards.

The plastic expansion tank is located on the right-hand side of the engine compartment, and collects the coolant which is displaced from the system as it expands due to the rise in temperature. The displaced coolant is returned to the radiator as the system cools.

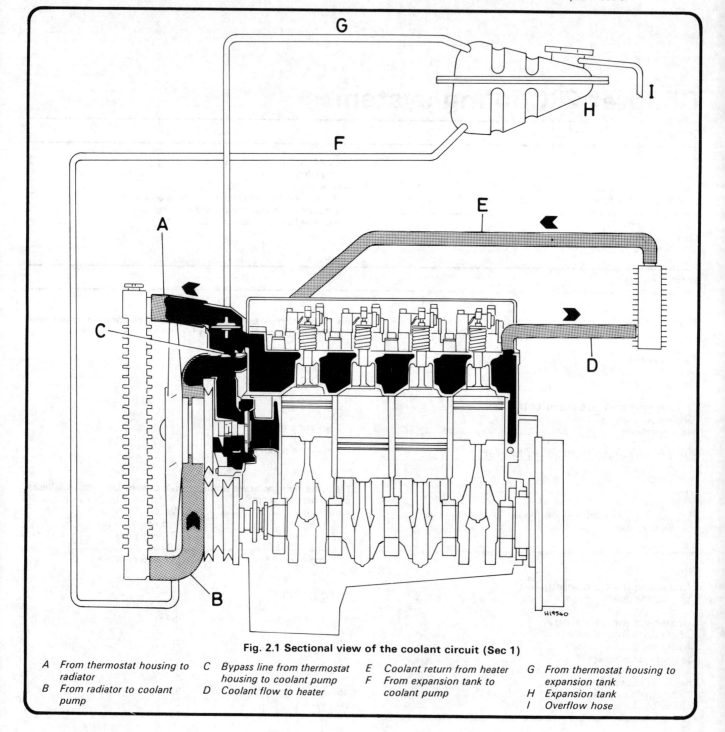

Fig. 2.1 Sectional view of the coolant circuit (Sec 1)

A From thermostat housing to radiator	C Bypass line from thermostat housing to coolant pump	E Coolant return from heater
B From radiator to coolant pump	D Coolant flow to heater	F From expansion tank to coolant pump
		G From thermostat housing to expansion tank
		H Expansion tank
		I Overflow hose

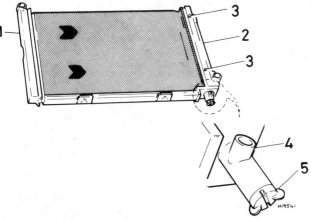

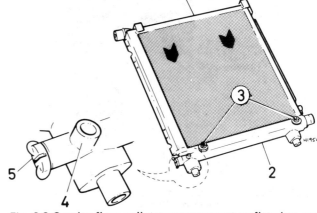

Fig. 2.2 Crossflow radiator arrangement as fitted to cars with air conditioning (Sec 1)

1 Left-hand plastic coolant compartment
2 Right-hand plastic coolant compartment
3 Fluid cooler unions (automatic transmission models)
4 Drain plug outlet
5 Drain plug

Fig. 2.3 Gravity flow radiator arrangement as fitted to cars without air conditioning (Sec 1)

1 Top plastic coolant compartment
2 Bottom plastic coolant compartment
3 Fluid cooler unions (automatic transmission models)
4 Drain plug outlet
5 Drain plug

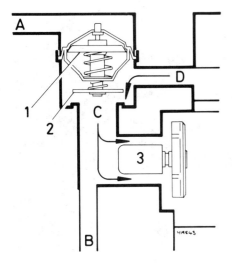

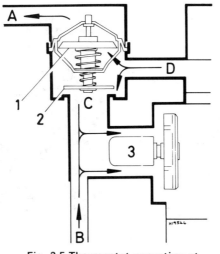

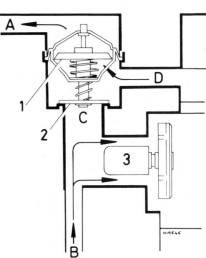

Fig. 2.4 Thermostat operation at temperatures below 87°C (Sec 1)

1 Main valve closed
2 Bypass valve fully open
3 Coolant pump
A No flow to radiator
B No return flow from radiator
C Coolant flow from open bypass valve
D Coolant return from engine to bypass valve

Fig. 2.5 Thermostat operation at temperatures from 87°C to 102°C (Sec 1)

1 Main valve partially open
2 Bypass valve partially open
3 Coolant pump
A Partial flow to radiator from engine
B Partial return flow from radiator to pump
C Coolant flow from partially open bypass valve to pump
D Coolant return from engine through main and bypass valve

Fig. 2.6 Thermostat operation at temperatures above 102°C (Sec 1)

1 Main valve fully open
2 Bypass valve closed
3 Coolant pump
A Full flow to radiator from engine
B Return flow from radiator to pump
C No flow through bypass valve
D Coolant return from engine through main valve

2 Maintenance and inspection

1 At weekly intervals, check the coolant level in the system when the engine is cold by viewing the coolant in the expansion tank on the right-hand side of the engine compartment. The level is correct when the coolant is up to the indicated mark on the side of the tank. If the engine is hot, the level will be slightly above the indicated mark.
2 If topping-up is necessary, wait until the engine is cold, then turn the pressure cap on the expansion tank anti-clockwise until it reaches the first stop. Wait until any pressure remaining in the system is released then push the cap down, turn it anti-clockwise to the second stop and lift off. Do not attempt to remove the pressure cap when the engine is hot, as there is a very great risk of scalding.
3 Add a mixture of water and antifreeze (see Section 6) through the expansion tank filler neck until the coolant is up to the level mark (photo). Refit the cap turning it clockwise as far as it will go to secure.
4 With a sealed-type cooling system, the addition of coolant should only be necessary at very infrequent intervals. If this is not the case, and frequent topping-up is required, it is likely there is a leak in the system. Check all hoses and joint faces for any signs of staining or actual wetness, and rectify if necessary. If no leaks can be found, it is advisable to have the system pressure tested, as this will often show up a small leak not previously visible.
5 At the intervals given in Routine Maintenance at the beginning of this manual, carefully inspect all hoses, hose clips, radiator and visible joint gaskets for cracks, corrosion, deterioration or leakage. Renew any components that are suspect.
6 Check the condition of the coolant pump and alternator drivebelt, renew the belt and/or adjust its tension as necessary. These procedures

Fig. 2.7 Expansion tank pressure cap (1) and coolant level marking (2) (Sec 2)

are covered in Chapter 12 of this manual.

7   At the (less frequent) service intervals given, drain, flush and refill the cooling system using fresh antifreeze as described in Sections 3, 4 and 5 respectively.

3   Cooling system – draining

1   It is preferable to drain the cooling system when the engine is cold. If the engine is hot, the pressure in the cooling system must be released before attempting to drain the system. Place a cloth over the expansion tank pressure cap and slowly turn the cap anti-clockwise until it reaches the first stop. Wait until the pressure has escaped, then press the cap downwards, slowly turn it further in an anti-clockwise direction until it reaches the second stop and lift off.

2   Place a suitable container beneath the left-hand side of the radiator on cars without air conditioning, or beneath the right-hand side on cars with air conditioning fitted.

3   Unscrew the radiator drain plug (photo) and allow the coolant to drain from the drain plug outlet into the container. Tighten the drain plug when all the coolant has drained.

4   Position the container beneath the right-hand side of the engine beneath the exhaust manifold.

5   Unscrew and remove the cylinder block drain plug (photo) and allow the remaining coolant in the engine to drain into the container. Refit the drain plug on completion.

4   Cooling system – flushing

1   With time, the cooling system may gradually lose its efficiency as the radiator core becomes choked with rust, scale deposits from the water and other deposits. This is more likely to occur if the specified concentration of antifreeze has not been maintained in the system, or if the antifreeze has not been renewed at the recommended intervals.

2   To flush the system, first drain the coolant as described in the previous Section.

3   Refer to Section 8 and remove the thermostat, then refit the thermostat housing cover.

4   Set the heater controls to the maximum heat position.

5   Fill the cooling system through the expansion tank using clean water only, until the water is up to the full level indicated on the side of the tank.

6   Leave the expansion tank pressure cap off, and run the engine at a fast idle until the temperature gauge moves off its stop to the first mark on the gauge (approximately 60 to 70°C). Add water to maintain the correct level in the tank during this time if necessary.

7   Refit the expansion tank pressure cap and continue running the engine until the temperature reaches 100°C, and then for a further five minutes thereafter.

8   Switch off and allow the engine to cool to approximately 50°C.

9   Refer to Section 3 and drain the system once more, but take care as the water will be hot and the system may still be under pressure.

10   Repeat this flushing procedure until only clean water, free from rust and sediment, drains from the system.

2.3 Topping-up the cooling system at the expansion tank

3.3 Gravity flow radiator drain plug (A) and outlet (B) (cars without air conditioning)

3.5 Cylinder block drain plug location (arrowed)

11 On completion refit the thermostat as described in Section 8, then fill the system as described in Section 5.

12 The use of chemical cleaners should only be necessary as a last resort in cases of severe contamination. Before using any form of de-scaling or de-rusting additives, the advice of a Mercedes-Benz dealer should be sought as to their suitability. The regular renewal of antifreeze should prevent excessive contamination of the system.

5 Cooling system – filling

1 Ensure that the heater controls are set to the maximum heat position, then slowly fill the system through the expansion tank, with the appropriate mixture of water and antifreeze, until the level is up to the full mark on the side of the tank.

2 Leave the expansion tank pressure cap off, and run the engine at a fast idle until the temperature gauge needle moves off its stop to the first mark (approximately 60 to 70°C). Add coolant to maintain the correct level in the tank during this time if necessary.

3 Refit the expansion tank pressure cap and continue to run the engine, increasing the speed periodically, until the temperature reaches approximately 90 to 100°C.

4 Switch the engine off and allow it to cool. When cold recheck the coolant level and top up if necessary.

6 Antifreeze mixture

1 The coolant used in the cooling system consists of a mixture of water and antifreeze to provide protection against freezing, protection against corrosion and also to raise the boiling point of the coolant.

2 For adequate corrosion protection, the proportion of antifreeze to water must never drop below 33%, which also provides antifreeze protection down to −20°C (−4°F), nor should it exceed 55%, which provides protection from freezing down to −45°C (−49°F), otherwise the heat dissipation properties of the coolant will be impaired.

3 The ideal quantities of antifreeze and water which should be maintained in the system at all times are shown in the Specifications.

4 The antifreeze should be renewed at the intervals given in Routine Maintenance, at which time the system should be completely drained and flushed, and all hoses checked for condition and security.

5 Always use an ethylene glycol-based antifreeze which is suitable for use in mixed metal cooling systems.

6 After filling with antifreeze, a label should be attached to the radiator stating the type and concentration of antifreeze used, and the date installed. Any subsequent topping-up should be made with the same type and concentration of antifreeze.

7 Do not use engine antifreeze in the screen washer system, as it will cause damage to the vehicle paintwork. Screen wash antifreeze is available from most accessory shops.

7 Radiator – removal, inspection, cleaning and refitting

1 Refer to Section 3 and drain the cooling system.

2 Slacken the clips and disconnect the top and bottom hoses at the radiator (photo).

3 Carefully prise out the retaining spring clips securing the top of the fan shroud to the radiator (photo). Disengage the shroud from the radiator and place it over the fan blades.

4 On cars without air conditioning, unscrew the plastic expander screws securing the side panels to the radiator and remove the expander body (photos).

5 On automatic transmission models, clamp the transmission fluid cooler hoses using self-grip wrenches with protected jaws or similar tools and unscrew the hose unions from the radiator bottom (photo) or side compartments as applicable. Carefully withdraw and cover the hoses.

6 Carefully prise out the retaining spring clips securing the top of the radiator to the body panel (photo).

7 Lift the radiator upwards to disengage the lower mounting lugs and remove it from the car, followed by the fan shroud (photos).

7.2 Radiator top hose attachments at radiator and thermostat housing cover

7.3 Removing the fan shroud retaining spring clips

7.4A Unscrew the plastic expander screws ...

7.4B ... located at the top and bottom of the side panels (arrowed) ...

7.4C ... then remove the expander body

7.5 Automatic transmission fluid cooler unions

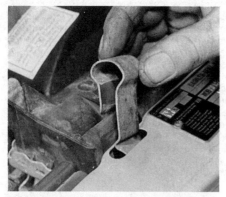

7.6 Remove the radiator retaining spring clips

7.7A Remove the radiator ...

7.7B ... followed by the fan shroud

7.9 Radiator lower mounting lug grommet

8.2 Removing the expansion tank hose from the thermostat housing cover

8.3A Lift off the thermostat housing cover ...

8   Carefully examine the radiator for signs of leaks, corrosion of the alloy core, or damage to the plastic side, top or bottom compartments. Should the radiator require attention, this work should be left to a specialist due to the nature of its construction. Clear the radiator core of flies, small leaves or other debris by brushing or hosing. Check the condition of all hoses, clips, mountings and retaining spring clips and renew as necessary.
9   Refitting the radiator is the reverse sequence to removal, but ensure that the lower mounting lugs properly engage with their rubber grommets (photo). Fill the cooling system as described in Section 5 after fitting, and on automatic transmission models, check the transmission fluid level as described in Chapter 6.

8   Thermostat – removal, testing and refitting

1   Refer to Section 3 and drain approximately 2.0 litres (3.5 pints) of coolant from the radiator.
2   Slacken the hose clips and remove the radiator top hose and expansion tank hose from the thermostat housing cover (photo).
3   Undo the three bolts and lift off the cover, followed by the O-ring seal (photos).
4   Withdraw the thermostat from the housing (photo).
5   To test whether the unit is serviceable, suspend it on a string in a saucepan of cold water, together with a thermometer. Do not allow the thermostat or thermometer to touch the bottom or sides of the pan. Heat the water and note the temperature at which the thermostat main valve begins to open. Continue heating the water until boiling point is reached, noting that at this temperature the main valve should be nearly fully open, and the bypass valve at the base of the unit should be in the closed position (ie it should move away from the thermostat body).
6   Remove the thermostat from the water, noting that as it cools, the main valve should close and the bypass valve should open.

7   If the thermostat valves did not operate as described during the test, or if the main valve did not start to open at the temperature given in the Specifications, the thermostat should be renewed.
8   Refitting the thermostat is the reverse sequence to removal, but renew the sealing O-ring if it shows any signs of deterioration. Tighten the thermostat housing cover retaining bolts to the specified torque and top up the cooling system on completion.

8.3B ... followed by the sealing O-ring ...

8.4 ... and remove the thermostat

9.2 Bypass hose retaining clips (arrowed)

9.3 Removing the thermostat housing

9 Thermostat housing – removal and refitting

1 Remove the thermostat as described in Section 8.
2 Slacken the hose clip securing the bypass hose to the coolant pump (photo).
3 Undo the two housing retaining bolts, and remove the housing from the coolant pump and cylinder head (photo).
4 Scrape away all traces of old gasket from the cylinder head and housing mating faces. Check the condition of the bypass hose and hose clips, and obtain replacements if necessary together with a new gasket.
5 Smear the gasket with jointing compound and place it in position on the housing.
6 Locate the housing and bypass hose in place, fit and tighten the bolts and secure the hose with the clip.
7 Refit the thermostat as described in Secion 8.

10 Electromagnetic fan and fan coupling – removal and refitting

1 Refer to Section 7 of this Chapter and remove the radiator.
2 Refer to Chapter 3 and remove the air cleaner.
3 Refer to Chapter 12 and release the drivebelt from the alternator and coolant pump pulleys.
4 Undo the centre retaining bolt securing the fan to the pump spindle (photo), and remove the fan.
5 Undo the four socket-headed bolts securing the pulley to the coolant pump spindle (photo) and remove the pulley.
6 On pre-October 1984 models with multiple ancillary drivebelts, undo the three bolts securing the fan coupling body to the coolant pump and pump bracket. Withdraw the coupling, disconnect the wiring plug, and remove the unit from the engine.
7 On post-October 1984 models with a single ancillary drivebelt

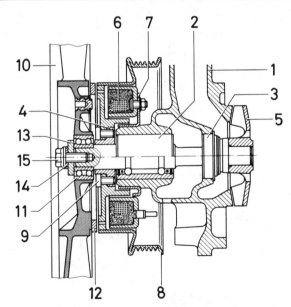

Fig. 2.8 Sectional view of the electromagnetic cooling fan assembly fitted to post-October 1984 models
(Sec 10)

1 Coolant pump body
2 Pump bearing
3 Sealing ring
4 Pump spindle flange
5 Impeller
6 Solenoid body
7 Solenoid body carrier
8 Pulley
9 Retaining bolts
10 Fan
11 Ball bearing
12 Armature
13 Spacer
14 Dished washer
15 Fan retaining bolt

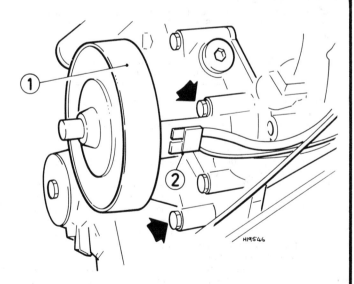

Fig. 2.9 Electromagnetic fan coupling body retaining bolts on left-hand side (arrowed) – pre-October 1984 models (Sec 10)

1 Fan coupling body
2 Wiring plug

Fig. 2.10 Electromagnetic fan coupling body-to-bracket retaining bolt (arrowed) – pre-October 1984 models (Sec 10)

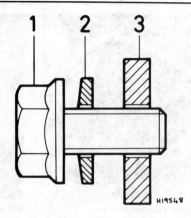

Fig. 2.11 Fan retaining bolt washer and spacer arrangement (Sec 10)

1   Fan retaining bolt   3   Spacer
2   Dished washer

arrangement, undo the bolts at the rear of the coupling body securing it to the mounting plate. Withdraw the coupling, disconnect the wiring plug and remove the unit from the engine.

8   Refitting is the reverse sequence to removal. Ensure that the arrangement of washers on the fan retaining bolt is as shown in Fig. 2.11, and tighten all retaining bolts to the torque wrench settings as given in the Specifications.

9   Refit and adjust the drivebelt (Chapter 12), refit the air cleaner (Chapter 3) and the radiator (Section 7), then fill the cooling system (Section 5).

11 Coolant pump – removal and refitting

1   Refer to Section 10 and carry out the operations described in paragraphs 1 to 5 inclusive.

2   Remove the thermostat housing as described in Section 9.

3   Slacken the clips and disconnect the radiator bottom hose and heater return hose at the coolant pump (photo).

4   Slacken the clip and disconnect the coolant auxiliary hose on the left-hand side of the pump body.

5   On pre-October 1984 models with multiple ancillary drivebelts, undo the three bolts securing the fan coupling body to the coolant pump and pump bracket. Withdraw the coupling, disconnect the wiring plug, and remove the unit from the engine.

6   On post-October 1984 models with single ancillary drivebelt arrangement, disconnect the electromagnetic fan coupling wiring and release the cable from any clips or ties.

7   Remove the alternator as described in Chapter 12, then undo the three bolts securing the alternator mounting bracket to the coolant pump (photo). Remove the bracket.

8   Undo the remaining bolts securing the coolant pump to the timing cover and remove the pump (photos). Make a note of the retaining bolt locations, as there are a number of different lengths used.

9   Clean away all traces of sealing compound from the mating faces prior to refitting the pump.

10 Smear a new gasket with jointing compound, and place it on the timing cover (photo). Note that during manufacture, the coolant pump-to-timing cover joint is sealed with a non-hardening silicone sealant, and a gasket is not used. In some instances, service replacement pumps may be supplied without a gasket, in which case a silicone sealant may be used again if a gasket cannot be obtained separately.

10.4 Undo the fan centre retaining bolt

10.5 Coolant pump pulley retaining bolts (arrowed)

11 Place the pump in position, fit the retaining bolts and tighten to the specified torque.

12 Refit the alternator mounting bracket and the alternator.

13 If previously removed, refit the electromagnetic fan coupling and secure with the three bolts.

14 Reconnect the coolant hoses and refit the thermostat housing (Section 9).

15 Refit the coolant pump pulley and secure with the four socket-headed bolts.

16 Place the fan over the pulley, fit the retaining bolt with the washer arranged as shown in Fig. 2.11, and tighten to the specified torque.

17 Refit and adjust the drivebelt (Chapter 12), refit the air cleaner (Chapter 3) and the radiator (Section 7), then fill the cooling system (Section 5).

18 Reconnect the fan coupling wiring (where applicable), and secure to the loom using new cable ties.

12 Coolant level indicator – description and testing

Later models are equipped with a dynamic coolant level indicator to monitor the coolant level in the expansion tank, and provide visual warning to the driver in the event of coolant loss or low coolant level.

The level sensor located in the expansion tank comprises a float which rises and falls with coolant level. Should the level fall below minimum, the float actuates the sensor contacts which cause a warning lamp bulb in the instrument panel to illuminate.

Should the warning lamp fail to illuminate when the coolant level falls below minimum, or if it is illuminated even when the level is correct, the circuit can be checked as follows.

1 Disconnect the wiring plug from the level sensor in the expansion tank (photo).

2 Connect an ohmmeter across the two sensor terminals and note the resistance. With the coolant level correct, the ohmmeter reading should be infinity. With the level below minimum, the reading should be approximately 5.0 ohms.

11.3 Radiator and heater hose connections at the coolant pump

3 If the readings are not as given above, renew the sensor. To do this, first drain the coolant in the expansion tank by releasing the return hose at the base of the tank. Make sure, however, that the engine is cold, and the pressure in the system is released by removing the pressure cap.

4 Extract the retaining circlip (photo) and withdraw the sensor and O-ring from the tank.

5 Fit the new new sensor and O-ring, noting that the unequal-sized lugs allow fitment one way only. Secure the sensor with the circlip, fit

11.7 Alternator mounting bracket retaining bolts (arrowed)

11.8A Coolant pump retaining bolts (arrowed) on left-hand side

11.8B Removing the coolant pump from the timing cover

11.10 Fitting a new pump gasket to the timing cover

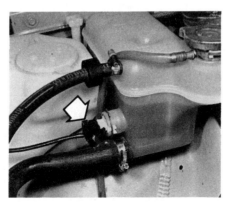

12.1 Coolant level sensor wiring plug (arrowed)

12.4 Coolant level sensor retaining circlip (arrowed)

the wiring plug and expansion tank hose, then top up the system.

6   If the ohmmeter readings were satisfactory, then the fault lies in the warning indicator or the wiring. To check the indicator, remove the instrument panel as described in Chapter 12 and connect the ohmmeter between terminal 12 of the instrument panel 15 terminal wiring plug, and a good earth. If the reading on the ohmmeter is infinity, then the warning indicator is faulty and should be renewed. If the reading is less than infinity, there is a wiring fault between the sensor and warning indicator, which should be investigated by a Mercedes-Benz dealer.

7   Remove the ohmmeter and refit the instrument panel as described in Chapter 12 on completion.

13 Fault diagnosis – cooling system

Symptom	Reason(s)
Overheating	Low coolant level (this may be the result of overheating for other reasons) Drivebelt slipping or broken Radiator blockage (internal or external) Thermostat defective Faulty electromagnetic fan coupling or thermal switch Expansion tank pressure cap faulty Ignition system fault Carburettor or fuel injection system fault Blown cylinder head gasket Brakes binding
Overcooling	Thermostat defective
Coolant loss – external	Loose hose clips Perished or cracked hoses Radiator core leaking Heater matrix leaking Expansion tank pressure cap seal faulty Boiling due to overheating Coolant pump or thermostat housing joint leakage Core plug leakage
Water loss – internal	Cylinder head gasket blown Cylinder head cracked or warped Cylinder block cracked
Corrosion	Incorrect antifreeze mixture or incorrect type of antifreeze Combustion gases contaminating coolant Infrequent draining or flushing

Chapter 3 Fuel and exhaust systems

Contents

Specifications

Part A: Carburettor models

Air cleaner

Type .... Renewable paper element, automatic air temperature control

Fuel pump

Type .... Mechanical, operated by eccentric on camshaft
Delivery pressure .... 0.25 to 0.38 bar (3.6 to 5.5 lbf/in²)

Carburettor

Type .... Variable choke sidedraught
Make .... Zenith-Stromberg 175 CDT
Cold start device .... Automatic choke
Idle speed .... 750 to 850 rpm
Fast idle speed .... 1600 to 1800 rpm
Idle mixture CO content .... 0.5 to 1.5%
Fast idle mixture CO content .... 5 to 7%
Fuel jet 100
Jet needle .... UC
Float level .... 18.0 to 19.0 mm (0.71 to 0.75 in)
Piston damper fluid type .... Mercedes-Benz approved ATF (Duckhams MB-Matic)

Fuel – general

Octane rating	98 RON (four-star)
Fuel tank capacity	55 litres (12.1 Imp gals) including 7.5 litres (1.65 Imp gals) reserve

Torque wrench settings

	Nm	lbf ft
Fuel tank retaining nuts	20	15
Fuel gauge sender unit cap nut	39	29
Carburettor to rubber mounting flange	50	37
Rubber mounting flange to inlet manifold	15	11
Carburettor air intake elbow adaptor bolts	30	22
Exhaust system U-bolt nuts	7	5
Downpipes to exhaust manifold	20	15
Exhaust system flange joint	20	15

Part B: Fuel injected models

General

System type	Bosch CIS-E electronically-controlled continuous injection system
System pressure	5.3 to 5.5 bar (76.8 to 79.7 lbf/in²)

Fuel pump

Type	12 volt electric roller cell type
Delivery quantity (minimum)	1.0 litre (1.76 Imp pts) in 40 seconds

Fuel injectors

Opening pressure:	
With new injectors	3.5 to 4.1 bar (50.7 to 59.4 lbf/in²)
With used injectors	3.0 bar (43.5 lbf/in²) minimum
Idle speed	750 to 850 rpm
Idle mixture CO content	0.5 to 1.5%

Fuel – general

Fuel octane rating	98 RON (four-star)
Fuel tank capacity	55 litres (12.1 Imp gals) including 7.5 litres (1.65 Imp gals) reserve

Torque wrench settings

	Nm	lbf ft
Fuel tank retaining nuts	20	15
Fuel gauge sender unit cap nut	39	29
Fuel line union nuts (reference value)	12	9
Air flow sensor rubber mounting nuts	10	7
Air guide housing to air flow sensor	10	7
Exhaust system U-bolt nuts	7	5
Downpipes to exhaust manifold	20	15
Exhaust system flange joint	20	15

PART A: CARBURETTOR MODELS

1 General description

The fuel system on carburettor engine models consists of an upright, centrally-mounted fuel tank, mechanical fuel pump driven by the engine intermediate shaft, and Zenith-Stromberg variable choke, sidedraught carburettor.

The air cleaner is of the automatic air temperature control type, and contains a disposable paper element.

The exhaust system is in two sections; the front section contains a resonator and twin downpipes from the manifold, while the rear section contains the two silencers. The system is suspended on rubber mountings at the centre and rear, and bolted via a flange joint to the cast iron manifold at the front.

Warning: *Many of the procedures in this Chapter entail the removal of fuel pipes and connections which may result in some fuel spillage. Before carrying out any operation on the fuel system refer to the precautions given in Safety First! at the beginning of this Manual and follow them implicitly. Petrol is a highly dangerous and volatile liquid and the precautions necessary when handling it cannot be overstressed.*

2 Maintenance and inspection

1 At the intervals given in Routine Maintenance at the beginning of this manual, carry out the following service operations on the fuel system.

2 With the car over a pit, raised on a vehicle lift, or securely supported on axle stands, carefully inspect the fuel pipes, hoses and unions for chafing, leaks and corrosion. Renew any pipes that are severely pitted with corrosion or in any way damaged. Renew any hoses that show signs of cracking or other deterioration.

3 Check the exhaust system flange bolts for tightness and check the system for leaks and security (see Section 18).

4 From within the engine compartment, check the security of all fuel hose attachments and inspect the fuel hoses and vacuum hoses for kinks, chafing and deterioration.

5 Renew the air cleaner element as described in Section 3.

6 Check the operation of the accelerator linkage, and lubricate the linkage and cable with a few drops of engine oil.

7 Unscrew the piston damper filler plug on the top of the carburettor (photo), and check that the fluid level is up to the bottom of the plug orifice. If necessary, top up using automatic transmission fluid (see Specifications) until the level is correct (photo).

8 Check and if necessary adjust the engine idle speed and mixture as described in Section 11.

3 Air cleaner and element – removal and refitting

1 To renew the air cleaner element, unscrew the retaining clips securing the air intake elbow to the carburettor and air cleaner (photos).

2.7A Unscrew the carburettor piston damper filler plug ...

2.7B ... and top up the fluid to the bottom of the plug orifice

3.1A Slacken the intake elbow clips at the carburettor ...

3.1B ... and air cleaner ...

3.2 ... and remove the elbow ...

3.3A Undo the air cleaner cover retaining nuts ...

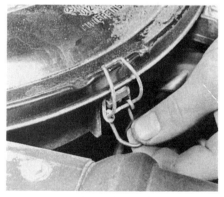

3.3B ... and spring back the clips

3.4 Removing the air cleaner element

3.9 Two of the air cleaner retaining nuts (arrowed)

2   Withdraw the elbow from the air cleaner and remove it from the car (photo).

3   Undo the nuts on the air cleaner cover, and spring back the retaining clips around the side (photos).

4   Lift off the cover and take out the air cleaner element (photo).

5   Wipe out the inside of the air cleaner body and the cover.

6   Place a new element in position, and refit the cover and intake elbow using the reverse of the removal procedure.

7   To remove the complete air cleaner assembly, first remove the air intake elbow as previously described.

8   Detach the cold air intake duct from the spout at the front of the car.

9   Undo the nuts securing the air cleaner to the rocker cover and inlet manifold (photo).

10 Lift the unit up and detach the hot air intake duct, followed by the crankcase breather and vacuum hoses. Remove the air cleaner assembly from the car.

11 Refitting the air cleaner is the reverse sequence to removal.

4   Air cleaner automatic air temperature control – description and testing

1   The air cleaner is fitted with an automatic air temperature control system to regulate the temperature of the intake air supplied to the carburettor.

2   The system consists of a thermostatic control element, flap valve, control rod and compression springs located in the air cleaner intake.

3   When the temperature of the ambient air around the thermostatic control element is below 13°C (55°F), the compression springs hold the flap valve fully open, blocking off the cold air intake and allowing only hot air from the exhaust manifold to enter the air cleaner.

4   At temperatures between 13°C (55°F) and 25°C (77°F), the thermostatic control element will act on the control rod, and the flap valve will start to move towards the closed position. Both the cold and hot air intakes will be open, and 'blended' warm air will be admitted to

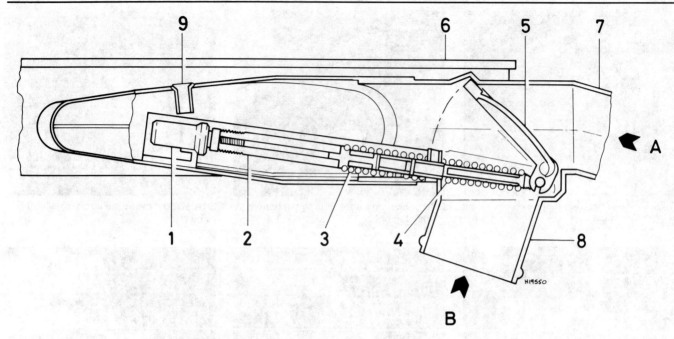

Fig. 3.1 Air cleaner flap valve in fully open position (Sec 4)

1 Thermostatic control element	4 Secondary compression spring	6 Air cleaner	9 Compensating air supply for control element
2 Control rod	5 Flap valve	7 Air intake	A Cold air supply
3 Main compression spring		8 Air intake	B Hot air supply

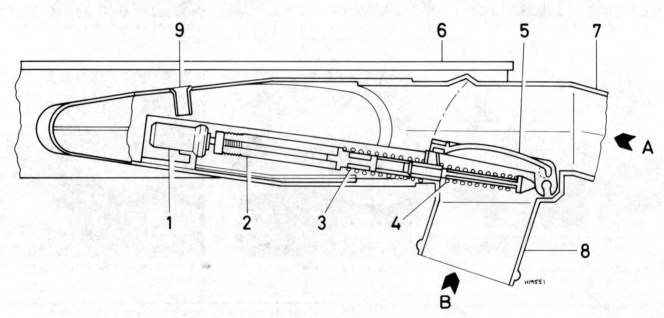

Fig. 3.2 Air cleaner flap valve in fully closed position (Sec 4)

1 Thermostatic control element	4 Secondary compression spring	6 Air cleaner	9 Compensating air supply for control element
2 Control rod	5 Flap valve	7 Air intake	A Cold air supply
3 Main compression spring		8 Air intake	B Hot air supply

the air cleaner.

5   At temperatures in excess of 25°C (77°F), the flap valve will be fully closed, blocking off the hot air intake and allowing only cold air to enter the air cleaner.

6   The position of the flap valve can be checked with the hot air duct disconnected, by using a mirror to view the flap valve from below. If the engine is cold and the ambient air temperature is below 13°C (55°F), the valve should be fully open to admit only hot air into the air

cleaner.

7   If the operation of the valve is suspect, its action can be checked with the air cleaner removed using a hair dryer and thermometer. Direct the hot air from the hair dryer into the intake and observe the operation of the valve at various temperatures.

8   If the unit does not function as previously described, undo the screws securing the assembly to the air cleaner at the side and renew the unit complete.

5.4 Disconnect the linkage return spring at the fuel pump bracket

5.5A Withdraw the bracket ...

5.5B ... then remove the pump

5.6A Withdraw the pushrod ...

5.6B ... followed by the insulating block

5 Fuel pump – removal and refitting

The fuel pump is located on the left-hand side of the engine, and is operated by a pushrod from the intermediate shaft eccentric. The pump is a sealed unit and cannot be dismantled for servicing or repair.
1 Disconnect the battery negative terminal.
2 Slacken the retaining clips and disconnect the fuel hoses at the pump, noting that the upper hose is the supply from the fuel tank, and the lower hose is the output to the carburettor.
3 Release the cable clip and detach the wiring from the bracket moulded into the fuel pump insulating block.
4 Disconnect the linkage return spring from the bracket on the pump lower mounting stud (photo).
5 Undo the two retaining nuts, remove the bracket from the lower stud and remove the fuel pump from the mounting studs (photos).
6 Withdraw the pushrod, followed by the insulating block (photos).
7 Check the condition of the O-ring seals in the insulating block, and renew the block if the O-rings have deteriorated. The O-rings are not available separately.
8 Refitting is the reverse sequence to removal, but note that the pushrod is fitted with its circlip towards the pump.

6 Fuel tank – removal and refitting

1 Removal of the fuel tank should be undertaken when the tank is almost empty, as a drain plug is not provided. Alternatively use a syphon or hand pump to remove the fuel, but ensure that this, and the fuel tank removal operations, are carried out in a well-ventilated area.
2 Raise the rear of the car and support it on axle stands. Do not position the car over an inspection pit.

3 Disconnect the battery negative terminal.
4 From under the car, disconnect the fuel supply and return hoses and the vent hose from the tank outlets. Plug the hoses and outlets after removal.
5 Release the large rubber closing grommet from the fuel tank outlets.
6 From within the luggage compartment, remove the floor carpet then release the tank lining panel retainers, first at the bottom, then along the top and sides of the panel (photos). Remove the panel from the luggage compartment.
7 Disconnect the fuel gauge sender unit wiring plug on the upper right-hand side of the tank (photo), and release the wiring from the cable clips.
8 Undo the fuel tank retaining nuts, lift the tank slightly, and pull out the drain hose.
9 Lift the tank upwards for clearance, then rearwards and remove it from the luggage compartment.
10 With the tank removed, unscrew the filter at the supply hose outlet and remove it from the tank. Blow the filter clean, and check the mesh screen for damage. Renew the filter if necessary.
11 If the tank is contaminated with sediment or water, remove the gauge sender unit as described in Section 7 and swill the tank out with clean fuel. If the tank is corroded or leaks, it should be repaired by specialists, or alternatively renewed. **Note:** *Do not, under any circumstances, solder or weld a fuel tank, for safety reasons.*
12 Before refitting, screw in the filter using a new gasket if necessary, and tighten securely. Also check that the damping pads at the bottom and rear faces of the tank are in place and secure. Attach them with a suitable adhesive if necessary, ensuring that the rear face pad is positioned approximately 190.0 mm (7.5 in) down from the tank upper edge.
13 Refitting the tank is the reverse sequence to removal.

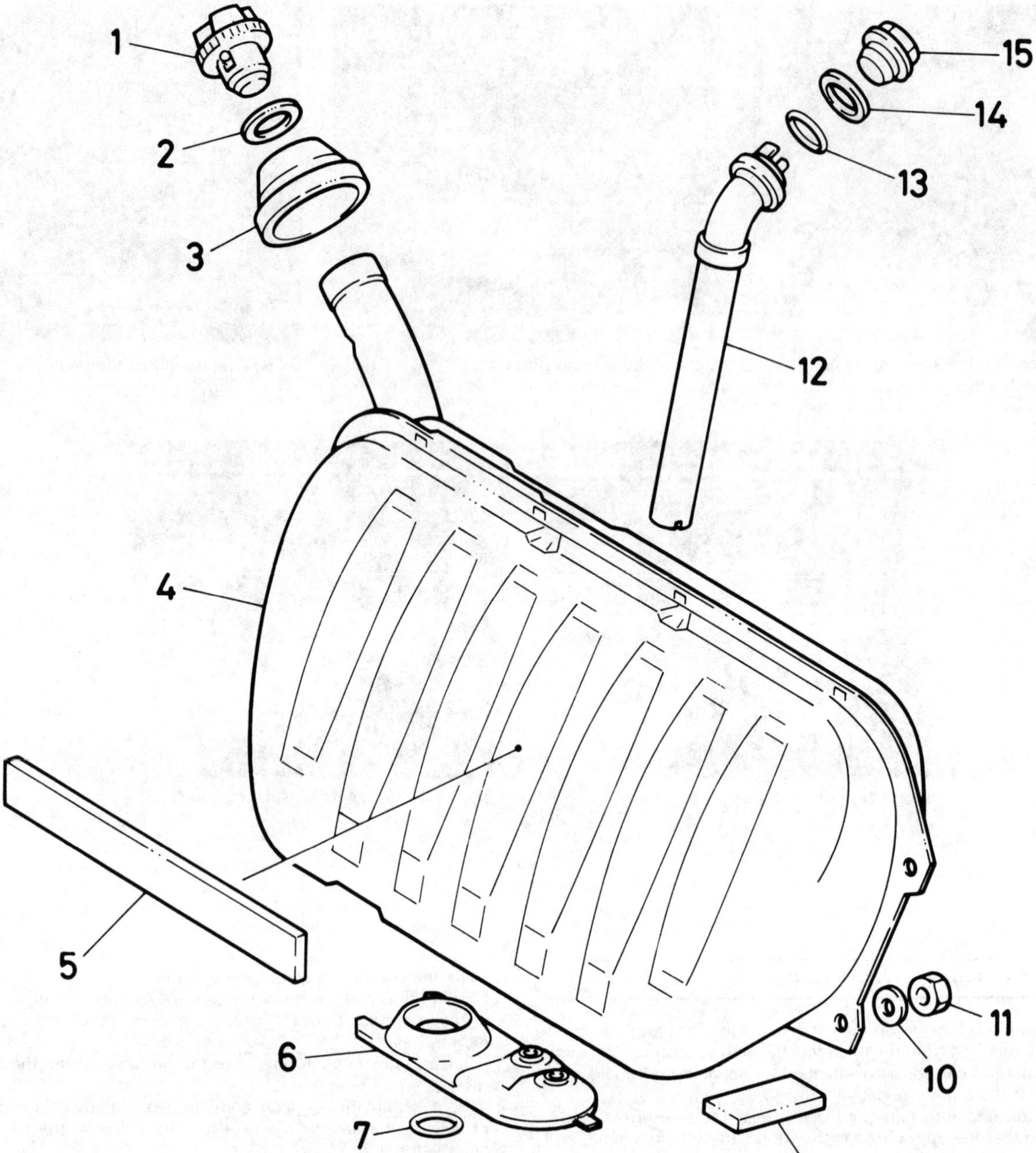

Fig. 3.3 Fuel tank and related components (Sec 6)

1 Filler cap	5 Rear damping pad	9 Bottom damping pad	13 Sealing O-ring
2 Sealing ring	6 Closing grommet	10 Washer	14 Sealing O-ring
3 Sealing sleeve	7 Filter seal	11 Nut	15 Sender unit cap nut
4 Fuel tank	8 Filter	12 Fuel gauge sender unit	

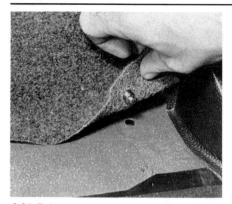

6.6A Release the fuel tank lining press studs ...

6.6B ... and flat clip retainers

6.7 Disconnect the fuel gauge sender unit wiring plug

7 Fuel gauge sender unit – removal and refitting

1   The fuel gauge sender unit is located on the upper right-hand side of the fuel tank, and can be removed and refitted from within the luggage compartment with the tank in place. Before removal it is necessary to remove 8 litres (14.1 Imp pts) of fuel from the tank (assuming it is full), by syphon or hand pump. Ensure that this and the following operations are carried out in a well-ventilated area.
2   Disconnect the battery negative terminal.
3   From within the luggage compartment, remove the floor carpet then release the fuel tank lining panel retainers, first at the bottom, then along the top and sides of the panel. Remove the panel from the luggage compartment.
4   Disconnect the wiring plug from the sender unit.
5   Unscrew the retaining cap nut and withdraw the sender unit upwards then rearwards from the tank.
6   Refitting is the reverse sequence to removal, but renew both sealing O-rings on the cap nut if they are in any way damaged. Ensure that the lug on the sender unit flange faces downwards when the unit is fitted.

8 Accelerator cable and linkage – adjustment

1   Run the engine until normal operating temperature is reached, then switch off.
2   Disconnect the accelerator cable end from the guide lever by releasing the square retainer from the lever (photo). Now slip the cable out of the slot on the side of the lever.
3   On cars equipped with automatic transmission, disconnect the control pressure cable end from the ball socket on the guide lever.
4   Slacken the clamp bolt on the connecting lever and move the guide lever until the roller rests against the idle speed end stop (photo). Hold the linkage in this position and tighten the connecting lever clamp bolt.
5   Reconnect the accelerator cable to the guide lever.
6   Have an assistant depress the accelerator pedal fully on cars with manual transmission, or down as far as the kickdown switch on cars with automatic transmisssion. Do not actuate the kickdown switch.
7   The throttle lever on the carburettor should now be in contact with the full throttle stop plate on the side of the carburettor (photo). Turn the cable adjuster (photo) as required to achieve this.
8   Release the accelerator pedal and allow the linkage to move to the idle position once more, with the roller resting against the guide lever idle speed end stop.
9   In this position, the stop nipple on the end of the accelerator cable should be in contact with the compression spring with no free play. If this is not the case, turn the adjuster at the accelerator pedal end of the cable, which is accessible from inside the car (photo) until the adjustment is correct.
10 Refer to Chapter 6, Section 19, and adjust the control pressure cable on cars equipped with automatic transmission.

8.2 Disconnect the accelerator cable end square retainer (arrowed)

8.4 Connecting lever clamp bolt (A) and linkage roller (B) against guide lever idle speed end stop

8.7A With the pedal depressed, the lever (A) should contact the full throttle stop plate (B)

8.7B Accelerator cable full throttle stop adjuster (arrowed)

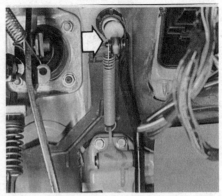

8.9 Accelerator cable idle speed end stop adjuster (arrowed)

9 Accelerator cable – removal and refitting

1   Disconnect the accelerator cable end from the guide lever by releasing the square retainer from the lever. Now slip the cable out of the slot on the side of the lever.

2   Compress the two legs of the outer cable retainer, and pull the cable up and out of the support bracket (photo).

3   From inside the car, extract the retaining circlip and remove the cable end from the accelerator pedal shaft.

4   Release the cable from the bulkhead and pull it through into the engine compartment.

5   Withdraw the grommet in the inner bulkhead and the retaining clips along the cable length.

6   Remove the cable from the car.

7   Refitting is the reverse sequence to removal, but adjust the cable as described in Section 8.

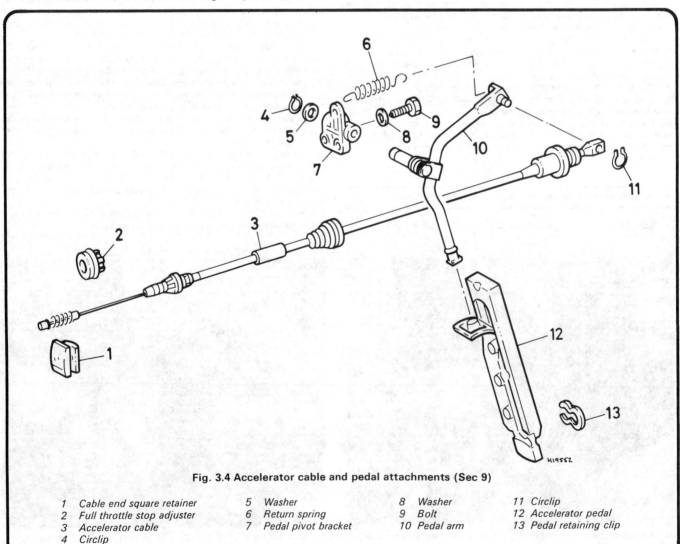

Fig. 3.4 Accelerator cable and pedal attachments (Sec 9)

1 Cable end square retainer	5 Washer	8 Washer	11 Circlip
2 Full throttle stop adjuster	6 Return spring	9 Bolt	12 Accelerator pedal
3 Accelerator cable	7 Pedal pivot bracket	10 Pedal arm	13 Pedal retaining clip
4 Circlip			

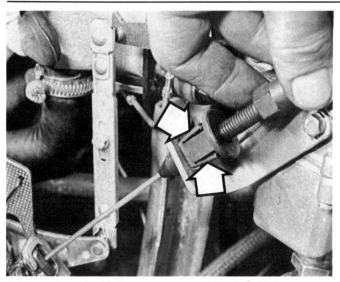

9.2 Compress the legs (arrowed) of the outer cable retainer

10.3 Earth cable retaining bolt (arrowed)

10 Carburettor – removal and refitting

1 Slacken the retaining clips and remove the air cleaner intake elbow from the air cleaner and carburettor.
2 Disconnect the accelerator cable from the carburettor as described in the previous Section.
3 Undo the bolt and remove the earth cable from the side of the carburettor flange (photo).
4 Carefully prise the linkage connecting lever off the throttle lever ball socket (photo).
5 Disconnect the electrical wiring plugs at the solenoid and choke housing (photo) and at the thermotime delay valve and fuel shut-off valve (photos).
6 Release the cooling system expansion tank pressure cap to relieve any pressure remaining in the cooling system.
7 Slacken the hose clips and remove the two coolant hoses from the automatic choke unit (photo). Plug each hose as soon as it is removed to minimise coolant loss.
8 Slacken the clips and remove the fuel supply and return hoses from the side of the carburettor. Plug these hoses also to avoid fuel spillage.
9 On cars fitted with automatic transmission, disconnect the control pressure cable from the guide lever ball socket and from the support bracket.
10 Disconnect the vacuum hose from the top of the carburettor flange.
11 Undo the four retaining bolts and remove the carburettor from the rubber mounting flange. Recover the flange gasket.
12 Refitting the carburettor is the reverse sequence to removal, but use a new flange gasket.

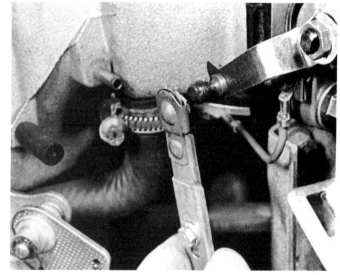

10.4 Disconnect the connecting lever at the ball socket

10.5A Disconnect the wiring plugs at the vent valve solenoid (A) and choke housing (B) ...

10.5B ... at the thermotime delay valve ...

10.5C ... and fuel shut-off valve

10.7 Remove the coolant hoses at the automatic choke

Fig. 3.5 Carburettor adjusting screw details
(Secs 11 and 12)

1 Choke lever connecting rod   3 Throttle lever
   (early version)   4 Idle speed adjusting screw
2 Fast idle adjusting screw

11 Carburettor idle speed and mixture – adjustment

Note: *The following adjustments should be carried out when the engine has just reached normal operating temperature after starting from cold, rather than after a long drive. Ideally the adjustments should be completed before the engine temperature exceeds 100°C (212°F).*

1 When carrying out the adjustments, the air cleaner must be in position with all vacuum and breather hoses connected. The tachometer inside the car is suitably accurate for idle speed adjustment. However, if for convenience an external instrument is being used, refer to the precautions given in Chapter 4 before connecting.

2 Start the engine and allow it to idle. On cars equipped with automatic transmission, move the selector lever to the 'P' (park) position. Ensure that the air conditioning system is turned off (if fitted).

3 Turn the idle speed adjusting screw (Fig. 3.5) as necessary until the engine is idling at the specified speed. Note that the idling speed adjusting screw is the longer of the two adjacent adjusting screws.

4 Accelerate the engine briefly, return it to idle and recheck the setting. Switch off when correct.

5 If the mixture setting is to be checked and adjusted, connect an exhaust gas analyser (CO meter) in accordance with the manufacturer's instructions.

6 If a tamperproof cap is fitted to the fuel shut-off valve, prise the cap apart using a screwdriver and discard it (Fig. 3.6).

7 Start the engine, accelerate it briefly and return it to idle.

8 Check the CO reading on the meter. If it is not as specified, slacken the fuel shut-off valve locknut and turn the valve body until the CO reading is correct (Fig. 3.7). Screwing the valve in will weaken the mixture, and screwing it out will richen it. Accelerate the engine briefly to clear the manifold between each adjustment.

9 When the CO reading is as specified, tighten the valve locknut.

10 Recheck the idle speed and readjust if necessary.

11 On automatic transmission models equipped with a vacuum governor on the side of the carburettor, the governor adjustment should be checked as follows.

12 With the engine idling, disconnect the vacuum hose at the diaphragm, and set the engine speed to 1250 rpm by turning the adjuster bolt on the end of the diaphragm rod (Fig. 3.8). Hold the diaphragm rod with a second spanner when turning the adjuster bolt.

13 Reconnect the vacuum hose and check that a small amount of free play (approximately 0.5 mm/0.02 in) exists between the adjuster bolt and the throttle lever.

14 Move the selector lever into D (drive), and also turn the steering onto full lock. Check that the vacuum governor maintains a smooth engine speed without stalling. If necessary make small adjustments by means of the large adjusting nut on the diaphragm rod.

15 On completion, switch off, and disconnect any instruments that were used.

Fig. 3.6 Tamperproof cap (arrowed) over the fuel shut-off valve (Sec 11)

Fig. 3.7 Fuel shut-off valve locknut (1) and shut-off valve body (2) (Sec 11)

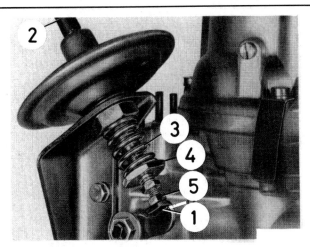

Fig. 3.8 Vacuum governor adjustment points (Sec 11)

1 Throttle lever
2 Vacuum hose connection
3 Spring
4 Diaphragm rod large adjusting nut
5 Diaphragm rod adjuster bolt

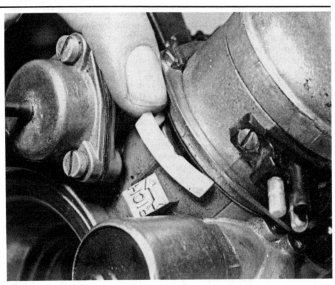

12.2A Remove the choke housing plastic cover ...

12 Carburettor automatic choke – adjustment

1 Check the idle speed and mixture adjustments as described in Section 11.
2 Remove the plastic cover from the choke housing, and check that the reference marks on the bi-metal spring housing and choke housing are in line (photos). If not, slacken the three retaining screws, align the marks and tighten the screws.
3 With the engine at normal operating temperature, and the CO meter still connected from the idle speed and mixture adjustment, start the engine and allow it to idle.
4 Hold the throttle linkage open by hand to increase the engine speed to approximately 2500 rpm. At the same time, insert a small screwdriver into the slot on the choke housing, exposed by removal of the plastic cover, and move the drive lever towards the engine until a noticeable stop is felt. Do not try to push the drive lever past the stop.
5 While holding the drive lever with the screwdriver, release the throttle linkage. The engine will now be running at the fast idle speed, which should be as given in the Specifications.
6 If the speed is not as specified, turn the fast idle adjusting screw (Fig. 3.5) as necessary until the speed is correct. Note that the fast idle adjusting screw is the shorter of the two adjacent adjusting screws.
7 Now check the fast idle mixture reading as shown on the CO meter with the engine still running at the fast idle speed. If the CO reading is not as given in the Specifications, hook out the tamperproof cap over the auxiliary air adjusting screw (Fig. 3.9).
8 Screw the adjusting screw in to richen the mixture or screw it out to weaken, until the specified value is obtained.
9 On completion switch off the engine, disconnect the instruments and refit the plastic cover to the choke housing.

13 Carburettor – dismantling and reassembly

1 Remove the carburettor from the engine as described in Section 10.
2 Undo the three screws and remove the dashpot cover complete with the piston damper (photo).
3 Undo the screws securing the dashpot to the carburettor body, noting that the thermotime delay valve is also retained by one of the screws. Withdraw the valve, then carefully lift off the dashpot (photos).
4 Lift out the piston spring, followed by the piston and diaphragm assembly (photos).
5 Undo the three screws and remove the bi-metal spring housing and gasket from the choke housing.
6 Release the connecting rod from the ball sockets on the choke and linkage levers, and remove the rod (photo).
7 Undo the three screws securing the choke housing to the carburettor and remove the housing and gasket (photos).

12.2B ... and check that the reference marks are aligned (arrowed)

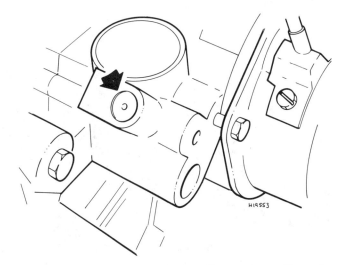

Fig. 3.9 Tamperproof cap (arrowed) over the auxiliary air adjusting screw (Sec 12)

8 Undo the three screws securing the vacuum diaphragm cover at the base of the carburettor (photo). Remove the cover, followed by the spring and diaphragm (photos).

9 Undo the float chamber retaining screws and carefully lift off the float chamber (photo). Lift out the compensating element, followed by the compression spring (photo). Note that the compensating element may have stayed in place on the fuel shut-off valve when the float chamber was removed.

10 Carefully prise the float pivot pin upwards to release it from its holders, disengage the float tag from the fuel needle valve retainer and remove the float (photo).

11 Unscrew and remove the fuel needle valve and sealing washer.

12 Further dismantling of the automatic choke is described in Section 14, and reference should be made to that Section if the operation of the unit is suspect.

13 With the carburettor dismantled, clean the parts as necessary in petrol and blow dry. Blow out all passages in the carburettor with compressed air; do not probe with wire or any sharp instruments.

14 Check the condition of all the diaphragms, gaskets, seals, and O-rings, and obtain new parts as necessary. Pay particular attention to the piston rubber diaphragm, and renew the diaphragm if there are any folds or creases in the rubber, or any signs of deterioration whatsoever. This is a critically important component, and if there is the slightest air leak through a small hole, the carburettor will not function.

15 To renew the diaphragm, undo the four retaining plate screws and remove the plate and diaphragm (photo). Fit the new diaphragm with the tag on the underside engaged with the slot in the piston, and secure with the retaining plate.

16 Check the condition of the jet needle for wear ridges, severe scuffing or distortion. If evident, renew the needle. To do this, unscrew

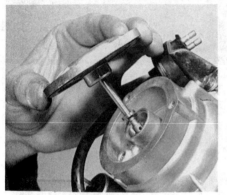
13.2 Remove the dashpot cover and piston damper

13.3A Thermotime delay valve retained by one of the dashpot screws

13.3B Removing the dashpot

13.4A Lift out the piston spring ...

13.4B ... followed by the piston and diaphragm

13.6 Release the connecting rod from the lever ball sockets

13.7A Remove the complete choke housing assembly ...

13.7B ... followed by the gasket

13.8A Undo the vacuum diaphragm cover screws ...

13.8B ... remove the cover ...

13.8C ... followed by the spring ...

13.8D ... and the diaphragm

13.9A Removing the float chamber complete with compensating element (arrowed) ...

13.9B ... and compression spring

13.10 Release the float tag (arrowed) from the fuel needle valve

the small grub screw in the side of the piston and withdraw the needle. Fit the new needle so that the plastic collar is flush with the base of the piston, and secure with the grub screw (Fig. 3.10).

17 With all the new parts obtained, begin reassembly by refitting the fuel needle valve and sealing washer.

18 Engage the float arm tag under the needle valve retainer and press the float pivot pin into its holders.

19 Blow through the fuel supply port, and check that the flow is interrupted as the float is raised, and restored as the float is lowered.

20 Turn the carburettor body upside down, so that the float is resting under its own weight and the fuel needle valve spring-loaded ball is completely pushed in. Check the float level with a ruler between the carburettor mating face and the highest point of the float (photo).

21 If the float level is not as given in the Specifications, first check that the sealing washer under the needle valve is of 1.5 mm (0.06 in) thickness. If this is not the case, renew the sealing washer and recheck the float level. If further adjustment is required, carefully bend the float arm tag as necessary until the correct level is obtained.

22 Place the compression spring and compensating element in the float chamber bore, then refit the float chamber using a new gasket. Secure with the retaining screws.

23 Place the vacuum diaphragm and spring on the carburettor body with the metal disc on the diaphragm towards the spring. Using a new gasket, refit the diaphragm cover and secure with the three screws.

24 Using a new gasket, refit the choke housing and secure with the retaining screws.

25 Refit the connecting rod to the ball sockets on the choke and linkage levers.

26 Place a new bi-metal spring housing gasket in position, locate the end of the bi-metal spring behind the drive lever, and position the housing over the gasket (photos). Align the marks on the two housings, then fit and tighten the three retaining screws.

27 Engage the piston needle through the jet in the fuel shut-off valve, and fit the piston and diaphragm to the carburettor body.

28 Engage the tag on the diaphragm with the slot in the body (photo), then refit the dashpot. With the thermotime delay valve in place, secure the dashpot with the retaining screws.

29 Refit and secure the dashpot cover with the three screws.

30 Unscrew the piston damper filler plug, and fill the damper using the specified grade of automatic transmission fluid, up to the bottom of the plug orifice. Refit the filler plug.

31 Refit the carburettor to the engine as described in Section 10, then adjust the carburettor and automatic choke as described in Sections 11 and 12 respectively.

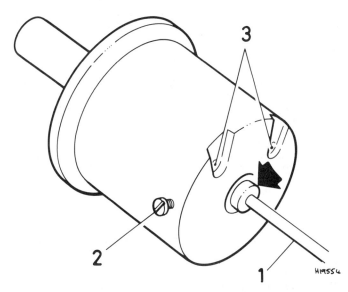

Fig. 3.10 Carburettor air piston and jet needle (Sec 13)

1 Jet needle
2 Grub screw
3 Air ports
Arrow shows plastic collar on jet needle

13.15 Piston diaphragm retaining screws
(arrowed)

13.20 Checking the float level

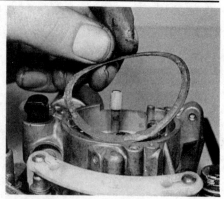

13.26A Using a new gasket ...

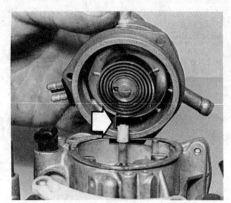

13.26B ... fit the bi-metal spring housing
with the spring end (arrowed) behind the
drive lever

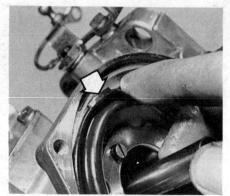

13.28 Engage the tag on the diaphragm
(arrowed) with the slot in the carburettor
body

14 Carburettor automatic choke – dismantling and reassembly

1   Disconnect the electrical wiring plugs at the solenoid and choke
housing, and the vacuum hoses at the pull-down unit.
2   Undo the three screws securing the bi-metal spring housing, and
remove the housing, leaving the coolant hoses still attached. Recover
the gasket.
3   Disengage the connecting rod from the ball socket on the choke
lever.
4   Undo the three screws securing the choke housing to the
carburettor body, withdraw the housing and remove the gasket.
5   With the unit on the bench, extract the circlip and remove the
choke lever, followed by the dirt guard (Fig. 3.11).
6   Undo the three screws and remove the pull-down diaphragm cover
and spring (photos). Recover the gasket.
7   Extract the circlip and slide the drive lever, together with the fast
idle cam, forwards to disengage the pull-down diaphragm rod (Fig.
3.12).
8   Withdraw the pull-down diaphragm and rod from the choke
housing (photo).
9   Withdraw the fast idle cam, drive lever, return spring and the spring
cup.
10 Unscrew the sealing plug on the side of the choke housing and
withdraw the plug, together with the washer, compression spring and
valve plate (photo).
11 Remove the dust sleeve and pull out the choke valve (Fig. 3.13).
12 With the choke now disconnected, clean all the parts and blow out
all the ports in the housing with compressed air.
13 Check that the choke valve slides easily in its bore, and if necessary
polish the valve with metal polish to achieve a perfect sliding fit.
14 Check the condition of the pull-down diaphragm, the operating
levers and all gaskets, and obtain any new parts as necessary. The dust

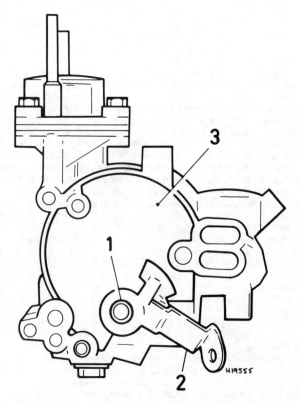

Fig. 3.11 Choke lever circlip (1), choke lever (2) and dirt
guard (3) (Sec 14)

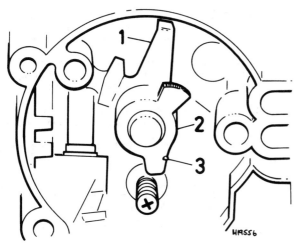

Fig. 3.12 Automatic choke drive lever (1), fast idle cam (2) and spring (3) (Sec 14)

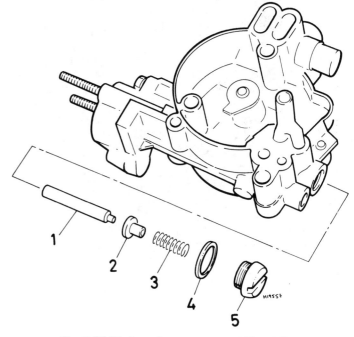

Fig. 3.13 Choke valve components (Sec 14)

1 Choke valve
2 Valve plate
3 Compression spring
4 Washer
5 Sealing plug

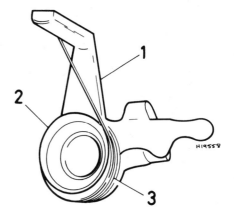

Fig. 3.14 Drive lever (1) with spring cup (2) and return spring (3) positioned ready for fitting (Sec 14)

sleeve for the choke valve must be renewed, as it will have been damaged during removal.

15 Ensure that all the parts are thoroughly clean and dry, and do not use any lubricant during reassembly.

16 With a new dust sleeve in place on the choke valve, insert the valve into its bore, then refit the valve plate, compression spring, washer and sealing plug. Tighten the plug securely.

17 Place the pull-down diaphragm and rod in position on the choke housing, and refit the spring and diaphragm cover using a new gasket. Secure the cover with the three screws.

18 Place the spring cup and return spring on the drive lever as shown in Fig. 3.14. Slide the drive lever onto the bearing shaft with its end engaged with the pull-down diaphragm rod. Engage the long end of the return spring with the retaining screw hole lug in the housing to tension the drive lever.

19 With the other return spring in place on the fast idle cam, place the cam on the bearing shaft and attach the spring end to the drive lever.

20 Secure the drive lever and fast idle cam with the retaining circlip.

21 Refit the choke lever without the dirt guard at this stage, so that the following adjustments can be carried out.

22 Push the diaphragm rod upwards to its stop, and push the drive lever to the left so that it rests against the diaphragm rod. The choke should now be resting in the centre of the second highest step on the fast idle cam (Fig. 3.16). If this is not the case, carefully bend the drive lever arm that contacts the fast idle cam as necessary.

23 Now push the drive lever to the left against its stop. The choke lever should now be resting on the highest step of the fast idle cam for a distance of 0.5 mm (0.02 in) (Fig. 3.17). Again, bend the drive lever arm if necessary to achieve this.

24 Finally, check that with the drive lever pushed fully to the right and the choke lever moved up, the fast idle cam moves so as to allow the choke lever to rest off the steps of the cam when the lever is released. Carefully file the edge of the fast idle cam if necessary.

14.6A Undo the pull-down diaphragm cover screws ...

14.6B ... and remove the cover and spring

14.8 Withdraw the pull-down diaphragm and rod

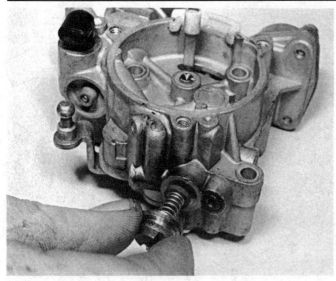

14.10 Withdraw the sealing plug together with washer, spring and valve plate

25 With the choke operating properly, remove the choke lever, fit the dirt guard, then refit the choke lever. Secure the lever with the circlip.
26 Refit the choke housing to the carburettor, using a new gasket, and secure with the three screws.
27 Place a new gasket on the choke housing and refit the bi-metal spring housing, ensuring that the spring end locates behind the drive lever. Align the marks on the spring housing and choke housing, then secure with the three screws.
28 Refit the connecting rod to the choke lever ball socket.
29 Reconnect the pull-down unit vacuum hoses and the wiring plugs at the solenoid and choke housing.
30 Adjust the carburettor and automatic choke as described in Sections 11 and 12 respectively.

15 Inlet manifold pre-heater – removal and refitting

1   Disconnect the wiring plug for the pre-heater, located on the underside of the inlet manifold.
2   Undo the bolts and move the inlet manifold support strut to one side for access.
3   Undo the retaining bolts, and carefully lever the pre-heater out of its location. Take care not to damage the insulating ring.
4   Remove the rubber sealing ring from the manifold.
5   Refitting is the reverse sequence to removal. Use a new sealing ring, and place this on the pre-heater before fitting the assembly to the manifold.

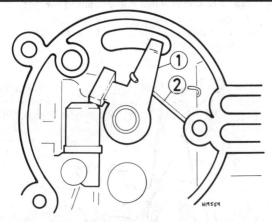

Fig. 3.15 Drive lever (1) in position and long end of return spring (2) engaged with screw hole lug (Sec 14)

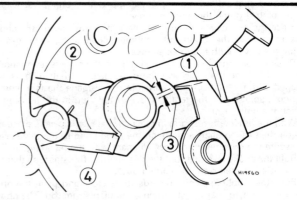

Fig. 3.16 Choke levers set in pull-down position (Sec 14)

1   Choke lever   3   Fast idle cam
2   Drive lever   4   Drive lever arm

Arrows indicate choke lever resting in the centre of second highest step on fast idle cam

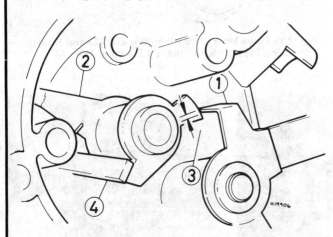

Fig. 3.17 Choke lever set in cold start position (Sec 14)

1   Choke lever   3   Fast idle cam
2   Drive lever   4   Drive lever arm

Arrows indicate choke lever resting on highest step of fast idle cam for a distance of 0.5 mm (0.2 in)

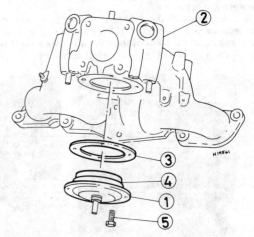

Fig. 3.18 Inlet manifold pre-heater components (Sec 15)

1   Pre-heater   4   Sealing ring
2   Inlet manifold   5   Retaining bolt
3   Insulating ring

16 Inlet manifold – removal and refitting

1 Disconnect the battery negative terminal.
2 Drain the cooling system as described in Chapter 2.
3 Remove the air cleaner as described in Section 3 of this Chapter.
4 Refer to Section 10 and remove the carburettor.
5 Unscrew the bolt and remove the brake servo vacuum hose banjo union and sealing washers from the manifold (photo).
6 Disconnect the vacuum supply hoses for the central locking system and automatic transmission, as applicable (photo).
7 Release the fuel and coolant hoses and the wiring loom from their support clips and cable ties on the manifold and the surrounding area.
8 Slacken the clips and disconnect the coolant hoses on the underside of the manifold.
9 Disconnect the electrical plug at the manifold pre-heater.
10 Undo the bolts and remove the manifold support strut.
11 Undo the two bolts securing the throttle linkage bracket to the cylinder head, and move the bracket aside.
12 Undo the nuts securing the manifold to the cylinder head. At the front, remove the coolant hose junction pipe (photo), and at the rear undo the additional bolt and remove the engine lifting bracket (photo).
13 Withdraw the manifold from the cylinder head and remove the gasket.
14 Refitting is the reverse sequence to removal, bearing in mind the following points:

(a) *Ensure that the manifold and cylinder head mating faces are clean, and use a new gasket*
(b) *Refit the carburettor and air cleaner as described in Sections 10 and 3 respectively*
(c) *Refill the cooling system as described in Chapter 2*

17 Exhaust manifold – removal and refitting

1 Jack up the front of the car and support it on axle stands.

2 Slacken the U-bolt nuts securing the exhaust downpipe to the transmission-mounted support bracket.
3 Undo the nuts securing the support bracket to the transmission, and move the bracket clear.
4 Support the exhaust downpipe on a jack.
5 Undo the bolts securing the downpipes to the manifold, and lower the jack to separate the joints. Recover the flange gasket(s).
6 Refer to Section 3 and remove the air cleaner.
7 Undo the nuts securing the manifold to the cylinder head, noting the location of the engine oil dipstick tube support clip (photos).
8 Withdraw the manifold from the cylinder head studs and remove the gaskets (photo).
9 Refitting is the reverse sequence to removal, but ensure that new gaskets are used, with the raised beading and the sheet metal sections towards the manifold.

18 Exhaust system – checking, removal and refitting

1 The exhaust system should be examined for leaks, damage and security at regular intervals (see Routine Maintenance). To do this, apply the handbrake and, in a well ventilated area, allow the engine to idle. Lie down on each side of the car in turn, and check the full length of the exhaust system for leaks whilst an assistant temporarily places a wad of cloth over the end of the tailpipe. If a leak is evident, stop the engine and use a proprietary repair kit to seal. If the leak is excessive, or damage is evident, renew the section. Check the rubber mountings for deterioration, and renew them, if necessary (photos).
2 The exhaust system is manufactured in two sections, but for repairs in service, a new rear section with silencer is available separately. This is attached by means of a push-on joint and U-clamp, after cutting off the original rear section.
3 When renewing any of the exhaust sections, it is best to remove the complete system from the car.
4 To remove the exhaust system, raise and support the car, and undo the nuts or bolts securing the downpipes to the manifold (photo).

16.5 Remove the brake servo vacuum hose banjo union

16.6 Disconnect the vacuum hose (arrowed) at the manifold outlet

16.12A Coolant hose junction pipe (arrowed) ...

16.12B ... and engine lifting bracket attachments

17.7A Exhaust manifold upper retaining nuts (arrowed) ...

17.7B ... and dipstick tube attachment

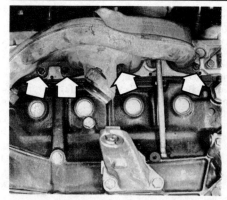

17.7C Exhaust manifold lower retaining nuts (arrowed)

17.8 Remove the manifold gaskets

18.1A Exhaust system centre rubber mounting ...

18.1B ... and rear rubber mountings

18.4 Exhaust downpipe to manifold connection

18.8 Exhaust front-to-rear section flange joint

5   Undo the nuts and remove the U-bolts securing the system to the transmission support bracket. Note the arrangement of the washers on the U-bolts (Fig. 3.19).

6   Support the system at the front and remove the transmission support bracket after undoing the retaining nuts.

7   Release the rubber rings securing the system at the centre and rear, and lower the exhaust to the ground.

8   Separate the front and rear sections at the flange joint (photo). Renew the sealing ring when refitting.

9   If a new rear section (tailpipe) has been obtained, lay this over the original system and mark the length of the new section. Add 80 mm (3.2 in) to this mark, and cut the system at that point (Fig. 3.20).

10 Connect the sections together loosely prior to refitting, and suspend the system on its mountings under the car.

11 Refit the downpipes to the manifold using new gaskets, and secure the system to the transmission support bracket.

12 Check that the system is well clear of the body and suspension components, and is not under strain, then tighten the section joints.

13 Run the engine and check for leaks.

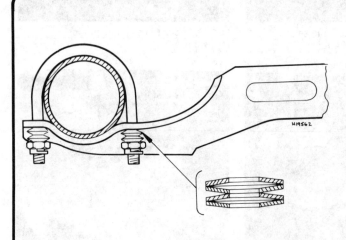

Fig. 3.19 Exhaust support bracket U-bolt washer arrangement (Sec 18)

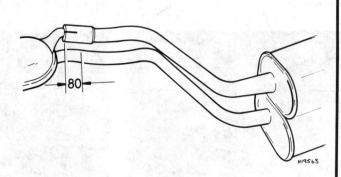

80

Fig. 3.20 Exhaust system cutting position for fitting separate rear section (Sec 18)

PART B: FUEL INJECTED MODELS

19 General description

The fuel system on fuel injected models consists of an upright, centrally-mounted fuel tank, electrically-operated fuel pump and Bosch CIS-E electronically-controlled fuel injection system.

The air cleaner is of the conventional dry filter type, containing a disposable paper element.

The exhaust system is in two sections; the front section contains a resonator and twin downpipes from the manifold, while the rear section contains the two silencers. The system is suspended on rubber mountings, and bolted via a flange joint to the cast iron manifold at the front.

Warning: *Many of the procedures in this Chapter entail the removal of fuel pipes and connections which may result in some fuel spillage. Before carrying out any operation on the fuel system refer to the precautions given in Safety First! at the beginning of this Manual and follow them implicitly. Petrol is a highly dangerous and volatile liquid and the precautions necessary when handling it cannot be overstressed.*

20 Maintenance and inspection

1 Apart from topping-up the carburettor piston damper, all the maintenance and inspection operations listed in Part A, Section 2, are applicable to fuel injected models, but with reference to the applicable Sections in Part B.
2 Additionally, the fuel filter must be renewed at the specified intervals, using the procedure given in Section 28.

21 Air cleaner and element – removal and refitting

1 Undo the nuts securing the air cleaner cover to the body (photo).
2 Spring back the retaining clips and lift off the cover complete with air cleaner element (photos).
3 Remove the element from the cover.
4 Wipe out the inside of the air cleaner body and the cover.
5 Place a new element in the cover and refit the cover to the air cleaner body. Secure with the clips and retaining nuts.
6 To remove the complete air cleaner assembly, first remove the cover and element as previously described.
7 Undo the nuts securing the air cleaner body to the rocker cover and the support brackets (photos).
8 Pull out the air intake duct and lift the air cleaner off the airflow sensor (photo).
9 Disconnect the engine breather hose from the base of the air cleaner, and remove the unit from the car (photo).
10 Refitting is the reverse sequence to removal, but ensure that the sealing ring locates squarely over the airflow sensor.

22 Fuel tank – removal and refitting

Refer to Part A: Section 6.

23 Fuel gauge sender unit – removal and refitting

Refer to Part A: Section 7.

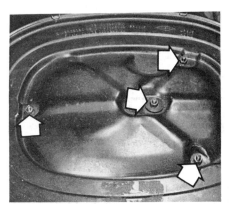

21.1 Undo the air cleaner cover retaining nuts (arrowed) ...

21.2A ... spring back the clips ...

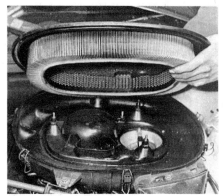

21.2B ... and lift off the cover and element

21.7A Undo the air cleaner front retaining nut (arrowed) ...

21.7B .. the centre nut (arrowed) ...

21.7C ... and rear nut (arrowed)

21.8 Pull out the air intake duct ...

21.9 ... lift up the air cleaner and disconnect the breather hose

24 Accelerator cable and linkage – adjustment

1 Check that the accelerator cable and linkage operate smoothly without stiffness in the linkage, and with no trace of binding or kinks in the cable.
2 Disconnect the accelerator cable end from the guide lever by releasing the square retainer from the lever. Now slip the cable out of the slot on the side of the lever.
3 Prise off the connecting lever from the guide lever ball socket. The connecting lever is the adjustable thin flat lever, connecting the guide lever on the main linkage with the throttle lever below on the throttle valve housing.
4 Move the guide lever until the roller rests against the idle speed end stop (photo). With the linkage in this position, adjust the length of the connecting lever if necessary, so that it can be fitted, free of tension, to the guide lever ball socket.

5 Reconnect the accelerator cable and connecting lever to the guide lever.
6 Have an assistant depress the accelerator pedal fully on cars with manual transmission, or down as far as the kickdown switch on cars with automatic transmission. Do not actuate the kickdown switch.
7 The throttle lever on the throttle valve housing should now be in contact with the full throttle stop. Turn the cable adjuster (photo) as required to achieve this.
8 Release the accelerator pedal and allow the linkage to return to the idle position, wth the roller resting against the guide lever idle speed end stop.
9 In this position, the stop nipple on the end of the accelerator cable should be in contact with the compression spring with no free play (photo). If this is not the case, turn the adjuster at the accelerator pedal end of the cable, which is accessible from inside the car, until the adjustment is correct.
10 Refer to Chapter 6, Section 19, and adjust the control pressure cable on cars equipped with automatic transmission.

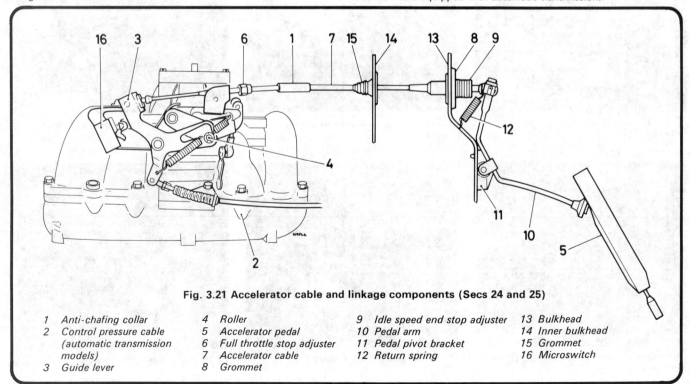
Fig. 3.21 Accelerator cable and linkage components (Secs 24 and 25)

1	Anti-chafing collar	4	Roller	9	Idle speed end stop adjuster	13	Bulkhead
2	Control pressure cable (automatic transmission models)	5	Accelerator pedal	10	Pedal arm	14	Inner bulkhead
3	Guide lever	6	Full throttle stop adjuster	11	Pedal pivot bracket	15	Grommet
		7	Accelerator cable	12	Return spring	16	Microswitch
		8	Grommet				

24.4 Linkage roller (arrowed) against guide lever idle speed end stop

24.7 Accelerator cable full throttle stop adjuster (arrowed)

24.9 Accelerator cable stop nipple (arrowed)

25 Accelerator cable – removal and refitting

Refer to Part A: Section 9, but on completion adjust the cable as described in the previous Section.

26 Fuel injection system – description and operation

The fuel injection system fitted is of the continuous injection type and supplies a precisely controlled quantity of atomized fuel to each cylinder under all operating conditions.

This system, when compared with conventional carburettor arrangements, achieves a more accurate control of the air/fuel mixture resulting in reduced emission levels and improved performance.

The main components of the system are listed below, together with a brief description of their operation, as follows:

The **fuel tank** is the same as that used on carburettor models, and is located behind a panel at the front of the luggage compartment.

The **fuel pump** is of electrically-operated, roller cell type. A pressure relief valve is incorporated in the pump to prevent excessive pressure build-up in the event of a restriction in the pipelines.

The **fuel accumulator** has two functions, (i) to dampen the pulsation of the fuel flow, generated by the pump and (ii) to maintain fuel pressure after the engine has been switched off. This prevents a vapour lock developing with consequent hot starting problems.

The **fuel filter** incorporates two paper filter elements to ensure that the fuel reaching the injection system components is completely free from dirt.

The **fuel distributor/airflow sensor assembly**. The fuel distributor controls the quantity of fuel being delivered to the engine, ensuring that each cylinder receives the same amount. The airflow sensor incorporates an air sensor plate and control plunger. The air sensor plate is located in the main airstream between the air cleaner and the throttle butterfly. During idling, the airflow lifts the sensor plate which in turn raises a control plunger which allows fuel to flow past the plunger and out of the metering slits to the injector valves. Increases in engine speed cause increased airflow which raises the control plunger and so admits more fuel. All mixture corrections are controlled electronically, by the **electromagnetic pressure actuator**, located on the side of the fuel distributor. The pressure actuator is directly controlled by a variable electric current, delivered by the fuel injection control module.

The **fuel injection control module** is located in the engine compartment behind the battery, and receives inputs from the various engine sensors concerning temperature, engine load, throttle movement, throttle position and starter actuation. This information modifies a program stored in its memory so that the electromagnetic pressure actuator, on receiving the signal from the module, can alter the mixture to suit all engine conditions.

The **throttle valve housing** is located beneath the airflow sensor, and contains the throttle plate, which is operated from the throttle linkage by means of a connecting lever. A throttle valve switch is located on the side of the housing, which sends inputs on throttle position to the control module. During manufacture, the throttle plate is adjusted so that it is fractionally open, to avoid the possibility of it

jamming shut, and it must not be re-positioned. Idle speed adjustment is provided for by means of a screw in the **idle speed air distributor** which, according to its setting, restricts the airflow through air bypass channels.

The **fuel injectors** are located in the inlet manifold, and are designed to open at a pre-determined fuel pressure.

The **fuel pressure regulator** is a vacuum-operated mechanical device which maintains the pressure differential between the inlet manifold depression and the system fuel pressure. When the pressure differential increases beyond a certain figure, excess fuel is diverted back to the fuel tank.

The **auxiliary air device** is located at the rear of the inlet manifold. It consists of a pivoted plate, bi-metal strip and heater coil. The purpose of this device is to supply an increased volume of fuel/air mixture during cold idling rather similar to the fast idle system on carburettor layouts.

The **cold start valve** system consists of an electrical injector and a **thermotime switch**. Its purpose is to spray fuel into the manifold to assist cold starting, the thermotime switch regulating the amount of fuel injected.

27 Fuel injection system – precautions and general repair information

1   Due to the complexity of the fuel injection system and the need for special gauges and Mercedes-Benz dedicated test equipment, any work should be limited to the operations described in this Chapter. Other adjustments and system checks are beyond the scope of most readers, and should be left to a Mercedes-Benz dealer or Bosch fuel injection specialists.

2   Before disconnecting any fuel lines, unions or components, thoroughly clean the component or connection and the adjacent area.

3   Place any removed components on a clean surface and cover them with plastic sheet or paper. Do not use fluffy rags for cleaning.

4   The system operates under pressure at all times, and care must be taken when disconnecting any fuel lines under pressure. Place an absorbent rag around the fuel line to be disconnected and slowly unscrew the union. Discard the rag safely once the pressure has been released and no further fuel escapes. If more than one union on a component is to be disconnected, the remaining unions will not normally be under pressure once the first one is undone. Refer to the warning note in Section 19, and always work with the battery negative terminal disconnected, and in a well-ventilated area.

5   Never start the engine when the battery is not firmly connected, and never disconnect the battery with the engine running.

6   If the battery is to be rapid-charged from an external source, it should be completely disconnected from the vehicle electrical system. If this is not done, there is a risk of damage to the fuel injection control module.

7   The control module must be removed from the car if temperatures are likely to exceed 80°C (176°F) as would be experienced, for example, in a paint spray oven, or if any electric welding is being carried out on the car. The ignition must be switched off when removing the control module.

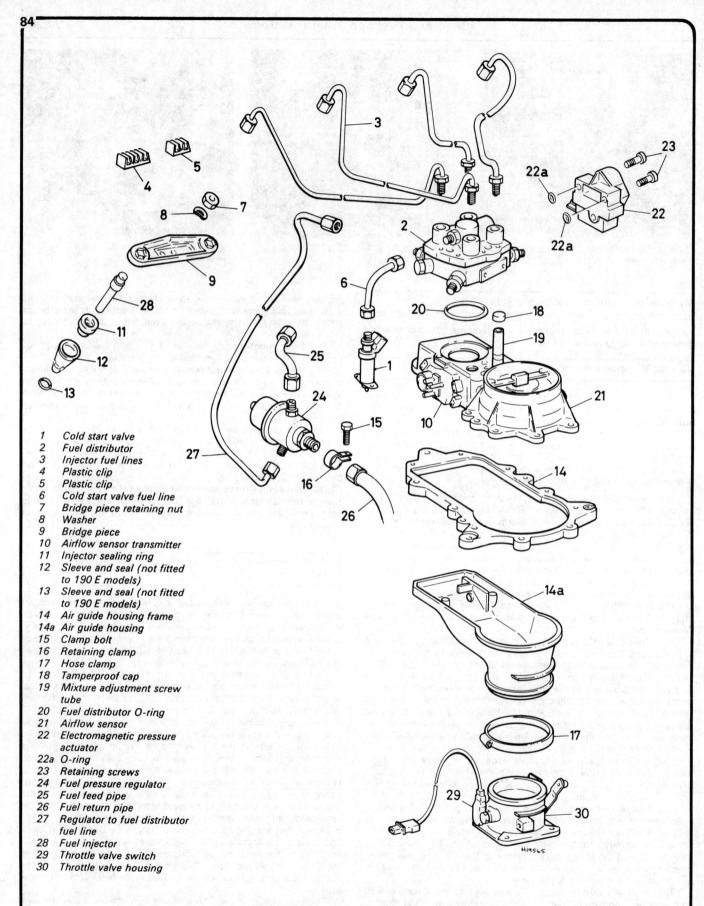

1 Cold start valve
2 Fuel distributor
3 Injector fuel lines
4 Plastic clip
5 Plastic clip
6 Cold start valve fuel line
7 Bridge piece retaining nut
8 Washer
9 Bridge piece
10 Airflow sensor transmitter
11 Injector sealing ring
12 Sleeve and seal (not fitted
   to 190 E models)
13 Sleeve and seal (not fitted
   to 190 E models)
14 Air guide housing frame
14a Air guide housing
15 Clamp bolt
16 Retaining clamp
17 Hose clamp
18 Tamperproof cap
19 Mixture adjustment screw
   tube
20 Fuel distributor O-ring
21 Airflow sensor
22 Electromagnetic pressure
   actuator
22a O-ring
23 Retaining screws
24 Fuel pressure regulator
25 Fuel feed pipe
26 Fuel return pipe
27 Regulator to fuel distributor
   fuel line
28 Fuel injector
29 Throttle valve switch
30 Throttle valve housing

**Fig. 3.22 Exploded view of the fuel injector and airflow
sensor assembly components (Sec 26)**

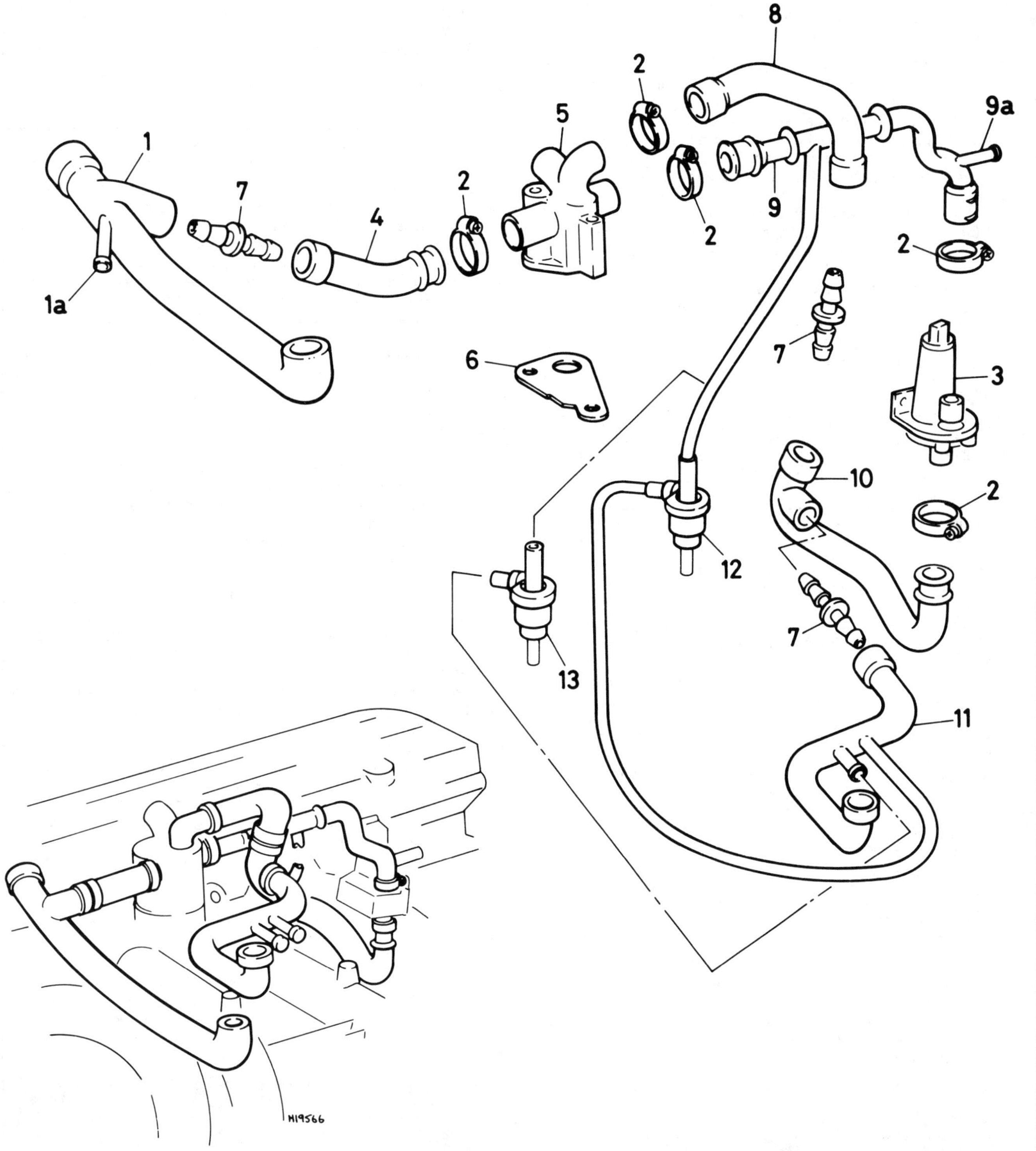

Fig. 3.23 Exploded view of the fuel injection air and vacuum hose arrangement (Sec 26)

1 Shaped hose
1a Take-off to fuel pressure regulator
2 Hose clamp
3 Auxiliary air device
4 Shaped hose
5 Idle speed air distributor
6 Gasket
7 Spacing element
8 Shaped hose
9 Shaped hose
9a Take-off to automatic transmission
10 Shaped hose
11 Shaped hose
12 Bypass valve for automatic transmission
13 Bypass valve for air conditioning compressor

28 Fuel filter – removal and refitting

1 Disconnect the battery negative terminal.
2 Release any excess pressure in the fuel tank by removing the filler cap.
3 Jack up the rear of the car and support it on axle stands.
4 Remove the plastic cover over the fuel filter, pump and accumulator assembly. To do this, undo the retaining bolts or if plastic fittings are used, unscrew the centre expander, then withdraw the retainer body (photos).
5 Using brake hose clamps or small G-clamps, pinch the two fuel hoses to prevent excessive fuel spillage.
6 Wipe clean the area around the fuel hose unions at both ends of the filter (photo).
7 Place a container beneath the filter to catch any escaping fuel, then undo the fuel outlet union on the left-hand end of the filter (photo). Withdraw the union and hose from the filter.
8 Unscrew the connecting pipe banjo union bolt, remove the bolt and the sealing washers (photo).
9 Undo the retaining strap screw (photo), swing the strap down and remove the filter.
10 Refitting is the reverse sequence to removal. Ensure that the retaining strap locates on the filter plastic sleeve only, and does not make metal-to-metal contact with the filter body. Use new sealing washers at the banjo union if the originals are in any way damaged.

29 Fuel pump – removal and refitting

1 Proceed as described in Section 28, paragraphs 1 to 5 inclusive.
2 Wipe clean the area around the fuel hose unions at both ends of the pump.
3 Place a container beneath the fuel pump to catch any escaping fuel, then slacken the clip on the fuel feed hose. Disconnect the hose from the pump.
4 Unscrew the connecting pipe banjo union bolt, remove the bolt and the sealing washers (photo).
5 Disconnect the electrical connections at the pump terminals.
6 Undo the two retaining strap screws, remove the strap and withdraw the pump.
7 Refitting is the reverse sequence to removal. Ensure that the retaining strap locates on the pump plastic sleeve only, and does not make metal-to-metal contact with the pump body. Position the pump with the electrical terminals in line vertically before securing the strap. Use new sealing washers on the banjo union if the originals are in any way damaged.

30 Fuel accumulator – removal and refitting

1 Proceed as described in Section 28, paragraphs 1 to 5 inclusive.
2 Wipe clean the area around the fuel hose unions at both ends of the fuel accumulator.
3 Place a container beneath the accumulator to catch any escaping fuel, then slacken the clip on the fuel hose. Disconnect the hose from the accumulator.

4 Unscrew the fuel pipe union nut at the other end of the accumulator.
5 Undo the retaining strap screw, remove the strap and withdraw the accumulator.
6 Refitting is the reverse sequence to removal.

31 Idle speed and mixture – adjustment

Note: *The following adjustments should be carried out when the engine has just reached normal operating temperature after starting from cold, rather than after a long drive. Ideally the adjustments should be completed before the engine temperature exceeds 100°C (212°F). On cars with air conditioning, the idling is electronically controlled and cannot be adjusted. If the idling speed is erratic on cars so equipped, the advice of a Mercedes-Benz dealer should be sought.*

1 When carrying out the adjustments, the air cleaner must be in position with all vacuum and breather hoses connected. The tachometer inside the car is suitably accurate for idle speed adjustment. However, if for convenience an external instrument is being used, refer to the precautions given in Chapter 4 before connecting. If the mixture is to be checked, connect an exhaust gas analyser (CO meter) in accordance with the manufacturer's instructions.
2 Start the engine and allow it to idle. On cars equipped with automatic transmission, move the selector lever to the 'P' (park) position. Ensure that the air conditioning system is turned off (if fitted).
3 Turn the idle speed adjusting screw, which is accessible through the gap between the rocker cover and air cleaner (photos) until the engine is idling at the specified speed.
4 Accelerate the engine briefly, return it to idle and recheck the setting. Switch off when correct.
5 To adjust the mixture, remove the air cleaner as described in Section 21 and hook out the tamperproof cap in the mixture adjustment screw tube (photo), unless this has been done previously. Refit the air cleaner.
6 Start the engine, accelerate it briefly and return it to idle.
7 Check the CO reading on the meter. If it is not as specified, insert an Allen key into the mixture adjustment screw tube, through the centre of the air cleaner (photo). Engage the Allen key with the adjusting device, push down against spring pressure until the adjusting device engages the mixture screw, then turn as required. Turning anti-clockwise weakens the mixture, turning clockwise richens it.
8 When the specified value is obtained, accelerate the engine briefly then return it to idle. Check the CO reading once more, and make any small corrections as necessary.
9 On completion, switch off, and disconnect any instruments that were used.

32 Fuel injectors – removal and refitting

1 Remove the air cleaner as described in Section 21.
2 Slacken the clips, and disconnect the shaped hoses at the rocker cover and idle speed air distributor as necessary for access (photos).
3 Undo the fuel line union nuts at the injectors and at the fuel distributor, and move the fuel lines to one side (photo). Hold the

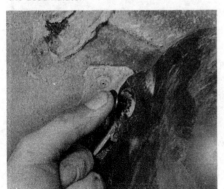
28.4A Remove the centre expander ...

28.4B ... followed by the plastic cover retainer body

28.6 Fuel pipe and wiring connections at the fuel filter (A) fuel pump (B) and fuel accumulator (C)

28.7 Fuel filter outlet union

28.8 Filter connecting pipe banjo union bolt

28.9 Filter retaining strap screw

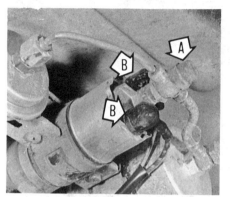

29.4 Fuel pump banjo union bolt (A) and electrical connections (B)

31.3A Insert a screwdriver between the rocker cover and air cleaner ...

31.3B ... to turn the idle speed adjusting screw (arrowed)

31.5 Hook out the tamperproof cap from the mixture adjustment screw tube ...

31.7 ... then adjust the mixture through the air cleaner opening

32.2A Disconnect the shaped hoses at the rocker cover ...

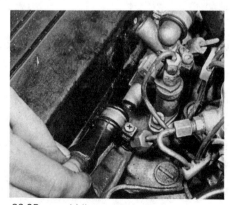

32.2B ... and idle speed air distributor

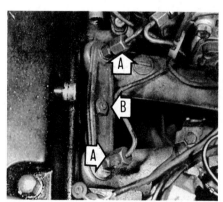

32.3 Fuel line union nuts (A) and injector bridge piece nut (B)

injector body with a second spanner when unscrewing the union nuts.
4 Undo the central nut and remove the retaining bridge piece securing each pair of injectors.
5 Withdraw the injector(s) from the manifold.
6 Refitting is the reverse sequence to removal, but renew the rubber sealing rings if they have deteriorated in any way.

33 Cold start valve – removal and refitting

1 Disconnect the battery negative terminal.
2 Disconnect the wiring plug at the cold start valve, which is located between the 2nd and 3rd fuel injector (photo).
3 Undo the fuel line union nuts and remove the fuel line (photo).
4 Undo the two socket-headed bolts and withdraw the valve from the manifold.
5 Refitting is the reverse sequence to removal.

34 Fuel distributor – removal and refitting

1 Disconnect the battery negative terminal.
2 Remove the air cleaner as described in Section 21.
3 Undo the fuel line union nuts for the four fuel injectors at the fuel distributor, and at the injectors. Ensure that the injector body is held with a second spanner as the union nuts are undone. Withdraw the fuel lines from the fuel distributor.
4 Similarly undo the union nuts for the cold start valve, pressure regulator and fuel supply pipe at the fuel distributor.
5 Disconnect the wiring multi-plug from the electromagnetic pressure actuator on the side of the fuel distributor.
6 Undo the three retaining screws on top of the unit, turn it from side to side while lifting upwards, and remove the unit from the airflow sensor (photo). Recover the sealing O-ring.
7 Refitting is the reverse sequence to removal, but use a new O-ring seal. Check for any signs of leaks on completion, and adjust the idle speed and mixture settings as described in Section 31.

33.2 Disconnecting the cold start valve wiring plug

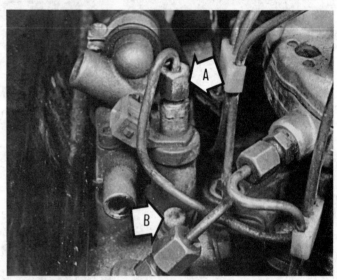
33.3 Cold start valve fuel line union (A) and front retaining bolt (B)

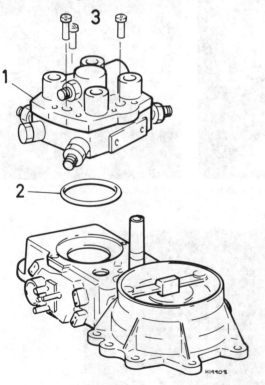
Fig. 3.24 Fuel distributor attachment details (Sec 34)

1 Fuel distributor
2 O-ring
3 Retaining screws

34.6 Fuel distributor retaining screws

35 Fuel pressure regulator – removal and refitting

1   Remove the air cleaner as described in Section 21.
2   Undo the three fuel line union nuts at the regulator located on the side of the airflow sensor (photo).
3   Disconnect the vacuum hose at the rear of the regulator.
4   Undo the clamp bolt and remove the unit from the airflow sensor.
5   Refitting is the reverse sequence to removal.

36 Airflow sensor – removal and refitting

1   Remove the fuel distributor as described in Section 34 and the fuel pressure regulator as described in Section 35.
2   Undo the two bolts and move the throttle linkage bracket aside (photo).
3   Disconnect the electric wiring plug at the airflow sensor transmitter (photo).
4   Slacken the hose clamp on the rubber connecting sleeve between the airflow sensor and the throttle valve housing below.
5   Undo the nuts securing the airflow sensor to its rubber mountings. Lift off the brackets under the nuts at the throttle linkage end (photo).
6   Lift the unit up, disconnect the idle speed air hose, and remove the airflow sensor from the car.
7   With the unit removed, the rubber air guide housing and its frame can be removed if required after undoing the retaining nuts.
8   Refitting is the reverse sequence to removal.

35.2 Fuel pressure regulator location and connections

36.2 Throttle linkage bracket retaining bolts (arrowed)

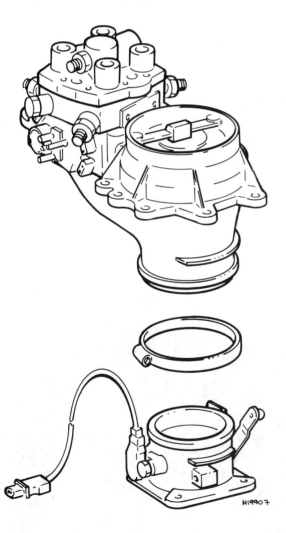

Fig. 3.25 Throttle valve housing attachment details (Sec 37)

1   Airflow sensor

36.3 Airflow sensor transmitter wiring plug

36.5 Airflow sensor-to-rubber mounting retaining nuts (arrowed)

38.5 Electromagnetic pressure actuator retaining screws (arrowed)

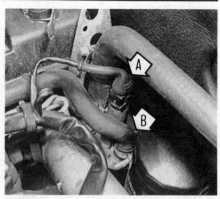

39.2 Wiring multi-plug (A) and air hose (B) at the auxiliary air device

37 Throttle valve housing – removal and refitting

1 Disconnect the battery negative terminal.
2 Remove the air cleaner as described in Section 21.
3 Undo the two bolts and move the throttle linkage bracket on the airflow sensor aside.
4 Disconnect the linkage return spring on the throttle valve housing and the linkage connecting rod.
5 Disconnect the vacuum hose at the throttle valve housing, and unplug the throttle valve switch wiring connector at the harness connection.
6 Undo the nuts securing the housing to the inlet manifold.
7 Slacken the hose clamp on the rubber connecting sleeve between the throttle valve housing and airflow sensor.
8 Undo the two nuts securing the airflow sensor to its rubber mountings at the throttle linkage end.
9 Unscrew the fuel return hose union nut at the rear of the fuel pressure regulator.
10 Lift the airflow sensor up until sufficient clearance exists to enable the throttle valve housing to be removed.
11 Cut the inlet manifold gasket at the throttle valve housing contact area, and remove the centre part of the gasket.
12 Refitting is the reverse sequence to removal, but use a new manifold gasket. Cut the gasket so that just the centre portion for the throttle valve housing is used.

38 Electromagnetic pressure actuator – removal and refitting

1 Disconnect the battery negative terminal.
2 Remove the air cleaner as described in Section 21.
3 Disconnect the wiring multi-plug from the pressure actuator, which is located on the side of the fuel distributor.
4 Reduce the fuel pressure by slackening the fuel line union on the pipe between the cold start valve and the fuel distributor at the fuel distributor end. Use an absorbent rag. Tighten the union after releasing the pressure.
5 Undo the two retaining screws and withdraw the pressure actuator from the fuel distributor (photo). Remove the two O-ring seals.
6 Refitting is the reverse sequence to removal, but use new O-ring seals.

39 Auxiliary air device – removal and refitting

1 Disconnect the battery negative terminal.
2 Disconnect the wiring multi-plug and the air hoses at the auxiliary air device, which is located at the rear of the inlet manifold, adjacent to the engine compartment bulkhead (photo).
3 Undo the retaining bolts, and lift the unit away.
4 Refitting is the reverse sequence to removal.

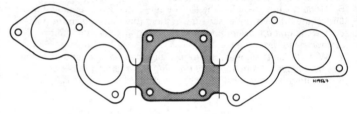

Fig. 3.26 Cut the inlet manifold gasket and remove the centre portion after removing the throttle valve housing (Sec 37)

40 Fuel injection control module – removal and refitting

1 The fuel injection control module is located in the engine compartment in the space behind the battery.
2 Remove the battery as described in Chapter 12.
3 On cars equipped wth ABS brakes, remove the braking system control unit as described in Chapter 9, Section 24.
4 Pull the control unit up and out of its location (photo).
5 Disconnect the wiring plug by depressing the spring tag at the cable end, lift the plug up at the cable end, then disengage the tab at the other end.
6 Refitting is the reverse sequence to removal, but ensure that the wiring plug engages with an audible click from the spring tag.

40.4 Fuel injection control module location in the compartment behind the battery

41 Inlet manifold – removal and refitting

1 Disconnect the battery negative terminal.
2 Remove the fuel injectors as described in Section 32.
3 Remove the cold start valve as described in Section 33.
4 Remove the airflow sensor as described in Section 36.
5 Remove the throttle valve housing as described in Section 37.
6 Disconnect the air hoses at the idle speed air distributor.
7 Unscrew the union nut and remove the brake servo vacuum hose. Release the hose from its support bracket.
8 Disconnect the remaining wiring plugs and vacuum hoses from their attachments and cable clips, after making a careful note of the location of each.
9 Undo the bolts and remove the support strut from beneath the manifold.
10 Undo the retaining nuts and one bolt securing the manifold to the cylinder head, withdraw the manifold from the studs, and remove the gasket.
11 If required, the manifold upper and lower halves can be separated after undoing the retaining nuts and bolts.
12 Refitting is the reverse sequence to removal. Use new gaskets and refit the manifold components with reference to the relevant Sections.

42 Exhaust manifolds – removal and refitting

Refer to Part A: Section 17.

43 Exhaust system – checking, removal and refitting

Refer to Part A: Section 18.

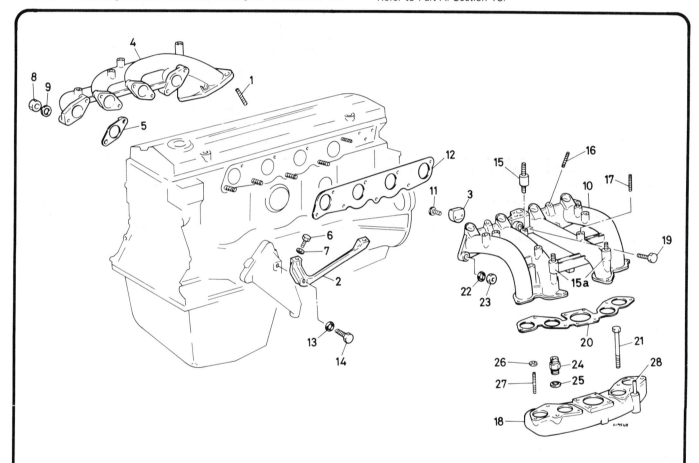

Fig. 3.27 Inlet and exhaust manifold details (Secs 41 and 42)

1	Stud	9	Washer	15a	Airflow sensor outer rubber
2	Support strut	10	Inlet manifold upper half		mountings
3	Closing cover	11	Rivet	16	Stud
4	Exhaust manifold	12	Gasket	17	Stud
5	Gasket	13	Washer	18	Inlet manifold lower half
6	Bolt	14	Bolt	19	Bolt
7	Washer	15	Airflow sensor inner rubber	20	Gasket
8	Nut		mounting	21	Bolt

22	Washer
23	Nut
24	Adaptor
25	Sealing ring
26	Washer
27	Stud
28	Vacuum connection

PART C: FAULT DIAGNOSIS

44 Fault diagnosis – fuel and exhaust systems (carburettor models)

Symptom	Reason(s)
Fuel consumption excessive	Air cleaner choked, giving rich mixture Leak from tank, pump or fuel lines Float chamber flooding due to incorrect level or worn needle valve Carburettor incorrectly adjusted Faulty or incorrectly adjusted choke Excessively worn carburettor
Lack of power, stalling or difficult starting	Punctured air piston diaphragm Faulty or incorrectly adjusted choke Leaking or disconnected vacuum hose Low piston damper oil level Carburettor incorrectly adjusted Fuel pump faulty Inlet manifold or carburettor flange gasket leaking
Poor or erratic idling	Carburettor incorrectly adjusted Faulty or incorrectly adjusted choke Leaking or disconnected vacuum hose Inlet manifold or carburettor flange gasket leaking Excessively worn carburettor

45 Fault diagnosis – fuel and exhaust system (fuel injected models)

Due to the need for special test equipment to carry out even the most routine fault diagnosis procedure, any fault occurring on the fuel injection system should be referred to a Mercedes-Benz dealer or Bosch fuel injection specialist. Before doing this however, make sure that the problem is not being caused by a disconnected or damaged hose or vacuum line, loose or disconnected wiring plug, or by some other simple fault that may be obvious under close visual inspection.

Chapter 4 Ignition system

Contents

Specifications

General
System type .... Constant energy transistorized electronic ignition

Distributor
Type .... Bosch electronic, breakerless
Rotor rotation .... Clockwise
Firing order .... 1-3-4-2 (No 1 at crankshaft pulley end)
Dwell angle range .... 7° to 34°

Coil
Type .... Bosch
Primary resistance .... 0.5 to 0.9 ohm
Secondary resistance .... 6.0 to 16.0 k ohm

Ignition timing
Stroboscopic at idle speed, with vacuum hose disconnected:
    Carburettor engines .... 10° to 16° BTDC
    Fuel injected engines:
        Pre-1985 (engine code 102.961) .... 10° to 16° BTDC
        1985 onwards (engine code 102.962) .... 12° to 18° BTDC
Centrifugal advance check – stroboscopic at 4500 rpm, with
vacuum hose disconnected .... 31° to 33° BTDC
Vacuum advance check (total advance) – stroboscopic at 4500
rpm, with vacuum hose connected .... 40° to 44° BTDC

Spark plugs
Type .... Bosch H7DC, Beru 14K-7DU, Champion BN9Y or S9YC
Electrode gap .... 0.8 mm (0.032 in)

Torque wrench setting

	Nm	lbf ft
Spark plugs	20	15

1 General description

A constant-energy electronic ignition system is fitted to all models covered by this manual, and comprises the battery, coil, distributor, electronic switching unit, spark plugs and associated leads and wiring.

The system is divided into two circuits, low tension and high tension. The high tension (HT) circuit is similar to that of a conventional ignition system, and consists of the high tension or secondary coil windings, distributor cap, rotor arm, spark plugs and HT leads. The low tension (LT) circuit consists of the battery, ignition switch, low tension or primary coil windings and a pulse generator operating in conjunction with the electronic switching unit. The pulse generator is located in the distributor, and comprises a permanent magnet, pick-up coil and trigger wheel (reluctor). The unit essentially performs the same function as the contact breaker points in a conventional system.

When the ignition switch is on, the ignition primary circuit is energized. As the distributor shaft rotates, the reluctor, which is a four-spoked disc fitted to the distributor shaft, changes the magnetic field, created by the permanent magnets, in which it rotates. Each time the magnetic field is interrupted, a voltage, sensed by the pick-up coil, is induced. This is sent to the electronic switching unit, which on receipt of the signal pulse, switches off the ignition coil primary current. The magnetic field in the coil collapses, and a high voltage is induced in the coil secondary windings which is conducted to the spark plug via the rotor arm, distributor cap and HT leads. A timing circuit in the electronic switching unit turns on the coil current again after the magnetic field has collapsed, and the process continues for each power stroke of the engine.

The distributor is fitted with centrifugal and vacuum advance mechanisms, to control the ignition timing according to engine speed and load respectively.

On models with carburettor engines, additional ignition advance, controlled by a check valve and thermovalve, is used to improve driving characteristics during the warm-up period. When the engine is cold, the thermovalve is closed and vacuum from the carburettor acts on the distributor vacuum unit via the check valve. The check valve maintains the vacuum and the ignition timing is advanced by a further 8° to 12° in addition to normal centrifugal advance. When the engine coolant reaches a pre-determined temperature, the thermovalve opens and the vacuum is exhausted to the carburettor. The vacuum unit now provides ignition advance conventionally according to throttle position and engine load.

A similar system is used on fuel injected engines, except that the vacuum is supplied via the inlet manifold and exhausted to the throttle valve housing.

2 Maintenance and inspection

1 At the intervals specified in Routine Maintenance at the beginning of this manual, check the condition and security of all leads and wiring associated with the ignition system. Make sure that no chafing is occurring on any of the wires, and that all connections are secure, clean and free of corrosion. Pay particular attention to the HT leads, which should be carefully inspected for any sign of corrosion on their end fittings which if evident, should be carefully cleaned away.

2 Renew the spark plugs as described in Section 9. If the spark plugs have been renewed within the service interval, clean them and reset the electrode gap also as described in Section 9.

3 Using the procedures given in Section 6, check and if necessary adjust the ignition timing.

4 Although not a specified service requirement, it is advisable periodically to remove the distributor cap and clean it inside and out with a dry lint-free rag. Examine the HT lead segments inside the cap. If the segments appear badly burnt or pitted, the cap should be renewed. Also check that the carbon brush in the centre of the cap is free to move and stands proud of its holder (photo).

2.4 Check the condition of the carbon brush and segments inside the distributor cap

4.1 Release the distributor cap clamps by turning through 90°

4.2A Remove the rotor arm ...

4.2B ... and the shield

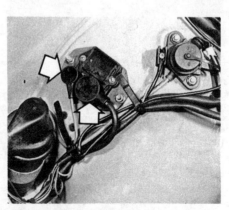
4.3 Wiring plug connections (arrowed) at the electronic switching unit

3 Ignition system – precautions

1 When working on the electronic ignition system, the following precautions must be strictly observed to prevent damage to the electronic components and to avoid the risk of personal injury.

2 The voltages produced are considerably higher than those produced by a conventional system. Extreme care must be taken if work is being done with the ignition switched on, and it is recommended that persons fitted with a cardiac pacemaker should not work on the system.

3 The ignition must be switched off before any ignition wiring, including HT leads or test equipment wiring, is disconnected or connected.

4 If for any reason the engine is to be turned over without starting (ie for checking valve clearances or cylinder compressions) either by hand or at starter motor speed, switch off the ignition and disconnect the LT wiring plug at the electronic switching unit (smaller of the two plugs, and having the green wire).

5 Do not run the engine with any ignition wiring or HT leads disconnected. For this reason, it is not permissible to pull of an HT lead with the engine running, or to check for a spark between the end of a disconnected HT lead and earth with the engine running or cranking on the starter.

6 When using a stroboscopic timing light to check ignition timing, the only timing light type allowable is one which receives its trigger signal from an external clamp around the HT lead. Do not use a timing light that requires the HT lead to be disconnected and plugged into an adaptor. When using an instrument with an external clamp, connect the clamp to the HT lead as near to the distributor as possible.

7 Do not connect any test instruments such as a tachometer or dwell meter, or any other form of instrument or device, between terminals 1 and 15 on the ignition coil. If any test instrument is being used which cannot be plugged directly into the diagnostic socket, consult a Mercedes-Benz dealer as to its suitability and correct method of connection.

4 Distributor – removal and refitting

1 Using a screwdriver, release the two distributor cap clamps by pushing and turning the screw head through 90° (photo).

2 Withdraw the rotor arm and shield (photos) then refit the rotor arm.

3 Disconnect the two wiring plugs at the electronic switching unit on the inner wing panel (photo). Also remove any cable ties retaining the distributor LT lead to the wiring loom.

4 Disconnect the hose from the distributor vacuum unit.

5 Pull off the HT lead and remove No 1 cylinder spark plug (nearest the front of the engine).

6 Using a socket and bar on the crankshaft pulley bolt, turn the engine over in the normal direction of rotation until the following conditions are present:

   (a) Compression can be felt building up in No 1 cylinder if a finger is placed over the spark plug hole as the engine is turned

   (b) The rotor arm is pointing towards the notch in the distributor body rim (photo)

   (c) The pointer on the timing cover is aligned with the TDC (OT) mark on the scale on the crankshaft pulley vibration damper (photo)

The engine is now positioned with No 1 piston at top dead centre (TDC) on compression.

7 As a further aid to refitting, scribe a line across the distributor body base and the timing cover.

8 Using an Allen key, unscrew the bolt securing the base of the distributor and slowly lift the unit out of its location (photo). As the distributor is removed, note that the rotor arm moves clockwise as the driving skew gears disengage. Mark this new position of the rotor arm on the distributor body (photo).

9 Before refitting, make sure that the engine is still positioned with No 1 piston at TDC as described in paragraph 6.

10 Position the rotor arm so that it is pointing towards the mark made on the distributor body after removal, and hold the distributor over the engine with the elongated mounting slot over the mounting bolt hole.

11 Insert the distributor fully, noting that the rotor arm should move

4.6A Rotor arm pointing toward notch (arrowed) in distributor body rim

4.6B Timing cover pointer (arrowed) aligned with TDC mark on vibration damper

4.8A Distributor retaining bolt (arrowed)

anti-clockwise and point towards the notch in the rim, with the line scribed on the distributor body base and timing cover also aligned.
12 Refit the retaining bolt, spark plug and lead, shield, rotor arm and distributor cap, then reconnect the wiring.
13 Adjust the ignition timing as described in Section 6.

4.8B Position of rotor arm relative to distributor body after disengagement of skew gears

5 Distributor vacuum unit – removal and refitting

1 Apart from the distributor cap and rotor arm, the only other distributor component which is available separately is the vacuum unit. The vacuum unit can be renewed without having to remove the distributor from the engine, although the accompanying photo shows the unit removed for clarity.
2 Release the two clamp screws and lift off the distributor cap.
3 Remove the rotor arm and shield.
4 Disconnect the hose from the vacuum unit.
5 Undo the two screws securing the vacuum unit to the distributor body.
6 Disengage the vacuum unit arm from the baseplate, and remove the unit from the distributor (photo).
7 Refitting is the reverse sequence to removal.

6 Ignition timing – adjustment

Note: *Before checking the ignition timing, ensure that the carburettor or fuel injection system adjustments are correct, and that the valve clearances (where applicable) and spark plug gaps are correctly set. A suitable stroboscopic timing light will be required for the following operations (see Section 3). On later models having a single drivebelt for the engine ancillaries, access to the timing marks is extremely limited due to the close proximity of the fan, drivebelt and the various pulleys. Exercise extreme caution when handling the timing light in this area.*

1 Turn the crankshaft using a socket on the pulley bolt until the timing marks on the pulley vibration damper are accessible. Before turning the crankshaft, disconnect the LT wiring plug at the electronic switching unit (the smaller of the two plugs, having the green wire – photo 4.3).
2 Refer to the Specifications for the ignition timing setting at idling speed, then using a dab of quick-drying white paint, highlight this value on the vibration damper scale (photo). Similarly highlight the timing cover pointer above the vibration damper.
3 Reconnect the LT wiring plug at the electronic switching unit and disconnect the vacuum hose at the distributor vacuum unit.
4 Start the engine and point the timing light at the scale on the vibration damper. With the engine idling, the highlighted mark and pointer will appear stationary and, if the timing is correct, will be in alignment.
5 If adjustment is necessary, slacken the distributor retaining bolt and move the distributor body as necessary until the mark and pointer align. Tighten the retaining bolt and re-check the setting.
6 If required, the operation of the distributor centrifugal and vacuum advance mechanisms can be checked as follows.
7 Refer to the Specifications for the centrifugal advance check figure and the corresponding engine speed.
8 Have an assistant run the engine at the specified speed with reference to the tachometer in the car.
9 Point the timing light at the vibration damper scale again, and this time the specified advance check figure on the damper scale should be aligned with the pointer. If this is not the case, or if the mark appears to 'jump' erratically, then the mechanism is worn or otherwise faulty and a new distributor will be required.
10 Similarly, the vacuum advance mechanism can be checked by running the engine at the specified speed and reconnecting the vacuum hose. As this is done, the specified vacuum advance check figure on the damper scale should align with the pointer. If this is not the case the vacuum unit is faulty and should be renewed.
11 On completion of the checks, switch off the engine and disconnect the timing light.

5.6 Removing the distributor vacuum unit

6.2 Timing scale on the vibration damper (arrowed)

7 Ignition system – testing

1   Should a fault develop on the ignition system, the following test procedure can be used to isolate the fault and the component concerned. To carry out these tests a good quality voltmeter, ohmmeter and dwell meter will be needed.

2   First check that the battery terminals are clean and secure, and that the battery is fully charged and supplying the correct system voltage (see Chapter 12).

3   Unscrew the cap on the diagnosis socket (photo) and connect the voltmeter between terminal 5 of the socket and earth. Switch on the ignition and check that battery voltage is present, then switch off the ignition. If the reading is less than battery voltage, there is a wiring fault or a break in the supply voltage via the ignition switch.

4   Connect the voltmeter between terminals 4 and 5 of the diagnosis socket (Fig. 4.2). With the ignition switched on, there should be no reading on the voltmeter. Switch off the ignition. If a reading of 0.1 volts or greater was indicated, the electronic switching unit is faulty and must be renewed. This may also have caused excessive heat

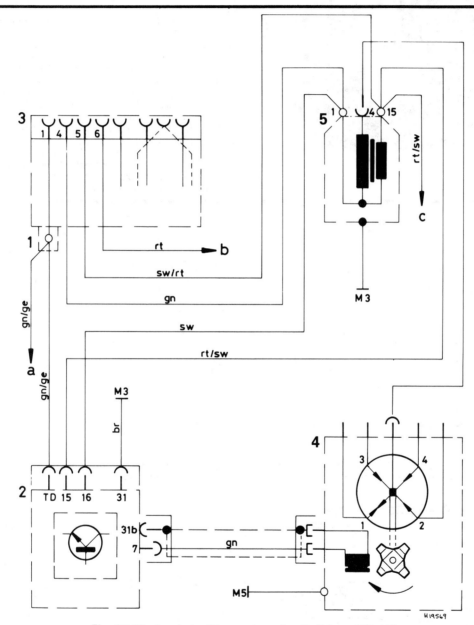

Fig. 4.1 Electronic ignition system circuit diagram (Sec 7)

1   Diagnosis socket terminal TD
2   Electronic switching unit
3   Diagnosis socket
4   Distributor
5   Ignition coil
a   To idle speed shut-off valve relay/tachometer
b   Central electric system coupler S jack 11
c   Central electric system coupler S jack 4
d   Ignition coil earth connection
e   Engine earth connection

Colour code
br = brown
ge = yellow
gn = green
rt = red
sw = black

7.3 Diagnosis socket location on inner wing panel

build-up, and internal damage to the ignition coil and this component should also be checked as described in Section 8.

5 Connect a dwell meter to the diagnosis socket terminals in accordance with the maker's instructions, or to terminal TD, which is the external screw terminal on the side of the diagnosis socket.

6 With the engine cranking, check that the dwell angle falls within the range given in the Specifications. If the dwell angle is greater than the value specified, renew the electronic switching unit. If the dwell angle is correct, or if there was no reading on the dwell meter, proceed to the next test, but first switch off the ignition and disconnect the meter.

7 Disconnect the LT wiring plug at the electronic switching unit (the smaller of the two plugs, and having the green wire). Connect the ohmmeter between the centre terminal (7) and the outer screening (3) (Fig. 4.3). The resistance should be between 500 and 700 ohms. If this value is not obtained, disconnect the wiring plug on the side of the distributor and connect the ohmmeter between the two terminals (Fig. 4.4). This resistance should be between 500 and 700 ohms also. If not, renew the distributor. If the values obtained are correct, refit the wiring plug to the distributor and proceed to the next test.

8 With the LT wiring plug at the electronic switching unit still disconnected, connect the ohmmeter betweeen terminal 3 and earth, then between terminal 7 and earth (Fig. 4.5). The resistance in each case should be 200 k ohms or greater. If these values are not obtained, disconnect the wiring plug at the distributor once more and connect the ohmmeter between one of the terminals and earth. If the resistance

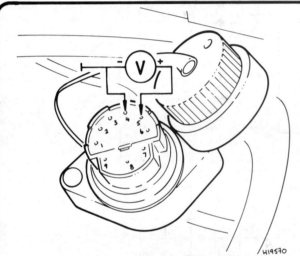

Fig. 4.2 Checking the voltage between terminals 4 and 5 of the diagnosis socket (Sec 7)

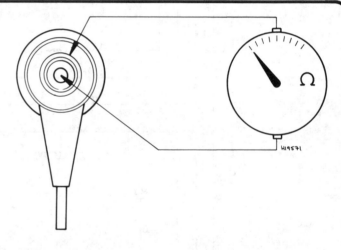

Fig. 4.3 Checking resistance at the LT wiring plug of the electronic switch unit (Sec 7)

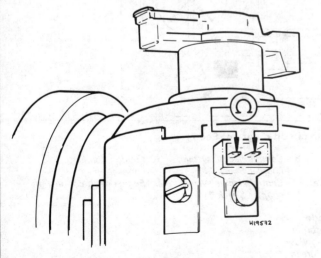

Fig. 4.4 Checking resistance at the distributor terminals (Sec 7)

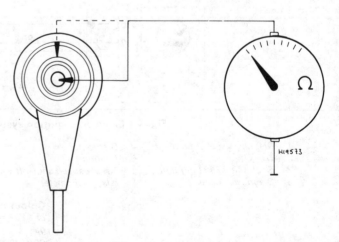

Fig. 4.5 Checking resistance between the LT wiring plug terminals and earth (Sec 7)

is now 200 k ohms or more, renew the green lead between the distributor and switching unit. If the resistance is still not as specified, renew the distributor. If the values obtained initially were correct, the system is in order and the wiring can be reconnected and the test instruments removed.

8 Ignition coil – testing, removal and refitting

1   The ignition coil is mounted on the inner wing panel on the left-hand side of the engine compartment.
2   Should the coil be suspect, the following checks can be made.
3   Remove the protective plastic cover over the coil terminals (photo), and observe the small round plug located on the coil face behind the centre HT terminal (Fig. 4.6). If there has been excessive heat build-up in the coil caused by a fault in the ignition system circuitry, any of the components, or the coil itself, this plug will be released. In this case the coil must be renewed, but before doing this it is necessary to determine the nature of the fault and effect a cure, otherwise the new coil will be similarly damaged.
4   To check the coil primary resistance, connect an ohmmeter between the two LT terminals (1 and 15). The resistance should be as given in the Specifications.
5   To check the secondary resistance, connect the ohmmeter between terminal 1 and the centre HT terminal (4). Again the resistance should be as specified.
6   If the correct resistance values are not obtained, the coil must be renewed. Only an identical Mercedes-Benz ignition coil may be fitted. If any other type is used, irreparable damage may be caused to the ignition system.
7   To remove the coil disconnect the HT lead from the centre terminal (photo) and unscrew the LT terminal nuts. Disconnect the LT leads from the terminal studs after identifying their colour and location for refitting.
8   Undo the mounting bracket bolts and remove the coil from the car.
9   Refitting is the reverse sequence to removal.

9 Spark plugs and HT leads – general

1   The correct functioning of the spark plugs is vital for the proper running and efficiency of the engine. The spark plugs should be renewed at the intervals given in Routine Maintenance at the beginning of this manual. If misfiring, hesitation or poor starting is experienced within the service period, the spark plugs should be removed, cleaned and re-gapped.
2   To remove the plugs, first pull off the HT leads by gripping the insulator portion, not the lead itself. The insulator is a tight fit over the plug, and a sharp pull is required. Using a spark plug spanner or suitable deep socket and extension bar, unscrew the plugs and remove them from their recesses in the cylinder head (photos).
3   Examination of the spark plugs will give a good indication of the condition of the engine.
4   If the insulator nose of the spark plug is clean and white, with no deposits, this is indicative of a weak mixture, or too hot a plug (a hot plug transfers heat away from the electrode slowly – a cold plug transfers heat away quickly). The plugs fitted as standard are detailed in the Specifications at the beginning of this Chapter.
5   If the top and insulator nose is covered with hard black-looking deposits, then this is indicative that the mixture is too rich. Should the plug be black and oily, then it is likely that the engine is fairly worn, as well as the mixture being too rich.
6   If the insulator nose is covered with light tan to greyish brown deposits, then the mixture is correct, and it is likely that the engine is in good condition.
7   If there are any traces of long brown tapering stains on the outside of the white portion of the plug, then the plug will have to be renewed, as this shows that there is a faulty joint between the plug body and the insulator and compression is being allowed to leak away.
8   Plugs should preferably be cleaned by a sand-blasting machine, which will free them from carbon better than cleaning by hand. The machine will also test the condition of the plugs under compression. Any plug that fails to spark at the recommended pressure should be renewed.

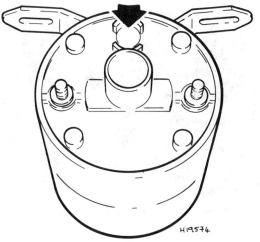

Fig. 4.6 Ignition coil over-pressure safety plug (arrowed) (Sec 8)

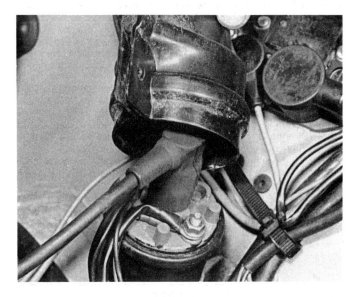

8.3 Remove the cover over the ignition coil terminals

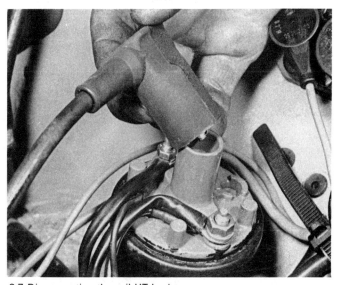

8.7 Disconnecting the coil HT lead

9.2A Pull the HT lead off the spark plug ...

9.2B ... undo the plug using a deep socket and extension bar ...

9.2C ... then remove the plug from its recess in the cylinder head

9 The spark plug gap is of considerable importance, because if it is either too large or too small the size of the spark and its efficiency will be seriously impaired. The spark plug gap should be set to the figures given in the Specifications.
10 To set it, measure the gap with a feeler gauge and then bend open, or close, the outer plug electrode until the correct gap is achieved. The centre electrode should never be bent as this may crack the insulation and cause plug failure, if nothing worse.
11 To refit the plugs, ensure that the thread is clean and dry and then screw each plug in by hand. Tighten the plugs to the specified torque. If a torque wrench is not available tighten them hand tight onto their seating and then tighten further by approximately 1/8 of a turn.
12 When refitting the HT leads, make sure that they are pushed fully home over the spark plug and into the cylinder head recess.
13 The plug leads themselves require no routine maintenance other than being kept clean and wiped over regularly. Should it be necessary to renew any of the leads, it is recommended that they be changed as a complete set. To do this, carefully prise off the plastic covers that retain them within the rocker cover. Disconnect each lead in turn from the spark plug and distributor cap, then fit a new lead of the same length. With all the new leads in place, refit the covers ensuring that each lead locates in its correct groove, corresponding to the cylinder numbering stamped on the plastic covers.

10 Fault diagnosis – ignition system

1 There are two distinct symptoms of ignition faults. Either the engine will not start or fire, or it starts with difficulty and does not run normally.
2 If the starter motor spins the engine satisfactorily, there is adequate fuel supply and yet the engine will not start, the fault is likely to be in the LT or primary side.
3 If the engine starts but does not run satisfactorily, it is more likely to be an HT or secondary circuit fault.

Engine fails to start
4 If the starter motor spins the engine satisfactorily, but the engine does not start, first check that the fuel supply to the engine is in order, with reference to Chapter 3.
5 Check for obvious signs of broken or disconnected wires or wiring plugs, particularly those to the coil, distributor and electronic switching unit, and for damp distributor cap and HT leads.
6 If all the above is in order follow the test procedure described in Section 7.

Engine starts but misfires
7 Bad starting and intermittent misfiring can be caused by an LT fault, such as an intermittent connection of either the distributor, coil or electronic switching unit wiring connections or plugs.
8 If these are satisfactory, look for signs of tracking or burning inside the distributor cap, then check the cap carbon brush, rotor arm, HT leads, spark plug caps and plug insulators.
9 If the engine misfires regularly, it indicates that the fault is in one particular cylinder. This can often be confirmed by removing the spark plugs and checking to see if any are badly sooted or even wet, indicating that that particular plug is not firing. If this is the case, clean and test, or renew, the spark plug, and run the engine again. If the fault persists, remove the HT lead and substitute it with one known to be satisfactory. If this clears the fault, renew the HT leads as a set. If the fault is not cured, check once again for tracking in the distributor cap. If these tests fail to cure the problem, there may be an internal engine fault on that cylinder, such as low cylinder compression.
10 If the misfire is of a more irregular nature, the test procedures described in Section 7 should be followed.

Warning: *When carrying out fault diagnosis tests or any checks on the ignition system, do not disconnect any wiring or leads (including spark plug HT leads) when the engine is running or the ignition is switched on.*

Chapter 5 Clutch

Contents

Specifications

Type .... Single dry plate, diaphragm spring with hydraulic operation

Driven plate
Friction lining thickness (new) .... 3.6 to 3.8 mm (0.14 to 0.15 in)
Friction lining thickness (minimum) .... 1.6 mm (0.06 in)
Maximum run-out .... 0.5 mm (0.02 in)

Pressure plate
Maximum wear of diaphragm spring fingers .... 0.3 mm (0.01 in)

Hydraulic fluid
Type .... Universal brake and clutch fluid to FMVSS 116 DOT 3 or DOT 4 (Duckhams Universal Brake and Clutch Fluid)

Torque wrench settings

	Nm	lbf ft
Clutch cover to flywheel	25	18
Pedal bracket assembly to bulkhead	20	15

1 General description

All manual transmission models are equipped with a single dry plate diaphragm spring clutch. The unit consists of a steel cover which is bolted to the flywheel and contains the pressure plate and diaphragm spring.

The clutch driven plate is free to slide along the splined gearbox input shaft, and is held in position between the flywheel and the pressure plate by the pressure of the diaphragm spring. Friction lining material is riveted to the driven plate, which has a spring-cushioned hub to absorb transmission shocks and help ensure a smooth take-up of the drive.

The clutch is operated hydraulically by a master and slave cylinder. The master cylinder is located inside the car, and is attached to the clutch pedal mounting bracket assembly. The slave cylinder is bolted to the gearbox bellhousing, and actuates the clutch by means of a pushrod, release fork and release bearing. Hydraulic fluid for the system is provided by a combined brake and clutch hydraulic fluid reservoir, located on the brake master cylinder.

The clutch is self-adjusting for wear of the driven plate linings, and apart from periodically checking the fluid level in the master cylinder, the system is entirely maintenance-free.

2 Clutch master cylinder – removal and refitting

The clutch master cylinder is located inside the car, attached to the clutch and brake pedal mounting bracket. Hydraulic fluid for the unit is supplied by a flexible rubber hose from the brake master cylinder reservoir in the engine compartment.

1 Disconnect the battery negative terminal.

2 Remove the cover below the steering column to gain access to the master cylinder and pedal assembly.

3 Remove the floor carpet and cover the floor beneath the pedals to protect against hydraulic fluid spillage.

4 To reduce hydraulic fluid loss, draw off a quantity of fluid from the appropriate chamber of the brake master cylinder reservoir, using a clean syringe, until the fluid level is below that of the supply hose outlet.

5 Disconnect the brake pedal return spring at the brake pedal end.

6 Disconnect the wiring plug from the brake light switch on the pedal bracket.

7 Extract the retaining wire clip and withdraw the brake servo pushrod clevis pin (photo).

8 Unscrew the hydraulic pipe union on the end of the clutch master cylinder, and carefully withdraw the pipe. Plug the pipe and master

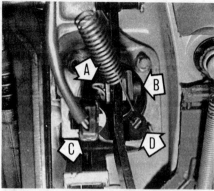

2.7 Brake servo pushrod retaining wire clip (A), clevis pin (B), brake light switch wiring plug (C) and pedal return spring attachment (D)

2.9 Pedal bracket upper retaining bolt (arrowed)

2.10 Pedal bracket and servo retaining nuts (arrowed)

2.14 Extract the pushrod-to-pedal retaining circlip

2.15 Undo the master cylinder retaining nuts

2.16 Fit the pushrod eye with the flanged side (arrowed) towards the pedal

cylinder orifice to prevent dirt ingress.

9 Undo the upper bolt securing the pedal bracket assembly to the bulkhead (photo).

10 Undo the four nuts securing the pedal bracket assembly and brake servo to the bulkhead (photo).

11 Disconnect the master cylinder fluid supply hose from the side of the brake master cylinder reservoir in the engine compartment. Push the hose a little way through the bulkhead, but not all the way.

12 Withdraw the pedal bracket assembly from the servo unit studs, and as soon as sufficient clearance exists, disconnect the fluid supply hose from the clutch master cylinder by pulling out the elbow connector.

13 Remove the pedal bracket assembly from the car.

14 With the assembly removed, extract the retaining clip securing the master cylinder pushrod to the clutch pedal (photo).

15 Undo the cylinder retaining nuts and remove the unit from the pedal bracket and pedal (photo).

16 Refitting is the reverse sequence to removal, but ensure that the master cylinder pushrod eye is fitted with the flanged side towards the pedal (photo). Bleed the clutch hydraulic system on completion, as described in Section 9.

3 Clutch master cylinder – overhaul

1 Remove the master cylinder from the car as described in Section 2.

2 Ease the dust cover on the pushrod away from the cylinder body to provide access to the circlip (photos).

3 Using circlip pliers, extract the circlip, then remove the retaining washer (photos).

4 Withdraw the pushrod and piston assembly from the cylinder bore, followed by the piston spring (photos).

5 Remove the end cap and check valve from the end of the piston (photo).

6 Wash all the parts in clean hydraulic fluid, then lay them out for inspection (photo).

7 Examine the cylinder bore and piston carefully for signs of scoring or wear ridges. If these are apparent, renew the complete master cylinder. If the condition of the components appears satisfactory, a new set of rubber seals must be obtained. Never re-use the old seals.

8 With the new parts obtained, remove the old seals from the piston, and carefully fit the new ones using the fingers only, and liberal quantities of clean hydraulic fluid. Ensure that the sealing lip edge of each seal is towards the spring end of the piston.

9 Lubricate the cylinder bore and the piston with hydraulic fluid, then insert the spring into the bore.

10 Place the check valve and end cap on the piston, and carefully enter the piston into the cylinder bore. Take care not to damage the seal lips.

11 Fit the retaining washer over the pushrod, followed by the circlip.

12 Push the piston down the bore slightly and engage the circlip in its groove. Ensure that it is fully seated.

13 Slide the dust cover into position and locate its end under the edge of the cylinder.

14 The master cylinder can now be refitted as described in Section 2.

4 Clutch slave cylinder – removal and refitting

1 Jack up the front of the car and support it on stands.

2 Unscrew the rigid pipe-to-flexible hose union at the connection located on the right-hand side of the transmission tunnel (photo). Place a suitable container beneath the bracket to collect the escaping fluid as the union is undone. Plug both the pipe and hose after separation to prevent further loss of fluid and dirt ingress.

3 Undo the two bolts securing the slave cylinder to the bellhousing, and withdraw the cylinder complete with pushrod, shim and flexible hose (photo).

4 To refit the cylinder, place the shim in position with the grooved side towards the bellhousing.

5 Introduce the cylinder and pushrod into the bellhousing, ensuring

3.2A Ease the pushrod dust cover away from the cylinder body (arrowed) ...

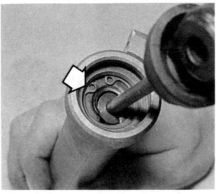

3.2B ... to provide access to the circlip (arrowed)

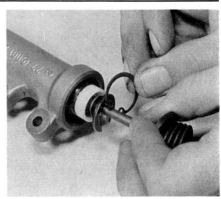

3.3A Remove the pushrod circlip ...

3.3B ... and then the retaining washer

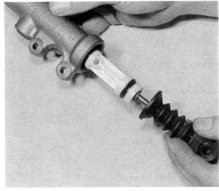

3.4A Withdraw the pushrod and piston assembly ...

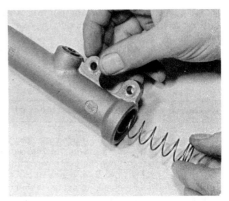

3.4B ... and remove the piston spring

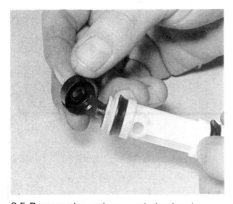

3.5 Remove the end cap and check valve from the piston

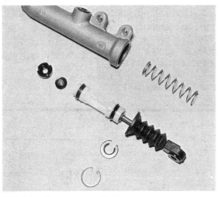

3.6 Clutch master cylinder components

4.2 Unscrew the slave cylinder rigid pipe-to-flexible hose union

that the pushrod engages with the spherical recess in the clutch release fork.
6   Fit and tighten the two retaining bolts, followed by the pipe-to-hose union.
7   Bleed the clutch hydraulic system as described in Section 9.

5   Clutch slave cylinder – overhaul

1   Remove the slave cylinder from the car as described in Section 4.
2   Using a screwdriver, carefully hook out the notched retaining ring and withdraw the pushrod assembly.
3   Tap the cylinder on a block of wood if necessary to release the piston, then remove the piston and spring (photos).

4   Wash all the parts in clean hydraulic fluid, then lay them out for inspection (photo).
5   Examine the cylinder bore and piston carefully for signs of scoring or wear ridges. If these are apparent, renew the complete slave cylinder. If the condition of the components appears satisfactory, a repair kit containing new rubber seals should be obtained. Never re-use the old seals.
6   With the new parts obtained, remove the old seal from the piston, and fit the new one using the fingers only, and liberal quantities of clean hydraulic fluid. Ensure that the sealing lip edge is towards the spring end of the piston.
7   Lubricate the cylinder bore and insert the spring, with the larger coils toward the bottom of the cylinder.
8   Carefully insert the piston, engaging the protruding end into the centre of the spring.

4.3 Removing the slave cylinder from the gearbox bellhousing

5.3A Withdraw the slave cylinder piston ...

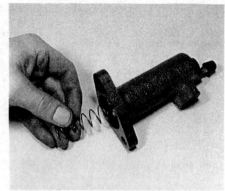

5.3B ... followed by the spring

9 Fit a new dust cover to the pushrod if necessary, and insert the pushrod assembly into the cylinder. The dust cover end of the pushrod faces the piston.
10 Press a new retaining ring into place and push it in firmly to secure the pushrod assembly.
11 The slave cylinder can now be refitted as described in Section 4.

6 Clutch driven plate – assessment of wear

On Mercedes-Benz 190 models covered by this manual, provision is made for assessing the wear of the driven plate friction linings without having to remove the gearbox or clutch assembly from the car. The check is carried out from below at the clutch slave cylinder, and requires the use of a checking gauge, which can easily be made from a thin strip of scrap metal or tin plate to the dimensions shown in Fig. 5.1. Having fabricated the gauge, proceed as follows.
1 Jack up the front of the car and support it on stands.
2 Insert the forked end of the gauge into the machined slot between the slave cylinder flange and the bellhousing.
3 With reference to Figs. 5.2 and 5.3, push the gauge in until the forked end contacts the slave cylinder pushrod. If the two notches on the checking gauge are not visible, the driven plate linings are in a satisfactory condition. If the two notches *are* visible, the driven plate linings have reached their wear limit, and the clutch assembly must be renewed (see Section 7).
4 After carrying out the check, remove the gauge and lower the car to the ground.

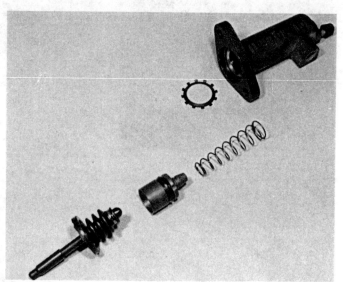

5.4 Clutch slave cylinder components

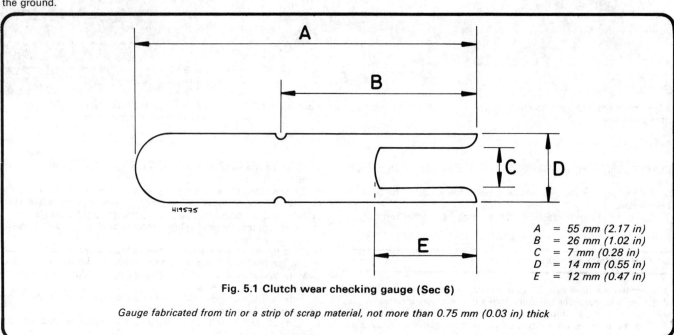

H19575

A = 55 mm (2.17 in)
B = 26 mm (1.02 in)
C = 7 mm (0.28 in)
D = 14 mm (0.55 in)
E = 12 mm (0.47 in)

Fig. 5.1 Clutch wear checking gauge (Sec 6)

Gauge fabricated from tin or a strip of scrap material, not more than 0.75 mm (0.03 in) thick

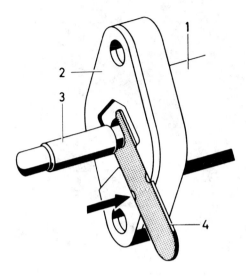

Fig. 5.2 Checking clutch wear – driven plate linings in satisfactory condition (Sec 6)

1   Slave cylinder   3   Pushrod
2   Slave cylinder shim   4   Checking gauge
Arrow indicates notches on gauge, not visible

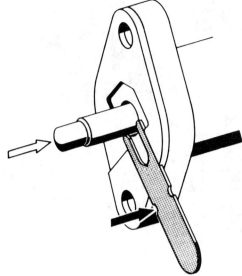

Fig. 5.3 Checking clutch wear – driven plate linings worn (Sec 6)

Light arrow – Pushrod movement as wear takes place
Dark arrow – Notches on gauge visible

7 Clutch assembly – removal, inspection and refitting

1   Remove the gearbox as described in Chapter 6.
2   In a diagonal sequence, half a turn at a time, slacken the bolts securing the clutch cover assembly to the flywheel.
3   When all the bolts are slack, remove them, then ease the cover assembly off the locating dowels. Be prepared to catch the driven plate, which will drop out as the cover assembly is removed.
4   With the clutch assembly removed, clean the parts with a damp cloth, ensuring that the dust is not inhaled. Because the dust produced by the wearing of the friction linings may contain asbestos, which is dangerous to health, parts should not be blown clean or brushed to remove dust.
5   Check the clutch driven plate linings for signs of oil contamination, cracks and insecure retaining rivets. Check that the linings have not worn down to, or below the minimum thickness as given in the Specifications. Also check that the torsion springs are not broken or loose, and that the splines do not exhibit wear ridges.
6   Check the fit of the driven plate hub on the gearbox input shaft splines, ensuring that the hub slides smoothly along the shaft with no sign of binding, and with minimal radial clearance between the input shaft and driven plate hub.
7   If there is reason to suspect that the driven plate hub is not running true, it should be checked by mounting the hub between centres and checking it with a dial gauge. Unless you have the proper equipment to do this, have the work carried out by a suitably-equipped garage.
8   Check the machined faces of the flywheel and pressure plate. If either is grooved or heavily scored, renewal is necessary. The clutch cover assembly must also be renewed if the pressure plate is warped, if any cracks are apparent, or if the diaphragm spring is damaged, its pressure suspect, or if a wear groove greater than 0.3 mm (0.01 in) is evident on the spring fingers.
9   Do not re-use any part which is suspect. Having gone to the trouble of dismantling the clutch, it is well worth ensuring that when reassembled, it will operate satisfactorily for a long time. Should any one of the components require renewal, it is advisable to renew all the parts together at the same time, ie cover assembly, driven plate, and release bearing (see Section 8).
10 Ensure that all the parts are clean, free of oil and grease, and are in a satisfactory condition before reassembling. If the cover assembly has been renewed, wipe off the protective grease coating on the pressure plate with methylated spirit before fitting.
11 To refit the clutch assembly, place the driven plate in position with

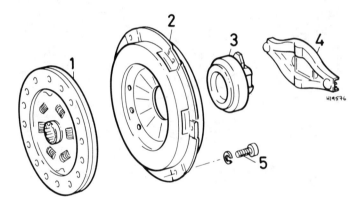

Fig. 5.4 Clutch assembly and release bearing components (Sec 7)

1   Driven plate   4   Release fork
2   Cover assembly   5   Cover bolt
3   Release bearing

the raised portion of the spring hub facing away from the flywheel (photo).
12 Hold the plate in place and refit the cover assembly loosely on the dowels. Refit the retaining bolts and tighten them finger-tight so that the driven plate is gripped, but can still be moved (photos).
13 The driven plate must now be centralised so that when the engine and transmission are mated, the input shaft splines will pass through the splines in the driven plate hub and engage with the spigot bearing in the end of the crankshaft.
14 Centralisation of the driven plate can be carried out in one of three ways; either by obtaining the manufacturer's centering tool, by obtaining a universal clutch aligning tool, which can be purchased from motor factors or hired from various tool hire companies (photo), or by aligning the driven plate visually as described below.
15 Insert a round bar through the centre of the driven plate hub so that the bar rests in the spigot bearing in the centre of the crankshaft. Moving the bar sideways or up and down will move the driven plate in whichever direction is necessary to achieve centralisation. With the bar removed, view the driven plate hub in relation to the hole in the end of the crankshaft and the circle created by the ends of the diaphragm

7.11 Fit the driven plate with the raised portion of the spring hub away from the flywheel

7.12A Refit the cover assembly ...

7.12B ... and secure with the retaining bolts finger-tight initially

7.14 Using a clutch aligning tool to centralise the driven plate

spring fingers. When the hub appears exactly in the centre, all is correct.
16 Tighten the cover retaining bolts gradually, and in a diagonal sequence, to the specified torque wrench setting.
17 Refit the gearbox as described in Chapter 6.

8 Clutch release bearing – removal, inspection and refitting

1   Remove the gearbox as described in Chapter 6.
2   Rotate the release bearing to disengage it from the release fork, and slide the bearing off the front cover sleeve over the input shaft (photo).
3   Move the end of the release fork nearest to the clutch slave cylinder away from the slave cylinder pushrod, then slide the fork sideways to disengage it from the pivot ball pin (photo). Remove the fork from the bellhousing.
4   Check the release bearing for smoothness of operation when spun and renew it if there is any harshness or roughness. Also check that the bearing is free to slide on the input shaft guide sleeve, but without excessive radial clearance.
5   Before refitting, carefully lubricate the guide sleeve, pivot ball pin (photo), slave cylinder pushrod, and all the points on the release fork

8.2 Remove the clutch release bearing ...

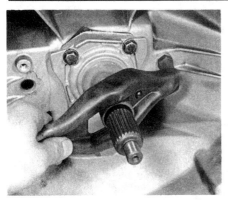

8.3 ... followed by the release fork

8.5 Lubricate the guide sleeve and pivot ball pin (arrowed) prior to refitting

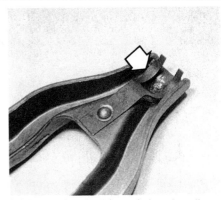

8.6 Ensure that the release fork spring clip (arrowed) locates around the rear of the pivot ball pin

9.6 Bleed tube (arrowed) connected to the brake caliper bleed screw

9.7 Connect the other end of the tube (arrowed) to the slave cylinder bleed screw

which contact the release bearing, with molybdenum disulphide grease.
6   Refit the release fork by engaging its end with the pivot ball pin so that the spring clip locates around the rear of the pin (photo). Move the other end of the fork towards the gearbox so that the slave cylinder pushrod rests in the ball shaped cut-out in the fork.
7   Slide the release bearing onto the guide sleeve and rotate the bearing so that it engages with the lateral-milled cut-outs in the fork.
8   Refit the gearbox as described in Chapter 6.

9   Clutch hydraulic system – bleeding

1   If any part of the hydraulic system is dismantled, or if air has accidentally entered the system, the system will have to be bled. The presence of air is characterised by the pedal having a 'spongy' feel (which lessens if the pedal is pumped a few times) and it results in difficulty in changing gear.
2   The design of the clutch hydraulic system does not allow bleeding to be carried out using the conventional method of pumping the clutch pedal. Instead, bleeding is carried out by utilising the hydraulic pressure of the vehicle braking system to force the air out of the clutch hydraulic system.
3   To bleed the system, first jack up the front of the car, support it on stands, and remove the right-hand front roadwheel.
4   Check the fluid level in the combined brake and clutch fluid reservoir on top of the brake master cylinder, and top up to the maximum level if necessary using the specified type of brake and clutch hydraulic fluid. Observe the fluid level during the bleeding operation and keep the reservoir topped up.
5   Obtain a length of rubber or plastic tubing which is long enough to reach from the right-hand front brake caliper to the clutch slave cylinder on the side of the transmission, and which is a snug fit on the brake caliper and slave cylinder bleed screws. The help of an assistant will also be required for the following operations.

6   Connect one end of the tube to the brake caliper bleed screw, and open the bleed screw approximately half a turn (photo). Have your assistant slowly depress the brake pedal until the tube is full of fluid free from air bubbles. Close the bleed screw then have your assistant release the brake pedal.
7   Connect the free end of the tube to the slave cylinder bleed screw, then open both bleed screws approximately half a turn (photo).
8   Have your assistant depress the brake pedal fully, close the brake caliper bleed screw whilst the pedal is depressed, then allow the pedal to be released. Open the bleed screw again and repeat the procedure until fluid free from air bubbles is being returned to the reservoir. Make sure that the brake caliper bleed screw is closed each time before the pedal is released, and keep the fluid level in the reservoir topped up as necessary during the bleeding operation.
9   On completion, close both bleed screws and check the operation of the clutch pedal. If it still has a 'spongy' feel, further bleeding is required. When the actuation of the pedal produces a firm, positive feel, all is satisfactory. Finally remove the tube, refit the roadwheel and lower the car to the ground.

10   Clutch and brake pedals – removal and refitting

1   Remove the pedal bracket assembly from the car as described in Section 2, paragraphs 1 to 14 inclusive.
2   With the assembly on the bench, remove the brake light switch by undoing the outer locknut or, on later models, by pushing the switch down and turning it through 90° (photo).
3   Move the clutch pedal upwards until the end of the off-centre spring can be released from the pedal bracket (photo). Now remove the off-centre spring leg from the stud on the clutch pedal.
4   Using circlip pliers, extract the circlip securing the clutch pedal to the pivot shaft (photo). Withdraw the washer and slide the pedal off the shaft.

5   Repeat paragraph 4 for the brake pedal if this is to be removed also.
6   Check the condition of the pedal bush, and renew it if worn or damaged. The bush is removed by knocking it out with a suitable tube or drift. Tap in the new bush so that its flange is towards the pedal bracket.

7   Lubricate the pedal shaft with molybdenum disulphide grease and refit the pedal(s) using the reverse sequence to removal. Refit the pedal bracket assembly to the car as described in Section 2.

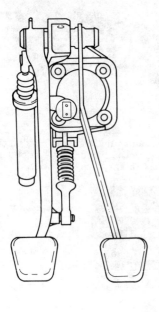
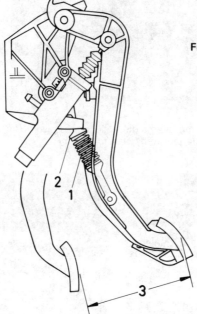

Fig. 5.5 Clutch and brake pedal bracket assembly (Sec 10)

1   Off-centre spring
2   Spring end
3   Pedal travel

10.2 Removing the later type brake light switch

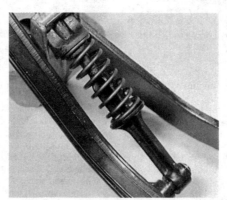

10.3 Move the clutch pedal upwards to release the off-centre spring end

10.4 Clutch and brake pedal retaining circlip (arrowed)

11 Fault diagnosis – clutch

Symptom	Reason(s)
Judder when taking up drive	Oil or grease contamination of friction linings Worn friction linings Excessive driven plate run-out Driven plate sticking on input shaft splines Faulty pressure plate or diaphragm spring
Clutch slip	Friction linings worn or contaminated Weak or broken diaphragm spring
Clutch drag (failure to disengage)	Driven plate sticking on input shaft splines Driven plate sticking to flywheel Input shaft seized in crankshaft spigot bearing Air in clutch hydraulic system
Noise evident when depressing clutch pedal	Dry or worn release bearing Dry clutch pedal shaft bushes

Chapter 6
Manual gearbox and automatic transmission

Contents

Specifications

Part A: Manual gearbox
Type .... Five forward speeds and reverse with synchromesh on all forward speeds

Identification code 717.411

Ratios
1st .... 3.91 : 1
2nd .... 2.17 : 1
3rd .... 1.37 : 1
4th .... 1.00 : 1
5th .... 0.77 : 1
Reverse .... 4.27 : 1

Synchromesh ring wear limit .... 1.0 mm (0.039 in)

Lubrication
Gearbox lubricant .... Mercedes-Benz approved ATF (Duckhams Fleetmatic A)
Lubricant capacity .... 1.5 litres (2.6 Imp pts)

Torque wrench settings

	Nm	lbf ft
Gearbox crossmember retaining bolts	45	33
Propeller shaft clamping nut	30 to 40	22 to 30
Centre support bearing to underbody	25	18
Propeller shaft flexible rubber coupling bolts	45	33
Gearbox front cover bolts	20	15
Gearbox flange collar nut	160	118
Gearbox rear cover/intermediate plate retaining bolts:		
Bolts stamped 8.8	20	15
Bolts stamped 10.9	28	21
Pivot pin plate retaining bolts	8	6
Reverse shaft locating bolt	20	15
Locking cage retaining bolts	8	6
Shift lever retaining bolts	25	18
Gearshift locking lever nut	20	15
Reverse lever bearing pin nut	20	15
Oil drain and filler plugs	60	44
Gear lever remote control assembly retaining bolts	6	4

Part B: Automatic transmission
Type .... Four-speed fully automatic with epicyclic gearbox, three element torque converter and standard or economy program selection

Identification codes:
190 models up to October 1984 .... 722.402
190 models from October 1984 onwards 722.411
190 E models 722.400

Ratios

1st	4.25 : 1
2nd	2.40 : 1
3rd	1.48 : 1
4th	1.00 : 1
Reverse	5.14 : 1

Lubrication

Transmission lubricant	Mercedes-Benz approved ATF (Duckhams MB-Matic)
Lubricant capacity:	
Total capacity	6.6 litres (11.6 Imp pts)
Drain and refill	5.5 litres (9.7 Imp pts)

Torque wrench settings

	Nm	lbf ft
Transmission crossmember retaining bolts	45	33
Propeller shaft clamping nut	30 to 40	22 to 30
Centre support bearing to underbody	25	18
Propeller shaft flexible rubber coupling bolts	45	33
Transmission-to-engine retaining bolts:		
M10 bolts	55	41
M12 bolts	65	48
Torque converter-to-drive plate bolts	42	31
Oil pan and torque converter drain plugs	14	10
Oil pan retaining bolts	8	6
Selector lever assembly retaining bolts	6	4

PART A: MANUAL GEARBOX

1 General description

The gearbox fitted to UK models covered by this manual is of Mercedes-Benz manufacture, and has five forward gears and one reverse gear. Synchromesh gear engagement is used on all forward gears, and a standstill synchronizing system is also used on reverse gear for smooth engagement, providing the car is at rest.

The gearbox comprises a main light alloy casing with integral bellhousing, an intermediate plate and a rear cover. Housed within the casing are the input shaft, mainshaft and layshaft assemblies, which carry constant mesh gear clusters, and are supported on plain and tapered roller bearings. Additionally, the front of the input shaft is supported in a needle roller bearing located in the end of the engine crankshaft. The synchromesh gear engagement is by baulk rings, which act under the movement of the synchro unit sliding sleeves. Gear selection is by means of a remote floor-mounted lever connected to the gearbox shift levers by three shift rods.

2 Maintenance and inspection

1 At the intervals given in Routine Maintenance at the beginning of this manual, carry out the following service operations on the gearbox.
2 Carefully inspect the gearbox joint faces and oil seals for signs of damage, deterioration, or oil leakage.
3 Check and if necessary top up the fluid in the gearbox. The filler/level plug is located on the right-hand side of the casing, and if a hexagonal removal key is not available, the plug can be undone using a suitable long nut and spanner (photo). Automatic transmission fluid is used in the gearbox (see Specifications), and the level is correct if the fluid just runs out of the orifice when the plug is removed. Top up if necessary, then refit and tighten the plug securely.
4 At the intervals specified, the fluid should be renewed. Drain the gearbox by removing the plug at the base of the casing (photo). After draining, refit and tighten the plug, then fill the gearbox as previously described.
5 At periodic intervals, a check should be made of the condition and security of the gear linkage shift rods, shift levers and the shift lever bushes.

2.3 Using a long nut and spanners to undo the gearbox filler/level plug

2.4 Gearbox drain plug location (arrowed)

3 Gearbox – removal and refitting

1 Position the car over an inspection pit, or on ramps or axle stands, and apply the handbrake firmly.
2 Disconnect the battery negative terminal.
3 Remove the full-length engine undertray, on cars so equipped, if this is likely to impede access to the gearbox.
4 Undo the nuts, and remove the bolts and washers, securing the exhaust system support bracket to the rear of the gearbox (photos).
5 Undo the U-clamp nuts securing the exhaust to the bracket and remove the bracket (photo).
6 Disconnect the exhaust system rubber ring mountings, lower the system by 150 to 250 mm (6 to 10 in), and support it in this position using wire or rope.
7 Support the gearbox on a suitable jack.
8 Undo the two bolts each side securing the gearbox crossmember to the chassis rails (photo).
9 Undo the nut securing the gearbox rubber mounting to the gearbox and remove the crossmember (photo).
10 Undo the four bolts and remove the exhaust heat shield over the front silencer.
11 Undo the three nuts and bolts securing the propeller shaft front flexible rubber coupling to the gearbox flange. To do this, undo the bolts using a socket and extension bar while holding the nuts from behind with a spanner. **Note:** *Further information on this and the following propeller shaft procedure will be found in Chapter 7, Section 3.*
12 Using a 41 mm open-ended spanner, slacken the propeller shaft clamping nut approximately two turns while using a second spanner to prevent the propeller shaft turning.
13 Slacken the two bolts securing the centre support bearing to the underbody.
14 Slide the propeller shaft front section towards the rear as far as the support bearing and clamping nut will allow. If the flexible coupling is tight on the gearbox flange, insert a bar or suitable screwdriver through

the bolt holes and move it up and down to release the locating sleeves from their recesses in the flange. Tie the propeller shaft up out of the way when it is clear.
15 Undo the speedometer cable clamp bolt on the right-hand side of the gearbox and withdraw the cable (photo).
16 Release the speedometer cable clips from the brackets below and on the left-hand side of the gearbox, and move the cable to one side (photos).
17 Undo the clutch fluid pipe-to-flexible hose union on the right-hand side of the gearbox, and separate the hose from the pipe (photo). Plug or tape over the two unions to minimise fluid loss.
18 Extract the retaining clips and withdraw the shift rods from the three gear lever remote control shift levers (photo).
19 Undo the bolts securing the starter motor to the engine and bellhousing, noting the location of the cable clip bracket behind the lower bolt head. Withdraw the starter and move it aside.
20 Position a second jack and wooden pad beneath and in contact with the engine sump at the rear.
21 Undo all the bolts securing the gearbox bellhousing to the engine, noting the location of the engine earth strap on the left-hand side bolt beneath the starter motor lower bolt.
22 Place a piece of sheet metal or similar protective material over the bulkhead insulation at the rear of the engine, so that the insulation is not damaged by the cylinder head when the engine is lowered.
23 While holding the gearbox in place, slowly lower the two jacks until sufficient clearance exists to allow withdrawal of the gearbox.
24 Pull the gearbox squarely away from the engine after releasing the locating dowels by use of a screwdriver between the bellhousing and engine flanges.
25 As soon as the gearbox is free of the dowels, turn it to the left and continue pulling it squarely to the rear until the input shaft is fully out of the clutch driven plate hub. Now lower the gearbox at the rear and remove it from under the car.
26 Refitting the gearbox is the reverse sequence to removal, bearing in mind the following points:

  (a) *Lubricate the gearbox input shaft splines with molybdenum disulphide grease prior to refitting*

3.4A Exhaust system support bracket bolts – first version (arrowed)

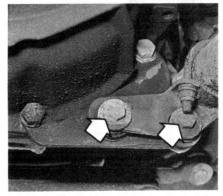
3.4B Exhaust system support bracket bolts – alternative version (arrowed)

3.5 Exhaust U-clamp retaining nuts (arrowed)

3.8 Gearbox crossmember right-hand retaining bolts

3.9 Removing the crossmember complete with rubber mounting

3.15 Removing the speedometer cable

3.16A Release the speedometer cable clips from the brackets below ...

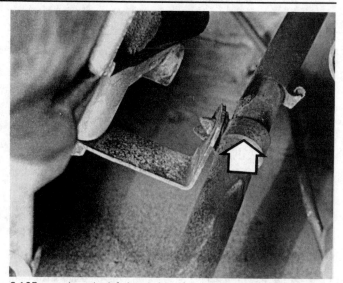

3.16B ... and on the left-hand side of the gearbox (arrowed)

3.17 Unscrew the clutch hydraulic fluid pipe (A) from the flexible hose union (B)

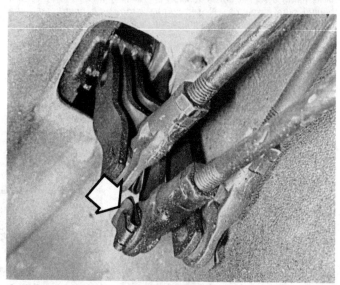

3.18 Extract the retaining clip (arrowed) from each shift rod

(b) *When refitting and when tightening the upper bellhousing bolts, avoid dislodging the brake pipe which runs over the transmission tunnel from its retaining clip. Ensure that there is a clearance between the brake pipe and gearbox after installation*

(c) *When connecting the propeller shaft, tighten the clamping nut after attaching the front flexible coupling and securing the centre support bearing*

(d) *Bleed the clutch hydraulic system as described in Chapter 5*

(e) *Refill or top up the transmission fluid in the gearbox with reference to Section 2*

4   Gearbox overhaul – general notes and precautions

Dismantling the gearbox into its major assemblies is reasonably straightforward, and can be carried out without recourse to the manufacturer's special tools. This will allow an initial assessment of any wear or damage to be carried out, and a decision can then be made as to the best course of action to take. The factors influencing that decision are firstly that gearbox parts are very expensive, and there can often be a problem with availability. Secondly, bear in mind that if further dismantling is to be undertaken, it will be necessary to have access to a press or hydraulic gear puller, together with a set of suitable

mandrels. Also, if any of the tapered roller bearing assemblies, the gearbox casings or the shafts require renewal, then the running clearances and endfloats will have to be adjusted, and this can really only be carried out successfully by a dealer with special tools and a large assortment of selective spacing washers for this purpose. It is worth seeking the advice of a dealer concerning this before proceeding with extensive dismantling of the gearbox. One final note of caution; it is perhaps inadvisable to undertake extensive dismantling or overhaul unless you have some previous gearbox experience, or know somebody who has and is willing to help. Taking all these points into consideration, it may be more economical or practical to consider obtaining an exchange reconditioned gearbox or alternatively carry out the removal, dismantling and reassembly work yourself, but with the help of a dealer to remove and refit the bearings and set up the clearances.

Whichever course of action is taken, read through all the procedures first so that you know what to expect, and if and when a special tool or alternative will be needed. It must be pointed out at this stage that undocumented changes are sometimes made to the design and specification of vehicle systems, particularly in the engine and transmission areas. Therefore some gearbox components may differ slightly from those shown in the photographs and described in the text. This should not present any problems, providing a logical approach is adopted, and if necessary, suitable notes taken as an aid to reassembly.

Before starting any work on the gearbox, drain the transmission fluid from the unit via the drain plug on the bottom of the casing, then clean the exterior using paraffin or a suitable solvent.

Make sure that an uncluttered working area is available with some small trays handy to store the various parts. Keep all related components together and where applicable in their fitted direction. Attach labels to the parts as they are removed if there is any likelihood of confusion on reassembly.

Before reassembly commences, all the components must be spotlessly clean and should be lubricated with the specified grade of automatic transmission fluid as they are fitted.

5 Gearbox – dismantling into major assemblies

1 Remove the gearbox from the car as described in Section 3, then remove the clutch release bearing, release fork and slave cylinder as described in Chapter 5.
2 Using a screwdriver or small punch, knock back the staking securing the gearbox flange collar nut to the mainshaft.
3 Using a socket and bar, unscrew the collar nut, noting that a new nut must be obtained prior to reassembly. To stop the flange turning as the nut is undone, wedge a small socket or similar item between one of the flange arms and a sturdy part of the casing.
4 Withdraw the gearbox flange from the mainshaft, together with any spacing washers that may be fitted.

5 On each side of the gearbox rear cover, undo the retaining bolt and pull out the pivot pin plates that support the 5th gearshift mechanism. Recover the O-rings from the pivot pins.
6 Undo the bolts securing the rear cover and remove the cover and gasket from the gearbox.
7 Withdraw the 5th gear synchro sleeve and shift mechanism as an assembly from the 5th gear synchro hub (photo).
8 Withdraw the speedometer drivegear from the mainshaft.
9 Using circlip pliers, extract the retaining circlip from the end of the layshaft (photo).
10 Withdraw the 5th gear synchro hub, followed by the 5th gear and synchro ring, from the layshaft.
11 Withdraw the 5th gear needle roller bearing and the thrustwasher.
12 Undo and remove the reverse shaft locating bolt from the left-hand side of the gearbox casing (photo).
13 Carefully lift the intermediate plate up and off the casing. Recover the gasket.
14 Undo and remove the two bolts and withdraw the locking cage from the left-hand side of the casing. Recover the gasket (photos).
15 Using an Allen key, unscrew the 1st/2nd gearshift lever socket-headed bolt and remove the shift lever (photo).
16 Undo the retaining bolt and pull out the pivot pin plate that supports the 1st/2nd gearshift mechanism. Recover the gasket behind the plate.
17 Lift the mainshaft and layshaft slightly, tip the layshaft away from the mainshaft and remove the mainshaft assembly from the casing.

5.7 Withdraw the 5th gear synchro sleeve and shift mechanism as an assembly

5.9 Extract the retaining circlip from the layshaft

5.12 Undo the reverse shaft locating bolt (arrowed)

5.14A Undo the two bolts ...

114

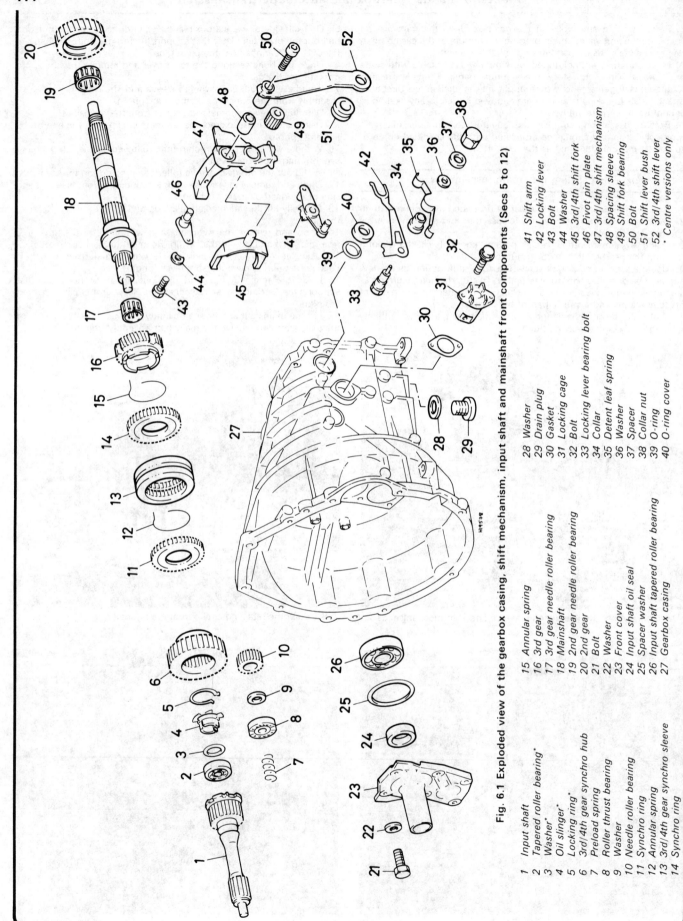

Fig. 6.1 Exploded view of the gearbox casing, shift mechanism, input shaft and mainshaft front components (Secs 5 to 12)

1	Input shaft	15	Annular spring	28	Washer
2	Tapered roller bearing*	16	3rd gear	29	Drain plug
3	Washer*	17	3rd gear needle roller bearing	30	Gasket
4	Oil slinger*	18	Mainshaft	31	Locking cage
5	Locking ring*	19	2nd gear needle roller bearing	32	Bolt
6	3rd/4th gear synchro hub	20	2nd gear	33	Locking lever bearing bolt
7	Preload spring	21	Bolt	34	Collar
8	Roller thrust bearing	22	Washer	35	Detent leaf spring
9	Washer	23	Front cover	36	Washer
10	Needle roller bearing	24	Input shaft oil seal	37	Spacer
11	Synchro ring	25	Spacer washer	38	Collar nut
12	Annular spring	26	Input shaft tapered roller bearing	39	O-ring
13	3rd/4th gear synchro sleeve	27	Gearbox casing	40	O-ring cover
14	Synchro ring				

41	Shift arm
42	Locking lever
43	Bolt
44	Washer
45	3rd/4th shift fork
46	Pivot pin plate
47	3rd/4th shift mechanism
48	Collar
49	Spacing sleeve
50	Shift fork bearing
51	Bolt
52	Shift lever bush
	3rd/4th shift lever

* Centre versions only

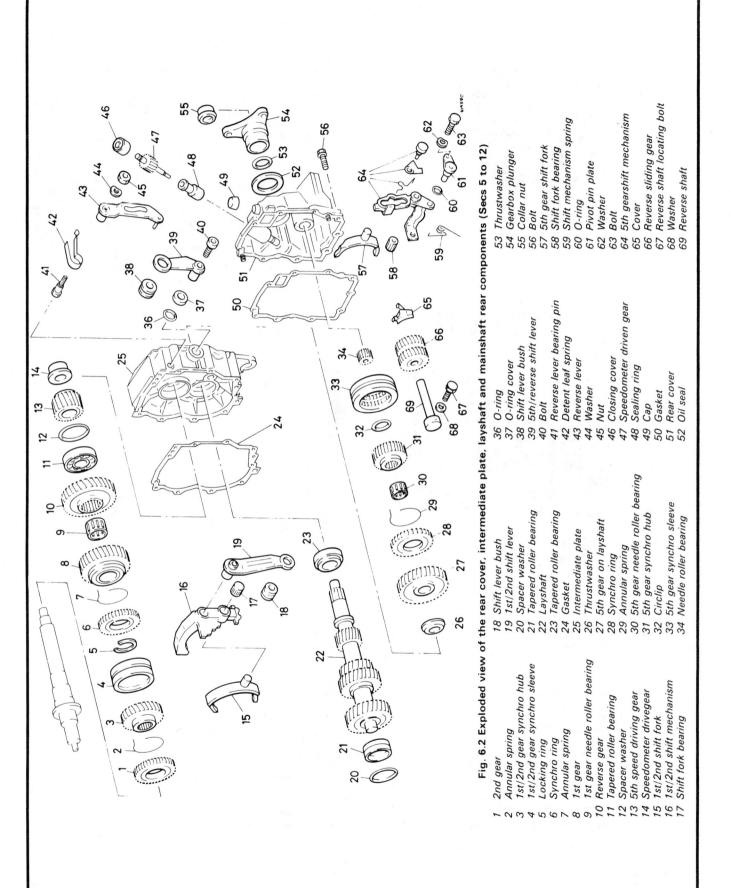

Fig. 6.2 Exploded view of the rear cover, intermediate plate, layshaft and mainshaft rear components (Secs 5 to 12)

1 2nd gear
2 Annular spring
3 1st/2nd gear synchro hub
4 1st/2nd gear synchro sleeve
5 Locking ring
6 Synchro ring
7 Annular spring
8 1st gear
9 1st gear needle roller bearing
10 Reverse gear
11 Tapered roller bearing
12 Spacer washer
13 5th speed driving gear
14 Speedometer drivegear
15 1st/2nd shift fork
16 1st/2nd shift mechanism
17 Shift fork bearing

18 Shift lever bush
19 1st/2nd shift lever
20 Spacer washer
21 Tapered roller bearing
22 Layshaft
23 Tapered roller bearing
24 Gasket
25 Intermediate plate
26 Thrustwasher
27 5th gear on layshaft
28 Synchro ring
29 Annular spring
30 5th gear needle roller bearing
31 5th gear synchro hub
32 Circlip
33 5th gear synchro sleeve
34 Needle roller bearing

36 O-ring
37 O-ring cover
38 Shift lever bush
39 5th/reverse shift lever
40 Bolt
41 Reverse lever bearing pin
42 Detent leaf spring
43 Reverse lever
44 Washer
45 Nut
46 Closing cover
47 Speedometer driven gear
48 Sealing ring
49 Cap
50 Gasket
51 Rear cover
52 Oil seal

53 Thrustwasher
54 Gearbox plunger
55 Collar nut
56 Bolt
57 5th gear shift fork
58 Shift fork bearing
59 Shift mechanism spring
60 O-ring
61 Pivot pin plate
62 Washer
63 Bolt
64 5th gearshift mechanism
65 Cover
66 Reverse sliding gear
67 Reverse shaft locating bolt
68 Washer
69 Reverse shaft

5.14B ... and remove the locking cage

5.15 Removing the 1st/2nd gearshift lever socket-headed bolt

5.18 Removing the 3rd/4th gearshift lever socket-headed bolt

5.19 Removing the 3rd/4th gearshift mechanism pivot pin plate and gasket

18 Unscrew the 3rd/4th gearshift lever socket-headed bolt and remove the shift lever (photo).
19 Undo the retaining bolt and pull out the pivot pin plate that supports the 3rd/4th gearshift mechanism. Recover the gasket behind the plate (photo).
20 Withdraw the 3rd/4th gear synchro sleeve and shift mechanism from the input shaft while lifting the layshaft slightly for clearance.
21 Withdraw the layshaft from the casing.
22 Withdraw the input shaft with 4th gear synchro ring from the casing.
23 Remove the needle roller bearing from the centre of the input shaft and, where fitted, the preload spring, roller thrust bearing and washers.

6 Mainshaft – dismantling and reassembly

1 Clamp the rear of the mainshaft in a vice having soft protected jaws.
2 Extract the retaining circlip from the input shaft end of the mainshaft (photo).
3 Slide off the 3rd/4th gear synchro hub, followed by 3rd gear and the 3rd gear synchro ring.
4 Remove the 3rd gear needle roller bearing.
5 Turn the mainshaft over so that the gears on the rear of the shaft are

uppermost, and support the shaft in the vice.
6 Using a puller with its legs located behind the 1st gear, draw off 1st gear, reverse gear, the mainshaft tapered roller bearing and the 5th speed driving gear together.
7 Remove the 1st gear synchro ring and 1st gear needle roller bearing.
8 Extract the locking ring securing the 1st/2nd gear synchro hub to the mainshaft (photo).
9 Slide off the 1st/2nd synchro sleeve, hub and shift mechanism as an assembly.
10 Remove the 2nd gear synchro ring, followed by 2nd gear and the needle roller bearing from the mainshaft.
11 With the mainshaft now dismantled, carry out a careful inspection of the mainshaft components as described in Section 11, and obtain any new parts as necessary.
12 Begin reassembly by placing the 2nd gear needle roller bearing in position on the mainshaft (photo).
13 Fit 2nd gear over the needle roller bearing, then place the synchro ring on the gear (photos). Ensure that the synchro ring lugs engage with the slots in the gear and the annular spring locates in the gear groove.
14 Place the 1st/2nd synchro sleeve on the mainshaft and over the synchro ring so that the side with the two machined grooves faces away from 2nd gear (photos).

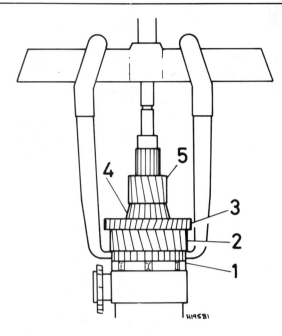

Fig. 6.3 Using a puller to remove the mainshaft gears (Sec 6)

1 Synchro ring	*4 Tapered roller bearing*
2 1st gear	*5 5th speed driving gear*
3 Reverse gear	

15 Slide on the 1st/2nd synchro hub, through the sleeve and with the wider hub flange towards 2nd gear (photo).

16 Secure the synchro hub with the locking ring, ensuring that it is fully located in its groove (photo).

17 Turn the fork of the 1st/2nd shift mechanism through 90° in relation to the mechanism body, and engage the fork with the groove in the 1st/2nd synchro sleeve (photo). When in position, the detent grooves in the mechanism body must be towards 2nd gear (photo).

18 Place the 1st gear needle roller bearing on the mainshaft (photo).

19 Fit 1st gear together with the synchro ring to the mainshaft (photo), ensuring that the synchro ring lugs engage with the slots in the gear, and the annular spring locates in the gear groove.

20 Fit reverse gear to the mainshaft, followed by the tapered roller bearing and the 5th speed driving gear (photos). Note that the wider collar of the 5th speed gear faces the bearing.

21 Using a press or hydraulic puller and suitable mandrels, press the 5th speed gear and tapered roller bearing fully home (photo).

22 At the other end of the mainshaft, place the 3rd gear needle roller bearing in position (photo).

23 Fit the 3rd gear and synchro ring with the synchro ring lugs engaged with the slots in the gear, and the annular spring located in the gear groove (photo).

24 Fit the 3rd/4th synchro hub and secure with the retaining circlip (photos). Ensure that the circlip seats fully into its groove.

7 Input shaft – dismantling and reassembly

1 Essentially, dismantling of the input shaft is carried out as part of the gearbox main dismantling procedure, and only the tapered roller bearing will now be left in place.

2 If it is necessary to remove the bearing, this can only be done using a press or hydraulic puller with suitable mandrels. The new bearing is then fitted in the same way.

3 Further reassembly of the input shaft is covered in later procedures in this Chapter.

6.2 Extract the circlip from the mainshaft

6.8 Extract the 1st/2nd gear synchro hub locking ring

6.12 Begin reassembly by fitting the 2nd gear needle roller bearing

6.13A Fit 2nd gear over the needle roller bearing ...

6.13B ... then place the synchro ring on the gear

6.14A Fit the 1st/2nd gear synchro sleeve ...

6.14B ... so that the side with the machined grooves (arrowed) faces away from 2nd gear

6.15 Fit the 1st/2nd gear synchro hub with the wider flange toward 2nd gear

6.16 Secure the synchro hub with the locking ring

6.17A Fit the 1st/2nd shift mechanism to the sleeve ...

6.17B ... with the detent grooves (arrowed) toward 2nd gear

6.18 Place the 1st gear needle roller bearing on the mainshaft

6.19 Fit 1st gear together with the synchro ring

6.20A Fit reverse gear ...

6.20B ... the tapered roller bearing ...

6.20C ... and the 5th speed driving gear

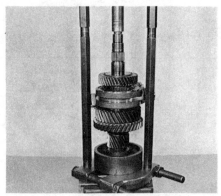

6.21 Using a hydraulic puller arrangement to press home the gear and bearing

6.22 Fit the 3rd gear needle roller bearing to the other end of the mainshaft

6.23 Place the 3rd gear synchro ring over the bearing

6.24A Fit the 3rd/4th gear synchro hub ...

6.24B ... and secure with the circlip

8 Layshaft – dismantling and reassembly

1   Dismantling and reassembly of the layshaft is limited to renewal, if necessary, of the tapered roller bearing at each end (photo).
2   To do this, the bearings must be drawn off using a press or hydraulic puller together with suitable mandrels. New bearings are then pressed on in the same way.

9 Intermediate plate – dismantling and reassembly

1   Using an Allen key, unscrew the socket-headed bolt securing the 5th/reverse shift lever to the shift arm inside the intermediate plate (photo). Withdraw the shift lever and the shift arm.
2   Unscrew the nut and remove the reverse lever bearing pin, together with the detent leaf spring (photo). Remove the reverse lever.
3   Support the intermediate plate, and drive out the reverse shaft together with the reverse sliding gear.
4   Remove the shift lever O-ring cover and the O-ring.
5   If the mainshaft and layshaft tapered roller bearing outer races are to be renewed, remove the outer races by tapping them out to the inside of the intermediate plate using a suitable drift. Recover any spacing washers that may be fitted behind the outer races.
6   With any new parts obtained as necessary, refit the outer races, together with their spacing washers (where fitted) by tapping them carefully and squarely into position.
7   Fit a new O-ring and O-ring cover to the shift lever bore.
8   With the sliding gear in place, attach the reverse shaft to the gearbox casing using the reverse shaft locating bolt. Lay the intermediate plate on the casing in its fitted position so that the reverse shaft enters its intermediate plate bore. Tap the plate down fully, then undo the locating bolt. Remove the intermediate plate complete with reverse shaft and sliding gear. Now finally tap the shaft home until its

end is flush with the intermediate plate face.
9   Engage the reverse lever peg with the reverse sliding gear, then fit the bearing pin and detent leaf spring (photo). Secure the bearing pin with the retaining nut.
10 Locate the shift arm end in the reverse lever elongated slot (photo).
11 Insert the shift lever into its bore and engage the sine-wave-like formed end of the lever with the shift arm. Secure the lever with the socket-headed retaining bolt.

10 Gearbox casing and rear cover – dismantling and reassembly

1   Undo the six bolts and remove the front cover from within the gearbox casing bellhousing (photo). Recover the spacing washers from the bearing seats in the cover (photo).
2   The input shaft oil seal in the front cover should be renewed as a matter of course (photo). To do this prise out the old seal using a screwdriver, and squarely tap in a new seal using a suitable mandrel.
3   Liberally grease the sealing lips of the new seal and also the open area within the seal itself.
4   If this work is being carried out in conjunction with gearbox overhaul, do not refit the front cover at this stage.
5   If the front cover was removed only for renewal of the oil seal, clean the cover and casing mating faces and apply an RTV sealing compound to the cover face.
6   Place the spacing washers in position and fit the cover to the casing. Apply thread sealer to the retaining bolts, then fit and tighten them to the specified torque.
7   Check the condition of the locking lever and detent leaf spring in the gearbox casing, and renew these components if necessary. Also renew the two O-ring seals for the shift levers in the side of the casing (photo).
8   If the input shaft and layshaft tapered roller bearings are to be

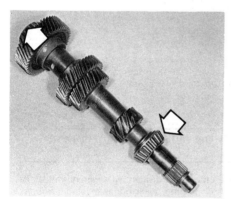

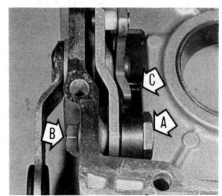

8.1 Tapered roller bearing locations (arrowed) on the layshaft

9.1 Undo the 5th/reverse shift lever retaining bolt (arrowed) on the intermediate plate

9.2 Reverse lever bearing pin (A), retaining nut (B), and detent leaf spring (C)

9.9 Reverse lever peg (arrowed) engaged with reverse sliding gear

9.10 Shift arm end engaged with reverse lever slot (arrowed)

10.1A Remove the front cover from the casing ...

10.1B ... and recover the spacing washers

10.2 Input shaft oil seal location (arrowed) in front cover

10.7 Locking lever assembly (A) and shift lever O-ring seals (B) in the gearbox casing

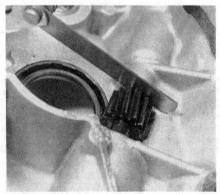

10.11 Using feeler gauges to check the speedometer driven gear clearance

10.12 Mainshaft oil seal (A) and needle roller bearing (B) in the rear cover

renewed, remove the two outer races by tapping them out of the casing using a suitable drift. Fit the two new outer races by carefully and squarely tapping them into place so that they protrude towards the front cover by approximately 5.0 mm (0.2 in).

9 Check the condition of the speedometer driven gear in the rear cover for signs of damage or wear of the teeth.

10 To renew the driven gear, tap out the closing cover using a thin punch from within the rear cover then withdraw the gear.

11 Fit the new gear, and tap in the closing cover until there is a clearance of 5.0 mm (0.2 in) between the gear and the register in the casing (photo).

12 Renew the rear cover mainshaft oil seal as a matter of course (photo) using the same procedure as for the front cover oil seal (paragraphs 2 and 3).

13 Renewal of the needle roller bearing in the rear cover requires the use of a special extractor tool, and if necessary this work should be carried out by a Mercedes-Benz dealer.

11 Gears, synchro units and shift mechanism – inspection and overhaul

1 With the mainshaft and input shaft dismantled, examine the shafts and gears for signs of pitting, scoring, wear ridges or chipped teeth. Check the fit of the gears on the shafts, and ensure that there is no lateral free play.

2 Check the smoothness of the bearings and check for any signs of

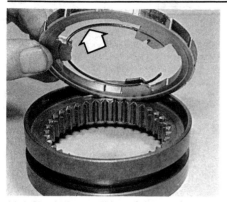

11.4 Check the condition of the synchro ring and annular spring (arrowed)

11.5 Using a depth gauge to check synchro ring wear

12.1 Fit the spacer washers to the front cover ...

scoring on the rollers, outer races or shafts.

3   Check the fit of the selector mechanism forks in their respective grooves in the synchro sleeves. Also check for wear ridges in the fork ends.

4   Examine each synchro ring for evidence of cracks, and check that the annular spring is not broken or distorted (photo).

5   Place the synchro rings, one at a time, in position on their respective sleeves. Using a depth gauge, measure the distance between the face of the ring and the edge of the sleeve at three points around the circumference (photo). If the mean measured dimension is greater than 1.0 mm (0.039 in), renew the synchro ring.

6   Obtain any new parts as necessary prior to reassembly.

12 Gearbox – reassembly

Note: *If, during overhaul, it was necessary to renew any of the tapered roller bearings, the gearbox casing or intermediate plate, or the mainshaft, input shaft or layshaft themselves, then the gearbox running clearances must be checked and if necessary re-adjusted. This is carried out by accurate measurement and the substitution of the selective spacing washers behind the bearing outer races in the front cover. It is recommended that the gearbox major assemblies be taken to a Mercedes-Benz dealer to have this work carried out. These clearances will not normally be affected if only the gears, synchro units or any other components not mentioned above have been renewed.*

1   Begin reassembly by placing the selected spacer washers in their respective recesses in the gearbox casing front cover (photo). Use a little grease to hold the washers in place.

2   Ensure that the mating faces are clean and dry, then apply an RTV sealing compound to the cover face.

3   Fit the cover (photo) and secure with the six retaining bolts, after first applying a thread sealer to the bolt threads. Tighten the bolts to the specified torque.

4   Refit the input shaft with synchro sleeve and shift mechanism (photos).

5   Fit the layshaft assembly to the gearbox casing. To do this, it is necessary to lift off the synchro sleeve and shift mechanism from the input shaft, enter the layshaft into its bearing race slightly, while at the same time placing the sleeve and shift mechanism back on the input shaft (photos).

6   Where fitted, refit the preload spring, washers and roller thrust bearing to the input shaft bore (photos).

7   Refit the mainshaft support needle roller bearing to the centre of the input shaft (photo).

8   Using a new gasket, fit the 3rd/4th gearshift mechanism pivot pin plate, while manipulating the shift mechanism to align the pivot pin hole (photo).

9   Apply a thread sealer to the retaining bolt, then fit and tighten the bolt to the specified torque (photo).

10 On the other side of the casing, align the shift mechanism with the shift lever bore in the casing (photo).

11 Fit the 3rd/4th gearshift lever, engage the sine-wave-like formed end in the lever with that in the shift mechanism, and fit the retaining bolt (photo). Tighten the bolt to the specified torque.

12 Locate the mainshaft assembly in position on the input shaft (photo). As the mainshaft is inserted, it will be necessary to lift and rotate the layshaft to allow the gears to engage. It will also be necessary to ease back the shift lever detent leaf spring with a screwdriver to allow the detents on the 1st/2nd shift mechanism to clear the spring (photo). The help of an assistant is useful here.

13 With the mainshaft in place, fit the 1st/2nd shift mechanism pivot pin plate with a new gasket, and secure with the retaining bolt tightened to the specified torque (photo).

14 Fit the 1st/2nd gearshift lever and secure with the retaining bolt tightened to the specified torque (photo).

15 Using a new gasket, insert the locking cage into the gearbox casing in such a manner that one ball points downwards toward the collar nut (photo). Fit the two retaining bolts and tighten to the specified torque.

16 Locate a new intermediate plate gasket on the gearbox casing (photo).

17 Move the locking lever in the gearbox casing to an upright position, ready to accept the shift lever in the intermediate plate (photo).

18 Carefully position the intermediate plate on the casing, while guiding the shafts into their bearing races, and the shift arm into the locking lever (photo). Tap the intermediate plate down using a soft mallet until it is fully seated on the gearbox casing.

19 Insert the reverse shaft locating bolt into the casing and tighten to the specified torque (photo).

20 Place the thrustwasher on the layshaft with the flanged side towards the bearing (photo).

21 Fit the needle roller bearing, followed by the 5th gear (photos).

22 Lay the 5th gear synchro hub over the layshaft splines (photo) and tap it fully home.

23 Secure the synchro hub using the retaining circlip, ensuring that the circlip fully enters the groove in the layshaft (photo).

24 Slip the speedometer drivegear onto the mainshaft, so that the flat side is towards the rear (photo).

25 Fit the 5th gear synchro sleeve and shift mechanism as an assembly, ensuring that the shift mechanism engages with the shift arm, and the spring end locates against the side of the intermediate plate (photos).

26 Locate a new rear cover gasket on the intermediate plate, then fit the rear cover (photos).

27 Using new O-rings, fit the pivot pin plates on each side of the rear cover that support the 5th gear shift mechanism (photo). Secure the pivot pin plates with the retaining bolts, tightened to the specified torque.

28 Fit the rear cover and intermediate plate retaining bolts and tighten to the specified torque (photo).

29 Fit the spacing washer (where fitted), followed by the gearbox flange (photos).

30 Screw on a new collar nut (photo) and tighten the nut to the specified torque. To stop the flange turning as the nut is tightened, wedge a small socket or similar item between one of the flange arms and a sturdy part of the casing (photo).

31 Using a small punch, stake the collar of the nut into the groove in the mainshaft after tightening.

32 Refit the clutch release bearing, release fork and slave cylinder as described in Chapter 5.

33 The gearbox can now be refitted to the car as described in Section 3.

12.3 ... then fit the front cover to the casing

12.4A Fit the input shaft assembly to the casing, complete with synchro sleeve and shift mechanism

12.4B Input shaft assembly in position

12.5A Fit the layshaft assembly while temporarily removing the sleeve and shift mechanism from the input shaft

12.5B As the gears mesh, locate the sleeve and shift mechanism back on the input shaft

12.6A Where fitted, place the preload spring in the input shaft bore ...

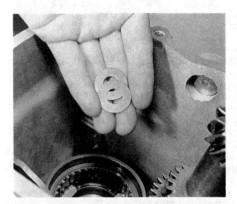
12.6B ... followed by the washers ...

12.6C ... and roller thrust bearing

12.7 Fit the mainshaft support bearing to the input shaft

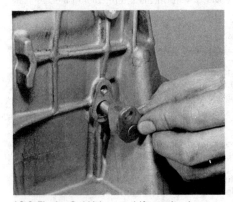
12.8 Fit the 3rd/4th gearshift mechanism pivot pin plate ...

12.9 ... and secure with the bolt after applying thread sealer

12.10 Align the shift mechanism with the shift lever bore ...

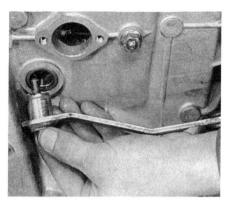

12.11 ... then fit the 3rd/4th gearshift lever

12.12A Locate the mainshaft assembly in position ...

12.12B ... while easing back the detent leaf spring with a screwdriver (arrowed)

12.13 Fit the 1st/2nd gearshift mechanism pivot pin plate

12.14 Fit the 1st/2nd gearshift lever

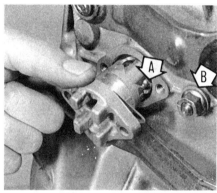

12.15 Insert the locking cage so that one ball (A) points towards the collar nut (B)

12.16 Locate a new intermediate plate gasket on the casing

12.17 Move the locking lever to an upright position ...

12.18 ... so that it engages the shift lever as the intermediate plate is fitted

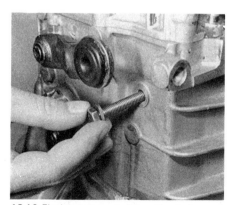

12.19 Fit the reverse shaft locating bolt

12.20 Place the thrust washer on the layshaft

12.21A Fit the needle roller bearing ...

12.21B ... followed by 5th gear ...

12.22 ... and the synchro hub

12.23 Secure the synchro hub with the circlip

12.24 Fit the speedometer drivegear with the flat side to the rear

12.25A Fit the synchro sleeve and shift mechanism with the shift arm (arrowed) engaged ...

12.25B ... and the spring end (arrowed) against the side of the intermediate plate

12.26A Place a new rear cover gasket in position ...

12.26B ... and fit the rear cover

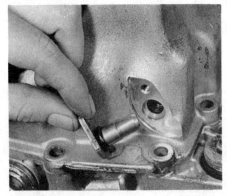
12.27 Fit the pivot pin plates on each side

12.28 Fit and tighten the rear cover retaining bolts

12.29A Fit the spacing washer ...

12.29B ... followed by the gearbox flange

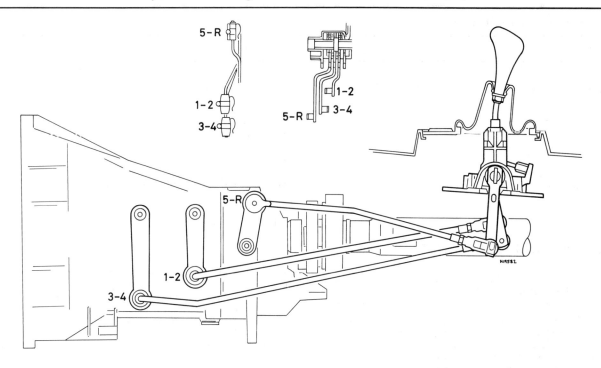

Fig. 6.4 Gearshift rods and shift lever arrangement (Sec 13)

13 Gearshift linkage – adjustment

1 Jack up the front of the car and support it on axle stands.
2 Place the gear lever in neutral.
3 From under the car, extract the retaining clips and withdraw the shift rods from the three gear lever remote control shift levers.
4 Lock the three shift levers in the neutral position by inserting a screwdriver, small punch or metal rod, having a diameter of 5.9 mm (0.23 in) and a length of approximately 40.0 mm (1.6 in), through the holes in the shift levers provided for this purpose (Fig. 6.5).
5 The shift rod ends should now just slip onto the pins of the shift levers. If adjustment is necessary, slacken the locknuts and adjust the length of each rod as required by turning the end fitting. Tighten the locknuts after adjustment.
6 Remove the locking tab and refit the shift rods to the shift levers. Secure each rod with its retaining clip.
7 Lower the car to the ground and check the operation of the linkage with the engine running.

14 Gear lever and remote control assembly – removal and refitting

1 Jack up the front of the car and support it on axle stands.
2 From under the car, extract the retaining clips and withdraw the shift rods from the three gear lever remote control shift levers.
3 From inside the car, remove the cover on the centre console for access to the remote control assembly. (Refer to Chapter 11 if necessary).
4 Unclip the reversing lamp switch from the remote control housing.
5 Undo the four bolts securing the housing to the floor and remove the assembly from inside the car.
6 Refitting is the reverse sequence to removal. Tighten the retaining bolts to the specified torque, then check the linkage adjustment as described in Section 13 before lowering the car to the ground.

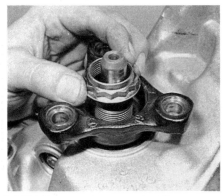

12.30A Screw on a new gearbox flange collar nut ...

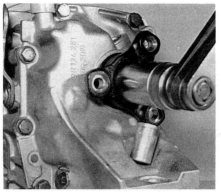

12.30B ... and tighten the nut while using a socket or similar to stop the flange turning

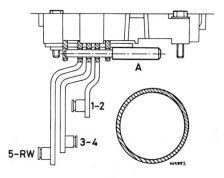

Fig. 6.5 Using a parallel punch (A) to lock the shift levers for adjustment purposes (Sec 13)

15 Fault diagnosis – manual gearbox

Symptom	Reason(s)
Ineffective synchromesh	Worn synchro rings
Jumps out of gear	Weak or broken detent spring Worn synchro unit or shift mechanism Excessive gearbox running clearances
Noisy operation	Worn bearings or gears
Difficult engagement of gears	Worn synchro unit or shift mechanism Incorrect gear linkage adjustment Clutch fault Input shaft spigot bearing in crankshaft seized

PART B: AUTOMATIC TRANSMISSION

16 General description

A Mercedes-Benz four-speed automatic transmission is available as an option on all models covered by this manual.

The transmission comprises two basic systems; the torque converter, which takes the place of the conventional clutch, and a torque/speed-responsive hydraulically-operated epicyclic gearbox.

The transmission also incorporates a program selector switch, which enables the unit to operate in Standard or Economy mode. In Standard mode, the transmission operates normally for maximum utilization of engine power according to load and throttle position. In Economy mode, the vehicle starts from rest with the transmission in 2nd gear, and up- and down-shifts occur at lower driving and engine speeds for quieter, comfort-orientated driving. The Economy mode is automatically switched off under full throttle kickdown conditions.

Because of the need for special test equipment, the complexity of some of the parts, and the need for scrupulous cleanliness when servicing automatic transmissions, the amount which the owner can do is limited, but those operations which can reasonably be carried out are detailed in the following Sections.

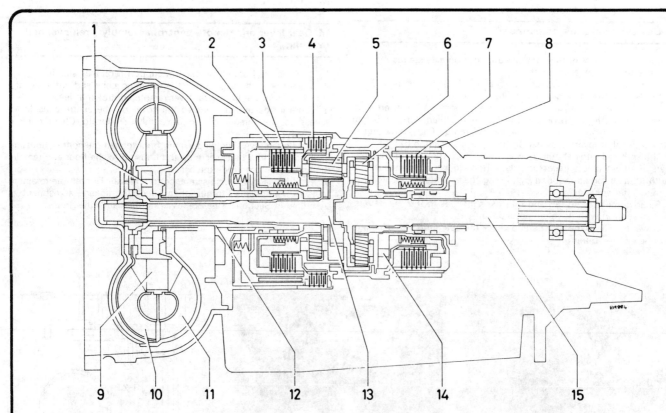

Fig. 6.6 Layout of the gear train and torque converter components within the automatic transmission (Sec 16)

1 One-way converter clutch	5 Ravigneaux planetary gear set	8 Brake band B2	12 Stator shaft
2 Brake band B1		9 Impeller	13 Input shaft
3 Clutch K1	6 Rear planetary gear set	10 Turbine wheel	14 One-way shift clutch F
4 Multiple disc brake B3	7 Clutch K2	11 Pump wheel	15 Output shaft

17 Maintenance and inspection

1   At the intervals specified in Routine Maintenance, the automatic transmission fluid level should be checked and if necessary topped up using the following procedures.
2   The fluid level should be checked when the transmission is at normal operating temperature, ie after a short journey if the car has been started from cold.
3   Park the car on level ground, with the engine idling and the selector lever in the 'P' (park) position. Lift up the locking catch on the transmission fluid dipstick which is located at the rear right-hand side of the engine compartment (photo). Withdraw the dipstick, wipe it on a clean lint-free rag, re-insert it fully, withdraw it once more and read off the fluid level. With the transmission at normal operating temperature, the level should be up to the upper ('max') mark on the dipstick (photo).
4   If topping-up is required, pour the required quantity of the specified fluid through a fine mesh filter into the dipstick tube. Take care not to overfill the transmission, noting that the difference between the upper and lower marks on the dipstick is 0.3 litre (0.5 Imp pt).
5   After topping-up, move the selector lever through all the gear positions, pausing a few seconds in each position, then return the lever to 'P'. Recheck the level once more and top up if necessary.
6   On completion, secure the dipstick in its tube by pressing down the locking catch, and switch off the engine.
7   Draining and refilling of the automatic transmission fluid should be carried out at the intervals specified in Routine Maintenance, using the procedure given in Section 18.

18 Automatic transmission fluid – draining and refilling

1   This job should not be attempted unless clean, dust-free conditions can be achieved.
2   Position the car over an inspection pit, or raise and support it at the front and rear, but ensure that it stays level.
3   Remove the full-length engine undertray, on cars so equipped, to provide access around the transmission oil pan.
4   Place the selector lever in the 'P' (park) position.
5   Clean the transmission oil pan, particularly around the drain plug, pan-to-transmission retaining bolts and the pan-to-transmission joint edge.
6   Unscrew the transmission drain plug (photo) using an Allen key, and allow the oil to drain into a suitable container. Refit the drain plug when all the oil has drained.
7   Turn the engine until the torque converter drain plug is accessible through the opening in the bottom of the converter housing (photo).
8   Unscrew the drain plug and allow the oil to drain into the container. Refit the plug after draining.
9   Unscrew the oil pan retaining bolts (photo), remove the clamp plates and withdraw the oil pan from the transmission. Tap the pan gently with a soft mallet if it is stuck. Recover the rubber seal.
10 Undo the screws and remove the filter screen.
11 Before refitting, thoroughly clean the oil pan inside and out, and dry with a lint-free cloth.
12 Fit a new filter screen and secure with the retaining screws.
13 Place the oil pan in position, and fit the retaining bolts and clamp plates. Tighten the retaining bolts to the specified torque.
14 Where applicable, refit the engine undertray.
15 Lower the car to the ground, then fill the transmission initially with approximately 4.0 litres (7.0 Imp pts) of the specified fluid, through the dipstick tube.
16 Start the engine and allow it to idle with the selector lever in the 'P' (park) position.
17 Continue adding fluid until the level is 12.0 mm (0.47 in) below the lower ('min') mark on the dipstick.
18 Move the selector lever through all the gear positions, pausing a few seconds in each position, then return the lever to the 'P' position.
19 Repeat paragraph 18 if topping-up is necessary.
20 Take the car for a short drive to bring the engine and transmission to normal operating temperature. Recheck the fluid level with the transmission warmed up, and this time, top-up if necessary to bring the level up to the upper ('max') mark on the dipstick.
21 On completion, switch off and secure the dipstick into its tube by pressing down the locking catch.

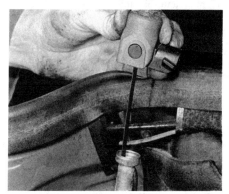
17.3A Lift up the locking catch and withdraw the transmission fluid dipstick

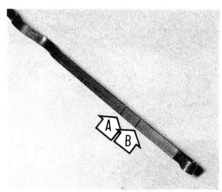
17.3B 'Max' mark (A) and 'min' mark (B) on the dipstick

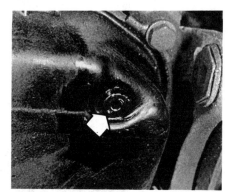
18.6 Transmission drain plug location (arrowed)

18.7 Torque converter drain plug (arrowed) acccessible through the converter housing opening

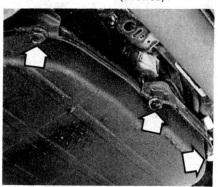
18.9 Transmission oil pan right-hand side retaining bolts (arrowed)

19 Control pressure cable – adjustment

Carburettor engines

1 Disconnect the control pressure cable end from the ball socket on the throttle linkage (Fig. 6.7).
2 Push the inner cable back into its outer cable (ie push it towards the transmission), then pull it out again until slight resistance is felt.
3 At the point where resistance is just felt, it should be possible to fit the cable end back onto the ball socket. If the cable is too long or too short to achieve this, turn the outer cable adjuster as necessary.
4 When the adjustment is correct, push the cable end firmly into place on its ball socket.

Fuel injected engines up to October 1984

5 The procedure is the same as described in paragraphs 1 to 4 for carburettor engines.

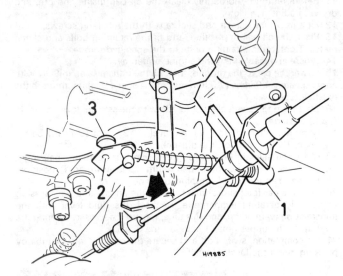

Fig. 6.7 Control pressure cable adjustment on carburettor engines (Sec 19)

1 Cable adjuster   3 Cable end
2 Ball socket on linkage

Arrow indicates inner cable pushed back into outer cable

19.6 Control pressure cable serrated adjusting nut (arrowed)

Fuel injected engines from October 1984 onwards

6 Screw in the serrated adjusted nut (photo) adjacent to the cable bracket, until there is approximately 1.0 mm (0.039 in) freeplay at the crush nipple on the spacing sleeve.
7 Now unscrew the adjusting nut until the tip of the indicator pointer is above the groove in the adjusting nut.

20 Starter inhibitor switch – removal, refitting and adjustment

1 Position the car over an inspection pit, raise it on a vehicle lift, or jack it up at the front and rear and supported it on axle stands.
2 Place the selector lever in the 'N' (neutral) position.
3 From under the car, extract the spring clip and disconnect the selector rod from the selector lever (photos).
4 Disconnect the exhaust system rear mountings, lower the system as far as possible without subjecting it to excessive strain, and support it using a length of wire.
5 Position a jack beneath the transmission crossmember and take the weight of the transmission.
6 Undo the two bolts each side securing the transmission crossmember to the chassis rails.
7 Lower the transmission just sufficiently to provide access to the starter inhibitor switch on the left-hand side of the transmission casing.
8 Disconnect the speedometer cable clip from the support bracket on the side of the transmission (photo).
9 Release the wiring plug locking clip by pushing it upwards (photo) then disconnect the wiring plug from the starter inhibitor switch.
10 Undo the two retaining bolts and remove the starter inhibitor switch from the transmission (photo).
11 To refit the switch, place it in position on the transmission, ensuring that the operating peg enters the gear selector arm opening. Fit the two retaining bolts but do not tighten at this stage.
12 Insert a 4.0 mm (0.16 in) diameter drill bit, or split pin of similar size, through the operating peg bore to lock the inhibitor switch and selector arm (photo). Now tighten the switch retaining bolts, then remove the drill bit or split pin.
13 Reconnect the wiring plug and slip the locking clip down to secure.
14 Raise the transmission on the jack, refit the crossmember bolts and tighten to the specified torque.
15 Reconnect the exhaust system to its mountings.
16 Reconnect the speedometer cable retaining clip.
17 Reconnect the selector rod to the selector lever.
18 Lower the car to the ground and check the operation of the starter inhibitor switch.

Fig. 6.8 Starter inhibitor switch adjustment (Sec 20)

1 Gear selector arm   4 Drill bit inserted in operating
2 Starter inhibitor switch   peg (arrowed)
3 Retaining bolts

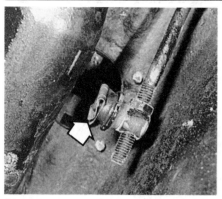
20.3A Extract the selector rod spring clip (arrowed) ...

20.3B ... and separate the rod from the selector lever

20.8 Disconnect the speedometer cable retaining clip

20.9 Push the wiring plug locking clip upwards to release the plug

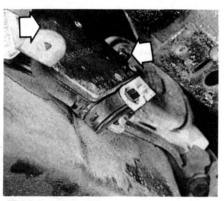
20.10 Starter inhibitor switch retaining bolt locations (arrowed)

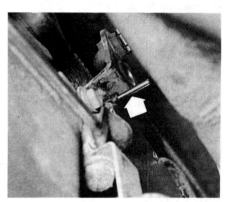
20.12 Locking split pin (arrowed) inserted through starter/inhibitor switch operating peg

21 Gear selector rod – adjustment

1 Jack up the front of the car and support it on axle stands.
2 Place the selector lever in the 'N' (neutral) position.
3 From inside the car, extract the spring clip and disconnect the selector rod from the selector lever.
4 Ensure that the selector arm on the side of the transmission is in the 'N' position by moving the arm through the range of positions with reference to Fig. 6.9.
5 Slacken the locknut on the selector rod. Now adjust the rod length by turning the end fitting until there is approximately 1.0 mm (0.039 in) clearance between the selector lever and the 'N' stop on the selector gate with the rod connected.
6 When the adjustment is correct, secure the selector rod with the spring clip, tighten the locknut, and lower the car to the ground.

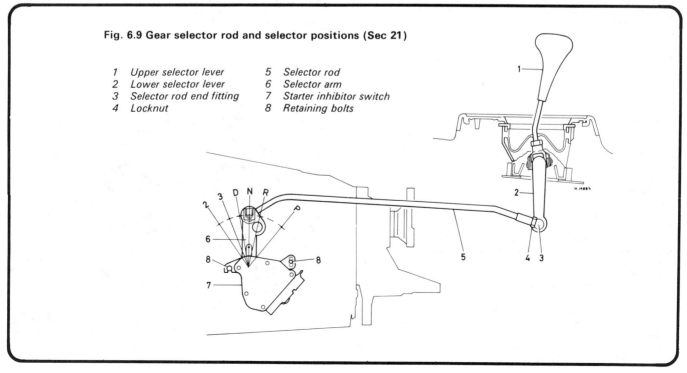

Fig. 6.9 Gear selector rod and selector positions (Sec 21)

1 Upper selector lever
2 Lower selector lever
3 Selector rod end fitting
4 Locknut
5 Selector rod
6 Selector arm
7 Starter inhibitor switch
8 Retaining bolts

22 Gear selector lever assembly – removal and refitting

1   Jack up the front of the car and support it on axle stands.
2   From under the car, extract the retaining clip and withdraw the selector rod from the lower selector lever.
3   From inside the car, remove the cover on the centre console for access to the selector assembly. (Refer to Chapter 11 if necessary).
4   Undo the four bolts securing the selector assembly to the floor, release the wiring and cable clips and remove the assembly from the car. Recover the rubber seal at the base of the unit.
5   Refitting is the reverse sequence to removal.

23 Automatic transmission – removal and refitting

1   Position the car over an inspection pit, or on ramps or axle stands, and apply the handbrake firmly.
2   Disconnect the battery negative terminal.
3   Disconnect the transmission fluid dipstick tube at the rear of the cylinder head and on the rocker cover.
4   On cars with carburettor engines, disconnect the control pressure cable end from the ball socket on the throttle linkage. Release the outer cable from the support bracket and move the cable clear.
5   On 190 E models up to October 1984, disconnect the control pressure cable end as described in paragraph 4.
6   On 190 E models from October 1984 onwards, disconnect the control pressure cable end by prising the support fixture apart using a screwdriver (Fig. 6.10), then withdrawing the cable end. Release the outer cable from the support bracket and move the cable clear.
7   Refer to Section 18 and drain the automatic transmission fluid from the oil pan and torque converter.
8   Remove the rubber grommet from the front face of the converter housing (photo).
9   Turn the engine until each pair of torque converter retaining bolts (from a total of six) becomes accessible through the converter housing opening (photo). Undo and remove the two bolts then repeat the procedure for the remaining bolts.
10 Undo the nuts and remove the bolts and washers securing the exhaust system support bracket to the rear of the transmission (photo).
11 Undo the U-clamp nuts securing the exhaust to the bracket, and remove the bracket.
12 Disconnect the exhaust system rubber ring mountings, lower the system by 150 to 250 mm (6 to 10 in) and support it in this position using wire or rope.
13 Support the transmission on a jack beneath the oil pan, using a block of wood to protect the pan.
14 Undo the two bolts each side securing the transmission crossmember to the chassis rails.
15 Undo the nut securing the crossmember rubber mounting to the transmission and remove the crossmember (photo).
16 Undo the four bolts and remove the exhaust heat shield over the front silencer.
17 Undo the three nuts and bolts securing the propeller shaft front flexible rubber coupling to the transmission flange. To do this, undo the bolts using a socket and extension bar while holding the nuts from behind with a spanner. **Note:** *Further information on this and the following propeller shaft procedures will be found in Chapter 7, Section 3.*
18 Using a 41 mm open-ended spanner, slacken the propeller shaft clamping nut approximately two turns, while using a second spanner to prevent the propeller shaft turning.
19 Slacken the two bolts securing the centre support bearing to the underbody.
20 Slide the propeller shaft front section towards the rear as far as the support bearing and clamping nut will allow. If the flexible coupling is tight on the transmission flange, insert a bar or suitable screwdriver through the bolt holes, and move it up and down to release the locating sleeves from their recesses in the flange. Tie the propeller shaft up out of the way when it is clear.
21 Undo the speedometer cable clamp bolt (photo) and withdraw the cable from the transmission. Release the cable clip from the support bracket and move the cable to one side.
22 Extract the retaining clip and remove the selector rod end fitting from the selector lever (photo).

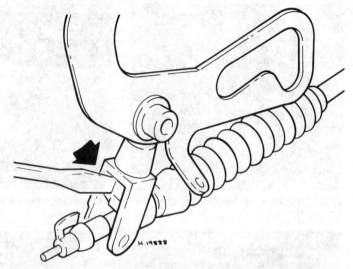

Fig. 6.10 Disconnecting the control pressure cable by using a screwdriver to prise apart the support fixture (arrowed) (Sec 23)

23.8 Remove the converter housing grommet ...

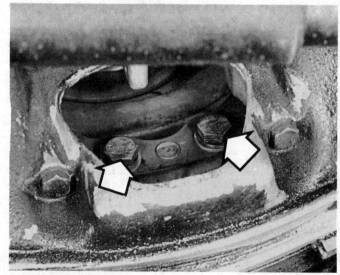

23.9 ... for access to the torque converter retaining bolts – two of six shown (arrowed)

23 Disconnect the cable for the kickdown solenoid valve at the rear of the transmission.

24 Lower the transmission slightly to provide access to the starter inhibitor switch on the left-hand side.

25 Release the wiring plug locking clip by pushing it upwards, then disconnect the wiring plug from the starter inhibitor switch.

26 Disconnect the vacuum pipe at the vacuum control unit adjacent to the starter inhibitor switch.

27 Unscrew the socket-headed retaining bolt and pull out the transmission fluid dipstick tube. Remove the tube from the car.

28 Unscrew the oil cooler pipe banjo unions on each side of the transmission (photos) and recover the sealing washers. Cover the unions after removal to prevent dirt ingress.

29 Undo the socket-headed bolts securing the oil cooler pipe support clips on each side of the converter housing (photos) and remove the clips. Position the pipes clear of the transmission.

30 Undo the bolts securing the starter motor to the engine and converter housing, withdraw the starter and move it aside.

31 Position a second jack beneath and in contact with the engine sump at the rear.

32 Place a piece of sheet metal or similar protective material over the bulkhead insulation at the rear of the engine, so that the insulation is not damaged by the cylinder head when the engine is tipped back.

33 Undo all the bolts securing the transmission to the engine, noting the location of the engine earth strap on the lower left-hand side (photo).

34 While holding the transmission in place, slowly lower the two jacks until sufficient clearance exists to allow the transmission to be pulled rearwards.

35 Release the engine-to-transmission locating dowels using a screwdriver between the two flanges, then withdraw the transmission complete with torque converter from the engine.

23.10 Exhaust system support bracket bolts (A) and crossmember retaining bolts (B)

23.15 Crossmember rubber mounting-to-transmission retaining nut (arrowed)

23.21 Speedometer cable clamp bolt (arrowed)

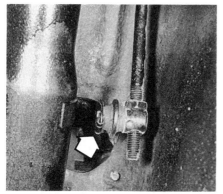

23.22 Selector rod-to-lever retaining clip (arrowed)

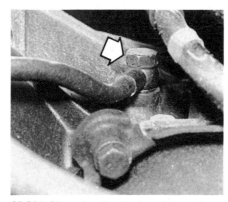

23.28A Oil cooler pipe banjo union on the transmission left-hand side (arrowed) ...

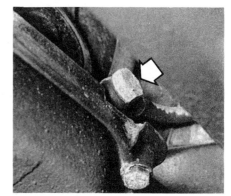

23.28B ... and on the right-hand side (arrowed)

23.29A Release the pipe support clip on the left-hand side (arrowed) ...

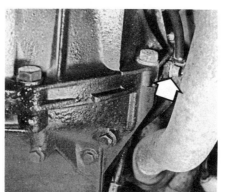

23.29B ... and right-hand side of the converter housing (arrowed)

23.33 Engine earth strap attachment at the transmission

36 Carefully lower the jack and remove the unit from under the car.
37 Refitting the transmission is the reverse sequence to removal, bearing in mind the following points:

    (a) Lightly lubricate the torque converter stub shaft prior to fitting
    (b) When connecting the propeller shaft, tighten the clamping nut after attaching the front flexible coupling and securing the centre support bearing
    (c) Use new sealing washers when refitting the oil cooler pipe banjo unions
    (d) Refill the transmission with the specified fluid using the procedure given in Section 18

24 Fault diagnosis – automatic transmission

1 Before the automatic transmission is removed for repair of a suspected malfunction, it is imperative that the cause be traced and confirmed. To do this requires specialist experience and various tools and gauges not normally found in the DIY mechanic's workshop.
2 If any fault arises that cannot be cured by attention to the fluid level and the adjustments described in this Chapter, take the vehicle to a Mercedes-Benz dealer for diagnosis and repair.

Chapter 7 Propeller shaft

Contents

Specifications

Type	....	Two-piece tubular steel propeller shaft with front and rear flexible rubber couplings, single universal joint and centre support bearing

Centering sleeves
Protrusion, front:

190	31.0 mm (1.22 in)
190E	33.0 mm (1.30 in)
Protrusion, rear	24.0 mm (0.95 in)

Torque wrench settings

	Nm	lbf ft
Flexible rubber coupling mounting bolts	45	33
Centre support bearing to underbody	25	18
Propeller shaft clamping nut	30 to 40	22 to 30
Transmission crossmember retaining bolts	45	33

1 General description

Drive is transmitted from the transmission to the final drive differential by means of a two-piece tubular steel propeller shaft. The propeller shaft is attached at each end to the transmission and final drive flanges through the flexible rubber couplings, and is supported at the centre by a rubber-mounted ball bearing. A vibration damper, located at the transmission end of the shaft, works in conjunction with the rubber couplings to eliminate transmission shocks and harmonically-induced vibrations. A universal joint located just to the rear of the centre bearing caters for slight movement of the propeller shaft and transmission on their mountings. The front and rear sections of the propeller shaft are joined by a sliding spline, which is locked by a clamping nut once the propeller shaft is fitted to the car.

134

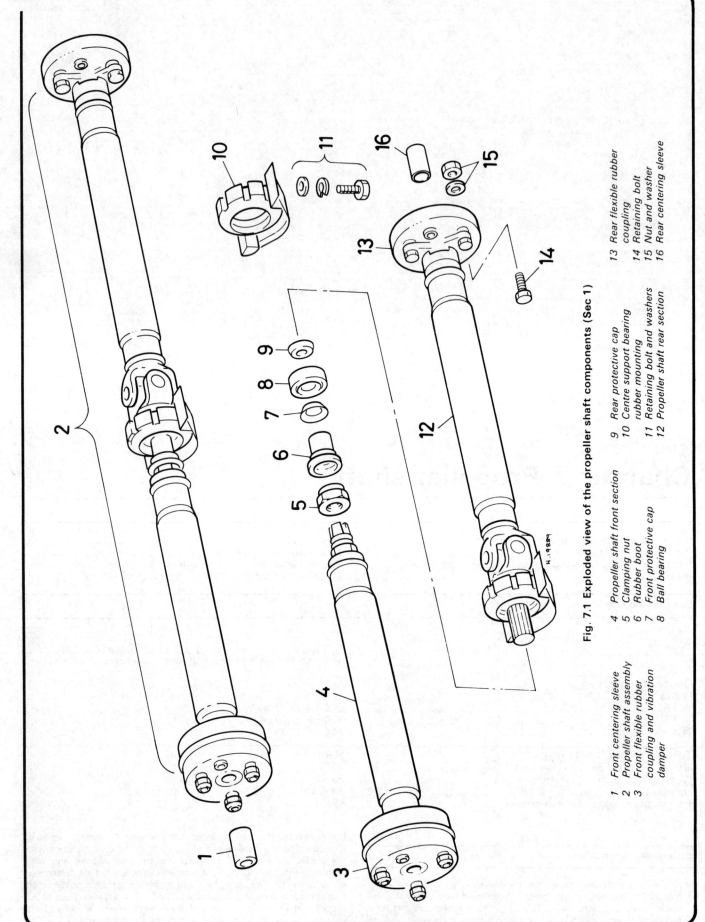

Fig. 7.1 Exploded view of the propeller shaft components (Sec 1)

1 Front centering sleeve
2 Propeller shaft assembly
3 Front flexible rubber coupling and vibration damper
4 Propeller shaft front section
5 Clamping nut
6 Rubber boot
7 Front protective cap
8 Ball bearing
9 Rear protective cap
10 Centre support bearing rubber mounting
11 Retaining bolt and washers
12 Propeller shaft rear section
13 Rear flexible rubber coupling
14 Retaining bolt
15 Nut and washer
16 Rear centering sleeve

2 Maintenance and inspection

1   At the intervals specified in Routine Maintenance at the beginning of this manual, position the car over an inspection pit, raise it on a ramp, or jack up and support it on axle stands so that the propeller shaft can be inspected over its entire length.
2   Check the two flexible rubber couplings at each end of the shaft carefully for signs of cracks, splits, deformation, or any signs of swelling of the rubber due to oil contamination. Should any of these conditions be apparent, renew the coupling concerned as described in Section 4.
3   At the centre of the shaft, check the condition of the centre support ball bearing and its rubber mounting. Examine the rubber for cracks, splits, oil contamination or other damage, and the bearing for obvious signs of excessive free play. Wear of the bearing may not be obvious visually, but may be indicated by a rumble from the centre of the car, consistent with road speed, when the car is driven. Should renewal of the bearing be necessary, refer to Section 5.
4   Check the condition of the universal joint by holding both propeller shaft sections and turning them in opposite directions. Any wear will appear as movement between the two yokes. Also check for signs of red rust deposits around the universal joint spider and the two yokes. This indicates that the joint is dry of lubricant, and in an advanced state of wear. Should the joint be worn, a new propeller shaft rear section must be obtained as the joint cannot be repaired.
5   Finally check the propeller shaft over its entire length for any other sign of damage, distortion or wear.

3 Propeller shaft – removal and refitting

1   Position the car over an inspection pit, raise it on a vehicle lift, or jack it up and securely support it on axle stands.
2   Undo the four bolts and remove the exhaust heat shield over the front silencer (photo).
3   Undo the three nuts and bolts securing the front flexible rubber coupling to the transmission flange. To do this, undo the bolts using a socket and extension bar while holding the nuts from behind with a spanner (photo). Clearance for the spanner is extremely limited, and if problems are encountered, support the transmission on a jack and remove the transmission crossmember. This will provide increased working clearance.
4   At the rear, undo the three nuts and bolts securing the flexible rubber coupling to the differential flange (photo).
5   Using a 41 mm open-ended spanner, slacken the propeller shaft clamping nut approximately two turns, while using a second spanner to prevent the propeller shaft turning (photo). When standing under the car looking towards the rear, the nut is turned clockwise to slacken.
6   Undo the two bolts securing the centre support bearing to the underbody.
7   Slide the propeller shaft rear section forwards until it is clear of the centering spigot on the differential flange (photo).
8   Slide the propeller shaft front section rearwards until it clears the transmission flange centering spigot (photo). If the flexible coupling is tight on the transmission flange, insert a bar or suitable screwdriver through the bolt holes and move it up and down to release the locating sleeves from their recesses in the flange.
9   With the propeller shaft free at both ends, lower it at the rear and remove it rearwards from under the car. Hold both front and rear sections together during removal otherwise they will come apart at the clamping nut splines.
10 If the two propeller shaft sections are to be separated after removal, check that some form of alignment marks are visible to ensure correct reassembly. These should be in the form of two humps on the rear section yoke, and a corresponding single hump on the front section just forward of the clamping nut. If no marks are apparent, make your own using dabs of white paint (photo).
11 With both sections suitably marked, the sections can be separated if required by releasing the rubber boot from the clamping nut groove and pulling the sections apart (photos).
12 Before refitting, liberally lubricate the centering sleeve cavities at each end of the propeller shaft, and also the rear section splines (if separated), with molybdenum disulphide grease.
13 Reconnect the two shaft sections, if previously separated, and slip

3.2 Undo the four bolts and remove the exhaust heat shield

3.3 Undo the front coupling and vibration damper retaining bolts

3.4 Rear flexible coupling-to-differential flange retaining bolts (arrowed)

the rubber boot into the clamping nut groove (photo). Do not tighten the clamping nut at this stage.

14 Engage the propeller shaft front and rear sections with the centering spigots on the transmission and differential. Fit the two bolts securing the centre bearing to the underbody, but leave the bolts finger-tight only at this stage.

15 Secure the front and rear flexible rubber couplings to their respective flanges, tightening the retaining bolts to the specified torque. Refit the transmission crossmember if previously removed for access.

16 Using the two open-ended spanners, securely tighten the propeller shaft clamping nut.

17 Tighten the propeller shaft centre bearing bolts to the specified torque, refit the exhaust shield, and lower the car to the ground.

4 Flexible rubber couplings and vibration damper – removal and refitting

Front coupling and vibration damper

1 Remove the propeller shaft from the car as described in Section 3.

2 Mark the vibration damper in relation to the three-arm flange of the propeller shaft, and also to the flexible coupling, before separating these components..

3 Using a socket and spanner in the same way as for removal of the propeller shaft from the car, undo the three nuts and remove the bolts and washers securing the coupling and damper to the propeller shaft (photo).

4 Remove the flexible rubber coupling, followed by the vibration damper, from the propeller shaft flange.

3.5 Propeller shaft clamping nut (A) and centre support bearing retaining bolts (B)

3.7 Slide the propeller shaft rear section forwards to clear the differential flange centering spigot (arrowed)

3.8 Front section clear of transmission flange centering spigot (arrowed)

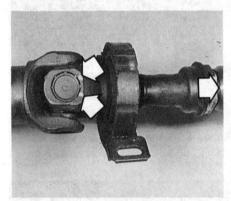

3.10 Alignment marks made on propeller shaft front and rear sections (arrowed)

3.11A Release the rubber boot from the clamping nut groove ...

3.11B ... and pull the two sections apart

3.13 Ensure correct seating of the rubber boot on reassembly

4.3 Front flexible coupling and vibration damper retaining nuts, bolts and washers (arrowed)

4.6A Fit the vibration damper ...

5   Check the condition of the flexible coupling and renew it if there is any sign of cracking, splits, or deformation of the rubber particularly around the retaining bolt locating sleeves.
6   Refit the vibration damper (photo), ensuring that the previously-made marks are aligned, followed by the flexible rubber coupling. On certain models, tangentially-soft couplings are used, which are identifiable by having off-centre retaining bolt locating sleeves, incorporating void holes. This type of coupling must be fitted with the wording 'DIESE SEITE ZUR GELENKWELLE' (this side towards propeller shaft) facing the vibration damper (photo).
7   Refit the mounting bolts, washers and nuts, with the bolt heads toward the propeller shaft, and tighten to the specified torque.
8   Refit the propeller shaft to the car as described in Section 3.

Rear coupling
9   Remove the propeller shaft from the car as described in Section 3.
10 Undo the three nuts, bolts and washers securing the coupling to the propeller shaft flange and remove the coupling.
11 Check the condition of the flexible coupling and renew it if there is any sign of cracking, splits, or deformation of the rubber, particularly around the retaining bolt locating sleeves.
12 Fit the new coupling and secure with the three bolts, nuts and washers. Ensure that the bolt heads are towards the propeller shaft, and tighten to the specified torque.
13 Refit the propeller shaft as described in Section 3.

5 Centre support bearing – removal and refitting

1   Remove the propeller shaft from the car and separate the front and rear sections as described in Section 3.
2   Securely clamp the propeller shaft rear section in a vice with the support bearing uppermost.
3   Slide the rubber boot off the propeller shaft splines (photo).
4   Using a suitable two- or three-legged puller, draw the centre support bearing assembly off the propeller shaft yoke (photo).
5   Prise off the rear protective cap still in position on the propeller shaft yoke. Lift off the front protective cap from the support bearing assembly.
6   If the ball bearing or rubber mounting are to be renewed, place the assembly on a tube or large socket of suitable diameter to contact the inner circumference of the rubber mounting. Using a mandrel in contact with the bearing outer race, drive the bearing out of the mounting (Fig. 7.2).
7   Assemble the new bearing and/or mounting using the reverse of the dismantling procedure, ensuring that the bearing seats fully against the flange in the mounting.
8   Fit the rear protective cap to the propeller shaft yoke.
9   Place the support bearing assembly over the splines on the yoke, and drive it fully home using a tube in contact with the ball bearing

4.6B ... followed by the flexible coupling with, where applicable, the wording facing the damper

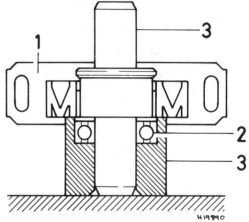
Fig. 7.2 Removing the centre support ball bearing from the rubber mounting (Sec 5)
1 Rubber mounting
2 Ball bearing
3 Mandrel for removing bearing and suitable socket or tube to support rubber mounting

5.3 Removing the rubber boot from the propeller shaft splines

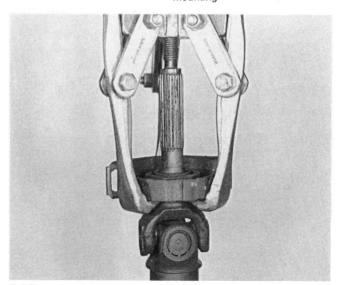
5.4 Removing the centre support bearing assembly using a puller

inner race. Make sure that the support bearing assembly is fitted the right way round. The bearing is offset to one side of the rubber mounting, and this offset side must be towards the propeller shaft universal joint.

10 Tap on a new front protective cap until it contacts the bearing inner race.

11 Fit the rubber boot, ensuring that the small end locates correctly.

12 The two propeller shaft sections can now be reconnected and refitted to the car as described in Section 3.

6 Propeller shaft centering sleeves – removal and refitting

1 In the event of wear or damage to the sealing lip in the propeller shaft front or rear section centering sleeves, which locate over the centering spigots in the transmission and differential flanges, the centering sleeves can be renewed as follows.

2 Remove the propeller shaft from the car as described in Section 3.

3 Refer to Section 4, and remove the front flexible rubber coupling and vibration damper if the front centering sleeve is to be renewed, or the rear flexible coupling if the rear sleeve is to be renewed.

4 Securely mount the front or rear propeller shaft section in a vice as applicable.

5 Knock the centering sleeve uniformly out of the propeller shaft using a hammer and flat chisel.

6 Protect the end of the new centering sleeve with a block of wood, and tap it into place in the propeller shaft. When fitted, the sleeve must protrude by the amount given in the Specifications (Fig. 7.4).

7 Fill the inside of the centering sleeve with approximately 6 g of molybdenum disulphide grease, then refit the rubber coupling and where applicable, the vibration damper as described in Section 4.

8 The propeller shaft can now be refitted to the car as described in Section 3.

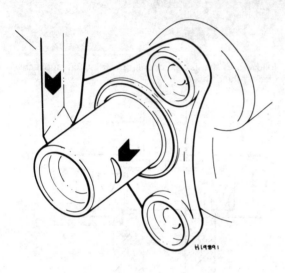

Fig. 7.3 Using a flat chisel for removal of a centering sleeve (Sec 6)

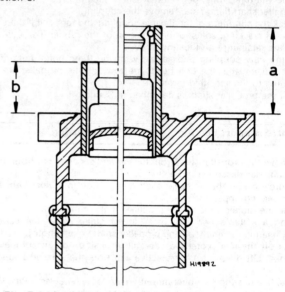

Fig. 7.4 Measuring centering sleeve protrusion (Sec 6)

a Protrusion at front
b Protrusion at rear

7 Fault diagnosis – propeller shaft

Symptom	Reason(s)
Vibration	Worn front or rear flexible rubber couplings
	Flexible rubber coupling mounting bolts loose
	Worn centre support bearing
	Propeller shaft front and rear sections incorrectly assembled
	Vibration damper incorrectly fitted
	Worn universal joint
'Clonk' on acceleration and deceleration	Worn front or rear flexible rubber couplings
	Flexible rubber coupling mounting bolts loose
	Worn universal joint
	Worn front-to-rear section connecting splines, or clamping nut loose
Noise	Worn centre support bearing
	Worn universal joint

Chapter 8 Final drive and driveshafts

Contents

Specifications

Final drive
Type .... Hypoid bevel gear with twin pinion differential
Lubricant type .... Hypoid gear oil, viscosity SAE 90 EP (Duckhams Hypoid 90S)
Lubricant capacity .... 0.7 litre (1.2 Imp pints)
Final drive ratio 3.23:1
Drive flange locking ring thicknesses .... 1.20 to 1.80 mm (0.047 to 0.071 in) in 0.05 mm (0.002 in) increments

Driveshafts
Type .... Solid steel with inner and outer constant velocity joints

Torque wrench settings

	Nm	lbf ft
Final drive housing rear retaining bolts	50	37
Final drive housing front retaining nut and bolt	45	33
Final drive housing rear cover bolts	45	33
Propeller shaft centre support bearing bolts	25	18
Propeller shaft flexible coupling to pinion flange	45	33
Propeller shaft clamping nut	35	26
Inner constant velocity joint to differential drive flange	70	52
Driveshaft retaining collar nut	280 to 320	207 to 236

1 General description

The conventional hypoid final drive differential assembly is bolted to a subframe at the rear of the car, which is in turn attached to the underbody by means of rubber-cushioned mountings.

Drive from the propeller shaft is taken to the bevel pinion and transmitted to the crownwheel and differential unit, which together form the differential assembly. A drive flange on each side, splined to the differential sun gears, allows the drive to be transmitted to the driveshafts and then to the rear wheels.

The solid steel driveshafts each contain two ball and cage type constant velocity joints, one at each end. The inboard joint is bolted to the differential drive flange, and the outboard joint is splined to the rear hub flange.

The procedures given in this Chapter relating to the differential assembly are limited to those considered feasible for the average owner to carry out. Due to the need for special tools, jigs, fixtures and expertise, it is not recommended that the owner should attempt to either remove, dismantle or make adjustments to, the differential unit itself. This work should be entrusted to a suitably equipped Mercedes-Benz dealer.

Removal of the driveshaft assemblies is straightforward but repair is limited to renewal of the rubber boots and inner constant velocity joints, these being the only parts available separately. The outer joint is supplied as part of a complete driveshaft assembly.

2   Maintenance and inspection

1   At the intervals specified in Routine Maintenance at the beginning of this manual, carry out the following service operations on the final drive differential and driveshafts.
2   Jack up the rear of the car and support it on axle stands.
3   Wipe the area around the filler/level plug on the left-hand side of the differential casing, unscrew the plug using a 14 mm hexagonal key, and check that the oil level is up to the plug orifice. Top up if required using the specified lubricant, then refit the plug (photo).
4   Check for signs of oil leakage around the drive flange and pinion shaft oil seals, and check the condition and security of all components and attachments within the final drive area.
5   Turn each driveshaft slowly, and carefully inspect the condition of the rubber boots on the inner and outer constant velocity joints. If any are split, damaged or in any way perished, they must be renewed immediately as described in Section 6 (photo).
6   Check for wear in the outer constant velocity joints by holding the roadwheel and attempting to turn the driveshaft. Any excessive movement of the driveshaft indicates wear in the joint. Check the inner constant velocity joint in a similar way, but hold the differential drive flange while attempting to turn the driveshaft. If the joints are suspect, remove the driveshaft from the car and carry out a careful inspection as described in later Sections of this Chapter.
7   At the specified intervals, drain and refill the final drive differential with fresh oil. Unscrew the drain plug at the bottom of the final drive housing, and allow the oil to drain into a suitable container. When the oil has drained, clean and refit the drain plug, and refill the final drive with the specified quantity and grade of oil, via the filler/level plug on the left-hand side of the differential casing.

3   Final drive differential assembly – removal and refitting

1   Jack up the rear of the car and support it on stands.
2   On cars equipped with ABS brakes, unscrew the drain plug at the bottom of the final drive housing using a 14 mm hexagonal key, and allow the oil to drain into a container (photo). Undo the socket-headed bolt and remove the rpm sensor from the side of the housing. Cover the probe end of the sensor after removal to protect it against damage. When all the oil has drained, refit the drain plug.
3   Undo the four bolts and remove the heat shield over the exhaust system centre section.
4   Using a 41 mm open-ended spanner, slacken the propeller shaft clamping nut, located just to the rear of the centre support bearing, approximately two turns. Use a second spanner to hold the propeller shaft stationary as the clamping nut is slackened.
5   Undo the two screws securing the propeller shaft centre support bearing to the underbody.
6   Undo the three nuts and remove the bolts securing the propeller shaft rear flexible coupling to the differential pinion flange.
7   Push the propeller shaft forwards as far as it will go to disengage the pinion flange centering sleeve. Move the disconnected propeller shaft to the side and support it using a length of wire tied to the handbrake cable.
8   Using a multi-toothed key or socket bit, unscrew the bolts securing both driveshaft inner constant velocity joints to the differential drive flanges. Remove the bolts and locking plates (photo).
9   Push the driveshafts outwards to clear the drive flanges and tie them up, using a length of wire, to the rear suspension camber strut.
10 Place a jack beneath the final drive housing and just take the weight of the unit.
11 Undo the bolts at the rear securing the final drive housing to the subframe, and remove the bolts together with the locking plates (photo).
12 Undo the nut and remove the socket-headed bolt securing the housing to the subframe at the front (photo).
13 Lower the jack and remove the final drive housing from under the car.
14 To refit the unit, position it centrally within the subframe and refit the front retaining bolt and nut finger-tight.
15 Refit the four rear retaining bolts and locking plates and tighten to the specified torque. Now tighten the front nut and bolt to the specified torque also.

2.3 Final drive differential oil filler/level plug (arrowed)

2.5 Check the condition of the constant velocity joint rubber boots for damage or deterioration

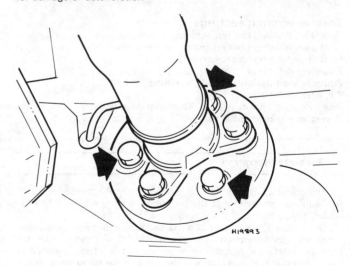

Fig. 8.1 Propeller shaft rear flexible coupling retaining bolts (arrowed) (Sec 3)

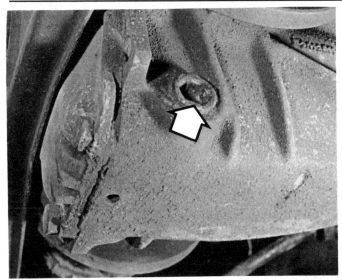

3.2 Final drive differential drain plug (arrowed)

3.8 Inner constant velocity joint retaining bolts (arrowed)

3.11 Final drive housing-to-subframe rear retaining bolts (arrowed)

3.12 Final drive housing-to-subframe front retaining bolt (arrowed)

16 Engage the propeller shaft over the pinion flange centering sleeve, and secure the flexible coupling to the pinion flange with the three nuts and bolts.
17 Refit the two centre support bearing retaining bolts, but tighten them finger-tight only at this stage.
18 With the propeller shaft in position, tighten the clamping nut, then fully tighten the centre bearing retaining bolts to the specified torque.
19 Refit the exhaust heat shield.
20 Lightly lubricate the driveshaft inner constant velocity joint-to-differential drive flange bolt threads with light oil, refit the bolts and locking plates, and tighten to the specified torque.
21 On cars with ABS brakes, refit the rpm sender and secure with the retaining bolt, after first removing any metallic particles which may have collected on the sensor magnetic probe.
22 Unscrew the housing filler/level plug and refill or top up the final drive oil to the level of the plug orifice, using the specified lubricant. Refit the plug and tighten securely.
23 Remove the stands and lower the car to the ground.

---

4   Differential drive flange oil seal – removal and refitting

1   Remove the final drive differential assembly from the car as described in Section 3.

2   Remove the drain plug at the base of the housing and drain the oil if this has not already been done. Refit the plug after draining.
3   Wipe away all traces of dirt from the housing in the region of the rear cover and the drive flange being worked on.
4   Undo the retaining bolts and remove the housing rear cover.
5   Using pliers or a suitable hook, pull the locking ring from the groove in the inner end of the drive flange that protrudes through the differential sun gear.
6   Withdraw the drive flange from the sun gear and housing.
7   Using a screwdriver, prise the oil seal from its recess in the side of the housing.
8   Before fitting the new seal, check the running surface of the drive flange for scoring or wear ridges and renew this component also if necessary.
9   Lubricate the new seal with the specified final drive oil and place it in position in the housing. Using a large socket, tube or other suitable mandrel, tap the seal fully into place. Take care not to damage the face of the seal during installation.
10 Lubricate the running surface of the drive flange and carefully insert it through the seal and sun gear.
11 Refit the locking ring and check that there is no noticeable end play of the drive flange. It should just be possible to turn the locking ring in its groove when in position. If this condition cannot be achieved, renew the locking ring with a slightly thinner or thicker one from the

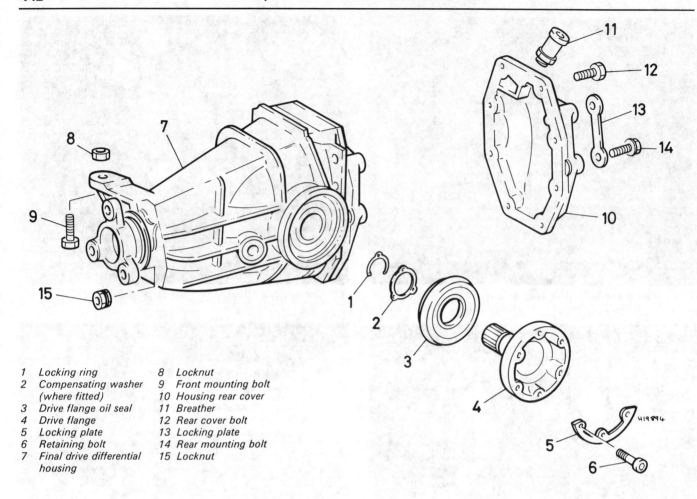

1 Locking ring
2 Compensating washer
   (where fitted)
3 Drive flange oil seal
4 Drive flange
5 Locking plate
6 Retaining bolt
7 Final drive differential
   housing
8 Locknut
9 Front mounting bolt
10 Housing rear cover
11 Breather
12 Rear cover bolt
13 Locking plate
14 Rear mounting bolt
15 Locknut

Fig. 8.2 Exploded view of the differential drive flange and oil seal components (Sec 4)

range available. Note that the original ring should also be renewed if it was at all damaged during removal.

12 Thoroughly clean the rear cover and the sealing face of the housing, then apply an RTV sealing compound to the cover contact face.

13 Fit the rear cover and secure with the retaining bolts tightened to the specified torque.

14 Refit the final drive differential as described in Section 3.

5 Driveshaft – removal and refitting

Note: *Removal and refitting of the driveshaft retaining collar nut entails the use of a 30 mm socket and a torque wrench capable of recording up to 350 Nm. Ensure that these tools are available before proceeding.*

1 With the car on the ground, remove the rear wheel trim and using a small punch or thin screwdriver, knock back the staking securing the driveshaft retaining collar nut to the stub shaft.

2 Using a 30 mm socket and long bar, unscrew and remove the collar nut (photo). Note that a new nut must be used when refitting the driveshaft.

3 Jack up the rear of the car and support it on stands. Remove the roadwheel.

4 Using a multi-toothed key or socket bit, unscrew the bolts securing the driveshaft inner constant velocity joint to the differential drive flange. Remove the bolts and locking plates.

5 Push the inner constant velocity joint outwards, and swivel the driveshaft upwards to clear the drive flange.

5.2 Unscrew the driveshaft collar nut with the car standing on its wheels

5.8 Peen the edge of the collar nut to the stubshaft groove after tightening

6   It should now be possible to push or gently tap the outer constant velocity joint out of the rear hub flange using a copper or plastic mallet. If the joint is tight however, it is advisable to use a suitable puller.
7   With the outer joint free, push the driveshaft down at its inner end and remove it from under the car.
8   Refitting is the reverse sequence to removal, bearing in mind the following points:

(a)   Lubricate the threads of the inner constant velocity joint retaining bolts with a little light oil before refitting and tighten them to the specified torque
(b)   Lightly tighten the new driveshaft retaining collar nut initially, then lower the car and tighten the nut fully to the specified torque with the car on the ground. Do not attempt to achieve this very high torque setting with the car suspended as there is a very great risk of tipping the vehicle off the stands
(c)   After tightening the collar nut, peen the edge of the collar into the stubshaft groove using a small punch (photo)

6   Constant velocity joint rubber boots – removal and refitting

1   Remove the driveshaft as described in Section 5.
2   Working on the inner constant velocity joint, slacken the rubber boot retaining clip screws and remove both retaining clips. If crimped type clips are fitted, cut them off with a pair of pincers or side cutters.
3   Using a suitable drift, carefully tap the end cover off the joint outer member. Take care to avoid damaging the end cover.
4   Similarly tap the rubber boot retaining cap off the joint outer member, and slide the rubber boot and cap down the driveshaft. Take care to avoid damaging the cap.
5   Wipe away the grease from the outer face of the constant velocity joint, and extract the circlip retaining the joint inner member to the driveshaft.
6   Support the inner face of the joint inner member in a vice and drive out the driveshaft using a hammer and soft metal drift.
7   Remove the rubber boot and retaining cap from the driveshaft.
8   If the outer constant velocity joint rubber boot requires renewal, remove the retaining clips, release the boot from the joint and slide it off the shaft.
9   Obtain a rubber boot repair kit for each joint as required, which contains a new rubber boot, two new clips and a quantity of special lubricating grease.
10 Using old rags, wipe away as much of the old grease as possible from the joint members. Do not use any form of solvent.
11 If the rubber boot on the outer joint is being renewed, lubricate the joint thoroughly, using 100 g of the special grease. Smear some grease onto the end of the driveshaft and slide on the boot. Fill the boot with the remainder of the grease and locate it in place over the joint. Secure the boot with the new clips, ensuring that the screw heads of both clips are together and in line (see also paragraph 18).
12 Slide the inner joint rubber boot and retaining cap onto the driveshaft, then securely mount the driveshaft in a vice.
13 Drive the inner constant velocity joint fully into position, using a mandrel or suitable tube in contact with the joint inner member. Do not strike or apply force to any other part of the joint assembly.
14 Refit the retaining circlip.
15 Lubricate the joint thoroughly using 100 g of the special grease, filling the rubber boot with any surplus.
16 Apply jointing compound such as Loctite 574 or Hylomar to the rubber boot retaining cap contact face on the joint outer member.

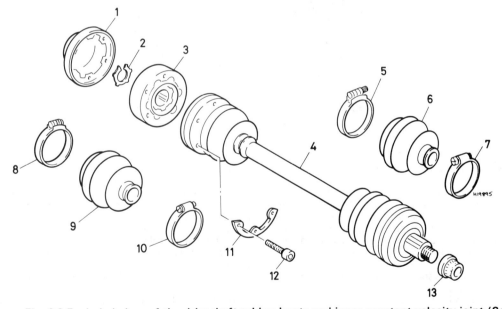

Fig. 8.3 Exploded view of the driveshaft rubber boots and inner constant velocity joint (Sec 6)

1 End cover	5 Retaining clip	8 Retaining clip	11 Locking plate
2 Circlip	6 Outer joint rubber boot	9 Inner joint rubber boot	12 Retaining bolt
3 Joint inner member	7 Retaining clip	10 Retaining clip	13 Driveshaft collar nut
4 Driveshaft assembly			

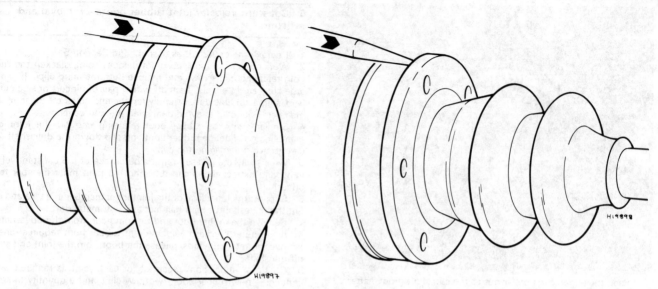

Fig. 8.4 Removing the constant velocity joint end cover (Sec 6)

Fig. 8.5 Removing the rubber boot retaining cap (Sec 6)

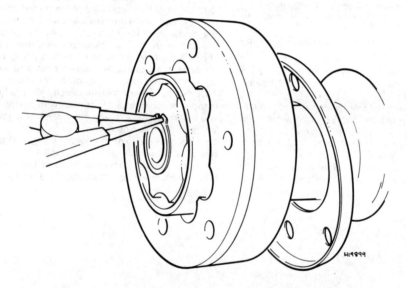

Fig. 8.6 Removing the inner member retaining circlip (Sec 6)

17 Locate the rubber boot and retaining cap in position, ensuring that the cap fits snugly against the joint.

18 Secure the rubber boot with new clips, ensuring that the screw heads (if screw type clips are being used) of both clips are together and on the opposite side of the driveshaft from those securing the outer joint rubber boot. If crimped type clips are being used, engage one of the slots in the clip end over the small tag, ensuring that the clip is as tight as possible. Fully tighten the clip by squeezing the raised portion with pincers.

19 Apply jointing compound to the end cover contact face on the joint outer member and tap the end cover into position.

20 Refit the driveshaft as described in Section 5.

7 Inner constant velocity joint – dismantling, inspection and reassembly

1 Refer to Section 6 and carry out the operations described in paragraphs 1 to 6 inclusive.

2 With the constant velocity joint on the bench, wipe away as much of the grease as possible at this stage.

3 Mark the relationship of the inner member, ball cage and outer member to each other so that these components can be fitted in their original position on reassembly.

4 Swivel the inner member and ball cage and remove the balls, one at a time, from their tracks.

5 With the balls removed, withdraw the inner member and ball cage together from the outer member.

6 Swivel the inner member through 90° and remove it from the ball cage.

7 Thoroughly clean all the parts and lay them out for inspection.

8 Check the running surfaces of the balls, ball cage and the tracks of the inner and outer members for pitting, scoring or evidence of wear. If badly damaged renew the complete constant velocity joint. If only light running traces and smooth spots are apparent, the joint is still serviceable and can be re-used.

9 Begin reassembly by holding the inner member at 90° to the ball cage, insert the member and turn it to its assembled position.

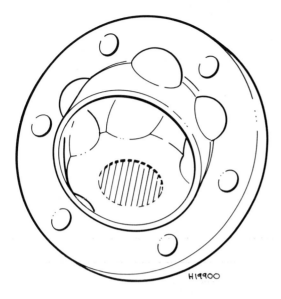

Fig. 8.7 Removing the balls from the constant velocity joint inner member and ball cage (Sec 7)

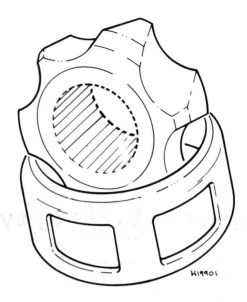

Fig. 8.8 Separating the constant velocity joint inner member from the ball cage (Sec 7)

10 Align the previously-made mark on the inner member and ball cage, then insert one of the balls into its track.
11 Introduce this assembly into the outer member, ensuring that the marks made prior to disassembly are all in line.
12 Swivel the inner member and ball cage as necessary and insert

each ball, one at a time.
13 The assembled joint can now be refitted to the driveshaft using a new rubber boot, retaining clips and quantity of special grease as described in Section 6.

8 Fault diagnosis – final drive and driveshafts

Symptom	Reason(s)
Vibration	Wear in driveshaft constant velocity joints Damaged or distorted driveshaft Roadwheels out of balance See also Fault diagnosis – propeller shaft
Noise	Insufficient lubricant Worn differential gears
'Clunk' on acceleration or deceleration	Incorrect crownwheel and pinion mesh Loose driveshaft retaining collar nut or flange bolts Wear in driveshaft constant velocity joints Excessive backlash due to wear in differential gears
Oil leakage	Faulty pinion or differential flange oil seals Poor seal of rear cover to differential housing

Chapter 9 Braking system

Contents

Specifications

System type .... Servo-assisted front-to-rear split dual circuit hydraulic, with front and rear disc brakes and cable-operated handbrake. Anti-lock braking system optionally available

Hydraulic fluid type .... Universal brake and clutch fluid to FMVSS 116 DOT 3 or DOT 4 (Duckhams Universal Brake and Clutch Fluid)

Front brakes
Type .... Disc with single piston floating calipers
Make .... Girling or Teves
Disc diameter .... 261.8 to 262.2 mm (10.31 to 10.33 in)
Disc thickness:
    New .... 11.0 mm (0.43 in)
    Wear limit .... 9.0 mm (0.35 in)
Minimum disc thickness after machining .... 9.5 mm (0.37 in)
Maximum disc run-out .... 0.12 mm (0.005 in)
Disc caliper piston diameter .... 54.0 mm (2.13 in)
Disc pad friction material:
    Thickness new .... 12.0 mm (0.47 in)
    Wear limit .... 3.5 mm (0.14 in)

Rear brakes
Type .... Disc with twin-piston fixed calipers
Make .... Teves
Disc diameter .... 257.8 to 258.2 mm (10.16 to 10.17 in)
Disc thickness:
    New .... 9.0 mm (0.35 in)
    Wear limit .... 7.3 mm (0.29 in)
Minimum disc thickness after machining .... 7.6 mm (0.30 in)
Maximum disc run-out .... 0.15 mm (0.006 in)
Disc caliper piston diameter .... 35.0 mm (1.38 in)
Disc pad friction material:
    Thickness new .... 9.0 mm (0.35 in)
    Wear limit .... 2.0 mm (0.08 in)

Handbrake
Type .... Cable-operated brake shoes with drum machined in rear disc hub
Drum diameter .... 163.8 to 164.2 mm (6.45 to 6.47 in)
Brake shoe friction material:
    Thickness new .... 2.65 mm (0.10 in)
    Wear limit .... 1.0 mm (0.04 in)

Master cylinder
Make .... Girling, Bendix or Teves
Piston diameter:
    Inner piston .... 17.46 mm (0.69 in)
    Outer piston .... 22.20 mm (0.87 in)

Torque wrench settings

	Nm	lbf ft
Disc caliper guide pin bolts	35	26
Disc caliper carrier bracket to steering knuckle	115	85
Rear disc caliper-to-hub carrier bolts	50	37
Front and rear brake disc retaining screws	10	7
Master cylinder to servo unit	20	15
Servo unit to bulkhead	20	15
Servo vacuum hose union	30	22
Brake hydraulic pipe and hose units	15	11
Wheel speed sensor retaining bolts (ABS)	22	16

1 General description

The braking system is of the servo-assisted, dual circuit hydraulic type, incorporating disc brakes at the front and rear. A front-to-rear split dual circuit hydraulic system is used, whereby one hydraulic circuit operates the front brakes and a separate hydraulic circuit operates the rear brakes from a tandem master cylinder. Under normal conditions both circuits operate in unison; however, in the event of hydraulic failure in one circuit, full braking force will still be available at two wheels.

The front brakes are operated by single piston floating type calipers, while at the rear, twin piston fixed type calipers are employed.

A cable-operated handbrake provides an independent mechanical means of rear brake application. The handbrake system utilizes two small brake shoes for each rear wheel, which contact a brake drum machined in the hub of each rear brake disc when the handbrake is applied.

Servo assistance for the braking system is provided by a vacuum-operated servo unit, mounted in-line with the brake master cylinder on the engine compartment bulkhead.

An anti-lock braking system (ABS) is available as an option on all models. Further information on this system will be found in the relevant Sections of this Chapter.

2 Maintenance and inspection

1 At the intervals given in Routine Maintenance at the beginning of this manual, the following service operations should be carried out on the braking system components.
2 Check that the brake hydraulic fluid level in the master cylinder reservoir is maintained between the MAX and MIN marks on the side of the reservoir. If necessary, top up with the specified fluid until the level is up to the MAX mark (photo). Periodically check the strainer in the reservoir filler neck for any signs of foreign matter (photo). If necessary remove the strainer, clean it in fresh brake fluid, blow it clear and refit.
3 The function of the low brake fluid warning lamp on the instrument panel can be checked by depressing the test buttons on top of the master cylinder reservoir (photo). With the ignition switched on, the lamp should illuminate when each button is depressed in turn.
4 Check the condition and thickness of the front and rear disc pads as described in Sections 3 and 7, and the condition of the discs themselves as described in Sections 6 and 10.
5 Check the hydraulic brake pipes and hoses for signs of corrosion, pitting or damage. At the same time check the condition of the handbrake cables, lubricate the exposed cables and linkages and, if necessary, adjust the handbrake as described in Section 11.
6 It is recommended by the manufacturers that the brake hydraulic fluid is renewed once a year, preferably in the spring, as described in Section 21.

3 Front disc pads – inspection and renewal

1 Jack up the front of the car and support it on axle stands. Remove both front roadwheels.
2 Carefully prise up the plastic cover over the disc pad wear sensor by inserting a small screwdriver in the two slots and releasing the lugs (photo).
3 Lift up the plastic cover and withdraw the wear sensor cable connector from its location in the wiring plug (photos).
4 On 1985 models onwards, which have the front flexible brake hose support bracket located on top of the front road spring turret, unscrew the caliper lower guide pin bolt while holding the guide pin with a spanner (photos). Pivot the caliper upwards, taking care not to foul the wear sensor, and secure the raised caliper using string or wire attached to the road spring (photo).
5 On pre-1985 models, undo the upper guide pin bolt and allow the caliper to pivot downwards.
6 Lift out the inner and outer disc pads from their locations in the carrier bracket (photos).
7 Brush the dust and dirt from the caliper, piston, disc and pads, but do not inhale it as it is injurious to health.
8 Rotate the brake disc by hand and scrape away any rust and scale. Carefully inspect the entire surface of the disc, and if there are any signs of cracks, deep scoring or severe abrasions the disc must be machined or renewed (see Section 6). Also inspect the caliper for signs of fluid leaks around the piston, corrosion or other damage. If leaks or damage are apparent, recondition the caliper as described in Section 5.
9 Check the disc pad friction material for wear, cracks, oil or fluid contamination, or other damage. If either of the pads is worn down to the minimum thickness as given in the Specifications, is contaminated, or in any way suspect, renew all four disc pads as a complete set. The pads should also be renewed if the wear sensor connector or the wire is damaged or chafed.
10 If new pads are to be fitted, push the caliper piston back into its bore using a G-clamp or suitable blocks of wood as levers. While doing this, check that brake fluid will not overflow from the master cylinder reservoir, and if necessary use a clean syringe to extract some fluid. **Note:** *Brake fluid is poisonous, and no attempt should be made to syphon the fluid by mouth.*
11 Refit the pads to the carrier, noting that the inner pad carries the brake pad wear sensor.
12 Swing the caliper into position, refit the guide pin bolt and tighten to the specified torque.
13 Coil up the wear sensor wire and insert the connector into the wiring plug. Close the plastic cover to secure the sensor.
14 Depress the brake pedal several times to bring the piston into contact with the pads.
15 Repeat the operations on the other front brake if all four pads are to be renewed.
16 On completion refit the roadwheels and lower the car to the

2.2A Top up the master cylinder reservoir with the specified fluid

2.2B Periodically clean the fluid strainer in the reservoir

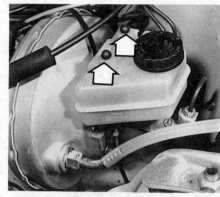

2.3 Low brake fluid warning lamp test buttons (arrowed)

3.2 Disc pad wear sensor plastic cover screwdriver slots (arrowed)

3.3A Lift up the plastic cover ...

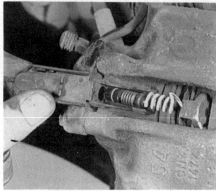

3.3B ... and release the wear sensor cable connector

3.4A Hold the caliper guide pin with a spanner while slackening the guide pin bolt ...

3.4B ... then remove the guide pin bolt from the caliper ...

3.4C ... and pivot the caliper upwards

3.6A Lift out the inner disc pad ...

3.6B ... and outer disc pad from the carrier bracket

ground. Check and if necessary top up the brake fluid in the master
cylinder reservoir.
17 If new pads have been fitted, allow them to bed in by braking
gently from approximately 50 to 25 mph a few times, allowing the
brakes to cool each time. Avoid heavy braking or panic stops if possible
for the first 20 to 50 miles.

4 Front disc caliper – removal and refitting

1   Jack up the front of the car and support it on axle stands. Remove
the appropriate front roadwheel.
2   Remove the dust cover on the caliper bleed screw and connect a
suitable hose or plastic tube to the bleed screw. Place the other end of
the hose in a clean container.
3   Open the bleed screw approximately one turn, then slowly pump
the brake pedal until all the fluid in the master cylinder reservoir primary
circuit compartment has drained into the container. Close the bleed
screw and remove the hose.
4   Carefully prise up the plastic cover over the disc pad wear sensor
on the caliper by inserting a small screwdriver in the two slots and
releasing the lugs.
5   Lift up the plastic cover and withdraw the wear sensor cable
connector from its location in the wiring plug.
6   Undo the retaining bolt and remove the wear sensor wiring plug
from the caliper body.
7   Clean the area around the flexible brake hose-to-rigid pipe union
under the wheel arch, and unscrew the union sufficiently to allow the
hose to swivel in its support bracket.
8   Unscrew the flexible brake hose at the caliper and plug the hose
and caliper after removal.
9   Undo the two bolts securing the disc caliper carrier bracket to the
steering knuckle (photo). **Note:** *The carrier retaining bolts are of the
encapsulated type, and incorporate a thread locking compound which
is activated when the bolt is fitted and tightened. The compound is
ineffective after removal of the bolt and new bolts must therefore be
obtained prior to refitting the caliper.*
10 Slide the caliper assembly off the disc (photo) and remove it from
the car.
11 To refit the caliper, slide it over the disc and align the bolt holes
with those in the steering knuckle.
12 Fit the two new encapsulated bolts and tighten to the specified
torque.
13 Secure the pad wear warning sensor wiring plug to the caliper,
then coil up the sensor wire and insert the connector into the plug.
Close the plastic cover to secure the sensor.
14 Refit the flexible brake hose to the caliper and tighten securely.
15 Engage the other end of the hose in its bracket, ensuring that the
hose is not twisted or kinked, and will not foul any suspension or
wheel arch components under steering or suspension travel. Hold the
hose in this position and tighten the rigid brake pipe union.
16 Refer to Section 21 and bleed the front brake hydraulic circuit, then
refit the roadwheel and lower the car to the ground.

5 Front disc caliper – overhaul

1   Remove the caliper as described in Section 4.
2   Undo the two guide pin bolts and remove the caliper from the
carrier bracket.
3   Remove the heat shielding plate from the piston, then using a foot
pump held against the brake hose union, blow the piston out of the
cylinder.
4   Remove the dust cap from the piston and carefully hook out the
piston seal from the cylinder bore groove using a blunt instrument such
as a knitting needle.
5   Wipe the components with a clean rag, and inspect the piston and
caliper bore for signs of scuffing or corrosion. Light corrosion deposits
on the piston can be removed with a soft brass wire brush, and in the
caliper bore with fine emery paper. However if the components are
heavily corroded or pitted the caliper should be renewed.
6   If the caliper is in a satisfactory condition, clean the components in
brake fluid and dry with a clean lint-free cloth. Also obtain a caliper
repair kit comprising new seals for reassembly.
7   Thoroughly lubricate the piston surface, cylinder bore and the seals

4.9 Disc caliper carrier bracket lower mounting bolt (arrowed)

4.10 Removing the caliper from the disc

with brake cylinder paste, then carefully fit the piston seal to the groove
in the caliper bore.
8   Position the dust cover over the innermost end of the piston so that
the caliper bore sealing lip protrudes beyond the base of the piston.
Using a blunt instrument if necessary, engage the sealing lip of the
dust cover with the groove of the caliper. Now push the piston into the
bore until the other sealing lip of the dust cover can be engaged with
the groove of the piston. Having done this, push the piston fully into its
bore. Ease the piston out again slightly and make sure that the dust
cover lip is correctly seating in the piston groove.
9   Fit the heat shielding plate, ensuring that the locating tags engage
in the piston upper groove.
10 Lift the disc pads off the carrier bracket, then release the dust boots
and remove the two guide pins.
11 Clean the carrier bracket, guide pins and the guide pin bores.
Inspect the guide pins and the carrier bracket for signs of damage and
renew if necessary.
12 If the components are satisfactory, lubricate the guide pins with a
high melting-point brake grease, then refit the pins and dust boots to
the carrier bracket. Use new dust boots if the originals show any signs
of deterioration.
13 Place the disc pads in the carrier with the pad containing the
warning lamp lead on the inside (nearest to the centre of the car with
the carrier installed).

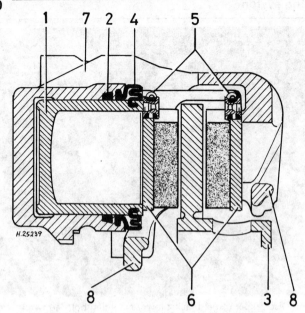

Fig. 9.1 Sectional view of the front disc caliper assembly
(Sec 5)

1 Piston   5 Pad steady springs
2 Piston seal   6 Disc pads
3 Brake disc   7 Caliper body
4 Dust cap   8 Carrier bracket

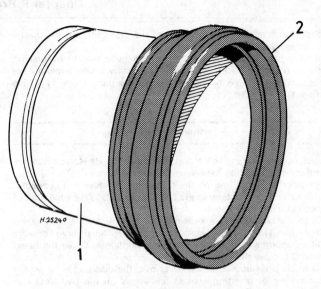

Fig. 9.2 Correct positioning of dust cap over end of
piston prior to fitting (Sec 5)

1 Piston   2 Dust cap

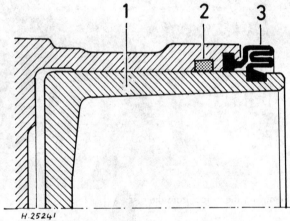

Fig. 9.3 Sectional view through piston and caliper
showing seal and dust cap arrangement (Sec 5)

1 Piston   3 Dust cap
2 Piston seal

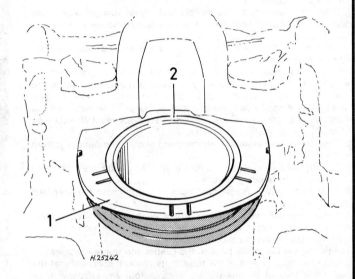

Fig. 9.4 Correct positioning of heat shielding plate (1)
over piston (2) (Sec 5)

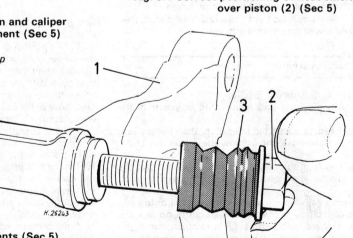

Fig. 9.5 Disc caliper guide pin components (Sec 5)

1 Carrier bracket 3 Dust boot
2 Guide pin

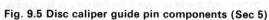

14 Position the caliper assembly over the pads, refit the guide pin bolts and tighten to the specified torque.
15 Refit the caliper to the car as described in Section 4.

6 Front brake disc – inspection, removal and refitting

1 Jack up the front of the car and support it on axle stands. Remove the appropriate front roadwheel.
2 Detach the pad wear warning sensor wire from the cable clip on the suspension strut.
3 Undo the two bolts securing the disc caliper carrier bracket to the steering knuckle. **Note:** *The carrier retaining bolts are of the encapsulated type, and incorporate a thread locking compound which is activated when the bolt is fitted and tightened. The compound is ineffective after removal and new bolts must therefore be obtained prior to refitting the caliper.*
4 Slide the caliper assembly, complete with pads, off the disc and suspend it from a convenient place under the wheel arch using string or wire (photo). Do not let the caliper hang unsupported from the brake hose.
5 Rotate the disc and examine it for cracks, deep scoring or grooving. Light scoring is normal, but if excessive the disc should be removed and ground by a Mercedes-Benz dealer or suitably equipped engineering works, providing that the machining operation will not reduce the disc to below the minimum specified thickness.
6 If brake judder has been experienced, or if the brake pedal travel tends to alter appreciably when driving, check the disc thickness at various points using a micrometer, and also check the disc run-out using a dial gauge if available. (Note that a variation in brake pedal travel may also be caused by incorrectly adjusted front hub bearings.)
7 To remove the disc, undo the socket-headed retaining screw (where fitted) using an Allen key, and withdraw the disc from the locating dowels (photo).
8 Before refitting the disc, remove all traces of rust or any burrs that may be evident on the hub flange or on the inside of the disc hub. Note also that new discs are supplied with a coating of nitro-cellulose paint to protect against corrosion, and this must be removed with a suitable solvent before fitting.
9 Locate the disc over the dowels, then fit and tighten the retaining screw, where applicable.
10 Place the caliper over the disc and fit the two new encapsulated retaining bolts, tightened to the specified torque.
11 Refit the roadwheel and lower the car to the ground.

7 Rear disc pads – inspection and renewal

1 Jack up the rear of the car and support it on axle stands. Remove both rear roadwheels.
2 Using a suitable punch, knock out the two pad retaining pins and remove the crucifix spring retaining plate (photos).
3 Withdraw the two disc pads from the caliper (photos). If the pads are to be re-used mark them suitably, inner and outer, on the backing plate so that they can be refitted in their original positions.
4 Brush the dust and dirt from the caliper, pistons, disc and pads, but do not inhale it as it is injurious to health.
5 Rotate the brake disc by hand and scrape away any rust and scale. Carefully inspect the entire surface of the disc and if there are any signs of cracks, deep scoring or severe abrasions the disc must be machined or renewed (see Section 10). Also inspect the caliper for signs of fluid leaks around the pistons, corrosion or other damage. If leaks or damage are apparent, recondition the caliper as described in Section 9. If the pads were tight in the caliper and hard to remove, scrape away the corrosion which will have caused this along the inner surfaces of the caliper contacted by the edges of the pad backing plates.
6 Check the disc pad friction material for wear, cracks, oil or fluid contamination, or other damage. If either of the pads is worn down to the minimum thickness as given in the Specifications, is contaminated, or in any way suspect, renew all four pads as a complete set.
7 If new pads are to be fitted, push the caliper pistons back into their bores using a G-clamp or small piece of wood as a lever. While doing this, check that brake fluid will not overflow from the master cylinder reservoir, and if necessary use a clean syringe to extract some fluid. **Note:** *Brake fluid is poisonous, and no attempt should be made to syphon the fluid by mouth.*

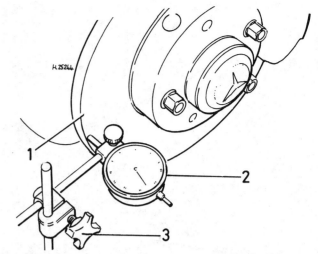

Fig. 9.6 Using a dial gauge to check front brake disc run-out (Sec 6)

1 *Disc*
2 *Dial gauge*
3 *Dial gauge stand*

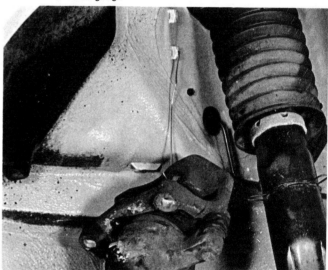

6.4 Suspend the caliper from a convenient place under the wheel arch

6.7 Removing the front brake disc retaining screw

7.2A Knock out the rear disc pad retaining pins ...

7.2B ... and remove the crucifix spring retainer

7.3A Withdraw the inner disc pad ...

7.3B ... and outer disc pad from the caliper

8 Lubricate the edges of the pad backing plates with a high melting-point brake grease and slide the pads into position in the caliper. Take care not to allow any grease to come into contact with the pad friction material.

9 Position the crucifix retaining spring over the pads, then tap in the upper and lower retaining pins.

10 Depress the brake pedal several times to bring the pistons into contact with the pads.

11 Repeat the operations on the other rear brake if all four pads are to be renewed.

12 On completion refit the roadwheels and lower the car to the ground. Check and if necessary top up the brake fluid in the master cylinder reservoir.

13 If new pads have been fitted, allow them to bed in by braking gently from approximately 50 to 25 mph a few times, allowing the brakes to cool each time. Avoid heavy braking or panic stops if possible for the first 20 to 50 miles.

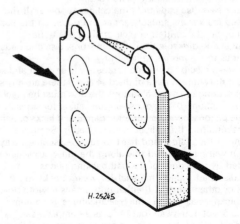

Fig. 9.7 Contact edges of rear disc pad backing plate (arrowed) to be lubricated with high melting-point brake grease prior to fitting (Sec 7)

8 Rear disc caliper – removal and refitting

1 Jack up the rear of the car and support it on axle stands. Remove the appropriate rear roadwheel.

2 Remove the dust cover on the caliper bleed screw and connect a

suitable hose or plastic tube to the bleed screw. Place the other end of the hose in a clean container.

3 Open the bleed screw approximately one turn, then slowly pump the brake pedal until all the fluid in the master cylinder reservoir secondary circuit compartment has drained into the container. Close the bleed screw and remove the hose.

4 Clean the area around the flexible brake hose-to-rigid pipe union under the wheel arch, and unscrew the union sufficiently to allow the hose to swivel in its support bracket.

5 Clean the area around the brake hose union on the caliper and unscrew the hose from the caliper. Plug the hose and caliper after removal.

6 Undo the two bolts securing the caliper to the rear hub carrier and slide the caliper off the disc (photos).
Note: *The caliper retaining bolts are of the encapsulated type, and incorporate a thread locking compound which is activated when the bolt is fitted and tightened. The compound is ineffective after removal of the bolt, and new bolts must therefore be obtained prior to refitting the caliper.*

7 If the caliper is to be renewed it is acceptable to fit a caliper of different manufacture, provided that the piston diameters are the same as the original, and the caliper is approved for use on the model concerned.

8 To refit the caliper slide it over the disc, align the mounting bolt holes and fit two new encapsulated bolts. Tighten the bolts to the specified torque.

9 Refit the flexible brake hose to the caliper and tighten securely.

10 Engage the other end of the hose in its bracket, ensuring that the hose is not twisted or kinked. Hold the hose in this position and tighten the rigid brake pipe union.

11 Refer to Section 21 and bleed the rear brake hyraulic circuit, then refit the roadwheel and lower the car to the ground.

8.6A Rear disc caliper mounting bolts (arrowed)

9 Rear disc caliper – overhaul

1 Remove the disc pads from the caliper as described in Section 7 then remove the caliper from the car as described in Section 8.

2 Using a small screwdriver, hook the two piston dust caps out of their locations in the caliper body grooves.

3 Using a small piece of wood and a G-clamp, retain one of the pistons in place, while blowing out the other piston using a foot pump held against the brake hose union on the side of the caliper.

4 With the first piston removed, seal off the caliper bore using the G-clamp and a flat piece of wood, then blow out the second piston in the same way.

5 Remove the dust caps from the pistons, and hook out the two piston seals from the caliper bore grooves using a blunt instrument such as a knitting needle.

6 Wipe the components with a clean rag and inspect the pistons and caliper bores for signs of scuffing or corrosion. Light corrosion deposits on the pistons can be removed with a soft brass wire brush, and in the caliper bores with fine emery paper. However if the components are heavily corroded or pitted, the caliper should be renewed.

7 If the caliper is in a satisfactory condition, clean the components in brake fluid and dry with a clean lint-free cloth. Also obtain a caliper repair kit comprising new seals for reassembly.

8 Thoroughly lubricate the piston surface, cylinder bore and the seals with brake cylinders paste, then carefully fit the piston seals to the grooves in the caliper bore.

9 Carefully fit the pistons to their respective caliper bores. Note that part of the pad contact face of each piston has been machined away, with the purpose of causing the pad to tip slightly under the action of the piston, thus reducing the possibility of disc pad squeal. With the caliper in its fitted position, the machined portion of each piston must face forwards at approximately 30° to the horizontal (Fig. 9.9). Set each piston in this position as it is inserted into its bore.

10 Engage the inner circumference of the new dust caps into their grooves in the pistons, push the pistons fully into their bores, then engage the outer circumference of the caps in their caliper grooves. Push the dust caps fully into place.

11 Refit the caliper to the car as described in Section 8 then refit the discs pads (Section 7) before bleeding the rear brake circuit (Section 21).

8.6B Removing the caliper from the disc

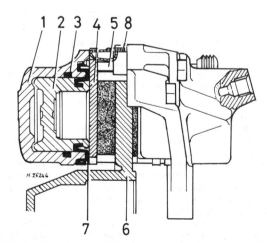

Fig. 9.8 Sectional view of the rear disc caliper assembly (Sec 9)

1	Caliper body	5	Pad retaining pin
2	Piston	6	Brake disc
3	Piston seal	7	Dust cap
4	Disc pad	8	Crucifix retaining spring

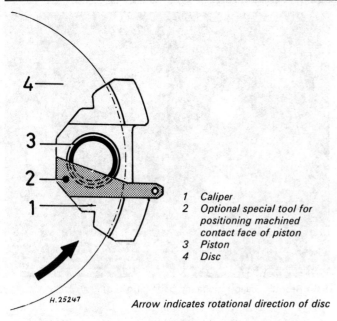

1 Caliper
2 Optional special tool for
   positioning machined
   contact face of piston
3 Piston
4 Disc

Arrow indicates rotational direction of disc

**Fig. 9.9 Correct positioning of piston in rear disc caliper
(Sec 9)**

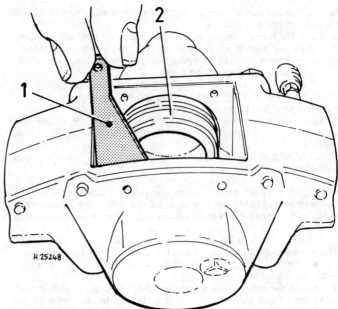

**Fig. 9.10 Using Mercedes tool (1) to position piston (2) in
rear caliper (Sec 9)**

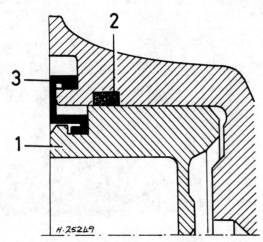

**Fig. 9.11 Sectional view through piston and caliper showing
seal and dust cap arrangement (Sec 9)**

1 Piston   3 Dust cap
2 Piston seal

10 Rear brake disc – inspection, removal and refitting

1   Jack up the rear of the car and support it on axle stands. Remove
the appropriate rear roadwheel.
2   Undo the two bolts securing the disc caliper to the rear hub carrier.
Note: *The caliper retaining bolts are of the encapsulated type, and
incorporate a thread locking compound which is activated when the
bolt is fitted and tightened. The compound is ineffective after removal,
and new bolts must therefore be obtained prior to refitting the caliper.*
3   Slide the caliper assembly, complete with pads, off the disc and
suspend it from the roadspring using string or wire. Do not let the
caliper hang unsupported from the brake hose.
4   Rotate the disc and examine it for cracks, deep scoring or grooving.
Light scoring is normal, but if excessive the disc should be removed
and ground by a Mercedes-Benz dealer or suitably equipped
engineering works, providing that the machining operation will not
reduce the disc to below the minimum specified thickness.
5   If brake judder has been experienced, or if the brake pedal travel
tends to alter appreciably when driving, check the thickness of the disc
at various points using a micrometer, and also check the disc run-out
using a dial gauge if available.

6   To remove the disc, make sure that the handbrake is not applied,
then undo the socket-headed retaining screw (where fitted) (photo).
7   Withdraw the disc from the locating dowel and remove it from the
car (photo). If the disc is tight, tap it from behind using a plastic mallet.
8   With the disc removed, check that the handbrake shoe linings are
not excessively worn and that the inner circumference of the disc hub,
which acts as the handbrake drum, is in a satisfactory condition.
9   Before refitting the disc, remove all traces of rust or any burrs that
may be evident on the hub flange or on the inside of the disc hub. Note
also that new discs are supplied with a coating of nitro-cellulose paint
to protect against corrosion, and this must be removed with a suitable
solvent before fitting.
10 Lightly lubricate the inner face of the disc hub at the wheel hub
contact areas with a high melting-point brake grease, as an aid to
future removal. Take care not to allow the grease to contaminate the
disc face or brake drum.
11 Locate the disc over the hub and secure with the retaining screw,
where applicable.
12 Place the caliper over the disc and fit the two new encapsulated
bolts. Tighten the bolts to the specified torque.
13 Refit the roadwheel and lower the car to the ground.

10.6 Undo the rear disc retaining screw using an Allen key

10.7 Removing the disc from the rear hub

11.4 Handbrake adjusting bolt (arrowed) on compensating mechanism

11.6A Turning the handbrake shoe adjusting wheel using a screwdriver through a wheel bolt hole

11.6B Handbrake shoe adjusting wheel shown with disc removed for clarity

12.2 Using pliers to remove the handbrake shoe hold-down spring

12.4 Disconnecting handbrake shoe upper return spring

11 Handbrake – adjustment

1   Adjustment of the handbrake should normally only be necessary after removal and refitting of any of the handbrake components, or to compensate for wear of the handbrake shoe linings (which will be minimal) or slight stretch of the cables.
2   If the handbrake lever can be pulled up by more than two notches of the ratchet without obtaining a braking effect, proceed as follows.
3   Jack up the rear of the car and support it on axle stands. Remove one wheel bolt from each rear roadwheel.
4   Release the handbrake fully, then from under the car, slacken the handbrake adjusting bolt on the compensating mechanism (photo) until both the cables are slack.
5   Turn the right-hand roadwheel until the bolt hole from which the wheel bolt was removed is positioned to the rear, at approximately 45° above the horizontal.
6   Insert a screwdriver through the bolt hole, and engage the toothed adjusting wheel of the handbrake shoe adjuster (photos).
7   Turn the adjusting wheel using the screwdriver until the shoes are in firm contact with the drum and the wheel can no longer be turned. On the right-hand brake, the screwdriver handle should be moved in a downwards direction to expand the handbrake shoes.
8   Now back off the adjusting wheel just sufficiently to allow the wheel to turn freely without dragging.
9   Repeat paragraphs 5 to 8 on the left-hand side, but in this case move the screwdriver handle in an upwards direction to expand the handbrake shoes.
10 Tighten the handbrake adjusting bolt on the compensating mechanism just enough to remove the slack from the cables.
11 Operate the handbrake lever energetically two or three times, then make further adjustments at the adjusting bolt until both wheels are locked after two clicks of the handbrake lever ratchet. Make sure however that both wheels are free to turn when the handbrake is released.
12 On completion, refit the wheel bolts and wheel trim then lower the car to the ground.

12 Handbrake shoes – removal and refitting

1   Remove the rear brake discs as described in Section 10.
2   Using a pair of needle-nose pliers inserted through one of the holes in the hub flange, depress the brake shoe hold-down spring, turn it through 90° to release it from the backplate and remove the spring (photo). Remove the other shoe hold-down spring in the same way.
3   Lift the brake shoe upper ends out of their locations in the adjusting wheel mechanism and remove the adjusting wheel.
4   Disconnect the upper return spring from both brake shoes and remove the spring (photo).

12.5 Handbrake shoe lower return spring removal

5 Lift the other end of the brake shoes out of the expander mechanism, disconnect the lower return spring (photo) and remove the two brake shoes.

6 Push out the pin securing the handbrake cable to the expander mechanism and remove the expander from the backplate.

7 Wipe clean the handbrake shoes, backplate and the expander and adjusting wheel mechanism. Examine the components for wear, damage or lack of free movement and renew any that are suspect. Renew the shoes if the linings are worn down to the specified minimum or show any sign of oil, grease or fluid contamination.

8 Lightly lubricate the sliding surfaces of the expander mechanism and the threads of the adjusting wheel with a high melting-point brake grease.

9 Refit the expander to the backplate and secure to the handbrake cable with the retaining pin.

10 Place the shoes in position on the backplate and connect the upper return spring to the slots in the brake shoe webs.

11 Set the adjusting wheel in the minimum adjustment position, spread the brake shoe ends and insert the adjusting wheel mechanism so that the adjusting wheel is towards the front of the car.

12 Insert the small hooked end of the lower return spring to the lower brake shoe and the large hooked end to the upper shoe (Fig. 9.13).

13 Spread the brake shoe ends and insert them into their locations in the expander mechanism.

14 Refit the hold-down springs to both brake shoes by depressing and turning each spring through 90°. Ensure that the springs are correctly connected to the backplate.

15 Refit the rear brake discs as described in Section 10 then adjust the handbrake as described in Section 11.

13 Handbrake lever – removal and refitting

1 Jack up the rear of the car and support it on axle stands.

2 From under the car disconnect the return spring at the handbrake cable compensating mechanism.

3 Refer to Chapter 11 and remove the centre console.

4 Release the warning lamp switch from the handbrake lever bracket.

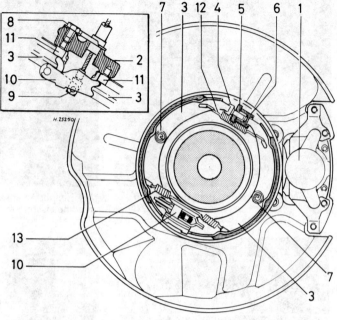

Fig. 9.12 Layout of the left-hand side handbrake shoe and expander mechanism components (Sec 12)

1 Brake caliper	9 Handbrake cable-to-expander mechanism pin
2 Rear hub carrier	
3 Handbrake shoes	10 Expander mechanism link
4 Thrust piece	
5 Adjusting wheel	11 Supporting bolt
6 Reaction member	12 Upper return spring
7 Handbrake shoe hold-down spring	13 Lower return spring
8 Handbrake cable retaining bolt	

Fig. 9.13 Handbrake shoe lower return spring large hooked end (arrowed) (Sec 12)

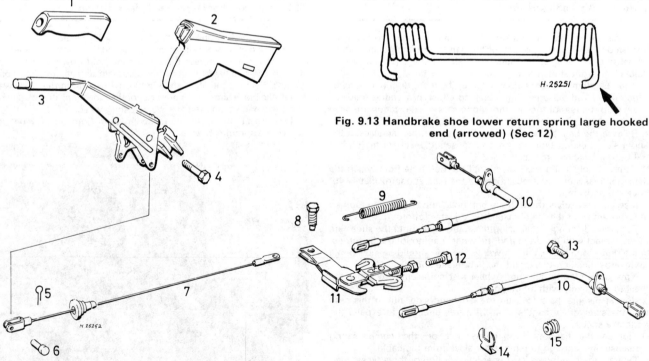

Fig. 9.14 Handbrake lever and cable arrangement (Secs 13 and 14)

1 Lever grip	5 Retaining circlip	9 Return spring	13 Rear cable retaining bolt
2 Lever cover	6 Clevis pin	10 Rear cables	14 Support bracket clip
3 Lever assembly	7 Front cable	11 Compensating mechanism	15 Grommet
4 Lever retaining bolt	8 Front cable retaining bolt	12 Adjusting bolt	

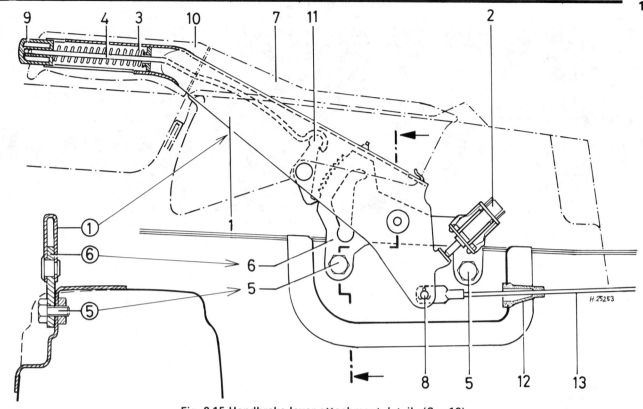

Fig. 9.15 Handbrake lever attachment details (Sec 13)

1 Handbrake lever	5 Retaining bolt	8 Clevis pin	11 Pawl
2 Warning lamp switch	6 Lever bracket	9 Push button	12 Grommet
3 Return spring	7 Lever cover	10 Lever grip	13 Front handbrake cable
4 Lever operating rod			

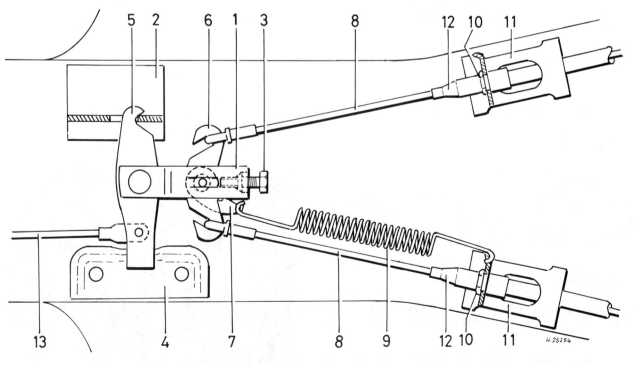

Fig. 9.16 Handbrake cable and compensating mechanism (Sec 14)

1 Adjusting bracket	5 Intermediate lever	8 Rear cables	11 Support bracket
2 Locating bracket	6 Compensating lever	9 Return spring	12 Grommet
3 Adjusting bolt	7 Spring clip	10 Retaining clip	13 Front cable
4 Guide bracket			

14.2 Handbrake front cable-to-intermediate lever retaining bolt (arrowed)

14.6 Handbrake rear cable-to-hub carrier retaining bolt (arrowed)

14.12 Handbrake rear cable-to-support bracket retaining clip (arrowed)

5   Undo the two bolts securing the lever assembly to the floor and lift up the lever.
6   Extract the retaining circlip and remove the clevis pin securing the front handbrake cable to the lever.
7   Remove the lever assembly from inside the car.
8   Refitting is the reverse sequence to removal. Check and if necessary adjust the handbrake as described in Section 11 on completion.

14 Handbrake cables – removal and refitting

Front cable
1   Remove the handbrake lever as described in Section 13.
2   Undo the bolt securing the front cable to the intermediate lever on the compensating mechanism under the car (photo).
3   Withdraw the cable through the grommet on the underbody and remove the cable from under the car.
4   Refitting is the reverse sequence to removal. Check and it necessary adjust the handbrake as described in Section 11 on completion.

Rear cables
5   Remove the handbrake shoes on the relevant side as described in Section 12.
6   Undo the bolt securing the handbrake cable to the rear hub carrier (photo) and withdraw the cable.
7   Disconnect the compensating mechanism return spring at the cable support bracket.
8   Slacken the handbrake adjusting bolt fully (photo 11.4).
9   Undo the bolt securing the front cable to the intermediate lever on the compensating mechanism.
10 Withdraw the hooked end of the intermediate lever from its locating bracket.
11 Disconnect the rear cable eye from the compensating lever.
12 Extract the retaining spring clip and withdraw the rear cable from its support bracket (photo) and guides.
13 Remove the cable from under the car.
14 Refitting is the reverse sequence to removal.

15 Brake pedal – removal and refitting

1   The brake and clutch pedals share a common bracket and pivot shaft assembly. Removal and refitting procedures for both pedals are given in Chapter 5.

16 Brake light switch – adjustment, removal and refitting

1   The brake lights are operated by a mechanical switch located on the brake pedal mounting bracket. The switch should activate the brake lights after a pedal movement of 3 to 20 mm (0.12 to 0.78 in).
2   If adjustment is necessary, remove the trim panel under the facia on the driver's side for access to the switch.

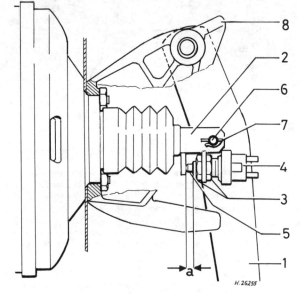
Fig. 9.17 Brake light switch attachment details (Sec 16)

1 Brake pedal
2 Servo limit pushrod
3 Adjusting locknuts
4 Brake light switch (adjustable type)
5 Plunger
6 Clevis pin
7 Retaining wire clip
8 Pedal bracket
a = 3 to 20 mm (0.12 to 0.78 in)

16.5 Brake light switch wiring plug (arrowed)

3   If the switch is provided with two locknuts for adjustment, slacken both locknuts and reposition the switch in its bracket as necessary. Tighten the locknuts and check the brake light operation. Repeat this procedure until the lights illuminate within the specified range of pedal travel.

4   If the switch does not incorporate adjusting locknuts, then it will be necessary carefully to bend the contact plate on the brake pedal slightly if the brake lights do not illuminate within the specified range of pedal travel.

5   To remove the switch disconnect the wiring plug (photo), then unscrew the inner locknut, or depress and turn the switch body through 90° according to the type of switch fitted.

6   Refitting is the reverse sequence to removal.

17 Master cylinder – removal and refitting

1   Remove the master cylinder reservoir filler cap, place a piece of polythene over the filler neck and refit the cap. This will minimise brake fluid loss during subsequent operations.

2   Using a small screwdriver, release the retaining lugs on the fluid level warning lamp wiring plug and disconnect the plug from the reservoir.

3   On manual transmission models, disconnect the clutch master cylinder fluid supply hose from the side of the reservoir. Plug or cap the outlet in the reservoir and the hose end as soon as the hose is released.

4   Unscrew the union nuts and withdraw the two brake pipe ends from the master cylinder body (photo). Plug or cap the cylinder orifices and pipe ends after removal. Carefully ease the brake pipe at the front of the cylinder, slightly to one side to provide clearance for removal of the master cylinder.

5   Undo the two nuts securing the master cylinder to the servo unit and withdraw the cylinder squarely off the studs. Do not tilt or twist the cylinder as it is removed, otherwise the lugs securing the pushrod in the servo unit may be damagd.

6   Recover the master cylinder-to-servo unit sealing ring, noting that the sealing ring must be renewed prior to refitting.

7   Refitting is the reverse sequence to removal. Ensure that the sealing ring is correctly located in its groove in the cylinder body, and bleed the brake hydraulic system as described in Section 21 after fitting.

18 Master cylinder – overhaul

1   Remove the master cylinder from the car as described in Section 17.

2   Remove the reservoir filler cap and pour the brake fluid into a container.

3   Carefully prise the reservoir out of the two rubber seals, then withdraw the seals from the cylinder ports.

4   Push the piston in slightly and extract the cylinder pin from the reservoir front port using needle-nose pliers.

5   Maintain pressure on the piston, and extract the piston retaining circlip from the end of the master cylinder bore using circlip pliers. Where fitted, remove the washer and O-ring seal from the cylinder.

6   Withdraw the two piston assemblies, together with their seals and springs, from the cylinder bore. Tap the end of the cylinder on a block of wood if necessary to eject the inner piston.

7   Examine the master cylinder bore for signs of scoring, wear ridges or corrosion, and if evident renew the complete master cylinder assembly. If the cylinder body is satisfactory, obtain a repair kit which consists of new pistons with their seals in place, and new O-rings and circlips as applicable.

8   Prior to reassembly, clean the cylinder body thoroughly in brake fluid and dry with a clean lint-free cloth.

9   Lubricate the cylinder bore thoroughly with clean brake fluid and insert the inner piston assembly with reference to Fig. 9.19. The guide slot on the piston must remain vertical during fitting. If necessary, turn the piston by means of a screwdriver engaged with the notch in the piston end.

10   Using a screwdriver or mandrel, push the piston in against spring pressure and fit the cylinder pin, chamfered end first, through the reservoir port. When fitted, the pin must not protrude by more than 2.0 to 3.0 mm (0.07 to 0.12 in).

17.4 Brake pipe union locations at the master cylinder (arrowed)

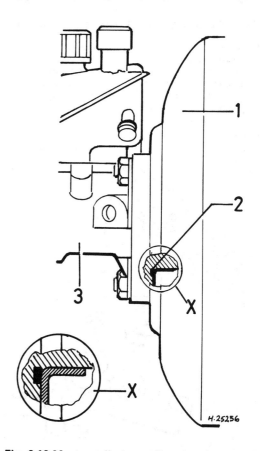

Fig. 9.18 Master cylinder sealing ring details (Sec 17)

1   *Servo limit*   3   *Master cylinder*
2   *Sealing ring*

11   Introduce the second piston into the cylinder bore, fit the O-ring and washer (where applicable), then push the piston down and fit the retaining circlip.

12   Lubricate the reservoir seals and fit them to the cylinder ports.

13   Insert one of the reservoir outlets into its seal, push down and engage the second outlet. Ensure that the reservoir outlets are fully engaged with their respective seals and the reservoir is sitting squarely.

14   The assembled master cylinder can now be refitted to the car as described in Section 17.

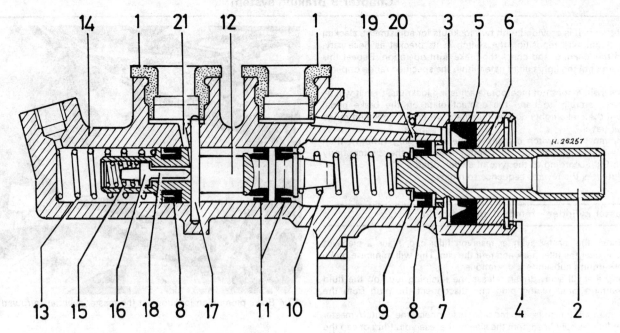

Fig. 9.19 Sectional view of the Bendix master cylinder – Girling and Teves units similar (Sec 18)

1 Reservoir seals	7 Filling disc	12 Inner piston	17 Cylinder pin
2 Outer piston	8 Piston seal	13 Compression spring	18 Valve pin
3 Washer	9 Supporting ring	14 Cylinder body	19 Filling bore
4 Circlip	10 Compression spring	15 Valve spring	20 Compensating bore
5 Secondary seal	11 Separating sleeve	16 Valve seal	21 Filling and compensating
6 Bush			bore

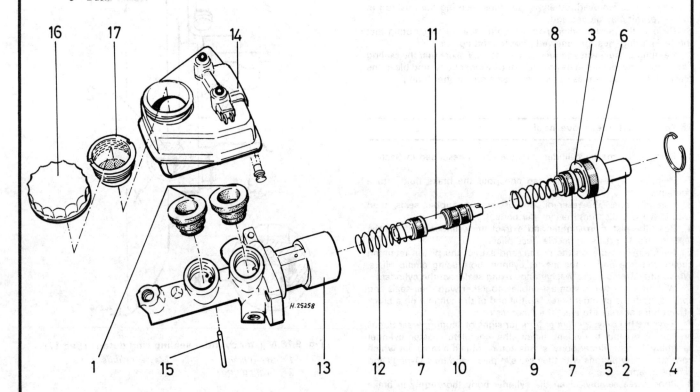

Fig. 9.20 Exploded view of the Bendix master cylinder components – Girling and Teves units similar (Sec 18)

1 Reservoir seals	6 Bush	10 Separating sleeve	14 Reservoir
2 Outer piston	7 Piston seal	11 Inner piston	15 Cylinder pin
3 Washer	8 Supporting ring	12 Compression spring	16 Filler cap
4 Circlip	9 Compression spring	13 Cylinder body	17 Strainer
5 Secondary seal			

19 Vacuum servo unit – removal and refitting

1 Remove the master cylinder as described in Section 17.
2 Undo the union nut and remove the vacuum hose from the front face of the servo unit.
3 Remove the trim panel under the facia on the driver's side.
4 Disconnect the brake pedal return spring at the pedal (photo).
5 Pull out the retaining wire clip, then withdraw the clevis pin securing the servo unit pushrod to the brake pedal.
6 Undo the four nuts securing the servo unit to the bulkhead and pedal bracket, then remove the servo from the engine compartment.
7 Refitting is a reversal of removal.

20 Hydraulic brake pipes and hoses – removal and refitting

1 Before removing a brake pipe or hose, unscrew the master cylinder reservoir filler cap, place a piece of polythene over the filler neck and refit the cap. This will minimise brake fluid loss during subsequent operations.
2 To remove a rigid brake pipe, unscrew the union nuts at each end, release the pipe from its retaining clips and withdraw the pipe from the car. Refitting is a reversal of removal.
3 To remove a flexible brake hose, unscrew the union nut securing the rigid brake pipe to the end of the flexible hose, while holding the hose end stationary. Remove the retaining clip and withdraw the hose from its bracket. Unscrew the other end of the hose from the brake caliper, release any retaining clips and remove the hose from the car. Refitting is a reversal of removal.
4 Bleed the hydraulic system as described in Section 21 after fitting a rigid pipe or flexible hose, and whenever a pipe or hose union is disconnected.

21 Hydraulic system – bleeding

1 The correct functioning of the brake hydraulic system is only possible after removal of all air from the components and circuit; this is achieved by bleeding the system. Note that only clean unused brake fluid, which has remained unshaken for at least 24 hours, must be used.
2 If there is any possibility of incorrect fluid being used in the system, the brake lines and components must be completely flushed with uncontaminated fluid and new seals fitted to the components.
3 *Never reuse brake fluid which has been bled from the system.*
4 During the procedure, do not allow the level of brake fluid to drop more than halfway down the reservoir.
5 Before starting work, check that all pipes and hoses are secure, unions tight and bleed screws closed. Take great care not to allow brake fluid to come into contact with the car paintwork, otherwise the finish will be seriously damaged. Wash off any spilled fluid immediately with cold water.
6 There are a number of one-man, do-it-yourself, brake bleeding kits currently available from motor accessory shops. Always follow the instructions supplied with the kit. If one of these kits is not available, it will be necessary to gather together a clean jar and suitable length of clear plastic tubing which is a tight fit over the bleed screw, and also to engage the help of an assistant.
7 If brake fluid has been lost from the master cylinder due to a leak in the system, ensure that the cause is traced and rectified before proceeding further.
8 If the hydraulic system has only been partially disconnected and suitable precautions were taken to prevent further loss of fluid it should only be necessary to bleed that part of the system (ie both front brakes or both rear brakes).
9 If the complete system is to be bled, then it should be done in the following sequence:

    (1) Left-hand rear brake
    (2) Right-hand rear brake
    (3) Left-hand front brake
    (4) Right-hand front brake

Note: *If the system is being bled after removal and refitting of the master cylinder, it may also be necessary to bleed the clutch hydraulic*

19.4 Brake pedal return spring attachment (arrowed)

system on manual transmission models. This should be done as described in Chapter 5.

Bleeding – two-man method
10 Gather together a clean jar and a length of rubber or plastic bleed tubing which will fit the bleed screw tightly. The help of an assistant will be required.
11 Take great care not to spill onto the paintwork as it will act as a paint stripper. If any is spilled, wash it off at once with cold water.
12 Clean around the bleed screw on the left-hand rear caliper and attach the bleed tube to the screw.
13 Check that the master cylinder reservoir is topped up, and then destroy the vacuum in the brake servo by giving several applications of the brake foot pedal.
14 Immerse the open end of the bleed tube in the jar, which should contain 50 to 76 mm (2 to 3 in) of hydraulic fluid. The jar should be positioned about 300 mm (12.0 in) above the bleed screw to prevent any possibility of air entering the system down the threads of the bleed screw when it is slackened.
15 Open the bleed screw half a turn and have your assistant depress the brake pedal to the floor and then slowly remove his foot to allow the pedal to return. Tighten the bleed screw at the end of each downstroke to prevent expelled air and fluid being drawn back into the system.
16 Observe the submerged end of the tube in the jar. When air bubbles cease to appear, fully tighten the bleed screw when the pedal is being held down by your assistant.
17 Top up the fluid reservoir. It must be kept topped up throughout the bleeding operations. If the connecting holes in the master cylinder are exposed at any time due to low fluid level, then air will be drawn into the system and work will have to start all over again.
18 Repeat the operations on the rest of the system in the sequence given in paragraph 9 (assuming that the whole system is being bled).
19 On completion, remove the bleed tube. Discard the fluid which has been bled from the system unless it is required for bleed jar purposes, **never** use it for filling the system.

Bleeding – with one-way valve
20 There are a number of one-man brake bleeding kits currently available from motor accessory shops. It is recommended that one of these kits should be used whenever possible as they greatly simplify the bleeding operation and also reduce the risk of expelled air or fluid being drawn back into the system.
21 Connect the outlet tube of the bleeder device to the bleed screw and then open the screw half a turn. Depress the brake pedal to the floor and slowly release it. The one-way valve in the device will prevent expelled air from returning to the system at the completion of each stroke. Repeat this operation until clean hydraulic fluid, free from air bubbles, can be seen coming through the tube. Tighten the bleed screw and remove the tube.

22 Repeat the procedure on the remaining bleed screws in the order described in paragraph 9. Remember to keep the master cylinder reservoir full.

Bleeding – with pressure bleeding kit
23 These are available from motor accessory shops, and are usually operated by air pressure from the spare tyre.
24 By connecting a pressurised container to the master cylinder fluid reservoir, bleeding is then carried out by simply opening each bleed screw in turn and allowing the fluid to run out, rather like turning on a tap, until no air bubbles are visible in the fluid being expelled.
25 Using this system, the large reserve of fluid provides a safeguard against air being drawn into the master cylinder during the bleeding operations.
26 This method is particularly effective when bleeding 'difficult' systems, or when bleeding the entire system at routine fluid renewal.

All methods
27 When bleeding is completed, check and top up the fluid level in the reservoir if necessary, then refit the filler cap.
28 Check the feel of the brake pedal. If it feels at all spongy, air must still be present in the system, and further bleeding is required.
29 Discard brake fluid which has been expelled from the system. It is almost certain to be contaminated with air and moisture, making it unsuitable for further use. Clean fluid should always be stored in an airtight container as it is hygroscopic (absorbs moisture readily). Any appreciable moisture content lowers its boiling point and could affect braking performance under severe conditions.

22 Anti-lock braking system – description and operation

Mercedes-Benz 190 models covered by this manual are available with an anti-lock braking system (ABS) as a factory-fitted option. The system is used in conjunction with the normal braking system to provide greater stability, improved steering control and shorter stopping distances under adverse braking conditions.

The roadwheels are provided with wheel speed sensors which monitor the wheel rotational speed. A separate sensor is used for each front wheel, while at the rear a single sensor monitors the speed of both rear wheels. The sensors consist of a magnetic core and coil and are mounted at a predetermined distance from a toothed rotor. The rotors for the front wheels are machined into the front wheel hubs, with the sensors mounted on the steering knuckles. At the rear, the rotor is pressed onto the final drive differential pinion with the sensor located in the side of the final drive housing. When each rotor turns it alters the magnetic field of the sensor, thus inducing an alternating voltage, the frequency of which varies according to wheel speed.

Signals from the wheel speed sensors are sent to an electronic control unit which can accurately determine whether a wheel is accelerating or decelerating in relation to a reference value. Information from the electronic control unit is sent to the hydraulic modulator, which contains three solenoids, one for each front wheel and one for both rear wheels. The solenoids each operate one inlet and one exhaust valve, and all work independently of each other in three distinct phases.

Pressure build-up phase: The solenoid inlet valves are open, and

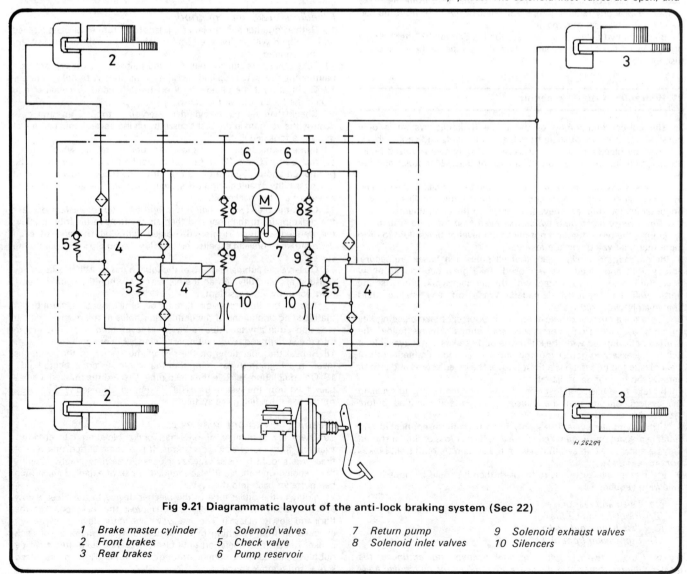

Fig 9.21 Diagrammatic layout of the anti-lock braking system (Sec 22)

1 Brake master cylinder	4 Solenoid valves	7 Return pump	9 Solenoid exhaust valves
2 Front brakes	5 Check valve	8 Solenoid inlet valves	10 Silencers
3 Rear brakes	6 Pump reservoir		

brake pressure from the master cylinder is applied directly to the brake calipers.

Constant pressure phase: The solenoid inlet and exhaust valves are closed and brake pressure at the calipers is maintained at a constant level even though master cylinder pressure may increase.

Pressure reduction phase: The solenoid inlet valve is closed to prevent further brake pressure reaching the caliper and, in addition, the exhaust valve is open to reduce existing pressure and release the brake. Fluid is returned to the master cylinder in this phase via the return pump in the hydraulic modulator.

The braking cycle for one wheel is therefore as follows, and will be the same for each front brake or both rear brakes, although independently.

Wheel rotational speed is measured by the wheel speed sensors and processed by the electronic control unit. By comparing the signals received from each wheel the control unit can determine a reference speed, and detect any variation from this speed, which would indicate a locking brake. Should a lock-up condition be detected, the control unit initiates the constant pressure phase and no further increase in brake pressure is applied to the affected brake. If the lock-up condition is still detected the pressure reduction phase is initiated to allow the wheel to turn. The control unit returns to the constant pressure phase until the wheel rotational speed exceeds a predetermined value, then the cycle repeats with the control unit re-initiating the pressure build-up phase. This control cycle is continuously and rapidly repeated until the brake pedal is released or the car comes to a stop.

Additional circuitry within the electronic control unit monitors the functioning of the system and informs the driver of any fault condition by means of a warning light. Should a fault occur, the system switches off allowing normal braking, without ABS, to continue.

23 Anti-lock braking system – precautions

Due to the complex nature of the anti-lock braking system the following precautions must be observed when carrying out maintenance and repair work to cars so equipped.
1   Whenever the battery terminals are disconnected, ensure that the terminal clamps are securely tightened when refitting.
2   Disconnect the electronic control unit wiring plug before using any electric welding equipment on the car.
3   Ensure that the battery earth terminal is disconnected before removing the hydraulic modulator.
4   Avoid subjecting the electronic control unit to prolonged high temperatures such as those experienced in a paint spray oven. Maximum acceptable temperatures are 95°C (203°F) for very short periods or 85°C (185°F) for up to two hours.

5   After any general maintenance or simple repair operation such as brake pad renewal, brake disc renewal, handbrake cable adjustment or renewal, or any work not directly involving the ABS components, road test the car and check that the ABS warning light does not come on when the vehicle reaches a speed of 4 mph (6 kph). If the warning light illuminates there is a fault in the system and the advice of a Mercedes-Benz dealer should be sought.
6   If any of the ABS components are removed, refitted, renewed or in any way disturbed, the operation of the system must be checked by a Mercedes-Benz dealer on completion.

24 Anti-lock braking system components – removal and refitting

Note: *Before proceeding, refer to Section 33.*

Hydraulic modulator
1   The hydraulic modulator is located at the front left-hand side of the engine compartment.
2   To remove the modulator control relays, disconnect the battery negative terminal, then undo the screw and lift off the modulator cover. Remove the relays by pulling them upwards out of their locations. The large relay controls the return pump operation, and the small relay controls the solenoid valve operation. Refitting is the reversal of removal.
3   To remove the complete modulator unit, first disconnect the battery negative terminal, then undo the screw and lift off the modulator cover.
4   Mark each brake pipe at the modulator to aid identification when refitting. Unscrew the pipe unions and withdraw the brake pipes from the modulator. Immediately plug the pipe ends and modulator orifices to minimise brake fluid loss.
5   Disconnect the earth strap from the return pump motor.
6   Undo the wiring multi-plug clamp screws and disconnect the wiring plug.
7   Slacken the modulator mounting retaining nuts and remove the unit from its mounting bracket. Do not attempt to dismantle the modulator as it is a sealed unit and no repairs are possible.
8   Refitting is the reverse sequence to removal. Bleed the brake hydraulic system as described in Section 21, then have the ABS operation checked by a Mercedes-Benz dealer.

Electronic control unit
9   The electronic control unit is located in the engine compartment, behind the battery.
10 Disconnect the battery negative terminal.

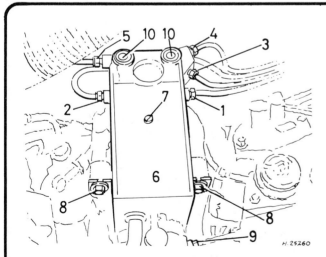

Fig. 9.22 Connections and attachments at the hydraulic modulator – anti-lock braking system (Sec 24)

1 to 5 Brake pipe connections	*9 Earth strap*
6 Modulator cover	*10 Valve plugs – Do not*
7 Cover retaining screw	*unscrew*
8 Mounting nuts	

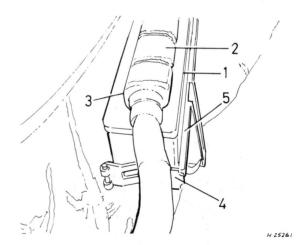

Fig. 9.23 Electronic control unit attachments – anti-lock braking system (Sec 24)

1 Electronic control unit	*4 Mounting bracket retainer*
2 Wiring plug	*5 Mounting bracket*
3 Spring tag	

11 Release the mounting bracket retainer and withdraw the control unit from its bracket.
12 Disconnect the control unit wiring plug by depressing the spring tag at the cable end, lift the plug up at the cable end, then disengage the tab at the other end.
13 Refitting is the reverse sequence to removal, but ensure that the wiring plug engages with an audible click from the spring tag.
14 Have the ABS operation checked by a Mercedes-Benz dealer on completion.

Front wheel speed sensors
15 Disconnect the battery negative terminal, then jack up the front of the car and support it on axle stands.
16 Remove the appropriate front roadwheel.
17 Withdraw the speed sensor wiring connector from its holder in the engine compartment adjacent to the suspension strut mounting turret. Disconnect the wiring at the connector.
18 Release the wiring from its support bracket under the wheel arch, and pull the wiring and grommet through from the engine compartment.
19 Release the wiring from the clips on the steering knuckle and suspension strut.
20 Using an Allen key, undo the two socket-headed retaining bolts and remove the wheel speed sensor from the steering knuckle. Recover the rubber grommet from the sensor body.

21 Refitting is the reverse sequence to removal. Ensure that there are no metallic foreign bodies on the sensor probe, and that the rubber grommet is in place prior to fitting.
22 Have the ABS operation checked by a Mercedes-Benz dealer on completion.

Rear wheel speed sensor
23 Disconnect the battery negative terminal.
24 Remove the rear seat cushion and backrest, referring to Chapter 11 if necessary.
25 Release the wiring from the holder bracket under the rear seat, and disconnect the wiring at the connector. Slacken the clip screws and release the wiring from the clips in the rear seat area.
26 Jack up the rear of the car and support it on axle stands.
27 From under the car, release the grommets in the car floor and rear subframe, then pull the wiring down and out of the car.
28 Using an Allen key, undo the socket-headed retaining bolt and remove the wheel speed sensor from the final drive differential housing.
29 Refitting is the reverse sequence to removal, but ensure that there are no metallic foreign bodies on the sensor probe prior to fitting. Renew the O-ring seal on the sensor body if it is in any way damaged.
30 Have the ABS operation checked by a Mercedes-Benz dealer on completion.

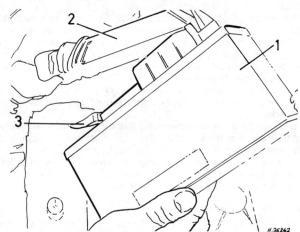

Fig. 9.24 Electronic control unit wiring plug removal – anti-lock braking system (Sec 24)

1 Electronic control unit   3 Spring tag
2 Wiring plug

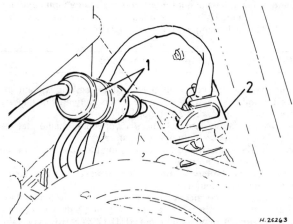

Fig. 9.25 Front wheel speed sensor wiring connector location – anti-lock braking system (Sec 24)

1 Wiring connector   2 Holder in engine compartment

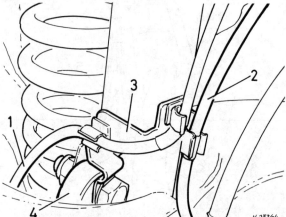

Fig. 9.26 Wheel speed sensor wiring clips on steering knuckle – anti-lock braking system (Sec 24)

1 Wiring to wheel speed sensor   3 Cable clip bracket
2 Wiring to disc pad wear sensor   4 Steering knuckle

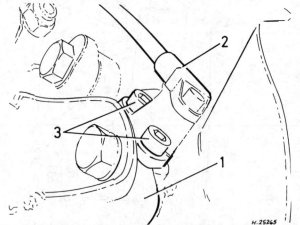

Fig. 9.27 Wheel speed sensor attachment at the steering knuckle – anti-lock braking system (Sec 24)

1 Steering knuckle   3 Retaining bolts
2 Wheel speed sensor

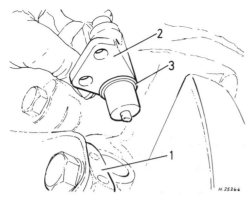

Fig. 9.28 Wheel speed sensor fitting details – anti-lock braking system (Sec 24)

1   Steering knuckle
2   Wheel speed sensor
3   Rubber grommet on sensor body

Fig. 9.30 Sectional view of the rear wheel speed sensor in the final drive differential housing – anti-lock braking system (Sec 24)

1   Wheel speed sensor
2   Retaining bolt
3   O-ring
4   Toothed rotor
5   Differential pinion
6   Final drive differential housing

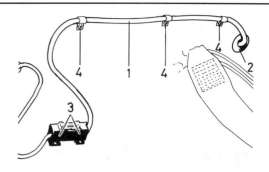

Fig. 9.29 Rear wheel speed sensor wiring attachments under rear seat – anti-lock braking system (Sec 24)

1   Wiring
2   Grommet
3   Wiring connector and holder
4   Clip retaining screws

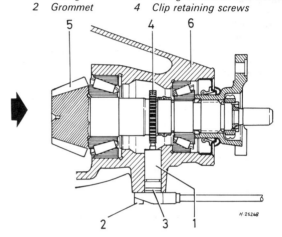

25 Fault diagnosis – braking system

Note: *Fault diagnosis on the anti-lock braking system (where fitted) should be entrusted to a suitably equipped Mercedes-Benz dealer due to the need for special gauges and test equipment.*

Symptom	Reason(s)
Excessive pedal travel	Air in hydraulic system Faulty master cylinder Excessive brake disc run-out Incorrectly adjusted front hub bearings
Brake pedal feels spongy	Air in hydraulic system Faulty master cylinder
Judder felt through brake pedal or steering wheel when braking	Excessive run-out or distortion of brake discs Disc pads excessively worn Disc caliper mounting bolts loose Worn front caliper guide pins Wear in suspension or steering components – see Chapter 10
Excessive pedal pressure required to stop car	Faulty vacuum servo unit Disc caliper piston(s) seized Disc pad linings worn or contaminated Incorrect grade of disc pads fitted Primary or secondary hydraulic circuit failure
Brakes pull to one side	Disc pad linings worn or contaminated Disc caliper piston seized Disc pads renewed on one side only Tyre, steering or suspension defect – see Chapter 10
Brakes binding	Disc caliper piston seized Handbrake incorrectly adjusted Handbrake cable or mechanism seized Faulty master cylinder

Chapter 10 Suspension and steering

Contents

Specifications

Front suspension

Type .... Independent, with MacPherson struts and separate coil springs, wide-based lower wishbones and anti-roll bar

Hub bearing endfloat .... 0.01 to 0.02 mm (0.0004 to 0.0007 in)

Hub bearing lubricant .... Mercedes-Benz high temperature bearing grease (Duckhams LB 10)

Rear suspension

Type .... Independent, with multiple locating struts, coil springs, telescopic shock absorbers and anti-roll bar

Steering

Type .... Power-assisted, recirculating ball

Power steering fluid .... Mercedes-Benz approved ATF (Duckhams Fleetmatic A)

Power steering reservoir capacity .... 0.6 litre (1.1 Imp pints)

Front wheel alignment

Toe setting .... 0°20′ ± 10′ (2.5 ± 1.0 mm) toe-in

Camber .... $0°\ {}^{+10′}_{-20′}$

Maximum camber variation between sides .... 0°20′

Castor .... 10°30′ ± 30′

Maximum castor variation between sides .... 0°30′

Rear wheel alignment

Toe setting .... $0°25′\ {}^{+10′}_{-5′}$ $(3.0\ {}^{+1.0}_{-0.5}\ mm)$

Camber .... −1°30′ (at kerb weight, vehicle level)

Track angle variation per wheel at 60 mm (2.36 in) suspension travel ... $0°05′\ {}^{+0′}_{-10′}$ toe-out

Maximum variation between sides .... 0°05′

Wheels

Type .... Pressed steel or light alloy

Size:

    Early models .... 5J x 14

    Later models .... 6J x 15

Tyres

Tyre sizes:

Early models with 14 in wheels:

190	175/70 R14 84 T
190 E	175/70 R14 84 H
Later models with 15 in wheels	185/65 R15 87 H

Tyre pressures:	Front	Rear
Normally laden:		
175/70 R14 84T	1.8 bar (26 lbf/in²)	2.0 bar (29 lbf/in²)
175/70 R14 84H	2.0 bar (29 lbf/in²)	2.2 bar (32 lbf/in²)
185/65 R15 87H	2.0 bar (29 lbf/in²)	2.2 bar (32 lbf/in²)
Fully loaded:		
175/70 R14 84T	2.0 bar (29 lbf/in²)	2.3 bar (33 lbf/in²)
175/70 R14 84H	2.2 bar (32 lbf/in²)	2.5 bar (36 lbf/in²)
185/65 R15 87H	2.2 bar (32 lbf/in²)	2.5 bar (36 lbf/in²)

Torque wrench settings

	Nm	lbf ft
Front suspension		
Front hub retaining nut socket-headed bolt	12	9
Disc caliper carrier bracket to steering knuckle	115	85
Brake disc retaining screw	10	7
Disc shield to steering knuckle	10	7
Suspension strut-to-steering knuckle lower bolts	110	81
Suspension strut-to-steering knuckle upper nut and bolt	75	55
Steering knuckle to wishbone balljoint pinch-bolt and nut	125	92
Steering arm-to-steering knuckle bolts	80	59
Suspension strut upper mounting to body	20	15
Suspension strut spindle to upper mounting	60	44
Front wishbone inner mounting bolts	120	89
Anti-roll bar clamp nuts	20	15
Rear suspension		
Rear subframe front and rear mountings	70	52
Camber strut to rear subframe	70	52
Camber strut to hub carrier	40	30
Pulling strut inner mounting	70	52
Pulling strut to hub carrier	40	30
Pushing strut to rear subframe	70	52
Pushing strut to hub carrier	45	33
Track rod to rear subframe	70	52
Track rod to hub carrier	35	26
Rear disc caliper to hub carrier	50	37
Spring support arm inner mounting	70	52
Spring support arm to hub carrier	120	89
Anti-roll bar to spring support arm	120	89
Anti-roll bar clamp retaining nuts	20	15
Shock absorber lower mounting bolt	45	33
Driveshaft retaining collar nut	280 to 320	207 to 236
Steering		
Steering wheel retaining bolt	80	59
Steering flexible coupling pinch-bolts	25	18
Steering column mounting bolts	20	15
Power steering gear-to-chassis member bolts	75	55
Track rod and drag link balljoint retaining nuts	35	26
Steering track rod inner clamp	10	7
Power steering high pressure hose unions	30	22
Power steering return hose unions	40	30
Steering damper retaining nuts	50	37
Power steering pump pulley bolts	30	22
Power steering pump mounting bolts	25	18
Steering idler arm retaining nut	95	70
Wheels		
Wheel bolts	110	81

1 General description

The independent front suspension is of the MacPherson strut type, incorporating single-tube telescopic damper (shock absorber) struts and separately-mounted coil springs, located inboard and to the front of each strut. Wide-based lower wishbones provide lateral and longitudinal location of each strut assembly, and an anti-roll bar is used to minimise body roll.

The independent rear suspension is of a unique multi-link arrangement, which comprises four individual upper and lower struts for lateral control, and a track rod to control fore-and-aft movement. Coil springs and telescopic shock absorbers are used in conjunction with an anti-roll bar, and the complete rear suspension assembly, including the final drive differential, is mounted on a subframe attached to the vehicle underbody.

The steering system is of the recirculating ball type, incorporating track rods, drag link, idler assembly and steering damper unit. Power-assistance is standard on all UK models.

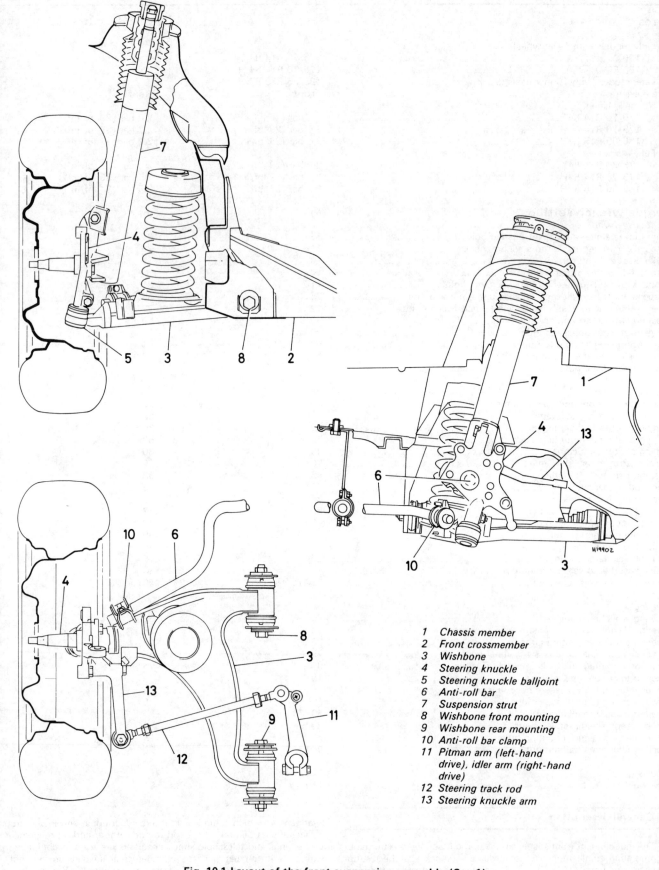

Fig. 10.1 Layout of the front suspension assembly (Sec 1)

1 Chassis member
2 Front crossmember
3 Wishbone
4 Steering knuckle
5 Steering knuckle balljoint
6 Anti-roll bar
7 Suspension strut
8 Wishbone front mounting
9 Wishbone rear mounting
10 Anti-roll bar clamp
11 Pitman arm (left-hand drive), idler arm (right-hand drive)
12 Steering track rod
13 Steering knuckle arm

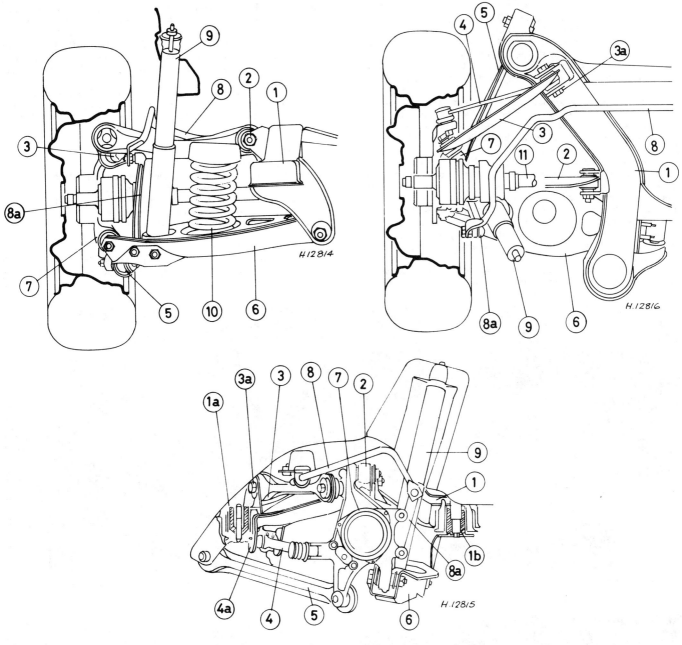

Fig. 10.2 Layout of the rear suspension assembly (Sec 1)

1 Rear subframe	3 Pulling strut	6 Spring support arm	9 Shock absorber
1a Subframe front mounting	4 Track rod	7 Rear hub carrier	10 Roadspring
1b Subframe rear mounting	4a Track rod inner mounting	8 Anti-roll bar	11 Driveshaft
2 Camber strut	5 Pushing strut	8a Anti-roll bar connecting link	

2 Maintenance and inspection

1 At the intervals given in Routine Maintenance at the beginning of this manual, a thorough inspection of all suspension and steering components should be carried out, using the following procedures as a guide.

Front suspension and steering
2 Jack up the front of the car and support it on axle stands.
3 Carry out a careful visual inspection of the steering gear, steering pump and the fluid pipes, hoses and unions for signs of fluid leaks, chafing of the pipes and hoses, or insecure components. Rectify any

problems found with reference to the relevant Sections of this Chapter.
4 Inspect the condition of the dust covers on the wishbone, track rod and drag link balljoints. The dust covers can be renewed separately, if necessary. However, if the dust covers have been damaged for some time, water and dirt will have entered the joint, causing rapid wear. If this is the case, renewal of the track rod or wishbone balljoints, or the complete drag link, will be necessary.
5 Check and if necessary adjust the front hub bearing play, using the procedure described in Section 3.
6 With the front hub bearings correctly adjusted, grasp the roadwheel at the 12 o'clock and 6 o'clock positions, and try to rock it. Very slight free play should be felt, but if the movement is appreciable, there is likely to be wear in the wishbone balljoint or wishbone inner

mountings. Renew the wishbone balljoint if worn, or the inner bushes if the wear is in this area (Sections 10 and 9 respectively).

7   Now grasp the wheel at the 9 o'clock and 3 o'clock positions, and try to rock it as before. Once again, slight movement only should be felt. If the movement is excessive, further investigation is required in the area of the track rod or drag link balljoints, or the idler assembly. Renew any worn components as described in the appropriate Sections of this Chapter.

8   Using a large screwdriver as a lever, check for wear in the anti-roll bar mountings and wishbone inner bushes by carefully levering against these components. Some movement is to be expected, as the mountings are made of rubber, but excessive wear should be obvious. Renew any bushes that are worn.

9   With the car standing on its wheels, have an assistant turn the steering wheel back and forth about one-eighth of a turn each way. With recirculating ball type steering there may be some lost movement between the steering wheels and the roadwheels, but this should be minimal. If the free play is excessive, closely observe the joints and mountings previously described, but in addition check the steering column couplings for wear, and also the steering gear itself. Any wear should be visually apparent, and must be rectified as described in the appropriate Sections of this Chapter.

10 Check the fluid in the power steering pump reservoir by unscrewing the cap nut, lifting off the cover and observing the fluid level (photos). If the car has just been driven and is at normal operating temperature, the fluid should be up to the punched or cast mark on the reservoir (approximately 20.0 mm/0.78 in) below the rim. If the fluid is cold, the level should be approximately 6.0 to 8.0 mm (0.23 to 0.31 in) below this mark. If topping-up is required, add the specified fluid to the reservoir until the level is correct (photo), then refit the cover and cap nut.

11 Check the condition, and if necessary adjust the tension, of the power steering pump drivebelt as described in Section 30 on cars with multiple drivebelts, or in Chapter 12 for later models with a single drivebelt arrangement.

Rear suspension

12 Jack up the rear of the car and support it on axle stands.

13 Visually inspect the rear suspension components, attachments and linkages for any visible sign of wear or damage.

14 Grasp the roadwheel at the 12 o'clock and 6 o'clock positions and try to rock it. Any excess movement here indicates worn hub bearings or wear in the suspension arm bushes.

Wheels and tyres

15 Carefully inspect each tyre, including the spare, for signs of uneven wear, lumps, bulges or damage to the sidewalls or tread face. Refer to Section 36 for further details.

2.10A Unscrew the cap nut ...

2.10B ... lift off the power steering pump reservoir cover ...

2.10C ... and top up the fluid to the punched or cast mark on the reservoir

2.16 Checking the torque of the wheel bolts

16 Check the condition of the wheel rims for distortion, damage or visibly excessive run-out. Also make sure that the balance weights are secure, with no obvious signs that any are missing. Check the torque of the wheel bolts and check the tyre pressures (photo).

17 The efficiency of the shock absorbers may be checked by bouncing the car at each corner. Generally speaking, the body will return to its normal position and stop after being depressed. If it rises and returns on a rebound, the shock absorber is probably suspect. Examine also the shock absorber upper and lower mountings for any sign of wear, and the body and piston areas for signs of fluid leakage. Renewal procedures are contained in Sections 6 and 21 for the front and rear units respectively.

3 Front hub bearings – adjustment

1 Jack up the front of the car and support it on axle stands. Remove the front roadwheel.

2 Refit two of the wheel bolts into diagonally opposite wheel bolt holes, and tighten them snugly to keep the disc firmly clamped to the hub.

3 Using a small punch or blunt chisel, carefully tap off the hub cap.

4 Remove the radio interference contact spring from the centre of the hub spindle.

5 Refer to Chapter 9 and remove the front disc pads.

6 Slacken the hub retaining nut socket-headed bolt using an Allen key, until the retaining nut is free to turn.

7 Tighten the retaining nut while turning the hub until the hub just becomes difficult to turn.

8 Slacken the retaining nut by approximately one-third of a turn, then strike the end of the hub spindle with a soft-faced mallet to relieve the tension on the bearing.

9 The hub endfloat, as given in the Specifications, should now be approximately correct. To check this, grasp the disc at two opposite points and pull it in and out. It should be just possible to detect the slightest trace of movement as this is done. Also, if the adjustment is correct, it should just be possible to turn the thrust washer behind the hub retaining nut smoothly with one finger and with minimal force (photo).

10 If a dial gauge is available, mount the gauge stand on the front face of the hub, with the gauge probe in contact with the end of the spindle. Zero the gauge scale, then pull the disc in and out as previously described. The hub endfloat will be shown accurately on the gauge (photo).

11 Repeat the adjustment procedure until the specified hub endfloat is obtained, then lock the retaining nut by tightening the socket-headed bolt.

12 Refit the radio interference contact spring to the hub spindle.

13 Fill the hub cap to the flanged edge with the specified grease, then tap the hub cap into place.

14 Remove the two disc retaining bolts, then refit the disc pads as described in Chapter 9.

15 Refit the roadwheel and lower the car to the ground.

4 Front hub and bearings – removal and refitting

1 Jack up the front of the car and support it on axle stands. Remove the front roadwheel.

2 Detach the disc pad wear warning sensor wire from the cable clip on the suspension strut.

3 Undo the two bolts securing the disc caliper carrier bracket to the steering knuckle. **Note:** *The carrier retaining bolts are of the encapsulated type, and incorporate a thread locking compound which is activated when the bolt is fitted and tightened. The compound is ineffective after removal, and new bolts must therefore be obtained prior to refitting the caliper.*

4 Slide the caliper assembly, complete with pads, off the disc, and suspend it from a convenient place under the wheel arch using string or wire. Do not let the caliper hang unsupported from the brake hose.

5 Using a small punch or blunt chisel, carefully tap off the hub cap.

6 Undo the socket-headed retaining screw (where fitted) using an Allen key, and withdraw the disc from the locating dowels (photos).

7 Remove the radio interference contact spring from the centre of the hub spindle (photo).

8 Slacken the hub retaining nut socket-headed bolt using an Allen

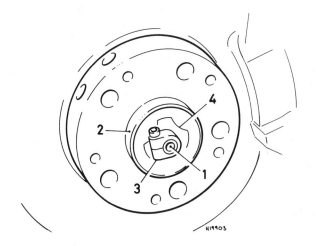

Fig. 10.3 Front hub bearing retaining nut components
(Sec 3)

1 Hub spindle	3 Socket-headed bolt
2 Hub	4 Thrust washer

3.9 The hub bearing adjustment is correct if the thrust washer can just be moved with one finger

3.10 Alternative method of checking the hub bearing adjustment, using a dial gauge

key (photo), then unscrew the nut from the spindle and remove the thrust washer (photo).

9   The front hub can now be withdrawn from the spindle, but if it is tight, which is quite likely, it will be necessary to use a two- or three-legged puller, or preferably a slide hammer (photo) to remove it. As the hub is removed, the inner bearing and inner race is likely to come apart and remain on the spindle. If this happens, draw off the bearing using a puller with its legs engaged behind the bearing rollers.

10   With the hub removed, lift out the outer bearing inner race, then turn the hub over and prise out the oil seal using a screwdriver (photo).

11   Lift out the inner bearing inner race.

12   Using a drift inserted through the centre of the hub, tap out the two bearing outer races (photo).

13   Wipe away the surplus grease from the bearings and hub bore, then clean these components thoroughly using paraffin or a suitable solvent. Dry with a lint-free rag. Remove any burrs or score marks from the hub bore using a fine file or scraper.

14   Carefully examine the bearing inner and outer races, the bearing rollers and roller cage for pitting, scoring, cracks or any sign of corrosion. Also check for any damage to the inner bearing caused by removal if it stayed in place on the spindle. Renew the bearings as a pair if at all suspect. It will also be necessary to renew the oil seal, as this will definitely have been damaged during removal.

15   Using a tube of suitable diameter, a large socket or a soft metal drift, drive the outer races into the hub until they contact their respective shoulders in the hub bore. Ensure that the races are kept square as they are fitted.

16   Weigh out 35 g (1.2 oz) of the specified grease and liberally lubricate the inner and outer bearings working the grease well into the rollers.

17   Place the inner bearing inner race in the hub, lubricate the sealing lip and cavity of the new oil seal, and carefully tap the seal into place using a hammer and block of wood.

18   Use the remaining grease to fill the space between the bearings in the bore, then place the hub in position over the spindle (photo).

19   Tap the hub fully home using a hammer and large socket or other suitable mandrel (photo).

20   Place the outer bearing inner race in the hub (photo), followed by

4.6A Undo the socket-headed retaining screw ...

4.6B ... and withdraw the disc from the hub flange

4.7 Remove the radio interference contact spring

4.8A Slacken the retaining nut socket-headed bolt and remove the nut ...

4.8B ... followed by the thrust washer

4.9 Using a slide hammer to remove the front hub

4.10 Prise out the hub oil seal using a screwdriver

4.12 Removal of the bearing outer race using a suitable drift

4.18 Refit the hub to the spindle ...

4.19 ... and tap it home using a socket or mandrel

4.20 Fitting the bearing inner race

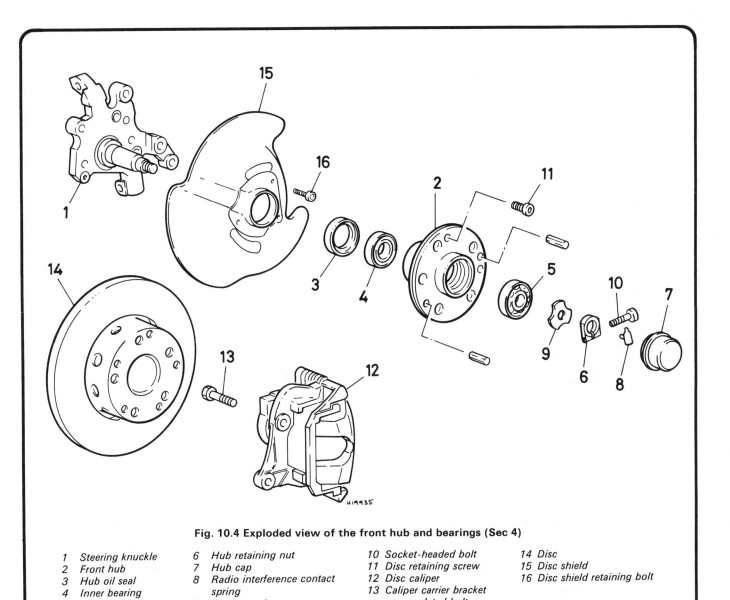

Fig. 10.4 Exploded view of the front hub and bearings (Sec 4)

1	Steering knuckle	6	Hub retaining nut	10	Socket-headed bolt	14	Disc
2	Front hub	7	Hub cap	11	Disc retaining screw	15	Disc shield
3	Hub oil seal	8	Radio interference contact	12	Disc caliper	16	Disc shield retaining bolt
4	Inner bearing		spring	13	Caliper carrier bracket		
5	Outer bearing	9	Thrust washer		encapsulated bolt		

the thrust washer and retaining nut. Tighten the retaining nut finger-tight only at this stage.
21 Refit the brake disc, ensuring that the disc and hub contact surfaces are clean and dry. Secure the disc with the socket-headed screw, where applicable.
22 Adjust the front hub bearings using the procedure described in Section 4.
23 Refit the radio interference contact spring, then tap on the hub cap, having first filled it up to the flanged edge with the specified grease.
24 Place the caliper over the disc, and secure it with two new encapsulated retaining bolts, tightened to the specified toruqe. Refit the wear sensor wire to its cable clip.
25 Refit the roadwheel and lower the car to the ground.

5 Steering knuckle – removal and refitting

1 Jack up the front of the car and support it on axle stands. Remove the front roadwheel.
2 Remove the front hub using the procedure described in Section 4.

3 On cars fitted with ABS brakes, remove the front wheel speed sensor from the steering knuckle, as described in Chapter 9.
4 Using an Allen key, undo the three socket-headed bolts securing the disc shield to the steering knuckle, and remove the shield (photos).
5 Undo the nut securing the track rod balljoint to the steering arm (photo). Release the joint from the steering arm using a balljoint separator tool.
6 Position a sturdy jack beneath the wishbone and in contact with it. Make sure that the jack is secure, as the full force of the roadspring will be taken by the jack when the steering knuckle is removed. It is advisable to retain the spring using coil spring compressors for added safety.
7 Undo the two lower bolts securing the suspension strut to the steering knuckle (photos). **Note:** *These two bolts are of the encapsulated type, and incorporate a thread locking compound which is activated when the bolt is fitted and tightened. The compound is ineffective after removal, and new bolts must therefore be obtained prior to refitting the steering knuckle.*
8 Undo the upper nut and bolt securing the strut to the steering knuckle, and ease the steering knuckle away from the strut (photo).

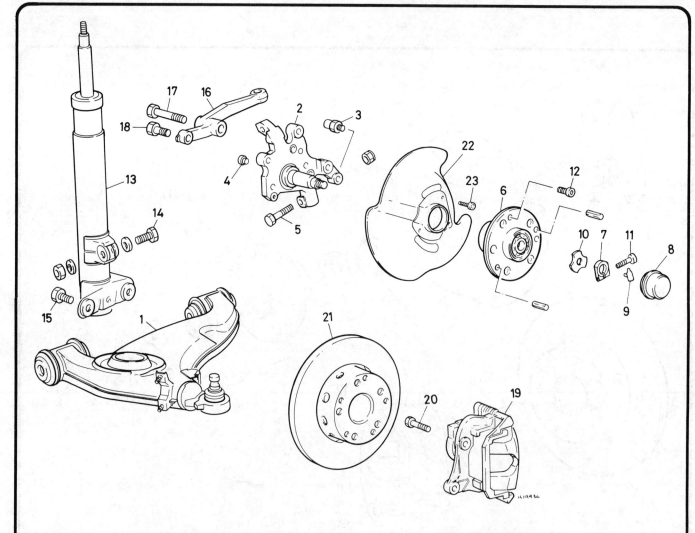

Fig. 10.5 Exploded view of the steering knuckle, suspension strut and related components (Secs 5 and 6)

1 Wishbone	8 Hub cap	14 Strut-to-steering knuckle upper retaining bolt	19 Disc caliper
2 Steering knuckle	9 Radio interference contact spring	15 Strut-to-steering knuckle lower retaining bolt	20 Caliper carrier bracket encapsulated bolt
3 Steering lock stop	10 Thrust washer	16 Steering knuckle arm	21 Disc
4 Locating peg	11 Socket-headed bolt	17 Arm retaining bolt (long)	22 Disc shield
5 Steering knuckle pinch bolt	12 Disc retaining screw	18 Arm retaining bolt (short)	23 Disc shield retaining bolt
6 Front hub	13 Suspension strut		
7 Hub retaining nut			

9 Undo the nut and remove the pinch-bolt securing the steering knuckle to the wishbone balljoint (photo).
10 Withdraw the steering knuckle from the balljoint shank and remove it from the car (photo). If the knuckle is tight on the balljoint shank due to corrosion, liberally apply penetrating fluid, then spread the knuckle clamp slightly using a sturdy screwdriver.
11 Check the steering knuckle for any signs of damage or distortion paying particular attention to the steering arm and the hub spindle areas. Check that the hub bearing oil seal contact area on the spindle is free from rust or wear grooves, and touch up with fine emery paper if necessary. If the contact area is scored or deeply grooved, renew the knuckle. Also check for scoring or damage on the hub bearing inner race contact areas on the spindle. Again, renew the knuckle if these are damaged.The steering arm can be renewed separately after undoing the two bolts if any damage or distortion is evident.
12 Refit the steering knuckle to the wishbone balljoint and secure with the pinch-bolt, tightened to the specified torque.

13 Locate the steering knuckle against the strut and fit the two new encapsulated bolts, but do not tighten the bolts at this stage.
14 Fit the upper knuckle-to-strut retaining bolt and nut, but tighten the nut only lightly at this stage.
15 Now tighten the two encapsulated bolts to the specified torque, followed by the upper nut and bolt.
16 Remove the spring compressors (if fitted) and the jack under the wishbone.
17 Refit the disc shield and secure with the three socket-headed bolts.
18 Engage the track rod balljoint with the steering arm and refit the retaining nut. Hold the balljoint shank using an Allen key, and tighten the retaining nut.
19 On cars with ABS brakes, fit the front wheel speed sensor as described in Chapter 9.
20 Refit the front hub, disc and caliper as described in Section 4, then adjust the front hub bearings as described in Section 3.
21 Refit the roadwheel and lower the car to the ground.

5.4A Undo the disc shield socket-headed bolts ...

5.4B ... and remove the shield

5.5 Undo the track rod balljoint retaining nut

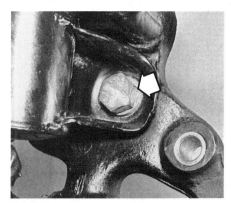
5.7A Undo the strut-to-steering knuckle left-hand lower bolt (arrowed) ...

5.7B ... and right-hand lower bolt (arrowed)

5.8 Undo the upper nut and bolt, and separate the strut from the steering knuckle

5.9 Remove the steering knuckle-to-wishbone nut and pinch-bolt

5.10 Withdraw the steering knuckle from the wishbone balljoint

6 Front suspension strut – removal and refitting

1   Jack up the front of the car and support it on axle stands. Remove the front roadwheel.
2   Place a sturdy jack beneath the wishbone and in contact with it. Make sure that the jack is secure, as the full force of the roadspring will be taken by the jack when the suspension strut is removed. It is advisable to retain the spring using coil spring compressors for added safety.
3   Undo the two lower bolts securing the suspension strut to the steering knuckle. **Note:** *These two bolts are of the encapsulated type, and incorporate a thread locking compound which is activated when the bolt is fitted and tightened. The compound is ineffective after removal, and new bolts must therefore be obtained prior to refitting the suspension strut.*
4   Undo the upper nut and bolt securing the strut to the steering knuckle, and ease the knuckle away from the strut (photo).
5   Disconnect any wiring, cables or hoses from their clips on the strut body.
6   From within the engine compartment, undo the three nuts securing the strut upper mounting to the body turret (photo), and withdraw the strut from under the wheel arch.
7   If required the upper mounting can be removed by undoing the retaining nut while holding the strut spindle with an Allen key (photo).

Withdraw the upper mounting, followed by the spindle dust cover and the bump-stop rubber buffer.
8   Examine the strut for signs of fluid leakage. Check the strut spindle for signs of wear or pitting along its entire legnth, and check the strut body for signs of damage. Test the operation of the strut, while holding it in an upright position, by moving the spindle through a full stroke, then through short strokes of about half the total spindle travel. In both cases, the resistance felt should be smooth and continuous. If the resistance is jerky or uneven, or if there is any visible sign of wear or damage to the strut, renewal is necessary.
9   Refit the bump-stop , dust cover and strut upper mounting, and secure the mounting with the retaining nut.
10 Position the strut under the wheel arch and engage the mounting studs with the turret holes. Fit and tighten the three upper mounting retaining nuts.
11 Fit the two new encapsulated bolts securing the lower part of the strut to the steering knuckle, then the upper nut and bolt Tighten the two lower bolts, followed by the upper nut and bolt, in that order, to the specified torque.
12 Remove the spring compressors (if fitted) and the jack under the wishbone.
13 Refit the wiring, cables or hoses as applicable to the clips on the strut body.
14 Refit the roadwheel and lower the car to the ground.

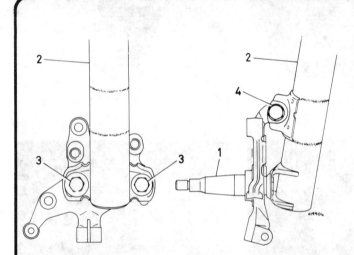

Fig. 10.6 Suspension strut-to-steering knuckle mounting details (Sec 6)

1 Steering knuckle	*3 Lower mounting bolts*
2 Suspension strut	* (encapsulated)*
	4 Upper nut and bolt

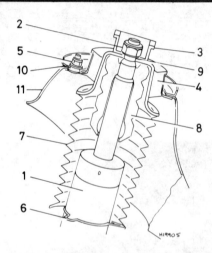

Fig. 10.7 Suspension strut upper mounting details (Sec 6)

1 Suspension strut	*6 Dust cover support ring*
2 Strut spindle retaining nut	*7 Dust cover*
3 Rebound stop	*8 Bump stop rubber buffer*
4 Upper mounting	*9 Washer*
5 Upper mounting retaining	*10 Washer*
* nut*	*11 Body turret*

6.4 Removing the suspension strut from the steering knuckle

6.6 Suspension strut upper mounting-to-body turret nuts (arrowed)

6.7 Hold the spindle and undo the retaining nut to remove the upper mounting

7   Front roadspring – removal and refitting

1   Jack up the front of the car and support it on axle stands. Remove the front roadwheel.

2   Detach the disc pad wear warning sensor wire from the cable clip on the suspension strut.

3   Undo the two bolts securing the disc caliper carrier bracket to the steering knuckle. **Note:** *The carrier retaining bolts are of the encapsulated type, and incorporate a thread locking compound which is activated when the bolt is fitted and tightened. The compound is ineffective after removal, and new bolts must therefore be obtained prior to refitting the caliper.*

4   Slide the caliper assembly, complete with pads, off the disc, and suspend it from a convenient place under the wheel arch using string or wire. Do not let the caliper hang unsupported from the brake hose.

5   On cars fitted with ABS brakes, disconnect the wiring at the plug connector alongside the suspension strut turret in the engine compartment. Release the grommet and pull the wiring through to the wheel arch.

6   Using coil spring compressors positioned on either side of the spring, compress the spring evenly until there is no tension on the upper spring seat or wishbone (photo).

7   Undo the nut securing the track rod balljoint to the steering arm. Release the joint from the steering arm using a balljoint separator tool.

8   Undo the two nuts securing the anti-roll bar clamp plate to the wishbone. Remove the plate and slide the rubber bush clear of the mounting.

9   Undo the pinch-bolt securing the steering knuckle to the wishbone balljoint.

10   Lever the wishbone down to release the balljoint shank from the steering knuckle. If the knuckle is tight on the balljoint shank due to corrosion, liberally apply penetrating oil, then spread the knuckle clamp slightly using a sturdy screwdriver.

11   From within the engine compartment, undo the three nuts securing the strut upper mounting to the body turret, and remove the strut assembly from under the wheel arch.

12   Using a stout bar, lever the wishbone down and withdraw the lower end of the spring from its wishbone seat. Pull the spring down out of its upper mounting and remove it from the car (photo).

13   If the spring is to be renewed, or left off the car for some time, carefully and evenly release the spring compressors and remove them from the spring. Remove the rubber upper mounting cup.

14   Before refitting, compress the spring evenly ensuring that with the compressors fitted on each side, the lower spring end faces forwards and to the right (photo).

15   Fit the rubber upper mounting cup over the top of the spring.

16   Lever the wishbone down and push the spring up and into its upper mounting (photo).

17   Engage the lower end of the spring in the wishbone with the spring end against the register (photo).

18   Engage the suspension strut upper mounting in the body turret and secure with the three retaining bolts, tightened to the specified torque.

19   Enter the wishbone balljoint shank into the steering knuckle, fit the pinch-bolt and tighten to the specified torque.

20   Remove the spring compressors.

21   Slide the anti-roll bar bush into its mounting, fit the clamp plate and secure with the two nuts.

22   On cars fitted with ABS brakes, feed the wiring through the wheel arch and fit the grommet to its location. Reconnect the wiring plug in the engine compartment.

23   Slide the disc caliper and pads over the disc, and secure the carrier bracket to the steering knuckle using two new encapsulated bolts, tightened to the specified torque.

24   Engage the track rod balljoint with the steering arm and refit the retaining nut. Hold the balljoint shank using an Allen key, and tighten the retaining nut.

25   Reconnect the disc pad wear warning sensor wire to the cable clip on the suspension strut.

26   Refit the roadwheel and lower the car to the ground.

7.6 Fitting coil spring compressors to the front roadspring

7.12 Front roadspring removal

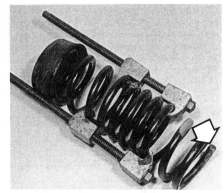

7.14 When refitting, position the spring compressors in relation to the spring end (arrowed) as shown

7.16 Locate the spring in its upper mounting ...

7.17 ... then engage the lower spring end with the register in the wishbone (arrowed)

8 Front wishbone – removal and refitting

1 Jack up the front of the car and support it on axle stands. Remove the front roadwheel.

2 Remove the engine undertray on cars so equipped.

3 Undo the two nuts securing the anti-roll bar clamp plate to the wishbone. Remove the plate and slide the rubber bush clear of the mounting.

4 Using coil spring compressors positioned on either side of the road spring, compress the spring evenly until there is no tension on the upper spring seat or wishbone.

5 Accurately mark the position of both wishbone inner mounting bolts, by drawing a vertical line on the chassis member above and directly in line with the bolt centre-line. The wishbone inner mountings are adjustable in a laterial plane, for camber and castor angle corrections, by means of an elongated bolt hole and an eccentric pin (mounting bolt). If the existing position of the mounting bolt is marked prior to removal the settings will not be lost on reassembly.

6 Undo the two inner mounting bolt retaining nuts and eccentric washers, then remove both the bolts. Tap the bolts out using a small punch if necessary.

7 Using a stout screwdriver ease the wishbone inner mountings out of their locations.

8 Undo the pinch-bolt and nut securing the steering knuckle to the wishbone balljoint, withdraw the balljoint from the knuckle and remove the wishbone from the car. If the balljoint shank is tight in the steering knuckle due to corrosion, liberally apply penetrating oil, then spread the knuckle clamp slightly using a sturdy screwdriver.

9 With the wishbone removed, check it carefully for signs of damage, and check the condition of the inner mounting bushes, balljoint dust cover and the balljoint itself. Should any of these components show signs of wear or damage, renew them using the procedures described elsewhere in this Chapter.

10 Begin refitting by engaging the balljoint shank in the steering knuckle, then refit the pinch-bolt and nut, and tighten the nut to the specified torque.

11 Lubricate the wishbone inner mounting bushes with rubber grease, then locate the mountings in the chassis member.

12 Insert the mounting bolts with their bolt heads facing each other, followed by the eccentric washers and retaining nuts. Do not tighten the nuts at this stage.

13 Remove the spring compressors from the road spring.

14 Slide the anti-roll bar rubber bush into position, refit the clamp plate and secure with the two nuts.

15 Refit the roadwheel and lower the car to the ground.

16 Roll the car forwards and backwards over half its length to settle the suspension.

17 Turn the inner mounting bolts, using a spanner on the bolt heads, until the bolt centre-line is positioned in line with the previously-made mark. Hold the bolts in position while tightening the retaining nuts to the specified torque.

18 Refit the engine undertray where applicable.

19 If a new wishbone has been fitted, new bushes installed, or if the bolt positions were not marked prior to removal, have the wheel alignment and steering angles checked by a Mercedes-Benz dealer (see Section 35).

9 Wishbone mounting bushes – renewal

1 Remove the front wishbone as described in Section 8.

Front mounting bush

2 Clamp the wishbone securely in a vice, with the front mounting bush uppermost.

3 Using a large drill bit, drill out the flared end of the clamping sleeve in the centre of the bush.

4 Using a punch, knock the clamping sleeve through, and remove it from the other end of the bush.

5 Using a drift against the bush collar, knock out the two bush halves from the wishbone front mounting.

6 Thoroughly clean the bush bore in the wishbone using fine emery paper if necessary to remove any corrosion.

7 Lubricate the two new bush halves with rubber grease, and place

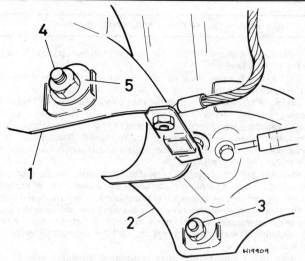

Fig. 10.8 Front wishbone inner mountings (Sec 8)

1 Chassis member	4 Rear mounting eccentric
2 Crossmember	bolt
3 Front mounting eccentric	5 Eccentric washer
bolt	

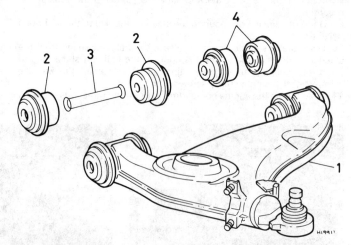

Fig. 10.9 Front wishbone mounting bushes (Sec 9)

1 Front wishbone	3 Clamping sleeve
2 Front bush halves	4 Rear bush halves

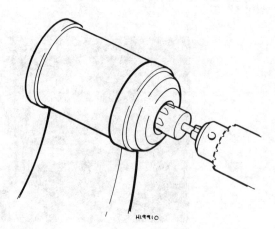

Fig. 10.10 Using a drill to remove the flared end on the wishbone front bush clamping sleeve (Sec 9)

one of them in position on the wishbone with the flat on the bush uppermost (Fig. 10.12).

8 Using a socket or tube of suitable diameter, press the bush into the wishbone with the aid of the vice.

9 Repeat paragraphs 7 and 8 for the other bush half.

10 Insert a new clamping sleeve through the centre of the bushes, then flare the end of the sleeve to secure the bushes. Use a tapered tool for this, such as the shank of a tapered drift.

Rear mounting bush

11 Clamp the wishbone securely in a vice, with the rear mounting uppermost.

12 Insert a large screwdriver or metal bar into the centre of one of the bush halves, and move it up and down to help free the bush from its location.

13 Tap out the bush, using a chisel against the bush flanged edge. With the first bush half removed, tap out the second, using a drift through the wishbone bush bore.

14 Thoroughly clean the bush bore in the wishbone using fine emery paper if necessary to remove any corrosion.

15 Position both new bush halves in the wishbone so that the slit in the bush metal jacket is towards and aligned with the welded seam of the wishbone.

16 Draw the bush halves into place using a long bolt, nut and flat washers.

17 On completion refit the wishbone to the car as described in Section 8.

10 Wishbone balljoint – removal and refitting

1 Remove the front wishbone as described in Section 8.

2 Prise out the retaining wire clips, and remove the dust cover over the balljoint.

3 The balljoint can now be pressed downwards out of the wishbone. It is possible to do this using a sturdy vice or hydraulic puller with suitable pieces of tubing as distance pieces, and mandrels, but the use of a press bed is preferable. Alternatively, take the wishbone to a suitably equipped garage, and have them press out the joint and fit the new one for you.

4 Fit the new balljoint using the same procedure as for removal, but ensure that the groove on the upper flange of the joint is towards the centre of the wishbone boss (Fig. 10.15).

5 Place the new dust cover over the balljoint and fit the retaining wire clips.

6 Refit the wishbone as described in Section 8.

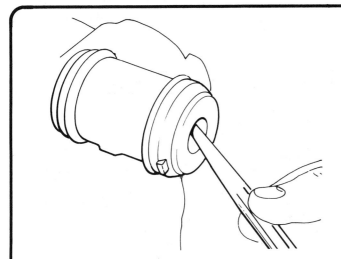

Fig. 10.11 Using a punch to knock out the wishbone front bush clamping sleeve (Sec 9)

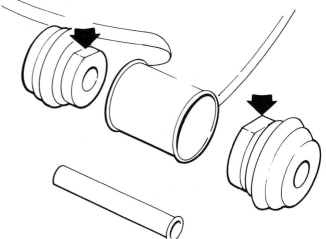

H.20446

Fig. 10.12 Wishbone front bushes must be fitted with their flats (arrowed) uppermost (Sec 9)

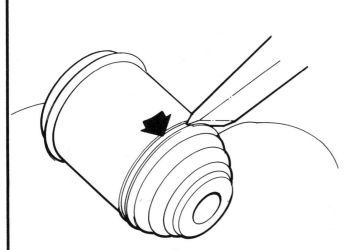

Fig. 10.13 Using a chisel to release the wishbone rear bush (Sec 9)

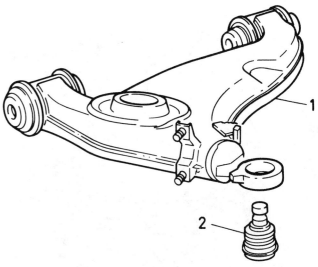

Fig. 10.14 Front wishbone (1) and balljoint (2) (Sec 10)

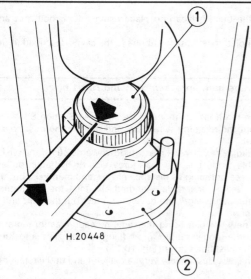

Fig. 10.15 Balljoint groove aligned with centre of wishbone boss (Sec 10)

1 Balljoint   2 Hydraulic puller and adaptor
                                   for fitting balljoint
Arrows indicate groove and wishbone centre-line

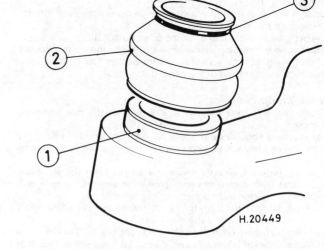

Fig. 10.16 Wishbone balljoint dust cover renewal (Sec 11)

1 Balljoint   3 Upper retaining clip
2 Dust cover

11 Balljoint dust covers – renewal

1   The dust covers over the wishbone, track rod and drag link balljoints can be individually renewed if their condition has deteriorated, or if they have been damaged during a removal and refitting operation. Should a damaged dust cover be discovered during routine maintenance, it is likely that water and dirt will have entered the balljoint, causing rapid wear. In this case the affected balljoint or drag link, as applicable, should be renewed complete.
2   Separate the balljoint shank from its component attachment with reference to the relevant Sections of this Chapter.
3   Remove the two retaining wire clips securing the dust cover to the balljoint housing and shank (photo).
4   Remove the dust cover and wipe out the old grease from the joint. Do not clean the joint with any solvents.
5   Pack the joint with molybdenum disulphide grease, then fit the new dust cover and secure with the two wire clips. When fitting the large wire clip, place a tube or socket over the dust cover, then slide the clip over the tube and into position.
6   Reconnect the balljoint shank to its component attachment.

12 Front anti-roll bar – removal and refitting

1   Jack up the front of the car and support it on axle stands. Remove both front roadwheels.
2   Undo the nuts and remove the clamp plates securing the anti-roll bar to both front wishbones, and to the mounting brackets on the front chassis members.
3   Withdraw the anti-roll bar forwards and remove it from under the car.
4   If the mounting bushes are to be renewed, slide them off the ends of the anti-roll bar, then slide on the new bushes after first lubricating them with rubber grease (photo).
5   Refitting is the reverse sequence to removal, but tighten the mounting nuts to the specified torque.

11.3 Using a small screwdriver to release the balljoint dust cover retaining clip

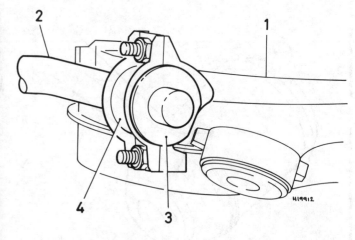

Fig. 10.17 Anti-roll bar mounting clamp details (Sec 12)

1 Wishbone   3 Mounting bush
2 Anti-roll bar   4 Clamp plate

12.4 Anti-roll bar rubber bush renewal

13 Rear hub carrier – removal and refitting

Note: *The following procedures necessitate removal and refitting of the driveshaft retaining collar nut and for this purpose a 30 mm socket and a torque wrench capable of recording up to 350 Nm will be required. Ensure that these tools are available before proceeding.*

1 With the car on the ground remove the rear wheel trim, and using a small punch or thin screwdriver, knock back the staking securing the driveshaft retaining collar nut to the stub shaft.

2 Using a 30 mm socket and long bar, unscrew and remove the collar nut. Note that a new nut must be used when refitting the hub carrier.

3 Jack up the rear of the car and support it on stands. Remove the roadwheel.

4 Undo the two bolts securing the disc caliper to the rear hub carrier.

Note: *The caliper retaining bolts are of the encapsulated type, and incorporate a thread locking compound which is activated when the bolt is fitted and tightened. The compound is ineffective after removal and new bolts must therefore be obtained prior to refitting the caliper.*

5 Slide the caliper assembly, complete with pads, off the disc, and suspend it from the roadspring using string or wire. Do not let the caliper hang unsupported from the brake hose.

6 Check that the handbrake is released, then where fitted undo the socket-headed retaining screw securing the brake disc to the hub flange. Remove the disc, tapping it off gently with a soft mallet if it is tight.

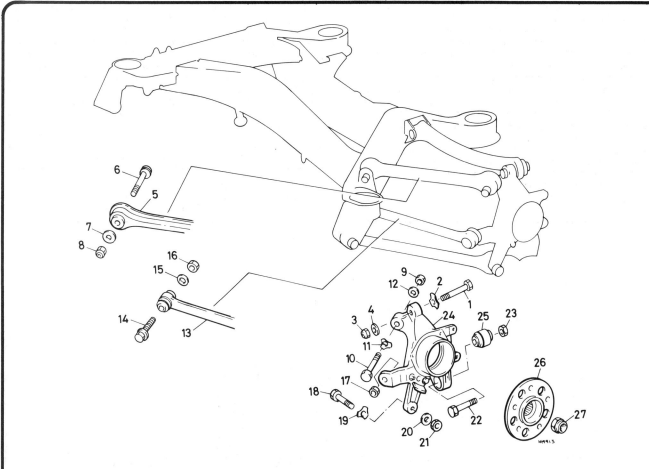

Fig. 10.18 Rear hub carrier attachment details (Sec 13)

1 Camber strut mounting bolt	8 Retaining nut	15 Eccentric washer	22 Spring support arm retaining
2 Contour disc	9 Retaining nut	16 Retaining nut	bolt
3 Retaining nut	10 Pulling strut mounting bolt	17 Retaining nut	23 Retaining nut
4 Washer	11 Contour disc	18 Pushing strut mounting bolt	24 Hub carrier
5 Pulling strut	12 Washer	19 Contour disc	25 Spring support arm bush
6 Pulling strut eccentric	13 Track rod	20 Washer	26 Hub flange
mounting bolt	14 Track rod eccentric	21 Retaining nut	27 Driveshaft retaining collar
7 Eccentric washer	mounting bolt		nut

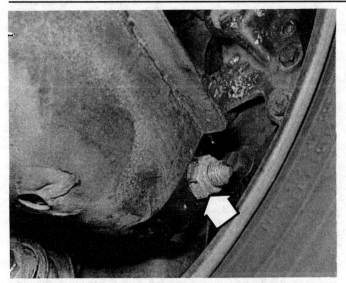

13.13 Spring support arm-to-hub carrier bolt and retaining nut (arrowed)

13.14 Using a puller to release the driveshaft constant velocity joint from the hub flange

7   Refer to Chapter 9 and remove the handbrake shoes.
8   Undo the bolt securing the handbrake cable to the rear hub carrier and withdraw the cable.
9   Refer to Section 16 and remove the pulling strut.
10 Refer to Section 18 and remove the rear track rod.
11 Unscrew the nut and washer, and remove the bolt and contour disc securing the camber strut to the hub carrier. Lever the camber strut sideways to release the mounting sleeve from the hub carrier.
12 Unscrew the nut and washer, and remove the bolt and contour disc securing the pushing strut to the hub carrier. Lever the pushing strut sideways to release the mounting sleeve from the hub carrier.
13 Undo the nut and remove the bolt securing the spring support arm to the hub carrier (photo).
14 Push, or gently tap, the outer constant velocity joint out of the hub flange, while at the same time withdrawing the hub carrier assembly from the car. If the constant velocity joint is tight, release it from the hub flange using a puller (photo).
15 Refitting the hub carrier is the reverse sequence to removal, but bear in mind the following points:

(a) Tighten all retaining nuts and bolts to the specified torque
(b) When refitting the camber strut and pushing strut, ensure that the contour disc is located behind the retaining bolt head and the washer (where fitted), behind the nut
(c) Before tightening the strut, track rod or spring support arm mountings, place a jack beneath the spring support arm and raise the suspension assembly until the driveshaft is horizontal
(d) Use new encapsulated bolts to retain the disc caliper, and a new driveshaft retaining collar nut
(e) Tighten the driveshaft collar nut with the car standing on its wheels, then stake the collar into the stub shaft groove using a small punch

14 Rear hub bearings – removal and refitting

1   Remove the rear hub carrier as described in Section 13.
2   Support the hub carrier securely in a vice, and drive out the hub flange using a hammer and drift or suitable tube.

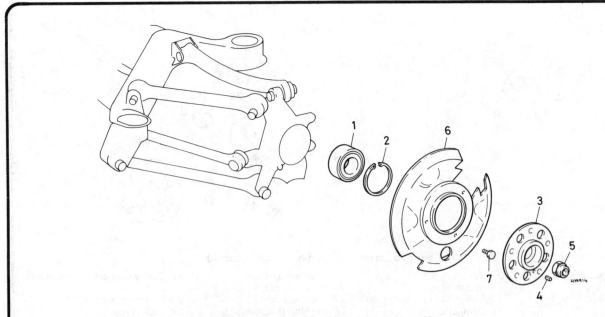

Fig. 10.19 Rear hub and bearing components (Sec 14)

1	Rear hub bearing	3	Hub flange	5	Driveshaft retaining collar nut
2	Circlip	4	Dowel		
				6	Disc shield
				7	Socket-headed bolt

3   As the hub flange is removed, the bearing will come apart and the inner race will then have to be removed from the hub flange. This is best done by obtaining an exhaust system U-clamp which is a snug fit in the inner race ball track. Place the U-clamp in the ball track and locate the legs of a puller behind the clamp. Use a washer or flat piece of metal over the end of the hub flange as a thrust piece for the puller, and draw off the bearing race.
4   Undo the socket-headed bolts and remove the disc shield from the hub carrier.
5   Using circlip pliers, extract the bearing retaining circlip.
6   Place the hub carrier face down in the vice, and drive the bearing down and out of the hub carrier using a hammer and drift.
7   Clean the hub carrier and remove any burrs from the bore using a scraper and fine emery paper.
8   Install the new bearing, either by pushing it in between the jaws of the vice, or by using a long bolt, nut and suitable washers to draw it into the hub carrier bore. Ensure that the bearing is inserted fully into the hub carrier until it contacts the hub carrier shoulder.
9   Refit the bearing retaining circlip.
10 Refit the disc shield and secure with the socket-headed bolts.
11 Using a similar method to that used for fitting the bearing, fit the hub flange, but make sure that the inner race is supported, otherwise it will be pushed out as the hub flange is installed. Fig. 10.20 shows the manufacturer's special tool for this purpose, to give an idea of the arrangement.
12 Refit the rear hub carrier to the car as described in Section 13.

15 Camber strut – removal and refitting

1   Jack up the rear of the car and support it on axle stands. Remove the roadwheel.
2   Undo the nut and remove the bolt securing the camber strut inner mounting to the rear subframe.
3   Undo the nut and washer, and remove the bolt and contour disc securing the camber strut to the hub carrier.
4   Lever the strut sideways to release the mounting sleeve from the hub carrier.
5   Release the inner end of the camber strut from its location, pull the hub carrier outwards, then remove the strut down and outwards from the car.
6   Check the camber strut rubber bushes for signs of deterioration, and if apparent renew the strut complete. The bushes cannot be individually renewed.
7   Refitting is the reverse sequence to removal, bearing in mind the following points:

(a) Tighten the retaining nuts to the specified torque, but before doing so, raise the rear suspension so that the driveshaft is horizontal by means of a jack under the spring support arm
(b) When refitting the outer retaining bolt, ensure that the contour disc is located behind the bolt head, and the washer behind the nut

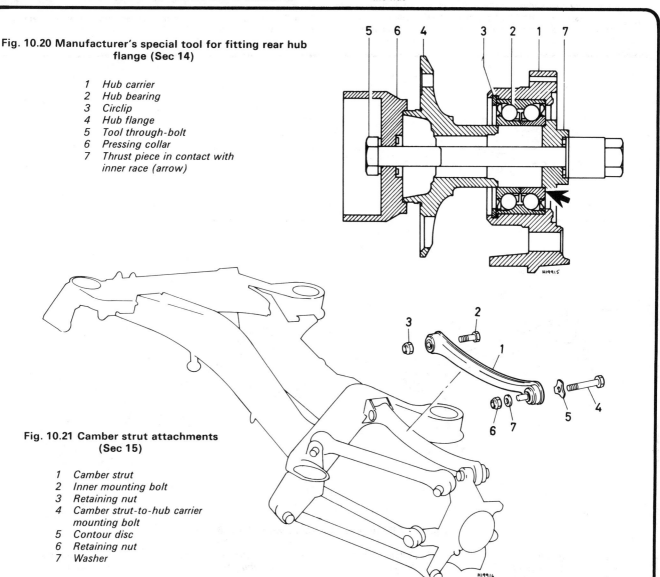

Fig. 10.20 Manufacturer's special tool for fitting rear hub flange (Sec 14)

1   Hub carrier
2   Hub bearing
3   Circlip
4   Hub flange
5   Tool through-bolt
6   Pressing collar
7   Thrust piece in contact with inner race (arrow)

Fig. 10.21 Camber strut attachments (Sec 15)

1   Camber strut
2   Inner mounting bolt
3   Retaining nut
4   Camber strut-to-hub carrier mounting bolt
5   Contour disc
6   Retaining nut
7   Washer

16 Pulling strut – removal and refitting

1   Jack up the rear of the car and support it on axle stands. Remove the roadwheel.
2   Using quick-drying white paint, draw a line across the camber strut inner mounting bolt, eccentric disc and chassis member. The pulling strut inner mounting is adjustable for suspension angle correction by means of an elongated bolt hole and an eccentric disc formed in the mounting bolt. If the existing position of the bolt and eccentric disc is marked prior to removal, the settings will not be lost on reassembly.
3   Undo the inner mounting nut and eccentric washer, then remove the mounting bolt.
4   At the hub carrier end, undo the retaining nut and washer, and remove the bolt and contour disc (photo).
5   Lever the pulling strut sideways to release the mounting sleeve from the hub carrier, then remove the pulling strut from the car.
6   Check the pulling strut bushes for signs of deterioration and if apparent, renew the strut complete. The bushes cannot be individually renewed.
7   Refitting is the reverse sequence to removal, bearing in mind the following points:

(a) Tighten the retaining nuts to the specified torque, but before doing so, raise the rear suspension so that the driveshaft is horizontal by means of a jack under the spring support arm
(b) Position the inner mounting bolt in line with the markings made prior to removal. If the bolt was not marked, or if any new parts have been fitted, the rear wheel alignment must be checked by a Mercedes-Benz dealer on completion (see Section 35)

(c) Ensure that the contour disc is fitted behind the outer retaining bolt head, and the washer behind the nut.

16.4 Pulling strut mounting at hub carrier end, showing retaining nut (A) and contour disc (B)

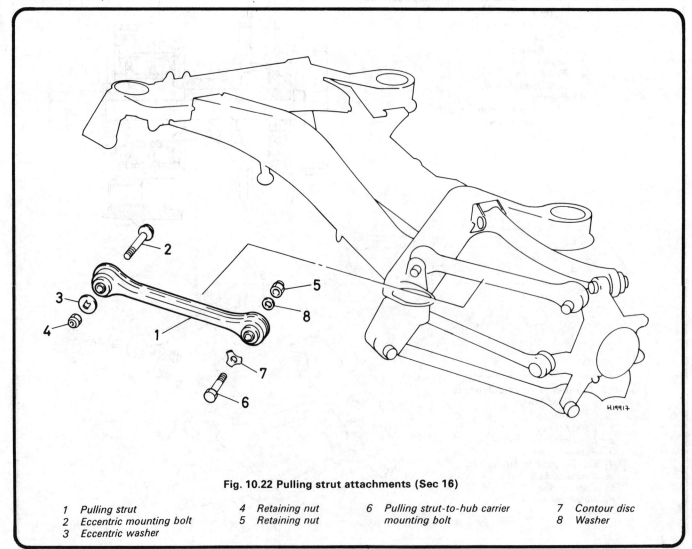

Fig. 10.22 Pulling strut attachments (Sec 16)

1 Pulling strut
2 Eccentric mounting bolt
3 Eccentric washer
4 Retaining nut
5 Retaining nut
6 Pulling strut-to-hub carrier mounting bolt
7 Contour disc
8 Washer

17 Pushing strut – removal and refitting

1   Jack up the rear of the car and support it on axle stands. Remove the roadwheel.
2   Remove the cover from the side of the pushing strut.
3   Undo the nut and remove the bolt securing the pushing strut to the rear subframe (photo).
4   Undo the nut and washer, and remove the bolt and contour disc securing the strut at the hub carrier end (photo).
5   Lever the pushing strut sideways to release the mounting sleeve from the hub carrier, and remove the strut from the car.
6   Check the pushing strut bushes for signs of deterioration and if apparent, renew the strut complete. The bushes cannot be individually renewed.
7   Refitting is the reverse sequence to removal, bearing in mind the following points:

(a) *Tighten the retaining nuts to the specified torque but before doing so raise the rear suspension so that the driveshaft is horizontal by means of a jack under the spring support arm*
(b) *Ensure that the contour disc is fitted behind the pushing strut-to-hub carrier retaining bolt head with the washer behind the nut*

18 Rear track rod – removal and refitting

1   Jack up the rear of the car and support it on axle stands. Remove the roadwheel.
2   Using quick-drying white paint, draw a line across the track rod

inner mounting bolt, eccentric disc and subframe member. The track rod inner mounting is adjustable for suspension angle correction by means of an elongated bolt hole and an eccentric disc formed in the mounting bolt. If the existing position of the bolt and eccentric disc is marked prior to removal, the settings will not be lost on reassembly.
3   Undo the inner mounting nut and eccentric washer, then remove the mounting bolt (photo).
4   At the hub carrier end, undo the nut securing the track rod balljoint, then release the balljoint from the hub carrier using a balljoint separator tool.
5   Prise the track rod inner mounting bush out of its location and remove the track rod from the car.
6   If the inner mounting bush shows signs of deterioration, this can be renewed separately by drawing it out using a long bolt and nut, a small tube of suitable diameter, and packing washers. Refit the new bush in the same way until it protrudes by equal amounts on both sides of the track rod.
7   Refitting is the reverse sequence to removal, bearing in mind the following points:

(a) *Position the inner mounting bolt in line with the markings made prior to removal. If the bolt was not marked, or if any new parts have been fitted, the rear wheel alignment must be checked by a Mercedes-Benz dealer on completion (see Section 35)*
(b) *Tighten the inner mounting nut to the specified torque, but before doing so, raise the rear suspension so that the driveshaft is horizontal by means of a jack under the spring support arm*
(c) *Tighten the track rod balljoint retaining nut to the specified torque, while holding the balljoint shank using an Allen key*

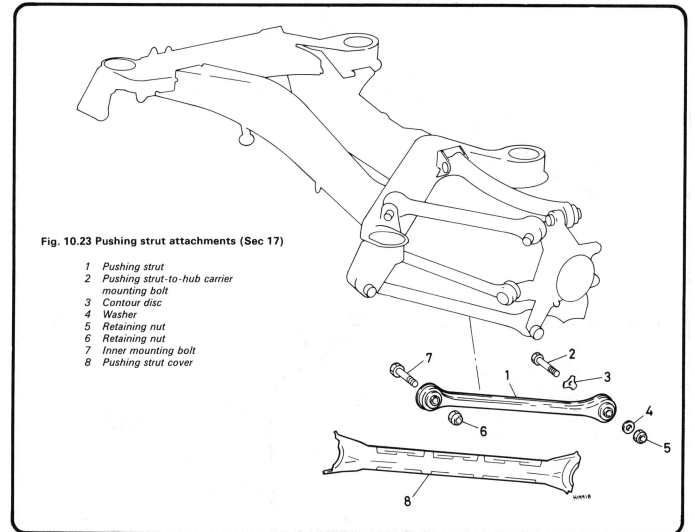

Fig. 10.23 Pushing strut attachments (Sec 17)

1   *Pushing strut*
2   *Pushing strut-to-hub carrier mounting bolt*
3   *Contour disc*
4   *Washer*
5   *Retaining nut*
6   *Retaining nut*
7   *Inner mounting bolt*
8   *Pushing strut cover*

17.3 Pushing strut-to-subframe retaining bolt (arrowed)

17.4 Pushing strut-to-hub carrier retaining bolt (arrowed) and contour disc

18.3 Track rod inner mounting on rear subframe

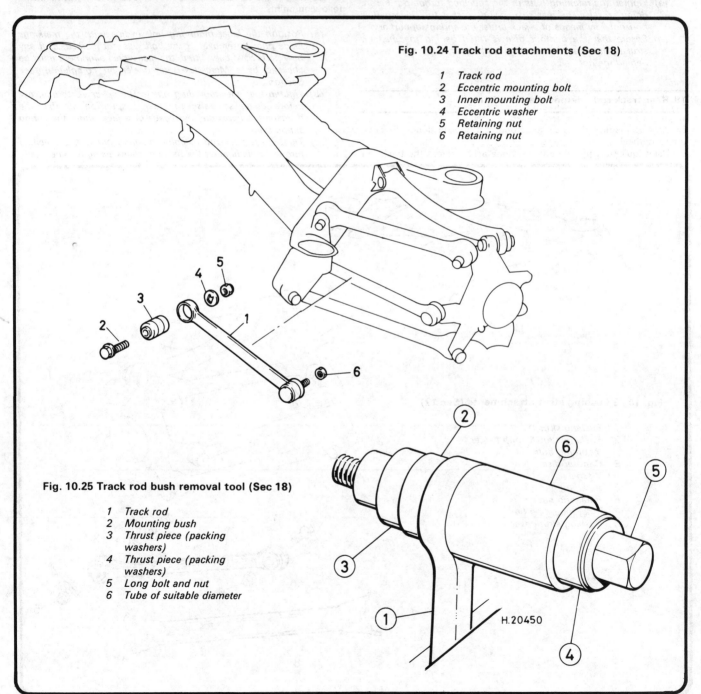

Fig. 10.24 Track rod attachments (Sec 18)

1   Track rod
2   Eccentric mounting bolt
3   Inner mounting bolt
4   Eccentric washer
5   Retaining nut
6   Retaining nut

Fig. 10.25 Track rod bush removal tool (Sec 18)

1   Track rod
2   Mounting bush
3   Thrust piece (packing washers)
4   Thrust piece (packing washers)
5   Long bolt and nut
6   Tube of suitable diameter

H.20450

19 Spring support arm – removal and refitting

Note: *For this operation it is recommended that the roadspring is retained using the manufacturer's special tool for this purpose, or some other form of coil spring compressor that can be fitted inside the spring through the opening in the support arm. Although it is possible to complete the procedure without such a tool, there is a risk of personal injury if extreme care is not taken.*

1   Jack up the rear of the car and support it on axle stands. Remove the roadwheel.

2   Refer to Section 21 and remove the rear shock absorber.

3   For increased working clearance, undo the two bolts securing the disc caliper to the rear hub carrier. **Note:** *The caliper retaining bolts are of the encapsulated type, and incorporate a thread locking compound which is activated when the bolt is fitted and tightened. The compound is ineffective after removal, and new bolts must therefore be obtained prior to refitting the caliper.*

4   Slide the caliper assembly, complete with pads, off the disc, and suspend it from a convenient place under the wheel arch. Do not let the caliper hang unsupported from the brake hose.

5   Slacken, but do not remove, the spring support arm inner mounting bolt nut (photo).

6   Fit the spring compressor (if used) to the roadspring, and compress the spring until the tension is removed from the spring support arm.

7   With the spring support arm securely supported on a jack, undo the nuts and washers securing the anti-roll bar, and hub carrier, retaining bolts to the spring support arm (photo).

8   Withdraw the anti-roll bar and hub carrier retaining bolts, then

slowly and carefully lower the jack (photo).

9   With the spring free of tension, withdraw it from its location in the support arm and subframe (photo).

10   Remove the retaining nut, washer and inner mounting bolt (photo), and withdraw the arm from its location.

11   If the inner mounting bush shows signs of deterioration, this can be renewed separately, by drawing it out using a long bolt and nut, a small tube of suitable diameter, and packing washers. Refit the new bush in the same way, after first lubricating it with rubber grease, until it protrudes by equal amounts on both sides of the support arm.

12   Begin refitting by engaging the inner end of the arm in its subframe location. Refit the inner mounting bolt and nut, but do not tighten at this stage.

13   Locate the spring in its subframe mounting, and in the recess in the spring support arm (photos).

14   Raise the support arm on the jack until the hub carrier and anti-roll bar mounting holes are aligned with those in the arm, and fit the retaining bolts. It may be necessary to lever down on one of the suspension upper struts, using a stout bar, to bring all the bolt holes into alignment (photos).

15   Refit the nuts and washers to the hub carrier and anti-roll bar bolts, but do not tighten at this stage. Remove the spring compressor, if one was used.

16   Raise the jack further until the driveshaft is horizontal, then tighten all the mounting nuts to the specified torque.

17   Refit the disc caliper to the hub carrier and secure with two new encapsulated bolts, tightened to the specified torque.

18   Refit the shock absorber as described in Section 21.

19   Refit the roadwheel and lower the car to the ground.

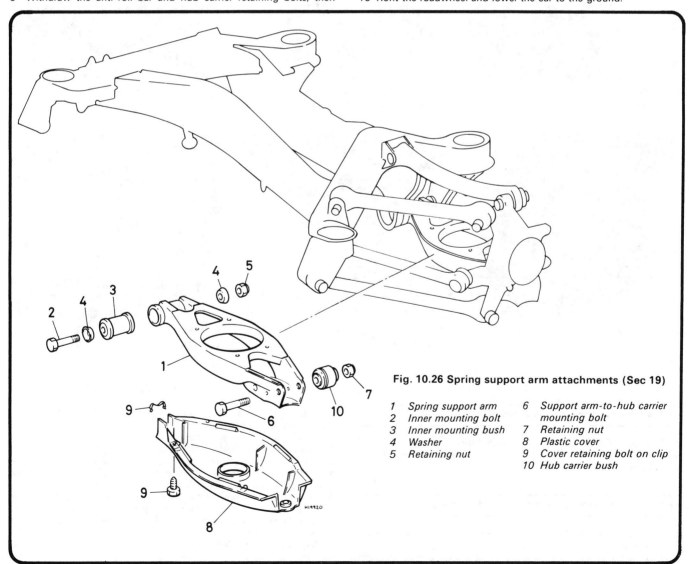

Fig. 10.26 Spring support arm attachments (Sec 19)

1   Spring support arm
2   Inner mounting bolt
3   Inner mounting bush
4   Washer
5   Retaining nut
6   Support arm-to-hub carrier mounting bolt
7   Retaining nut
8   Plastic cover
9   Cover retaining bolt on clip
10   Hub carrier bush

19.5 Slacken the spring support arm inner mounting nut (arrowed)

19.7 Undo the nuts from the anti-roll bar (A) and hub carrier (B) retaining bolts

19.8 Remove the bolts and carefully lower the supporting jack

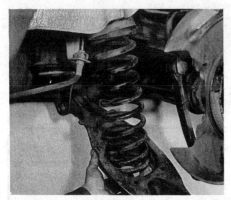

19.9 Remove the roadspring when it is free from tension

19.10 Remove the spring support arm inner mounting nut and bolt

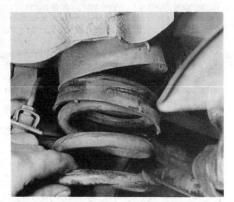

19.13A Refit the spring in its upper mounting ...

19.13B ... and in the spring support arm

19.14A Raise the supporting jack to align the mounting holes ...

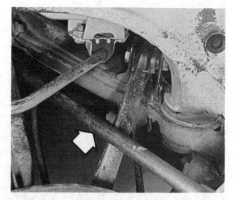

19.14B ... and lever down using a stout bar (arrowed) if necessary, until the bolts can be fitted

20 Rear roadspring – removal and refitting

1   This operation is part of the spring support arm removal and refitting procedure, and reference should be made to the relevant paragraphs of Section 19.

21 Rear shock absorber – removal and refitting

1   Jack up the rear of the car and support it on axle stands. Remove the roadwheel.
2   Remove the plastic cover over the spring support arm by releasing

the retaining clips on early models, or by undoing the small bolts (photo) on later versions.
3   Position a sturdy jack beneath the spring support arm, and raise the jack slightly to take the tension of the road spring.
4   Undo the nut and washer, then remove the shock absorber lower mounting bolt from the spring support arm. Ease the shock absorber lower mounting from the arm (photo).
5   From inside the boot, release the retaining buttons and plastic clips securing the vertical trim covering over the fuel tank. This need only be done on the side being worked on, and just sufficiently to fold back the covering for access.
6   Remove the moulded plastic trim panel over the shock absorber (photo).

7 Using two spanners, slacken the shock absorber upper mounting locknuts and remove the upper nut (photo).
8 Remove the lower nut, followed by the washer and rubber mounting (photos).
9 Push the shock absorber down, and remove it from under the wheel arch.
10 Test the operation of the shock absorber, while holding it in an upright position, by moving the spindle through a full stroke, then through short strokes of about half its total travel. In both cases, the resistance felt should be smooth and continuous. If the resistance is jerky or uneven, or if there is any visible sign of wear or damage to the unit, renewal is necessary.
11 Refitting is the reverse sequence to removal, ensuring that the mountings are tightened to the specified torque.

22 Rear anti-roll bar – removal and refitting

1 Jack up the rear of the car and support it on axle stands. Remove the rear roadwheels.
2 Undo the nuts and bolts securing the anti-roll bar to the spring support arm connecting links on both sides.
3 Undo the two nuts each side securing the mounting clamp plates, and remove both plates.
4 Manipulate the anti-roll bar sideways, and remove it from under the right-hand wheel arch.
5 If required, the mounting bushes can be renewed by sliding them off the ends of the bar. Lubricate the new bushes with rubber grease prior to fitting.
6 Refitting is the reverse sequence to removal.

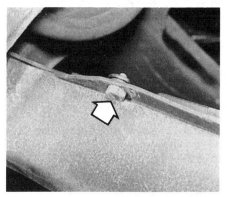
21.2 Spring support arm cover retaining bolt (arrowed)

21.4 Release the shock absorber lower mounting (arrowed)

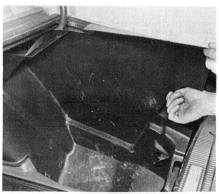
21.6 Remove the side trim panel in the boot

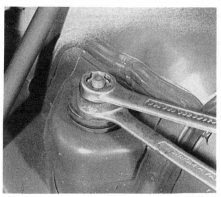
21.7 Slacken the shock absorber mounting locknuts

21.8A Remove the two nuts ...

21.8B ... followed by the washer ...

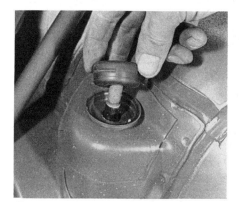
21.8C ... and rubber mounting

23.2 Prise out the steering wheel trim motif

23.3 Undo the retaining bolt with an Allen key socket bit

23 Steering wheel – removal and refitting

1   Set the roadwheels in the straight-ahead position.
2   Using a small screwdriver, carefully prise out the trim motif from the centre of the steering wheel pad (photo).
3   Using an Allen key type socket bit and extension bar, unscrew the steering wheel retaining bolt, with the help of an assistant if necessary to hold the wheel (photo).
4   Withdraw the steering wheel from the shaft.
5   Before refitting the steering wheel, check if there is a marking line or notch on the end of the steering shaft. If so, ensure that this is uppermost.
6   Position the steering wheel on the shaft with the spokes horizontal, and the slightly-curved spoke at the bottom.
7   Fit the retaining bolt and tighten to the specified torque.
8   Refit the trim motif.

24 Steering column – removal and refitting

1   Remove the trim panel under the facia on the driver's side.
2   Remove the steering wheel as described in Section 23.
3   Remove the instrument panel as described in Chapter 12.
4   Jack up the front of the car and support it on axle stands.
5   From under the car, undo the two socket-headed pinch-bolts securing the flexible rubber coupling to the steering gear spindle and steering column lower shaft.
6   Slide the rubber coupling off the steering gear spindle.
7   From inside the car, undo the three screws securing the combination switch to the column.
8   Withdraw the combination switch and remove the one-piece steering column shroud.
9   Remove the complete steering lock assembly as described in Section 26.
10 Undo the two nuts and remove the column upper mounting bolts (photo).

11 Undo the two nuts and remove the column lower mounting bolts (photo).
12 Release the rubber guide sleeve from the floor at the base of the column, then remove the column assembly from the car.
13 Check the condition of the flexible rubber coupling on the column lower shaft, and renew the shaft if there is any sign of deterioration of the coupling. The shaft should also be renewed if the corrugated section shows any sign of distortion, damage, or evidence of compression to any of the corrugations.
14 Before refitting the steering column, the steering gear must be centered with the roadwheels in the straight-ahead position. To do this, unscrew the hexagon-headed plug from the steering gear adjacent to the Pitman arm (photo). Slowly turn the steering gear by means of the steering gear spindle, while viewing through the plug orifice. When a centering hole appears in the piston being viewed through the orifice, the steering is centered. Ideally, the steering gear should be locked in this position by obtaining a suitable long bolt that will screw into the plug orifice, then file a point at the end. This will then engage and lock the piston, preventing any movement of the steering gear.
15 Lubricate the sealing ring at the base of the column lower shaft, and position the column assembly and rubber guide sleeve in the car.
16 Refit the column upper and lower mounting bolts and nuts, but leave them slack at this stage.
17 Refit the steering column lock assembly as described in Section 26.
18 Tighten the column upper and lower mountings to the specified torque.
19 Engage the flexible rubber coupling with the steering gear spindle, then fit and tighten the two pinch-bolts.
20 From under the car, remove the bolt used to lock the steering gear, and refit the plug bolt.
21 Refit the steering column shrouds and the combination switch.
22 Slip the rubber guide sleeve into its location in the floor.
23 Refit the instrument panel as described in Chapter 12.
24 Refit the steering wheel as described in Section 23.
25 Refit the trim panel under the facia and lower the car to the ground.

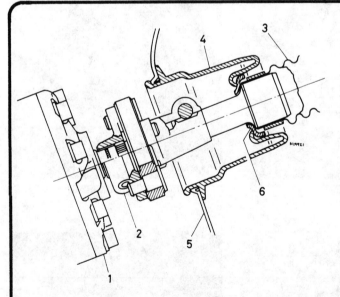

Fig. 10.27 Steering column coupling and rubber guide sleeve details (Sec 24)

1 Steering gear
2 Flexible rubber coupling
3 Steering column lower shaft
4 Rubber guide sleeve
5 Floorpan
6 Sealing ring

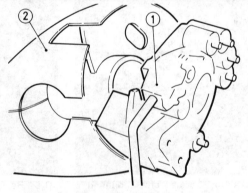

Fig. 10.28 Removing the combination switch (1) and steering column shroud (2) (Sec 24)

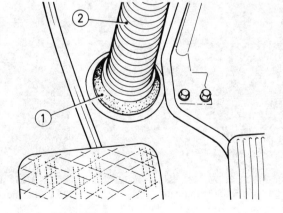

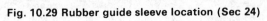

Fig. 10.29 Rubber guide sleeve location (Sec 24)

1 Rubber guide sleeve
2 Steering column lower shaft

Chapter 10 Suspension and steering

24.10 Steering column upper mountings (arrowed)

24.11 Steering column lower mountings (arrowed)

24.14 Steering gear centering hole plug bolt (arrowed)

25 Steering column – dismantling and reassembly

1   Remove the steering column as described in Section 24.
2   With the column assembly on the bench, undo the pinch-bolt at the upper rubber coupling, and separate the column lower shaft from the upper shaft.
3   At the base of the upper shaft, extract the circlip and remove the spring disc and supporting ring.
4   Push the shaft upwards slightly, then push the support ring at the top of the shaft down to allow removal of the locking ring. With the locking ring removed, slide off the support ring.
5   Slide the steering shaft down the column, and place a flat piece of metal behind the upper bearing. Firmly push the shaft up, to force the bearing out of the column.

6   Repeat this procedure to remove the lower bearing, then remove the shaft from the column.
7   Check all the dismantled parts for wear, and renew as necessary.
8   Using a socket, tube or other suitable mandrel, tap the lower bearing into place in the column.
9   Insert the steering shaft from above into the column, then fit the upper bearing using the same procedure as in the preceding paragraph.
10 Slide the support ring onto the shaft so that its lug engages with the shaft groove.
11 Refit the locking ring to the shaft groove.
12 At the base of the upper shaft, refit the supporting ring, spring disc and circlip. Use a tube to push the circlip down until it enters its groove in the shaft.
13 Refit the column lower shaft and secure the coupling with the pinch-bolt, tightened to the specified torque.

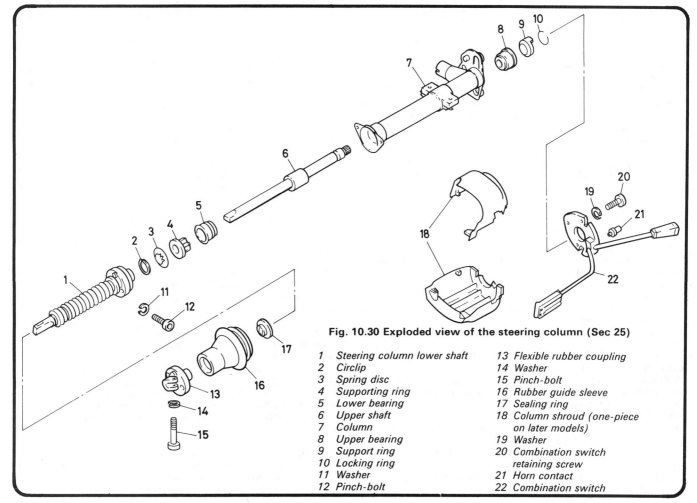

Fig. 10.30 Exploded view of the steering column (Sec 25)

1   Steering column lower shaft
2   Circlip
3   Spring disc
4   Supporting ring
5   Lower bearing
6   Upper shaft
7   Column
8   Upper bearing
9   Support ring
10 Locking ring
11 Washer
12 Pinch-bolt
13 Flexible rubber coupling
14 Washer
15 Pinch-bolt
16 Rubber guide sleeve
17 Sealing ring
18 Column shroud (one-piece on later models)
19 Washer
20 Combination switch retaining screw
21 Horn contact
22 Combination switch

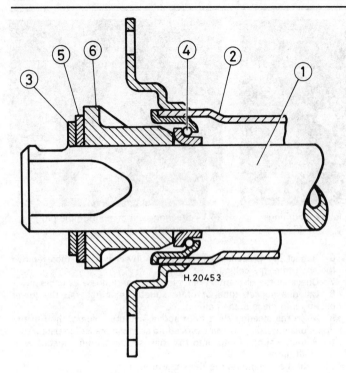

Fig. 10.31 Sectional view of the column lower bearing
components (Sec 25)

1	Upper shaft	4	Lower bearing
2	Column	5	Spring disc
3	Circlip	6	Supporting ring

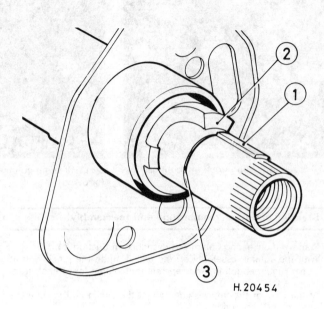

Fig. 10.32 Steering column upper bearing components
(Sec 25)

1	Upper shaft
2	Supporting ring
3	Locking ring

26 Steering lock – removal and refitting

1   The steering lock is a three-part assembly comprising the electrical
part of the ignition switch, the ignition switch lock barrel, and the
mechanical part of the steering lock mechanism. All three parts can be
removed and refitted separately as follows.

Ignition switch
2   Disconnect the battery negative terminal.
3   Remove the trim panel under the facia on the driver's side.
4   Refer to Section 23 and remove the steering wheel.
5   Refer to Chapter 12 and remove the instrument panel.
6   Using a small screwdriver, carefully prise off the trim ring around
the ignition switch.
7   Insert the ignition key and turn the switch to position 'I'.
8   Working through the instrument panel aperture, pull off the wiring
multi-plug at the rear of the switch.
9   Undo the three screws securing the combination switch to the
steering column.
10 Withdraw the combination switch and remove the one-piece
steering column shroud.
11 Slacken the bolt to release the clamp around the steering lock
body.
12 Depress the locking pin located behind the clamp, and slightly
withdraw the lock body.
13 Remove the ignition key, then swivel the lock body so that it clears
the ignition switch hole in the facia. If necessary, undo the facia
retaining screw adjacent to the steering column and ease the facia
outwards for increased clearance.
14 Withdraw the lock body from the steering column and disconnect
the wiring plug at the contact switch.
15 Reinsert the ignition key, turn it to position 'I' and remove the
contact switch.
16 Undo the three screws securing the ignition switch to the rear of
the lock body and remove the switch.

17 To refit the switch, place it in position on the lock body, ensuring
that the tag on the switch engages with the notch in the body. Secure
the switch with the three screws.
18 The remainder of the procedure is the reverse sequence to removal.
Ensure that the locking pin is depressed as the lock body is fitted, and
that the pin enters its locating hole. When depressing the pin, and
when fitting the contact switch and the main wiring multi-plug, the
ignition key must be inserted and turned to position 'I'.

Ignition switch lock barrel
19 Using a small screwdriver, carefully prise off the trim ring around
the ignition switch.
20 Insert the ignition key and turn the switch to position 'I'.
21 Bend a suitable length of 2.0 mm (0.07 in) diameter wire (a piece
of welding rod is ideal) into a U-shape, and file a 60° chamfer on each
end, facing inwards.
22 Insert the releasing wire into the slots on each side of the lock
barrel, and push the wire in to compress the detents.
23 Withdraw the lock barrel using the ignition key.
24 Remove the releasing wire and ignition key, then withdraw the lock
barrel from its sleeve.
25 To refit, insert the lock barrel into the steering lock body, with the
raised section engaged in the lock body groove.
26 Position the sleeve over the lock barrel with its detent towards the
steering column.
27 Insert the ignition key, turn it to position 'I' and push both the lock
barrel and cover fully into the steering lock body. **Note:** *The edge of
the ignition key must point towards the mark on the cover while fitting,
thus indicating that the cover detent is in correct alignment.*
28 Check the lock and lock barrel for correct operation, then refit the
trim ring.

Steering lock mechanism
29 Removal of the steering lock mechanism complete is included in
the procedures at the beginning of this Section. Carry out paragraphs 2
to 18 inclusive, with the exception of paragraph 16.

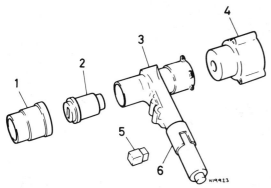

Fig. 10.33 Exploded view of the steering lock components (Sec 26)

1	Lock barrel sleeve	4	Ignition switch
2	Lock barrel	5	Contact switch
3	Lock body	6	Locking pin

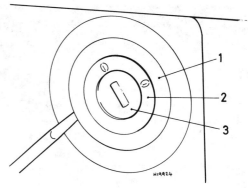

Fig. 10.34 Using a screwdriver to prise off the ignition switch trim ring (Sec 26)

1	Trim ring	3	Lock barrel
2	Lock barrel sleeve		

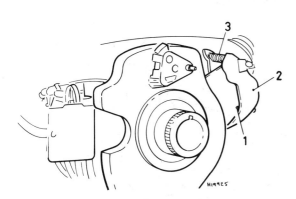

Fig. 10.35 Steering lock body clamp details (Sec 26)

1	Locking pin	3	Clamp bolt
2	Clamp		

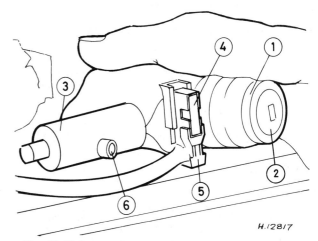

Fig. 10.36 Steering lock assembly removal (Sec 26)

1	Lock barrel sleeve	4	Contact switch
2	Lock barrel	5	Contact switch wiring plug
3	Steering lock	6	Locking pin

27 Power steering gear – removal and refitting

1 Unscrew the power steering pump reservoir cap nut, lift off the cover and draw off the fluid in the reservoir using a clean syringe such as a poultry baster.
2 Unscrew the high-pressure hose and return hose union nuts at the steering gear, while using a second spanner to hold the union adaptors. Remove the two hoses and plug or tape over their ends, and the adaptors on the steering gear, to prevent dirt ingress.
3 Jack up the front of the car and support it on axle stands.
4 Undo the two socket-headed pinch-bolts securing the flexible rubber coupling to the steering gear spindle and steering column lower shaft.
5 Slide the rubber coupling upwards off the steering gear spindle.
6 Undo the two nuts securing the drag link and track rod balljoints to the steering gear Pitman arm (photo). Release the balljoints from the arm using a balljoint separator tool.
7 From under the wheel arch, undo the three bolts securing the steering gear to the chassis member.
8 Remove the steering gear from under the car.
9 Before refitting, the steering gear must be centered and locked in the straight-ahead position, using the procedure described in Section 24, paragraph 14.
10 Place the steering gear in position and secure to the chassis member using three new retaining bolts, tightened to the specified torque.
11 Turn the steering wheel to the straight-ahead position, ie with the top of the wheel boss horizontal.

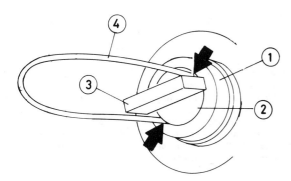

Fig. 10.37 Ignition switch lock barrel removal (Sec 26)

1	Lock barrel sleeve	3	Ignition key in position '1'
2	Lock barrel	4	Releasing wire

27.6 Drag link (A) and track rod (B) attachments at the steering gear Pitman arm (C)

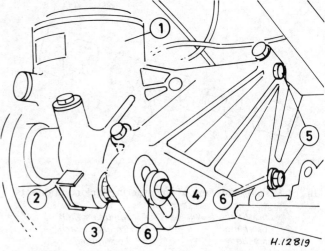

Fig. 10.38 Power steering pump mounting details (Sec 28)

1 Power steering pump   4 Adjuster lockbolt
2 Locking nut   5 Mounting bolts
3 Toothed adjuster   6 Washers

12 Slide the flexible rubber coupling onto the steering gear spindle, screw in the two pinch-bolts, and tighten to the specified torque.
13 Remove the bolt used to lock the steering gear and refit the plug bolt.
14 Refit the drag link and track rod balljoints to the Pitman arm, screw on the retaining nuts, and tighten the nuts while holding the balljoint shanks with an Allen key.
15 Lower the car to the ground.
16 Refit the high-pressure and return hoses to the steering gear, and tighten the unions securely.
17 Fill the power steering pump reservoir with the specified fluid.
18 Start the engine and turn the steering wheel several times to full-left, then full-right lock, while keeping the fluid level in the reservoir topped-up. When the fluid level remains constant, top up finally to the correct level (see Section 2, paragraph 10), then refit the cover and cap nut.

28 Power steering pump (pre-October 1984 models) – removal and refitting

Note: *The following procedure covers models in which multiple drivebelts are used to drive the engine ancillaries. On cars with a single drivebelt layout, refer to Section 29.*
1 Unscrew the cap nut and lift off the cover on the power steering pump reservoir.
2 Unscrew the nut from the long stud in the centre of the reservoir, and remove the pressure spring from the stud.
3 Withdraw the filter cartridge from the reservoir.
4 Using a clean syringe such as a poultry baster, draw off the fluid from the reservoir.
5 Unscrew the high-pressure and return hose pipe unions on the side of the pump and withdraw the pipes. Plug or tape over the pipe ends and pump orifices to prevent dirt ingress.
6 At the rear of the pump mounting bracket, slacken the adjuster lockbolt furthest from the engine, and the two mounting bolts nearest to the engine.
7 Turn the toothed adjuster bolt using an open-ended spanner to move the pump towards the engine and relieve the tension on the drivebelt.
8 Slip the drivebelt off the pump pulley.
9 Undo the three bolts securing the pulley to the pump flange and remove the pulley.
10 Undo and remove the two mounting bolts at the rear of the pump mounting bracket, and recover the threaded retaining plate from the front.
11 Undo and remove the adjuster lockbolt from the rear of the pump, and recover the locking nut and toothed adjuster.
12 Remove the pump from the engine.

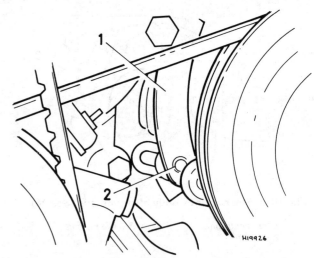

Fig. 10.39 Power steering pump threaded retaining plate (1) and mounting bolt (2) (Sec 28)

13 Refitting is the reverse sequence to removal, bearing in mind the following points:

(a) With the drivebelt in position, adjust its tension as described in Section 30
(b) When refitting the filter cartridge pressure spring and nut, tighten the nut just sufficiently to pre-load the spring
(c) On completion of refitting, fill the reservoir with the specified fluid, then start the engine and turn the steering onto full-left, then full-right lock a few times, topping-up the fluid as necessary. When the fluid level remains constant, top up finally to the correct level (see Section 2, paragraph 10), then refit the cover and cap nut

29 Power steering pump (October 1984 models onwards) – removal and refitting

Note: *The following procedure covers models in which a single drivebelt is used to drive the engine ancillaries. On cars with a multiple drivebelt layout, refer to Section 28.*
1 For increased working access, remove the air cleaner assembly as described in Chapter 3.

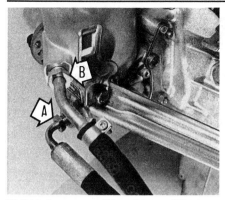

29.6 High-pressure (A) and return (B) pipe unions at the power steering pump

29.8 Pulley-to-pump flange retaining bolts

29.10 Power steering pump-to-mounting bracket bolts (arrowed)

2   Unscrew the cap nut and lift off the cover on the power steering pump reservoir.
3   Unscrew the nut from the long stud in the centre of the reservoir, and remove the plastic sleeve and pressure spring from the stud.
4   Withdraw the filter cartridge from the reservoir.
5   Using a clean syringe such as a poultry baster, draw off the fluid from the reservoir.
6   Unscrew the high-pressure and return hose pipe unions on the side of the pump and withdraw the pipes (photo). Plug or tape over the pipe ends and pump orifices to prevent dirt ingress.
7   Referring to the procedures given in Chapter 12, Section 6, slacken the drivebelt and remove it from the pump pulley.
8   Undo the three bolts, and remove the pulley from the pump flange (photo).
9   Undo the bolt securing the support strut to the rear of the pump, and slacken the bolt securing the strut to the engine. Swivel the strut clear of the pump.
10 Undo the two bolts and nuts securing the pump to the mounting bracket, and remove the unit from the engine (photo).
11 Refitting is the reverse sequence to removal, bearing in mind the following points:

(a) With the drivebelt in position, adjust its tension as described in Chapter 12, Section 6
(b) When refitting the filter cartridge, pressure spring plastic sleeve and nut, tighten the nut just sufficiently to pre-load the spring
(c) On completion of refitting, fill the reservoir with the specified fluid, then start the engine and turn the steering onto full-left, then full-right lock a few times, topping-up the fluid as necessary. When the fluid level remains constant, top up finally to the correct level (see Section 2, paragraph 10), then refit the cover and cap nut

30 Power steering pump drivebelt – removal, refitting and adjustment

Note: *The following procedure covers models in which multiple drivebelts are used to drive the engine ancillaries (up to approximately October 1984). On later cars with a single drivebelt layout, refer to Chapter 12, Section 6*

1   Refer to Chapter 12, Section 6 and remove the alternator drivebelt.
2   At the rear of the power steering pump mounting bracket, slacken the adjuster lockbolt furthest from the engine and the two mounting bolts nearest to the engine.
3   Turn the toothed adjuster bolt using an open-ended spanner to move the pump towards the engine, then slip the drivebelt off the pulleys.
4   Examine the belt for cracks, fraying, signs of oil contamination or evidence of the belt bottoming in the vee of the pulleys. Renew the belt if at all suspect.
5   Refit the belt over the pulleys, then turn the adjuster bolt until it is just possible to deflect the drivebelt by approximately 12.0 mm (0.5 in) under moderate finger pressure midway between the two pulleys.
6   Tighten the adjuster lockbolt, followed by the two mounting bolts.

31 Steering damper – removal and refitting

1   Jack up the front of the car and support it on axle stands.
2   Undo the nuts and remove the bolts securing the damper to the drag link and chassis bracket (photos).

31.2A Steering damper-to-drag link retaining nut (arrowed) ...

31.2B ... and damper mounting at the chassis bracket (arrowed)

3 Remove the damper from under the car.
4 Check the operation of the damper by compressing and releasing it through two or three full strokes, then several half strokes. At all times, the resistance felt should be continuous and even. If the resistance is jerky or uneven, or if there is any damage to the damper body or mounting bushes, obtain a new unit.
5 Refitting is the reverse sequence to removal, but note that the piston (large) end of the damper must be fitted to the chassis bracket. Tighten the retaining nuts to the specified torque.

32 Drag link – removal and refitting

1 Jack up the front of the car and support it on axle stands.
2 Undo the nut and bolt securing the steering damper to the drag link.
3 Undo the retaining nuts, and release the drag link balljoints from the steering gear Pitman arm and the idler arm, using a balljoint separator tool.
4 Remove the drag link from under the car.
5 Check the condition of the drag link balljoints, which should be reasonably stiff to move. If they are sloppy or have excessive free play, renew the drag link. The drag link should also be renewed if the balljoint dust covers have deteriorated, or are damaged or split. If, however, the damage was caused during removal, the dust covers can be renewed separately as described in Section 11.
6 Refitting is the reverse sequence to removal. Tighten the balljoint retaining nuts to the specified torque while holding the balljoint shank with an Allen key.

33 Steering track rod – removal and refitting

1 Jack up the front of the car and support it on axle stands. Remove the front roadwheel.
2 Undo the nut securing the track rod outer balljoint to the steering arm, and release the balljoint using a separator tool (photos).
3 Undo the nut securing the track rod inner balljoint to the steering gear Pitman arm or idler arm (photo). Release the balljoint using the separator tool.
4 Remove the track rod from the car.
5 Check the condition of the track rod balljoints, which should be reasonably stiff to move. If they are sloppy or have excess free play, renew the balljoint(s). The balljoint should also be renewed if the dust cover has deteriorated, or is damaged or split. If, however, the damage was caused during removal, the dust cover can be renewed separately as described in Section 11.
6 To renew a balljoint, first record the number of exposed threads between the balljoint and track rod. if the outer balljoint is being renewed, slacken the two locknuts. If the inner balljoint is being renewed, slacken the clamp nut and bolt. Now grip the track rod and unscrew the balljoint.
7 To refit the balljoint, first transfer the two locknuts if a new outer joint is being fitted, then screw the balljoint into the track rod until the

same number of threads as noted during removal are showing. If both balljoints are being refitted or renewed, set the distance between their ballpin centres as shown in Fig. 10.40, and with the same number of exposed threads on each.
8 Tighten the two locknuts or the clamp nut and bolt as applicable.
9 Fit the track rod to the car, with the balljoint having the two locknuts attached to the steering knuckle arm.
10 Refit the locknuts and tighten while holding the ball-pin with an Allen key (photo).
11 Refit the roadwheel and lower the car to the ground.
12 Check the front wheel alignment as described in Section 35.

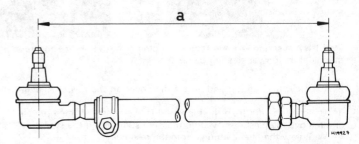

Fig. 10.40 Steering track rod fitting dimension (Sec 33)

a = 333.0 to 337.0 mm (13.12 to 13.28 in)

33.2A Release the balljoint taper using a separator tool ...

33.2B ... and remove the balljoint from the steering arm

33.3 Undo the nut (arrowed) securing the inner balljoint to the Pitman arm

33.10 Tighten the retaining nut while holding the ball-pin with an Allen key

34 Steering idler arm assembly – removal and refitting

1 Jack up the front of the car and support it on axle stands.
2 Unscrew the retaining nuts, and release the track rod and drag link balljoints from the idler arm, using a balljoint separator tool.
3 Undo the idler arm retaining nut and remove the sealing washer (photo).
4 Withdraw the through-bolt, idler arm and dust cap upwards from the idler bracket, and remove them from the car. Recover any washers, if fitted, from between the idler arm and dust cap.
5 If necessary the idler bushes can be renewed as follows.
6 Lift up the sealing lip of the rubber slide bearing using a screwdriver, and withdraw the slide bushing from the slide bearing.
7 The slide bearings can be renewed by drawing them out using a tube of suitable diameter, long bolt, nut and packing washers. Fit the new slide bearings in a similar way.
8 Fit the slide bushing to the slide bearing, while lifting up the sealing lip as done during removal.
9 Fit the dust cap to the top of the slide bearing assembly, then fit the idler arm, through-bolt, and any washers recovered during removal.
10 Refit the lower washer and retaining nut, and tighten to the specified torque.
11 Locate the drag link and track rod balljoints into the idler arm, refit the retaining nuts and tighten while holding the ball pins with an Allen key.
12 Lower the car to the ground.

35 Front and rear wheel alignment, and steering angles

1 Accurate front and rear wheel alignment is necessary to provide positive steering and handling characteristics and to prevent excessive tyre wear.

Front suspension
2 The front wheel alignment consists of four factors:
Camber is the angle at which the front wheels are set from the vertical when viewed from the front of the car. 'Positive camber' is the amount (in degrees) that the wheels are tilted outwards at the top from the vertical.
Castor is the angle between the steering axis and a vertical line when viewed from the side of the car. 'Positive castor' is when the steering axis is inclined rearwards.
King pin inclination is the angle (when viewed from the front of the car) between the vertical and an imaginary line drawn between the suspension strut upper mounting and the wishbone balljoint.
Toe setting is the amount by which the distance between the front inside edges of the roadwheels (measured at hub height) differs from the diametrically opposite distance, measured between the rear inside edges of the roadwheels.
3 Camber and castor are both adjustable by means of the front wishbone eccentric mounting bolts. The front mounting being mainly responsible for camber angle adjustment, while the rear mounting can be used to adjust the castor. Adjustment of one variable also affects the other, and both affect the kingpin inclination.

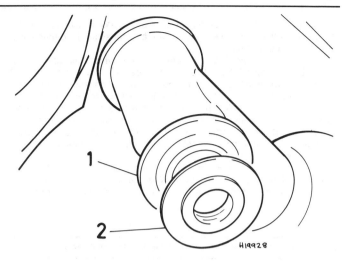

Fig. 10.41 Idler assembly bush renewal (Sec 34)

1 Rubber slide bearing   2 Slide bushing

4 The toe setting is adjustable by altering the length of the two steering track rods.
5 With the exception of the toe setting, all other adjustments can only be carried out accurately using Mercedes-Benz setting gauges, or optical wheel alignment equipment. These settings will not normally require adjustment unless the car has been involved in an accident, or new components have been fitted.

Rear suspension
6 The rear wheel alignment is adjustable for toe setting and track angle change. The toe setting is as described in paragraph 2, and is controlled by means of an eccentric bolt at the track rod inner mounting. The track angle change is the variation in toe setting with suspension travel, and this is adjustable by means of the eccentric bolt on the pulling strut inner mounting.
7 All the rear suspension adjustments require the use of special equipment, and can only be carried out by a Mercedes-Benz dealer.

Checking and adjustment
8 As mentioned previously, the only adjustment which can be carried out without sophisticated workshop equipment is the front toe setting, and this can be done as follows.
9 Before making any checks or adjustments, check that the tyres are correctly inflated, the front wheels are not buckled or their rims damaged, and the steering linkage and suspension joints are in good order, without slackness or wear.
10 Two methods are available to the home mechanic for checking the toe setting. One method is to use a gauge to measure the distance between the front and rear inside edges of the roadwheels. The other method is to use a scuff plate, in which each front wheel is rolled across a movable plate which records any deviation, or scuff, of the tyre from the straight-ahead position as it moves across the plate.

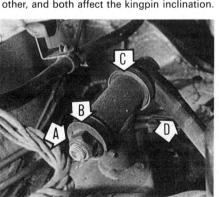

34.3 Steering idler arm assembly showing the retaining nut (A), sealing washer (B), dust cap (C) and idler arm (D)

35.12A Steering track rod locknuts (arrowed) ...

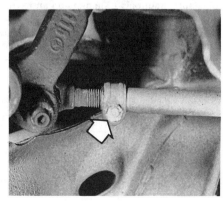

35.12B ... and inner clamp (arrowed)

Relatively inexpensive equipment of both types is available from accessory outlets to enable these checks, and subsequent adjustments, to be carried out at home.

11 If, after checking the toe setting using whichever method is preferable, it is found that adjustment is necessary, proceed as follows.

12 Slacken the two locknuts at the outer end of each steering track rod (photo) and the clamp nut and bolt at the track rod inner end (photo).

13 Using a pair of grips, turn both track rods by small, equal, amounts to increase or decrease their length as necessary, then recheck the adjustment. Be sure that the steering is in the straight-ahead position at all times, and if a gauge is being used, roll the car forwards (never backwards) before checking.

14 Repeat the above procedure, making small corrections to the track rods each time, until the toe setting is as specified.

15 On completion, tighten the two clamp nuts and bolts first, followed by the outer locknuts.

36 Wheels and tyres – general care and maintenance

Wheels and tyres should give no real problems in use provided that a close eye is kept on them with regard to excessive wear or damage. To this end, the following points should be noted.

Ensure that tyre pressures are checked regularly and maintained correctly. Checking should be carried out with the tyres cold and not immediately after the vehicle has been in use. If the pressures are checked with the tyres hot, an apparently high reading will be obtained owing to heat expansion. Under no circumstances should an attempt be made to reduce the pressures to the quoted cold reading in this instance, or effective underinflation will result.

Underinflation will cause overheating of the tyre owing to excessive flexing of the casing, and the tread will not sit correctly on the road surface. This will cause a consequent loss of adhesion and excessive wear, not to mention the danger of sudden tyre failure due to heat build-up.

Overinflation will cause rapid wear of the centre part of the tyre tread coupled with reduced adhesion, harsher ride, and the danger of shock damage occurring in the tyre casing.

Regularly check the tyres for damage in the form of cuts or bulges, especially in the sidewalls. Remove any nails or stones embedded in the tread before they penetrate the tyre to cause deflation. If removal of a nail *does* reveal that the tyre has been punctured, refit the nail so that its point of penetration is marked. Then immediately change the wheel and have the tyre repaired by a tyre dealer. Do *not* drive on a tyre in such a condition. In many cases a puncture can be simply repaired by the use of an inner tube of the correct size and type. If in any doubt as to the possible consequences of any damage found, consult your local tyre dealer for advice.

Periodically remove the wheels and clean any dirt or mud from the inside and outside surfaces. Examine the wheel rims for signs of rusting, corrosion or other damage. Light alloy wheels are easily damaged by 'kerbing' whilst parking, and similarly steel wheels may become dented or buckled. Renewal of the wheel is very often the only course of remedial action possible.

The balance of each wheel and tyre assembly should be maintained to avoid excessive wear, not only to the tyres but also to the steering and suspension components. Wheel imbalance is normally signified by vibration through the vehicle's bodyshell, although in many cases it is particularly noticeable through the steering wheel. Conversely, it should be noted that wear or damage in suspension or steering components may cause excessive tyre wear. Out-of-round or out-of-true tyres, damaged wheels and wheel bearing wear/maladjustment also fall into this category. Balancing will not usually cure vibration caused by such wear.

Wheel balancing may be carried out with the wheel either on or off the vehicle. If balanced on the vehicle, ensure that the wheel-to-hub relationship is marked in some way prior to subsequent wheel removal so that it may be refitted in its original position.

General tyre wear is influenced to a large degree by driving style – harsh braking and acceleration or fast cornering will all produce more rapid tyre wear. Interchanging of tyres may result in more even wear, but this should only be carried out where there is no mix of tyre types on the vehicle. However, it is worth bearing in mind that if this is completely effective, the added expense of replacing a complete set of tyres simultaneously is incurred, which may prove financially restrictive for many owners.

Front tyres may wear unevenly as a result of wheel misalignment. The front wheels should always be correctly aligned according to the settings specified by the vehicle manufacturer.

Legal restrictions apply to the mixing of tyre types on a vehicle. Basically this means that a vehicle must not have tyres of differing construction on the same axle. Although it is not recommended to mix tyre types between front axle and rear axle, the only legally permissible combination is crossply at the front and radial at the rear. When mixing radial ply tyres, textile braced radials must always go on the front axle, with steel braced radials at the rear. An obvious disadvantage of such mixing is the necessity to carry two spare tyres to avoid contravening the law in the event of a puncture.

In the UK, the Motor Vehicles Construction and Use Regulations apply to many aspects of tyre fitting and usage. It is suggested that a copy of these regulations is obtained from your local police if in doubt as to the current legal requirements with regard to tyre condition, minimum tread depth, etc.

37 Fault diagnosis – suspension and steering

Note: *More detailed fault diagnosis on the power steering gear entails the use of special test equipment. Apart from the general references listed below, faults on this system should be referred to a Mercedes-Benz dealer.*

Symptom	Reason(s)
Excessive play in steering	Worn steering gear
	Worn track rod or drag link balljoints
	Worn idler arm bushes
	Worn wishbone balljoint or mountings
Car wanders or pulls to one side	Incorrect wheel alignment
	Worn track rod or diag link balljoints
	Worn wishbone balljoint or mountings
	Uneven tyre pressures
	Faulty tyre
	Accident damage
	Binding brakes

Symptom	Reason(s)
Heavy or stiff steering	Power steering pump drivebelt slipping or broken Incorrect wheel alignment Incorrect tyre pressures Seized suspension or steering balljoint Power steering gear fault Bent or distorted steering column or steering shaft Partially seized steering damper
Wheel wobble and vibration	Roadwheels out of balance Roadwheels damaged Faulty tyre Faulty steering damper Weak shock absorber Excessive play in hub bearings
Excessive tyre wear	Incorrect tyre pressures Incorrect wheel alignment Roadwheels out of balance Faulty tyre Wear in steering or suspension components

Chapter 11 Bodywork

Contents

1 General description

The body is of unitary all-steel construction, and incorporates computer-calculated impact crumple zones at the front and rear, with a central safety cell passenger compartment. During manufacture the body is dip-primed, fully sealed and undercoated then painted with multi-layered base and top-coats.

The bodyshell on all models covered by this manual is of four-door saloon configuration.

2 Maintenance – bodywork and underframe

The general condition of a vehicle's bodywork is the one thing that significantly affects its value. Maintenance is easy but needs to be regular. Neglect, particularly after minor damage, can lead quickly to further deterioration and costly repair bills. It is important also to keep watch on those parts of the vehicle not immediately visible, for instance the underside, inside all the wheel arches and the lower part of the engine compartment.

The basic maintenance routine for the bodywork is washing – preferably with a lot of water, from a hose. This will remove all the loose solids which may have stuck to the vehicle. It is important to flush these off in such a way as to prevent grit from scratching the finish. The wheel arches and underframe need washing in the same way to remove any accumulated mud which will retain moisture and tend to encourage rust. Paradoxically enough, the best time to clean the underframe and wheel arches is in wet weather when the mud is thoroughly wet and soft. In very wet weather the underframe is usually cleaned of large accumulations automatically and this is a good time for inspection.

Periodically, except on vehicles with a wax-based underbody protective coating, it is a good idea to have the whole of the underframe of the vehicle steam cleaned, engine compartment included, so that a thorough inspection can be carried out to see what minor repairs and renovations are necessary. Steam cleaning is available at many garages and is necessary for removal of the accumulation of oily grime which sometimes is allowed to become thick in certain areas. If steam cleaning facilities are not available, there are one or two excellent grease solvents available which can be brush applied. The dirt can then be simply hosed off. Note that these methods should not be used on vehicles with wax-based underbody protective coating or the coating will be removed. Such vehicles should be inspected annually, preferably just prior to winter, when the underbody should be washed down and any damage to the wax coating repaired. Ideally, a completely fresh coat should be applied. It would also be worth considering the use of such wax-based protection for injection into door panels, sills, box sections, etc, as an additional safeguard against rust damage where such protection is not provided by the vehicle manufacturer.

After washing paintwork, wipe off with a chamois leather to give an unspotted clear finish. A coat of clear protective wax polish will give added protection against chemical pollutants in the air. If the paintwork sheen has dulled or oxidised, use a cleaner/polisher combination to restore the brilliance of the shine. This requires a little effort, but such dulling is usually caused because regular washing has been neglected. Care needs to be taken with metallic paintwork, as special non-abrasive cleaner/polisher is required to avoid damage to the finish. Always check that the door and ventilator opening drain holes and pipes are completely clear so that water can be drained out. Bright work should be treated in the same way as paint work. Windscreens and windows can be kept clear of the smeary film which often appears by the use of a proprietary glass cleaner. Never use any form of wax or other body or chromium polish on glass.

3 Maintenance – upholstery and carpets

Mats and carpets should be brushed or vacuum cleaned regularly to keep them free of grit. If they are badly stained remove them from the vehicle for scrubbing or sponging and make quite sure they are dry before refitting. Seats and interior trim panels can be kept clean by wiping with a damp cloth. If they do become stained (which can be more apparent on light coloured upholstery) use a little liquid detergent and a soft nail brush to scour the grime out of the grain of the material. Do not forget to keep the headlining clean in the same way as the upholstery. When using liquid cleaners inside the vehicle do not over-wet the surfaces being cleaned. Excessive damp could get into the seams and padded interior causing stains, offensive odours or even rot. If the inside of the vehicle gets wet accidentally it is worthwhile taking some trouble to dry it out properly, particularly where carpets are involved. *Do not leave oil or electric heaters inside the vehicle for this purpose.*

4 Minor body damage – repair

The colour bodywork repair photographic sequences between pages 32 and 33 illustrate the operations detailed in the following sub-sections.
Note: *For more detailed information about bodywork repair, the Haynes Publishing Group publish a book by Lindsay Porter called The Car Bodywork Repair Manual. This incorporates information on such aspects as rust treatment, painting and glass fibre repairs, as well as details on more ambitious repairs involving welding and panel beating.*

Repair of minor scratches in bodywork
If the scratch is very superficial, and does not penetrate to the metal of the bodywork, repair is very simple. Lightly rub the area of the scratch with a paintwork renovator, or a very fine cutting paste, to remove loose paint from the scratch and to clear the surrounding bodywork of wax polish. Rinse the area with clean water.

Apply touch-up paint to the scratch using a fine paint brush; continue to apply fine layers of paint until the surface of the paint in the scratch is level with the surrounding paintwork. Allow the new paint at least two weeks to harden; then blend it into the surrounding paintwork by rubbing the scratch area with a paintwork renovator or a very fine cutting paste. Finally, apply wax polish.

Where the scratch has penetrated right through to the metal of the bodywork, causing the metal to rust, a different repair technique is required. Remove any loose rust from the bottom of the scratch with a penknife, then apply rust inhibiting paint to prevent the formation of rust in the future. Using a rubber or nylon applicator fill the scratch with bodystopper paste. If required, this paste can be mixed with cellulose thinners to provide a very thin paste which is ideal for filling narrow scratches. Before the stopper-paste in the scratch hardens, wrap a piece of smooth cotton rag around the top of a finger. Dip the finger in cellulose thinners and then quickly sweep it across the surface of the stopper-paste in the scratch; this will ensure that the surface of the stopper-paste is slightly hollowed. The scratch can now be painted over as described earlier in this Section.

Repair of dents in bodywork
When deep denting of the vehicle's bodywork has taken place, the first task is to pull the dent out, until the affected bodywork almost attains its original shape. There is little point in trying to restore the original shape completely, as the metal in the damaged area will have stretched on impact and cannot be reshaped fully to its original contour. It is better to bring the level of the dent up to a point which is about ⅛ in (3 mm) below the level of the surrounding bodywork. In cases where the dent is very shallow anyway, it is not worth trying to pull it out at all. If the underside of the dent is accessible, it can be hammered out gently from behind, using a mallet with a wooden or plastic head. Whilst doing this, hold a suitable block of wood firmly against the outside of the panel to absorb the impact from the hammer blows and thus prevent a large area of the bodywork from being 'belled-out'.

Should the dent be in a section of the bodywork which has a double skin or some other factor making it inaccessible from behind, a different technique is called for. Drill several small holes through the metal inside the area – particularly in the deeper section. Then screw long self-tapping screws into the holes just sufficiently for them to gain a good purchase in the metal. Now the dent can be pulled out by pulling on the protruding heads of the screws with a pair of pliers.

The next stage of the repair is the removal of the paint from the damaged area, and from an inch or so of the surrounding 'sound' bodywork. This is accomplished most easily by using a wire brush or abrasive pad on a power drill, although it can be done just as effectively by hand using sheets of abrasive paper. To complete the preparation for filling, score the surface of the bare metal with a screwdriver or the tang of a file, or alternatively, drill small holes in the affected area. This will provide a really good 'key' for the filler paste.

To complete the repair see the Section on filling and re-spraying.

Repair of rust holes or gashes in bodywork
Remove all paint from the affected area and from an inch or so of the surrounding 'sound' bodywork, using an abrasive pad or a wire brush on a power drill. If these are not available a few sheets of abrasive paper will do the job just as effectively. With the paint removed you will be able to gauge the severity of the corrosion and therefore decide whether to renew the whole panel (if this is possible) or to repair the affected area. New body panels are not as expensive as most people think and it is often quicker and more satisfactory to fit a new panel than to attempt to repair large areas of corrosion.

Remove all fittings from the affected area except those which will act as a guide to the original shape of the damaged bodywork (eg headlamp shells etc). Then, using tin snips or a hacksaw blade, remove all loose metal and any other metal badly affected by corrosion. Hammer the edges of the hole inwards in order to create a slight depression for the filler paste.

Wire brush the affected area to remove the powdery rust from the surface of the remaining metal. Paint the affected area with rust inhibiting paint; if the back of the rusted area is accessible treat this also.

Before filling can take place it will be necessary to block the hole in some way. This can be achieved by the use of aluminium or plastic mesh, or aluminium tape.

Aluminium or plastic mesh is probably the best material to use for a large hole. Cut a piece to the approximate size and shape of the hole to be filled, then position it in the hole so that its edges are below the level of the surrounding bodywork. It can be retained in position by several blobs of filler paste around its periphery.

Aluminium tape should be used for small or very narrow holes. Pull a piece off the roll and trim it to the approximate size and shape required, then pull off the backing paper (if used) and stick the tape over the hole; it can be overlapped if the thickness of one piece is insufficient. Burnish down the edges of the tape with the handle of a screwdriver or similar, to ensure that the tape is securely attached to the metal underneath.

Bodywork repairs – filling and re-spraying
Before using this Section, see the Sections on dent, deep scratch, rust holes and gash repairs.

Many types of bodyfiller are available, but generally speaking those proprietary kits which contain a tin of filler paste and a tube of resin hardener are best for this type of repair. A wide, flexible plastic or nylon applicator will be found invaluable for imparting a smooth and well contoured finish to the surface of the filler.

Mix up a little filler on a clean piece of card or board – measure the hardener carefully (follow the maker's instructions on the pack) otherwise the filler will set too rapidly or too slowly. Using the applicator apply the filler paste to the prepared area; draw the applicator across the surface of the filler to achieve the correct contour and to level the filler surface. As soon as a contour that approximates to the correct one is achieved, stop working the paste – if you carry on too long the paste will become sticky and begin to 'pick up' on the applicator. Continue to add thin layers of filler paste at twenty-minute intervals until the level of the filler is just proud of the surrounding bodywork.

Once the filler has hardened, excess can be removed using a metal plane or file. From then on, progressively finer grades of abrasive paper should be used, starting with a 40 grade production paper and finishing with 400 grade wet-and-dry paper. Always wrap the abrasive paper around a flat rubber, cork, or wooden block – otherwise the surface of the filler will not be completely flat. During the smoothing of the filler surface the wet-and-dry paper should be periodically rinsed in water. This will ensure that a very smooth finish is imparted to the filler at the final stage.

At this stage the 'dent' should be surrounded by a ring of bare metal, which in turn should be encircled by the finely 'feathered' edge of the good paintwork. Rinse the repair area with clean water, until all of the dust produced by the rubbing-down operation has gone.

Spray the whole repair area with a light coat of primer – this will show up any imperfections in the surface of the filler. Repair these imperfections with fresh filler paste or bodystopper, and once more smooth the surface with abrasive paper. If bodystopper is used, it can be mixed with cellulose thinners to form a really thin paste which is ideal for filling small holes. Repeat this spray and repair procedure until you are satisfied that the surface of the filler, and the feathered edge of the paintwork are perfect. Clean the repair area with clean water and allow to dry fully.

The repair area is now ready for final spraying. Paint spraying must be carried out in a warm, dry, windless and dust free atmosphere. This condition can be created artificially if you have access to a large indoor working area, but if you are forced to work in the open, you will have to pick your day very carefully. If you are working indoors, dousing the floor in the work area with water will help to settle the dust which would otherwise be in the atmosphere. If the repair area is confined to one body panel, mask off the surrounding panels; this will help to minimise the effects of a slight mis-match in paint colours. Bodywork fittings (eg chrome strips, door handles etc) will also need to be masked off. Use genuine masking tape and several thicknesses of newspaper for the masking operations.

Before commencing to spray, agitate the aerosol can thoroughly, then spray a test area (an old tin, or similar) until the technique is mastered. Cover the repair area with a thick coat of primer; the thickness should be built up using several thin layers of paint rather than one thick one. Using 400 grade wet-and-dry paper, rub down the surface of the primer until it is really smooth. While doing this, the work area should be thoroughly doused with water, and the wet-and-dry paper periodically rinsed in water. Allow to dry before spraying on more paint.

Spray on the top coat, again building up the thickness by using several thin layers of paint. Start spraying in the centre of the repair area and then, using a circular motion, work outwards until the whole repair area and about 2 inches of the surrounding original paintwork is covered. Remove all masking material 10 to 15 minutes after spraying on the final coat of paint.

Allow the new paint at least two weeks to harden, then, using a paintwork renovator or a very fine cutting paste, blend the edges of the paint into the existing paintwork. Finally, apply wax polish.

Plastic components

With the use of more and more plastic body components by the vehicle manufacturers (eg bumpers, spoilers, and in some cases major body panels), rectification of more serious damage to such items has become a matter of either entrusting repair work to a specialist in this field, or renewing complete components. Repair of such damage by the DIY owner is not really feasible owing to the cost of the equipment

and materials required for effecting such repairs. The basic technique involves making a groove along the line of the crack in the plastic using a rotary burr in a power drill. The damaged part is then welded back together by using a hot air gun to heat up and fuse a plastic filler rod into the groove. Any excess plastic is then removed and the area rubbed down to a smooth finish. It is important that a filler rod of the correct plastic is used, as body components can be made of a variety of different types (eg polycarbonate, ABS, polypropylene).

Damage of a less serious nature (abrasions, minor cracks etc) can be repaired by the DIY owner using a two-part epoxy filler repair material. Once mixed in equal proportions, this is used in similar fashion to the bodywork filler used on metal panels. The filler is usually cured in twenty to thirty minutes, ready for sanding and painting.

If the owner is renewing a complete component himself, or if he has repaired it with epoxy filler, he will be left with the problem of finding a suitable paint for finishing which is compatible with the type of plastic used. At one time the use of a universal paint was not possible owing to the complex range of plastics encountered in body component applications. Standard paints, generally speaking, will not bond to plastic or rubber satisfactorily. However, it is now possible to obtain a plastic body parts finishing kit which consists of a pre-primer treatment, a primer and coloured top coat. Full instructions are normally supplied with a kit, but basically the method of use is to first apply the pre-primer to the component concerned and allow it to dry for up to 30 minutes. Then the primer is applied and left to dry for about an hour before finally applying the special coloured top coat. The result is a correctly coloured component where the paint will flex with the plastic or rubber, a property that standard paint does not normally possess.

5 Major body damage – repair

Where serious damage has occurred, or large areas need renewal due to neglect, it means that the complete new panels will need welding in, and this is best left to professionals. If the damage is due to impact, it will also be necessary to check completely the alignment of the bodyshell, and this can only be carried out accurately by a Mercedes-Benz dealer using special jigs. If the body is left misaligned, it is primarily dangerous as the car will not handle properly, and secondly, uneven stresses will be imposed on the steering, suspension and possibly transmission, causing abnormal wear, or complete failure, particularly to such items as the tyres.

6 Bonnet – removal and refitting

1 Raise the bonnet to the vertical position by pressing the catch on the left-hand hinge, releasing the retaining wire clip on the support strut, and pushing upwards.
2 Extract the retaining clip and withdraw the support strut from its lower mounting stud (photo).
3 Disconnect the windscreen washer hose(s) at the check valve on the right-hand side and release the hose clips on the bonnet hinge.
4 Pull the wiring for the heated washer jets out of the bonnet cavity adjacent to the jet(s) and disconnect the wiring plug connections.
5 Tie a length of string to the main feed cable and pull the wiring out of the bonnet cavity from the hinge end. As soon as the end of the string appears, untie it and remove the wire. When refitting, tie the cable to the string to draw it back into position.
6 Remove the hinge retaining straps by releasing the upper bent-over locking portion from the hinge pin, then withdrawing the straps upwards (photo).
7 Mark the position of the lower threaded hinge bolts on both sides so that the bonnet can be refitted in its original position.
8 With the help of an assistant to support the bonnet, undo the lower retaining nut each side, withdraw the hinge bolts and hinge pins and carefully lift off the bonnet.
9 To refit the bonnet, push the hinge pin and hinge bolt bushes into the hinges, if these came out during removal.
10 Place the bonnet in position and insert the lower hinge bolt. Turn the bolt until the square collar engages with the retangular hole in the hinge lever.
11 Insert the upper hinge pin and turn it until the slot in the hinge pin head is horizontal.
12 Refit the hinge nut, position the bonnet so that the previously

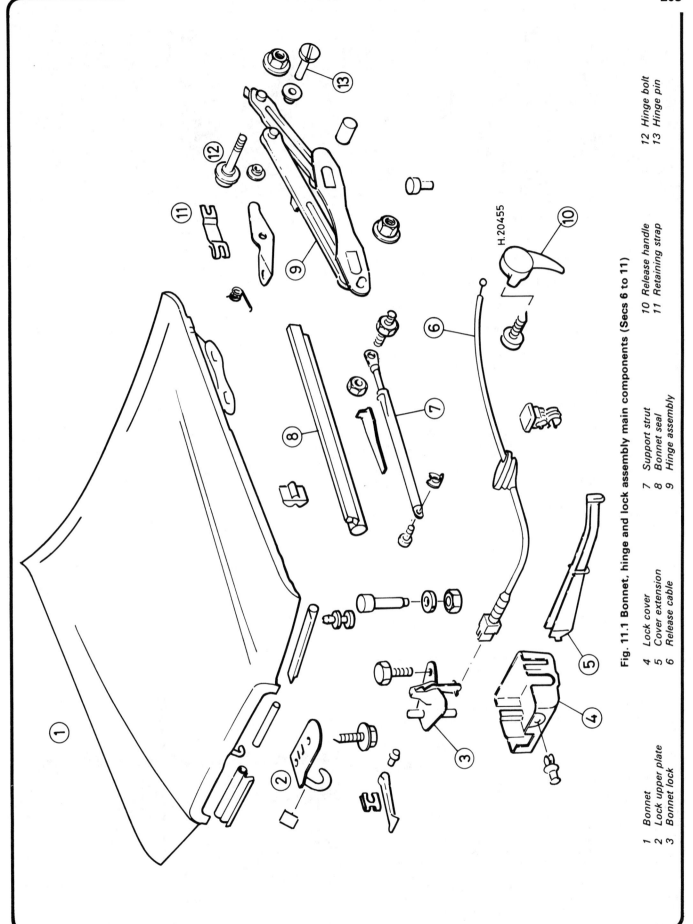

Fig. 11.1 Bonnet, hinge and lock assembly main components (Secs 6 to 11)

1 Bonnet
2 Lock upper plate
3 Bonnet lock
4 Lock cover
5 Cover extension
6 Release cable
7 Support strut
8 Bonnet seal
9 Hinge assembly
10 Release handle
11 Retaining strap
12 Hinge bolt
13 Hinge pin

H.20455

6.2 Bonnet support strut retaining clip (arrowed)

6.6 Bonnet hinge retaining strap (arrowed)

7.2 Bonnet lock upper plate retaining bolts (arrowed)

made marks are aligned, then tighten the nut. Refit the hinge retaining strap, then repeat these operations for the hinge on the other side.

13 Tie the washer jet wiring to the drawstring and pull the wires through the bonnet into place. Reconnect the wiring plug(s).

14 Reconnect the washer hose(s) at the check valve, and secure with new hose clips to the bonnet hinge.

15 Locate the support strut on the mounting stud and secure with the retaining clip.

16 Lower the bonnet and check its fit and alignment. If necessary adjust the bonnet position as described in Section 7.

7 Bonnet – adjustment

1 With the bonnet closed, check the gap between the bonnet and front wings on both sides (transverse adjustment), the alignment of the front edge of the bonnet with the front edge of the wing when looking down, (longitudinal adjustment – Fig. 11.2) and the height of the bonnet front edge and top edge in relation to the wing (height adjustment – Fig. 11.3).

Transverse adjustment
2 Open the bonnet and slacken the two bolts securing the lock upper plate to the bonnet (photo)
3 By trial and error, move the upper plate until a gap of approximately 5.0 mm (0.2 in) exists between the bonnet and the front wings on each side.

Longitudinal adjustment
4 Remove the bonnet support strut as described in Section 9.
5 Remove the plastic wheel arch covering from under the wheel arch, on the side being adjusted, for access to the bonnet hinge retaining nuts.
6 From within the engine compartment, slacken the locknut and screw down the bonnet rubber buffer behind the hinge.
7 Slacken the four bonnet hinge retaining bolts from under the wheel arch.
8 With the bonnet closed, position it in such a way that when viewed from the front looking down, the edge of the bonnet and the edge of the front wing are in alignment.
9 Tighten the hinge nuts with the bonnet closed and correctly aligned.
10 Refit the wheel arch covering and bonnet support strut, then check the height adjustment.

Height adjustment
11 From within the engine compartment, slacken the locknut and screw down the bonnet rubber buffer behind the hinge.
12 Slacken the nut on the bonnet-to-hinge lower retaining bolt.
13 By trial and error, move the bonnet as necessary, tightening the hinge bolt each time until the bonnet upper edge and front wing edge are aligned.
14 Now raise the rubber buffer a few turns at a time until the front edge of the bonnet and the edge of the wing, when viewed from the front, are aligned. Tighten the buffer locknut when adjustment is correct.

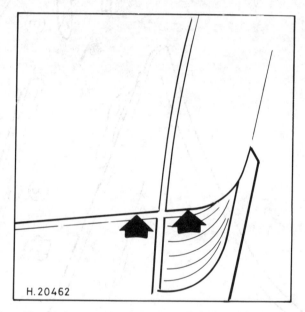

Fig. 11.2 Bonnet longitudinal adjustment (Sec 7)

Front edge of bonnet aligned with front edge of wing when correct

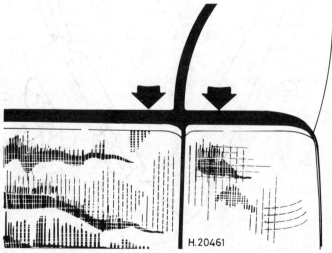

Fig. 11.3 Bonnet height adjustment (Sec 7)

Height of bonnet front edge and front wing identical when correct

8 Bonnet hinge – removal and refitting

1 Remove the bonnet as described in Section 6.
2 Remove the plastic wheel arch covering from under the wheel arch for access to the hinge retaining nuts.
3 Undo the four hinge retaining nuts and remove the hinge.
4 Refitting is the reverse sequence to removal. Adjust the bonnet as described in Section 7 after fitting.

9 Bonnet support strut – removal and refitting

1 Open the bonnet to the vertical position by pressing the catch on the left-hand hinge, releasing the retaining wire clip on the support strut and pushing the bonnet upwards until the hinge locks.
2 Extract the strut lower retaining clip, undo the upper retaining nut and remove the strut.
3 Refitting is the reverse sequence to removal.

10 Bonnet release cable – removal and refitting

1 Release the locking stud on the front panel adjacent to the support strut and remove the cover under the lock. **Note:** *On cars with air conditioning, undo the two screws and move the fan, then release the four upper clips and move the radiator rearwards for access.*
2 Disconnect the release cable at the lock lever and support bracket.
3 From inside the car, remove the cover under the facia on the left-hand side.
4 Undo the screw and remove the release handle, then disconnect the cable.
5 Push out the rubber grommet at the cable entry point on the bulkhead.
6 Tie string to the release cable so that as the cable is pulled through the bulkhead it will pull the string with it.
7 Pull out the cable in a forward direction. When the drawstring appears, untie it and remove the cable from the car.
8 Refitting is the reverse sequence to removal – use the string to draw the new cable through the bulkhead into the car.

11 Bonnet lock – removal and refitting

1 Release the locking stud on the front panel adjacent to the support strut and remove the cover under the lock. **Note:** *On cars with air conditioning, undo the two screws and move the fan, then release the four upper clips and move the radiator rearwards for access.*
2 Disconnect the release cable at the lock lever and support bracket.
3 Undo the two retaining bolts and remove the lock from the front panel (photo).
4 Refitting is the reverse sequence to removal. Minor adjustment of the closing action can be carried out by slackening the front panel support strut lower mounting bolt, and moving the strut and panel up or down slightly as necessary.

12 Radiator grille – removal and refitting

1 Open the bonnet, and from the inside at the front, undo the six retaining bolts.
2 Remove the grille surround and grille from the bonnet.
3 Release the pin clamps securing the grille to the grille surround on both sides.
4 Undo the lower screw and the upper nut that also retains the Mercedes badge. Remove the badge, then lift the grille out of the grille surround.
5 Refitting is the reverse sequence to removal.

13 Mercedes star – removal and refitting

1 From the underside of the bonnet, pull the spring clip down using heavy duty pliers, against considerable spring tension, and turn the clip 90° to the left. Make sure that the spring clip enters into the grooves of the rosette.
2 Pull the star upwards out of the grille surround to remove.
3 Refitting is the reverse sequence to removal.

14 Boot lid – removal and refitting

1 Disconnect the battery negative terminal.
2 Prise out the luggage compartment lamp, disconnect the wiring and remove the lamp.
3 Withdraw the wiring harness from the boot lid cavity.
4 Mark the outline of the hinges on the boot lid using a pencil.
5 Place some rags beneath the lower corners of the boot lid and, with the help of an assistant, undo the hinge retaining bolts (photo). Remove the boot lid from the car.
6 Refitting is the reverse sequence to removal, but align the hinges with the outline marks made prior to removal before tightening the bolts. Adjust the lock striker plate as necessary to achieve satisfactory opening and closing of the boot lid (photo).

15 Boot lid lock – removal and refitting

1 Open the boot lid, undo the two bolts and withdraw the lock (photo).
2 If central locking is fitted, undo the three solenoid retaining screws (photo) and disconnect the operating rod from the lock prior to removal.
3 To remove the solenoid, disconnect the vacuum hose and withdraw the unit from the boot lid aperture.
4 Refitting is the reverse sequence to removal. Adjust the lock striker plate as necessary to achieve satisfactory opening and closing of the boot lid.

11.3 Bonnet lock retaining bolts (arrowed)

14.5 Boot lid-to-hinge retaining bolts (arrowed)

14.6 Boot lid striker plate retaining bolts (arrowed)

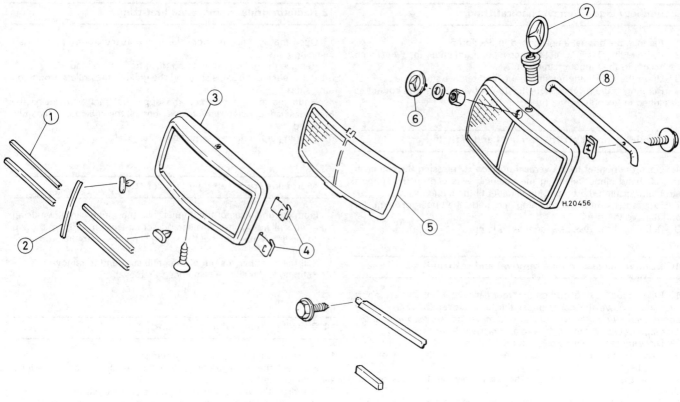

Fig. 11.4 Radiator grille components and attachments (Secs 12 and 13)

1 Horizontal bars	3 Grille surround	5 Grille panel	7 Mercedes star
2 Vertical bar	4 Pin clamps	6 Mercedes badge	8 Clamp rail

16 Front and rear bumpers – removal and refitting

Front bumper

1   Undo the single bolt each side securing the bumper laterally to the side support members.
2   Undo the two nuts and remove the washers on each side at the front securing the bumper to the chassis members.
3   Push out the clips along the top edge of the bumper in front of the radiator.
4   Carefully pull the bumper forwards and remove it from the car.
5   Refitting is the reverse sequence to removal.

Rear bumper

6   From inside the luggage compartment, open the flaps in the trim panels and undo the bumper retaining bolts on each side (photo).
7   Carefully pull the bumper rearwards and remove it from the car.
8   Refitting is the reverse sequence to removal.

17 Bumpers – dismantling and reassembly

1   The front and rear bumpers comprise a protective strip, foam member, trim covering and stiffener sandwiched together to form an assembly. Dismantling of both front and rear bumpers is as follows, with reference to the accompanying illustrations.
2   Undo the side retaining screws at the extreme ends on both sides.
3   Push back the holding straps, top and bottom, in pairs starting from the outside and working towards the centre.
4   Remove the protective strip and the foam member.
5   Push back the clips and remove the trim from the stiffener.
6   Push back the detent on the threaded holders on both sides, while at the same time sliding the holder down to remove.
7   Undo the nuts and bolts securing the front holders, and remove the holders.
8   Reassembly is the reverse sequence to dismantling.

15.1 Undo the bolts (arrowed) and withdraw the boot lock

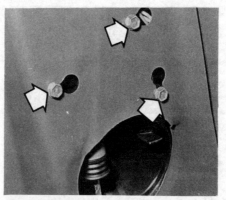

15.2 Central locking solenoid retaining bolts (arrowed)

16.6 Rear bumper retaining bolts (A). Additional bolt may be fitted at (B)

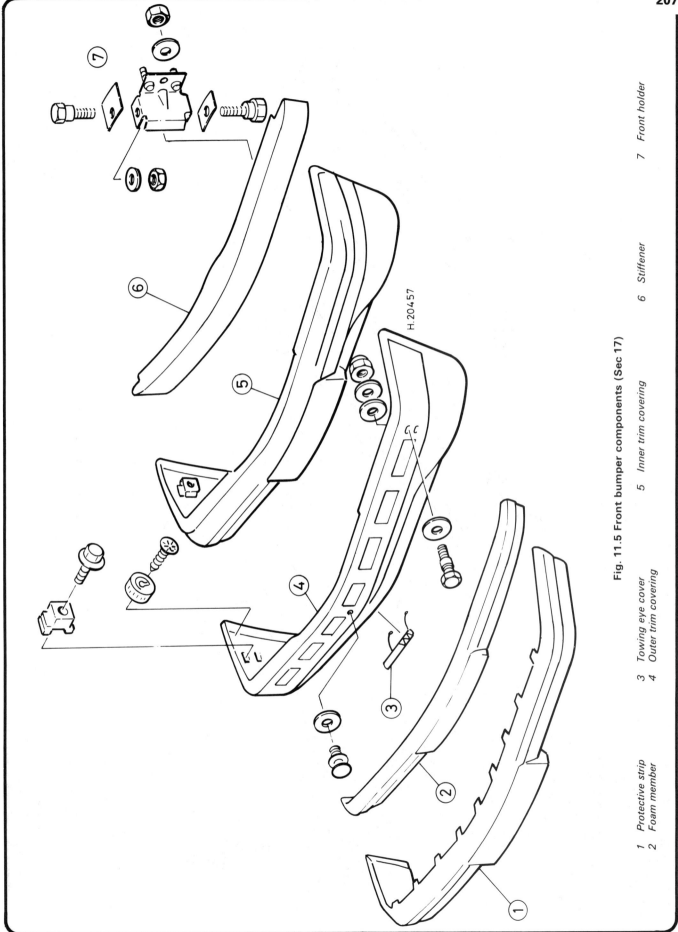

H.20457

Fig. 11.5 Front bumper components (Sec 17)

1 Protective strip
2 Foam member

3 Towing eye cover
4 Outer trim covering

5 Inner trim covering

6 Stiffener

7 Front holder

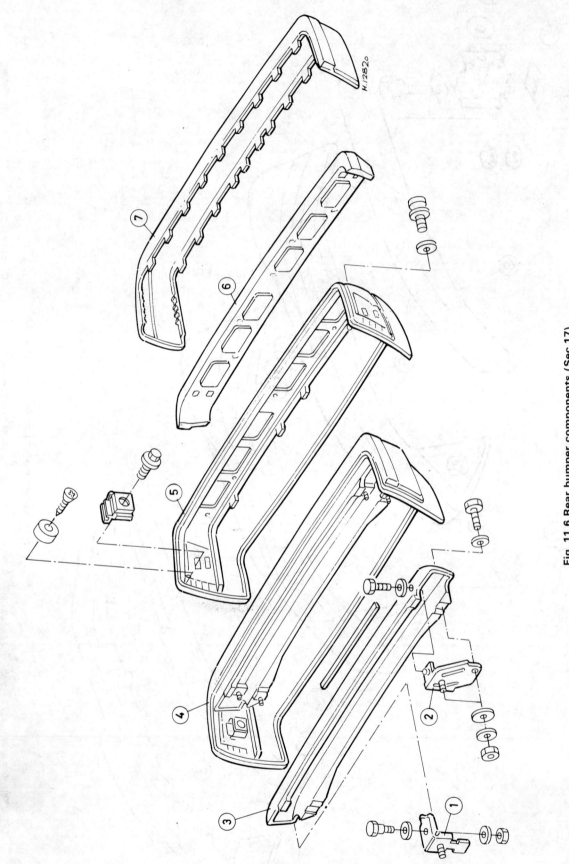

H.1282o

Fig. 11.6 Rear bumper components (Sec 17)

1 Holder
2 Holder

3 Stiffener
4 Inner trim covering

5 Outer trim covering

6 Foam member

7 Protective strip

18 Door inner trim panel – removal and refitting

1 Undo the screw and remove the door lock trim capping (photo).
2 Carefully prise off the plastic cover at the top of the grab handle (photo).
3 Undo the grab handle retaining bolt (photo).
4 Ease the interior release handle out of the trim panel, while at the same time sliding the complete housing forwards to release the internal retaining hooks (photo).
5 Disengage the lock operating rod from the rear of the interior release handle, and remove the handle and housing from the door.
6 On cars with manually operated window regulators, slide the regulator handle trim off the handle, after releasing the detent by pressing down with a small screwdriver (photo).
7 Withdraw the regulator handle and the trim disc (photos).
8 Lift the trim panel upwards to release the hooked retainers at the rear of the panel at the centre, bottom and sides (photo). When the panel is free, lift it over the interior lock button and remove it from the door.
9 For access to the door internal components, carefully peel back the waterproof sheet and remove it from the door (photo).
10 Refitting is the reverse sequence to removal. When engaging the panel hooked retainers, first engage the longer one at the centre of the panel (photo), then lift the panel just sufficiently to engage the rest without disengaging the centre one.

18.1 Remove the door lock trim capping

18.2 Prise off the grab handle plastic cover

18.3 Undo the grab handle retaining bolt

18.4 Release the interior handle hooks (A) and disengage the operating rod (B)

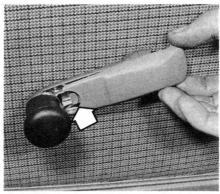
18.6 Remove the regulator handle trim after pressing down the detent (arrowed)

18.7A Withdraw the regulator handle ...

18.7B ... and the trim disc

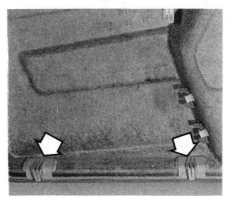
18.8 Door trim panel lower rear hooked retainers (arrowed)

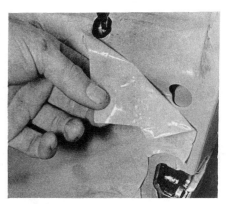
18.9 Carefully peel back the waterproof sheet

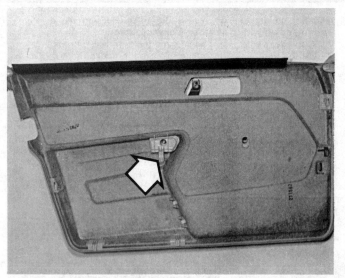

18.10 Engage the panel centre hooked retainer first (arrowed) when refitting

19 Front door window regulator – removal and refitting

1   Remove the door inner trim panel as described in Section 18.
2   Lower the window until the nut securing the regulator arm to the window regulator channel is accessible through the small aperture at the front of the door (photo).
3   Support the window in this position either by using a wooden wedge between the window and door, or by using masking tape over the top of the door frame (photo).
4   With the window supported, undo the regulator arm to channel retaining nut.
5   On cars with electric windows, disconnect the wiring at the cable connector terminals.
6   Undo the two nuts securing the guide rail to the door panel (photo) and release the rail from the panel.
7   Undo the four bolts (photo) on cars with manual windows, or three bolts on cars with electric windows, securing the regulator assembly to the door.
8   On cars with manual windows, temporarily refit the regulator handle, and turn it as if to lower the window until the two detents (photo) are swivelled out of their location. Remove the regulator handle.
9   Disengage the regulator rear arm from the regulator channel, and withdraw the regulator assembly out through the door lower aperture (photos).

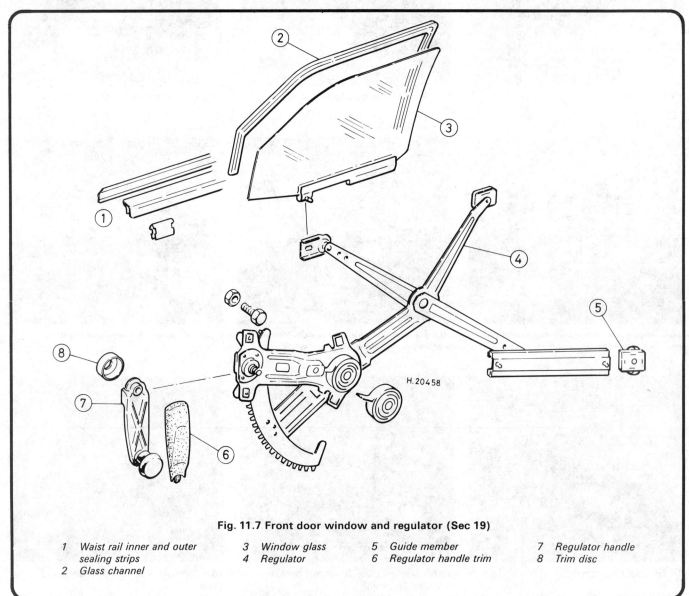

Fig. 11.7 Front door window and regulator (Sec 19)

1	Waist rail inner and outer sealing strips	3	Window glass
2	Glass channel	4	Regulator

5	Guide member	7	Regulator handle
6	Regulator handle trim	8	Trim disc

10 Refitting is the reverse sequence to removal, but only tighten the regulator arm to regulator channel nut, and the two guide rail nuts finger-tight initially, then adjust the window operation as follows, before refitting the trim panel.

11 Wind the window down to the fully-open position.

12 Push the window down and forwards at the front, into the front guide channel, and rearwards at the top into the rear guide channel.

13 With the window held in this position, tighten the regulator arm to regulator channel retaining nut.

14 Push the guide rail rear nut downwards and tighten, then tighten the guide rail front nut.

15 Check the window operation and refit the trim panel as described in Section 18.

20 Front door window glass – removal and refitting

1 Remove the door inner trim panel as described in Section 18.

2 Lower the window fully, and undo the nut securing the regulator arm to the regulator channel at the front (photo).

3 Undo the two nuts securing the guide rail to the door panel.

4 Disengage the regulator rear arm from the regulator channel, and the guide member from the guide rail (photo).

5 Remove the guide member from the regulator channel, then lift the glass upwards and out on the inside of the door frame (photo).

6 Refitting is the reverse sequence to removal, but adjust the regulator as described in Section 19, paragraphs 10 to 15.

19.2 Undo the regulator arm to regulator channel nut

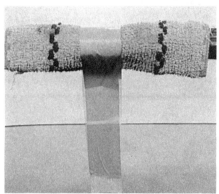
19.3 Using masking tape to support the window

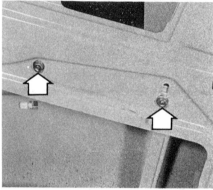
19.6 Undo the guide rail retaining nuts (arrowed)

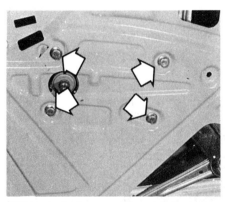
19.7 Undo the four regulator retaining bolts (arrowed)

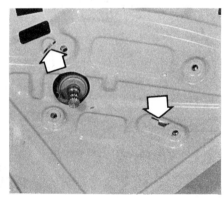
19.8 Release the detents (arrowed)

19.9A Disengage the regulator rear arm ...

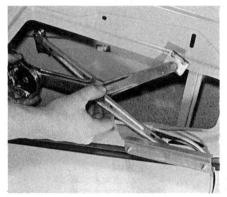
19.9B .. and remove the regulator

20.2 Undo the regulator arm nut (arrowed)

20.4 Disengage the guide member (arrowed) from the guide rail

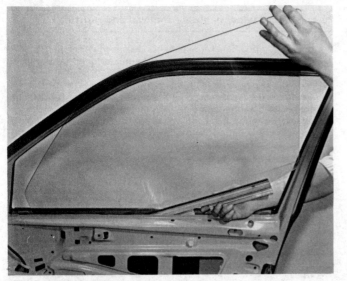

20.5 Remove the glass on the inside of the door frame

21 Rear door window regulator – removal and refitting

1 Remove the door inner trim panel as described in Section 18.
2 Open the window until the guide member of the regulator guide rail is accessible through the aperture in the top centre of the door panel.
3 Support the window in this position either by using a wooden wedge between the window and the door, or by using masking tape over the top of the door frame and onto the glass on the inside and outside.
4 On cars with electric windows, open the wiring plug connection and release the two wires for the window lift motor.
5 Remove the locking clip securing the window glass to the guide member of the regulator guide rail.
6 Undo the two regulator retaining bolts on manual windows, or the three regulator nuts on electric windows.
7 Undo the regulator guide rail lower retaining bolt.
8 Swivel the regulator rearwards to release the guide member from the channel at the bottom of the window glass.
9 On cars with electric windows, remove the motor wiring cable connector from the door panel.
10 Manipulate the regulator assembly out of the large aperture in the door panel.
11 Refitting is the reverse sequence to removal.

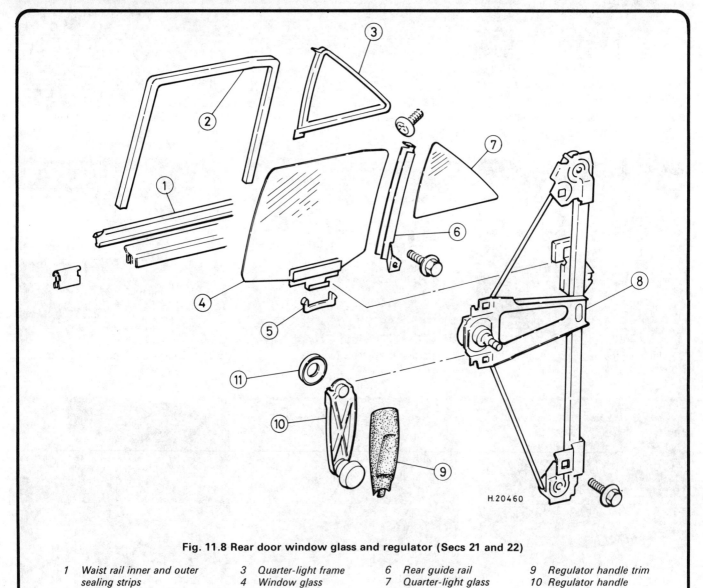

Fig. 11.8 Rear door window glass and regulator (Secs 21 and 22)

1 Waist rail inner and outer sealing strips
2 Glass channel
3 Quarter-light frame
4 Window glass
5 Locking clip
6 Rear guide rail
7 Quarter-light glass
8 Regulator
9 Regulator handle trim
10 Regulator handle
11 Trim disc

22 Rear door window glass – removal and refitting

1   Remove the door inner trim panel as described in Section 18.
2   Lower the window fully.
3   Using a plastic wedge or similar tool, carefully prise up the inner and outer sealing strips at the top of the door panel.
4   Remove the locking clip securing the window glass to the guide member of the regulator guide rail.
5   Move the window glass to the rear to release the channel at the bottom of the glass from the guide member.
6   Pull the flexible guide channel out of the rear guide rail, then undo the lower bolt securing the rail to the door panel and the upper screw securing the rail to the door frame.
7   Slide the guide rail downwards and remove it from one of the door panel apertures.
8   Lift the window glass upwards and remove it on the inside of the door frame.
9   Refitting is the reverse sequence to removal.

23 Rear door fixed quarter-light – removal and refitting

1   Refer to Section 22 and carry out the operations listed in paragraphs 1 to 7 inclusive.
2   Pull the quarter-light forwards and remove it from the door.
3   Refitting is the reverse sequence to removal, but lubricate the quarter-light sealing channels with a soapy solution to ease insertion.

24 Front door exterior handle – removal and refitting

1   Remove the door inner trim panel as described in Section 18.
2   Remove the closing plug from the rear edge of the door (photo).
3   Using an Allen key inserted through the closing plug hole, undo the lock cylinder retaining grub screw (photo).
4   Insert the key into the door lock cylinder and turn it approximately 60° to the rear (photo). At the same time, push the lock cylinder rearwards to disengage the internal tang, and withdraw it from the door handle (photo).
5   Push the door exterior handle to the rear, while at the same time pulling outwards, then disengage the tangs at the front from the mounting bracket (photo).
6   Remove the rubber escutcheon from the handle front location (photo).
7   Undo the three mounting bracket retaining screws and remove the mounting bracket from the aperture in the inner door panel (photos).
8   Refitting is the reverse sequence to removal. When inserting the handle, ensure that the rear operating leg slides behind the wire spring of the mounting bracket as well as the lock lever, (photo) then slide the handle forwards to secure. The tag on the handle rear rubber escutcheon fits between the door panel and the mounting bracket (photo).

25 Front door lock – removal and refitting

1   Remove the front door exterior handle as described in Section 24.
2   Release the inner door handle connecting rod from the door guide (photo) then disengage it from the lock lever (photo).
3   On cars equipped with central locking, release the retaining clip on the top edge of the door and remove the plastic water deflector from the door aperture (photos). Disconnect the wiring and vacuum connections at the central locking solenoid (photo).
4   Undo the screws securing the door lock to the door (photo).
5   On cars equipped with central locking, undo the screws securing the central locking solenoid to the door (photo).
6   Lower the door lock and remove it, complete with central locking solenoid (where fitted), through the door panel aperture (photo).
7   Refitting is the reverse sequence to removal. When fitting the water deflector on cars with central locking, the deflector must slide up behind the window guide channel before clipping onto the top edge of the door.

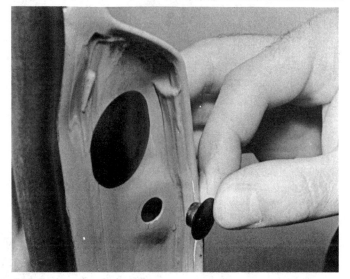
24.2 Remove the closing plug

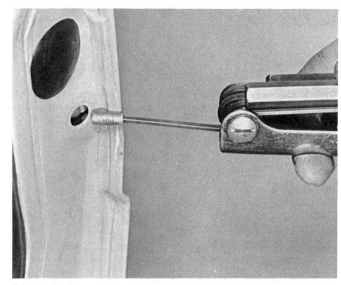
24.3 Undo the grub screw

24.4A Turn the key 60° to the rear ...

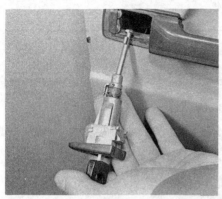
24.4B ... and remove the lock cylinder

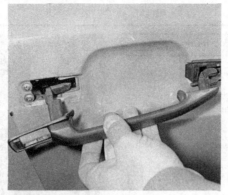
24.5 Remove the exterior handle

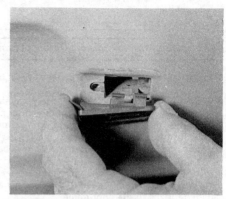
24.6 Remove the rubber escutcheon

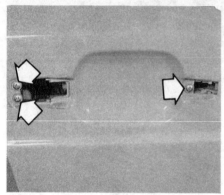
24.7A Undo the mounting bracket screws (arrowed) ...

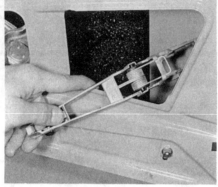
24.7B ... and remove the mounting bracket

24.8A The exterior handle leg must fit behind the lock lever (arrowed) when refitting ...

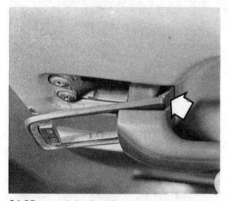
24.8B ... and the handle escutcheon tag (arrowed) locates between the door and bracket

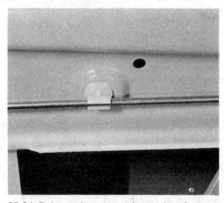
25.2A Release the connecting rod at the guide ...

25.2B ... and lock lever

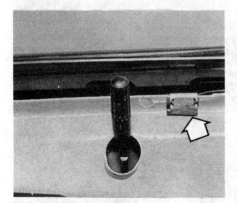
25.3A Release the clip arrowed ...

25.3B ... and remove the water deflector

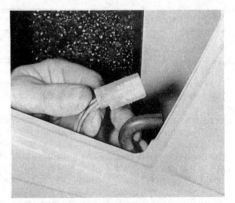
25.3C Disconnect the wiring and vacuum hose at the solenoid

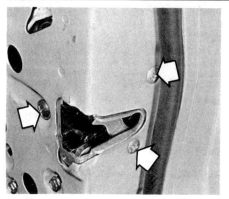

25.4 Undo the door lock retaining screws (arrowed) ...

25.5 ... and central locking solenoid screws (arrowed)

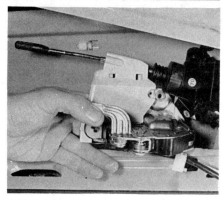

25.6 Remove the lock and solenoid from the door

26 Rear door exterior handle – removal and refitting

1   The procedure is the same as for the front door handle as described in Section 24, except that there is no lock cylinder to remove. Instead, remove the plastic trim covering by pushing it to the rear.

27 Rear door lock – removal and refitting

1   The procedure is the same as for the front door lock as described in Section 25.

28 Door lock solenoids (central locking system) – removal and refitting

1   Remove the door lock, complete with solenoid, from the front or rear doors as applicable, as described in Section 25 or 27.
2   Carefully prise off the plastic cover over the solenoid and lock connecting levers (photo).
3   Push the retaining clip end upwards, then remove it from the interior lock button rod (photo).
4   Withdraw the interior lock button rod to release the solenoid operating rod, and withdraw the solenoid (photos).
5   Refitting is the reverse sequence to removal.

29 Front and rear doors – removal and refitting

1   On cars equipped with central locking or electric windows, remove the inner trim panel as described in Section 18 and disconnect the applicable wiring or vacuum hose connections. Release the convoluted hose between the door and pillar, and pull the wiring and hoses out of the door.
2   Remove the rubber seal from the door check strap (photo), extract the retaining clip and washer, and drive out the check strap pin upwards using a punch.
3   Accurately mark the outline of the upper and lower hinge plates on the pillar using a pencil.
4   With an assistant supporting the door, undo the two upper and two lower bolts securing the hinge plates to the body pillar (photos).
5   Withdraw the door rearwards from the car.
6   Refitting is the reverse sequence to removal, but ensure that the hinge plates are aligned with the previously made marks. Adjustments can be made at the hinge plates and at the door striker (photo) to provide an equal gap all round the door, and to align the contour of the door panel with that of the front wing.

30 Windscreen and rear window – removal and refitting

1   Due to the methods of attachment, and the special equipment

required to complete the task successfully, removal and refitting of the windscreen and rear window should be entrusted to a dealer or auto glass replacement specialist.

31 Driver's door mirror glass (manual mirror) – renewal

1   Using a plastic wedge, very carefully prise the ball on the rear face of the mirror glass out of the plastic socket on the mirror body (photos).
2   If the mirror is electrically heated, disconnect the wiring plug at the rear of the mirror glass (photo).
3   Pull the mirror rearwards to disengage the adjuster at the front and remove it from the mirror body.
4   To refit the glass, reconnect the wiring plug, where applicable, then engage the front of the glass with the adjuster (photo).
5   Engage the ball stud with the socket, and press the glass in the centre until the ball fully engages with the socket.

32 Driver's door mirror assembly (manual mirror) – removal and refitting

1   Extract the small plastic clip from the adjustment lever by carefully prising it out with a screwdriver (photo).
2   Withdraw the adjustment lever cover (photo).
3   Prise off the trim panel at the top, disengage its bottom edge from the door trim panel and remove (photo).
4   If the mirror glass is electrically heated, separate the wiring at the connector (photo).
5   Undo the three screws (photo) and remove the mirror assembly from the door (photo).
6   Refitting is the reverse sequence to removal.

33 Driver's door mirror glass (electrically operated mirror) – renewal

1   Using a plastic wedge, very carefully prise the mirror glass off the three engagement points on the reverse side of the glass.
2   Align the engagement points on the adjusting motor to accept the sockets on the new glass. Align the upper engagement point horizontally and the lateral points vertically.
3   Place the glass in position and press it in until it is heard to engage in the three places.

34 Driver's door mirror assembly (electrically operated mirror) – removal and refitting

1   Prise off the trim panel for the mirror attachment at the top, disengage its bottom edge from the door trim panel and remove. Remove the foam fabric shim.
2   Unscrew the wiring plug retaining screw and disconnect the plug.

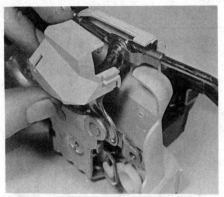

28.2 Prise off the plastic cover

28.3 Remove the retaining clip (arrowed)

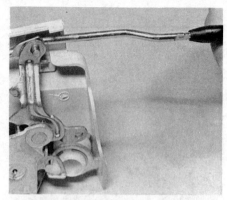

28.4A Withdraw the lock button rod ...

28.4B ... release the solenoid operating rod ...

28.4C ... and withdraw the solenoid

29.2 Remove the rubber seal from the check strap (arrowed)

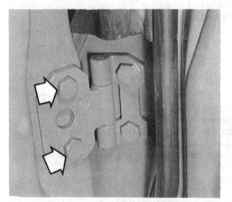

29.4A Hinge plate to door pillar bolts for the front door (arrowed) ...

29.4B ... and rear door

29.6 Front door striker plate

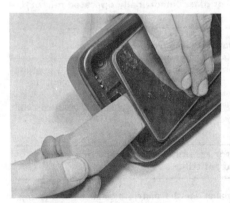

31.1A Prise out the mirror glass using a plastic wedge ...

31.1B ... to release the ball from the socket (arrowed)

31.2 Disconnect the wiring plug on electrically heated mirrors

31.4 Engage the front of the glass with the adjuster when refitting

32.1 Extract the small plastic clip

32.2 Withdraw the lever cover

32.3 Remove the trim panel

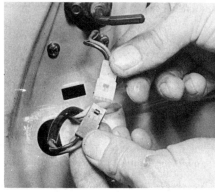

32.4 Disconnect the wiring connector

32.5A Undo the three screws ...

32.5B ... and remove the mirror assembly

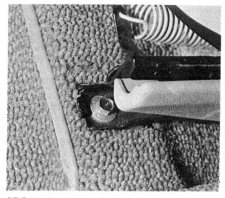

35.2 Undo the seat front guide rail bolts ...

35.4 ... and the rear guide rail bolts

3   Undo the three screws and remove the mirror from the door.
4   To remove the adjustment motor, remove the mirror glass as described in Section 33, then undo the three motor retaining screws.
5   Hinge the mirror back and hold it in this position with a suitable distance piece.
6   Turn the wiring socket in a clockwise direction and remove the motor and wiring from the mirror body.
7   Refitting is the reverse sequence to removal.

35 Front seats – removal and refitting

Driver's seat

1   Move the driver's seat to the rear and set the height adjuster to its lowest position.

2   Undo the two bolts at the front securing the guide rails to the floor (photo).
3   Move the driver's seat forwards and set the height adjuster to its highest position.
4   Undo the two bolts at the rear securing the guide rails to the floor (photo).
5   Slightly raise the driver's seat and pull it forwards out of the slide rail.
6   Refitting is the reverse sequence to removal.

Passenger's seat

7   Move the passenger's seat to the rear and undo both front guide rail retaining bolts.
8   Slide the seat forwards and remove the covers on the guide rails at the rear.

9 Undo the guide rail rear retaining bolts, then pull the seat forwards out of the slide rail.
10 Refitting is the reverse sequence to removal.

36 Rear seat – removal and refitting

Seat bench
1 Push in the detent clip on the left- and right-hand sides of the seat bench at the bottom (photo), while at the same time lifting up the seat bench.
2 Withdraw the seat bench and remove it from the car.
3 Refitting is the reverse sequence to removal.

Seat back rest
4 Remove the seat bench.
5 Undo the three retaining screws at the bottom of the back seat.
6 Push the back rest upwards to disengage the four upper tags, then remove the back rest from the car.
7 Refitting is the reverse sequence to removal, but ensure that the upper tags engage with their holders.

37 Seat belts – removal and refitting

Front belt
1 Undo the two centre pillar trim panel lower retaining screws (photo).
2 Swivel the seat belt rearwards, remove the cap over the lower mounting bolt by sliding it off the bottom of the belt (ie forwards), then undo the seat belt lower mounting bolt.
3 Pull off the door rubber sealing weatherstrip around the centre pillar.
4 Move the centre pillar trim downwards to release the upper retaining clip, and remove the trim.
5 Undo the seat belt upper guide retaining bolt and the inertia reel retaining bolt, then remove the belt.
6 If the seat belt stalk is also to be removed, first remove the driver's or passenger's seat as applicable, as described in Section 35.
7 Hold the stalk and undo the retaining bolt on the side of the seat. Remove the stalk.
8 Refitting is the reverse sequence to removal.

Rear belt
9 Remove the rear seat bench as described in Section 36.
10 Undo the bolt securing the seat belt mounting to the floor (photo).
11 Pull off the door rubber sealing weatherstrip around the trim panel on the rear pillar.
12 Carefully push off the trim panel clips at the front towards the centre of the car by means of a wedge.
13 Push the trim panel upwards and remove it from the rear pillar.
14 Remove the rear seat back rest as described in Section 36.
15 Undo the belt upper guide retaining bolt on the rear pillar.
16 Unclip the sound-deadening material around the rear inertial reel.

17 Undo the inertia reel retaining bolt and remove the seat belt from the car.
18 If the stalk(s) are to be renewed, undo the single bolt, remove the separating plate and remove the relevant stalk (photo).
19 Refitting is the reverse sequence to removal.

38 Sunroof – general

1 A sliding sunroof, either mechanically or electrically operated, is available as a factory fitted option.
2 Adjustment or repair of the sunroof or its component parts should be left to a dealer, as the complexity of the unit and the need for special tools and equipment renders these operations beyond the scope of the average owner.

39 Central locking system vacuum pump – removal and refitting

1 Disconnect the battery negative terminal.
2 Remove the rear seat bench as described in Section 36.
3 Lift up the cover on the sound proofing box and lift the unit out of its location (photos).
4 Disconnect the vacuum hoses and wiring plug, and remove the unit from the car (photo).
5 Refitting is the reverse sequence to removal.

40 Centre console – removal and refitting

1 On manual gearbox models, release the gear lever boot from the console cover and slide the boot up the lever (photo). Using the fingers at the rear of the plastic centre part of the console cover, lift the cover at the rear, then slide it to the rear and lift off (photos). Note that the cover is secured by two extremely tight rear tags and two lugs at the front (photo).
2 On automatic transmission models, lift the console cover at the rear by means of a plastic wedge inserted in the gap between the selector position plate and the cover. Move the cover to the rear to disengage the two front lugs and lift off.
3 Disconnect the wiring plugs at the console cover switches, after identifying their locations, and remove the cover (photo).
4 Refer to Chapter 9 and slacken the handbrake adjuster under the car so that the lever can be pulled up to the nearly-vertical position.
5 Remove the front ashtray, then undo the two upper screws securing the ashtray housing to the facia (photo).
6 Withdraw the ashtray housing, disconnect the wiring and illumination bulb and remove the housing (photos).
7 Remove the floor mats on both sides from the footwells.
8 Undo the retaining screw each side securing the facia and console edges (photo).
9 Release the spire clip and retaining screw (where fitted) and remove the footrest on the driver's side (photo).

36.1 Push in the detent clip (arrowed) to release the rear seat bench

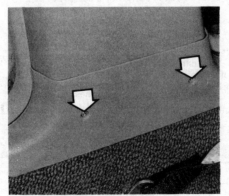

37.1 Centre pillar trim panel screws (arrowed)

37.10 Rear seat belt mounting bolt

37.18 Rear seat belt stalk retaining bolt

39.3A Lift up the sound proofing box cover ...

39.3B ... and take out the vacuum pump

39.4 Disconnect the vacuum hoses and wiring plug

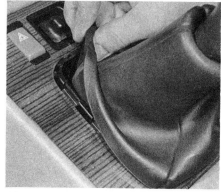

40.1A Release the gear lever boot ...

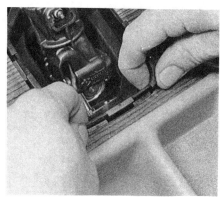

40.1B ... lift the console cover at the rear ...

40.1C ... then slide it rearwards to remove

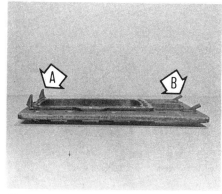

40.1D Console cover rear tags (A) and front lugs (B)

40.3 Disconnect the wiring at the console cover switches

40.5 Undo the front ashtray housing screws

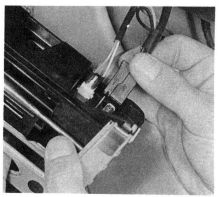

40.6A Disconnect the wiring ...

40.6B ... and illumination bulbholder at the ashtray housing

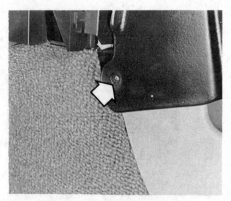

40.8 Undo the side retaining screw (arrowed)

40.9 Release the footrest retaining spire clip

40.11A Undo the kick panel retaining screw ...

40.11B ... and remove the panel

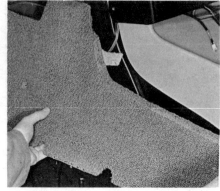

40.12 Remove the console side cover carpets

40.13A Pull off the handbrake lever grip ...

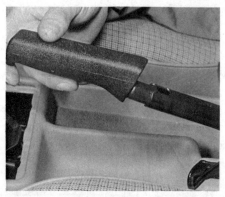

40.13B ... and remove it from the lever

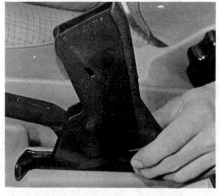

40.14 Remove the handbrake lever lower lining

40.15 Undo the front retaining bolt

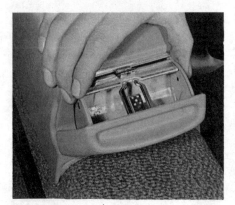

40.16A Remove the rear ashtray ...

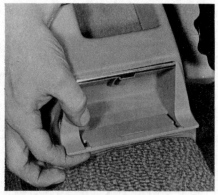

40.16B ... and the ashtray housing

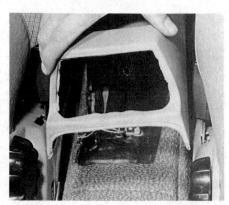

40.19A Lift up the console at the rear ...

10 Remove the front carpets on both sides.
11 On the passenger's side undo the lower retaining screw and remove the front kick panel (photos).
12 Undo the central retaining screw and remove the console side cover carpet on both sides (photo). On the drivers side the cover carpet is also secured by an additional spire clip.
13 With extreme effort, pull off the grip on the handbrake lever and slide it off the front of the lever (photos).
14 Pull the handbrake up and remove the lower lever lining (photo).
15 Undo the console retaining bolt in front of the gear lever or selector housing (photo).
16 Remove the rear ashtray, then remove the ashtray holder by prising up the lower holding clip (photos).
17 Working through the ashtray aperture, undo the console rear retaining bolt.
18 Move both front seats towards the rear, and pull the handbrake lever up as far as it will go.
19 Lift the console at the rear, and disengage it from the facia at the front (photos).
20 Lift the console up over the handbrake lever and remove it from the car.
21 Refitting is the reverse sequence to removal. Adjust the handbrake as described in Chapter 9 on completion.

41 Glovebox – removal and refitting

1 Disconnect the battery negative terminal.
2 Prise out the glovebox lamp, disconnect the wiring and remove the lamp (photo).
3 Undo the two screws and remove the latch bracket (photo).
4 Remove the expanding rivets by prising out the rivet expander with a screwdriver, then remove the expander and rivet body (photos).
5 Withdraw the glovebox, pull the lamp wiring through the aperture and remove the glovebox from the facia (photo).
6 Refitting is the reverse sequence to removal.

42 Facia – removal and refitting

1 Remove the instrument panel as described in Chapter 12.
2 Remove the glovebox as described in Section 41.
3 Remove the covers under the facia on both sides. On the driver's side, the cover is retained by four screws and a spire clip, and on the passenger's side, by three screws. Prise off the trim caps for access to the screws (photo).

4 Pull away the door seal weatherstrip on the front body pillar on both sides (photo).
5 Remove both front pillar trim panels by pushing the panel in the area of the retaining clips away from the pillar using a plastic wedge (photo).
6 Undo the retaining screw and remove the speaker grille from the top of the facia on both sides.
7 Undo the upper retaining bolt on each side adjacent to the speakers (photo).
8 Using pliers and a protective cloth, pull off the knob on the light switch, then undo the switch retaining nut (photo). Disconnect the wiring and remove the switch.
9 Prise out the headlamp beam adjustment rotary switch, disconnect the wiring and vacuum hoses and remove the switch. Note that the hose attachments are lilac at the top and lilac/yellow at the bottom.
10 Prise out the facia upper switches, or push them out from behind, idenftify the wiring plug connections and disconnect the wiring plugs. Remove the switches.
11 Undo the two side retaining bolts, left and right, securing the facia to the body stiffener (photo).
12 Pull off the air ducts on the left and right outer air nozzles (photo).
13 Identify their locations, then disconnect the wires at the glovebox lamp switch (photo).
14 Undo the bolt securing the underside of the facia to the body stiffener (photo).
15 Undo the screw securing the facia to the centre console on both sides (photo).
16 Using pliers and a protective cloth, pull off the three heater control knobs (photo).
17 Pull off the blower control switch knob (photo).
18 Undo the three heater control retaining nuts (photo).
19 Using pliers and a protective cloth, pull out the centre vent grilles (photo).
20 Undo the screws on each side of the centre vent grille apertures (photo).
21 Carefully prise off the ignition switch trim surround (photo).
22 Close the fresh air flap and undo the bolt, working through the lever slot (photo).
23 Pull the air hose off the rear of the centre vent nozzles (photo).
24 Undo the retaining bolt behind the glovebox cover (photo), and the inner nut at the bottom right-hand side.
25 Pull out the demister nozzles on the heater box and withdraw the facia from the car.
26 Refitting is the reverse sequence to removal.

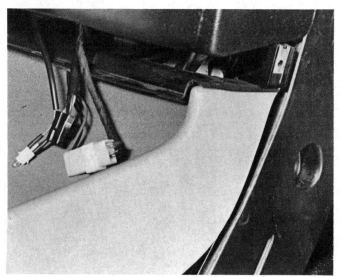
40.19B ... and disengage it at the front

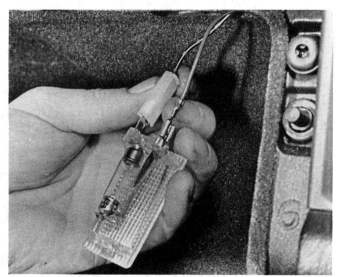
41.2 Remove the glovebox lamp

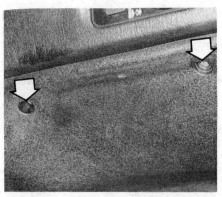
41.3 Undo the latch bracket screws

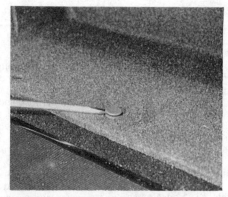
41.4A Prise out the rivet expander ...

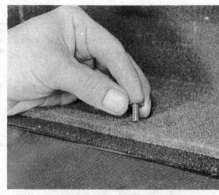
41.4B ... then remove the rivet expander ...

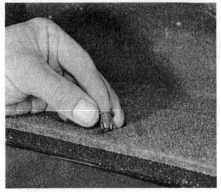
41.4C ... and rivet body

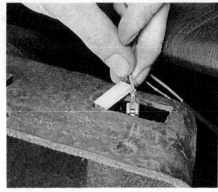
41.5 Withdraw the wires as the glovebox is removed

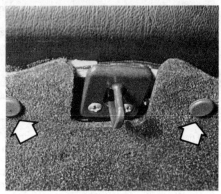
42.3 Prise off the trim caps (arrowed) and undo the screws

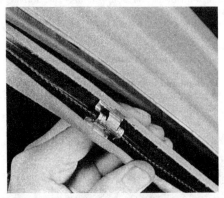
42.4 Pull away the door seal weatherstrip

42.5 Remove the front pillar trim panels

42.7 Undo the upper bolt by the speaker each side

42.8 Undo the light switch retaining nut (arrowed)

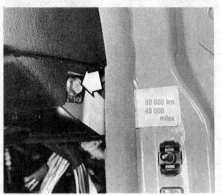
42.11 Undo the facia side retaining bolts (arrowed)

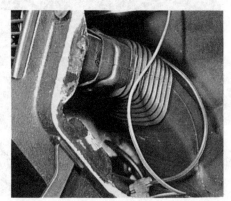
42.12 Pull off the air ducts on the outer nozzles

42.13 Disconnect the glovebox lamp switch wires (arrowed)

42.14 Undo the facia-to-stiffener lower bolt

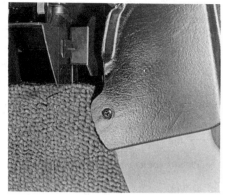

42.15 Undo the side retaining screws

42.16 Pull off the heater control knobs

42.17 Pull off the blower control switch knob

42.18 Undo the heater control retaining nuts

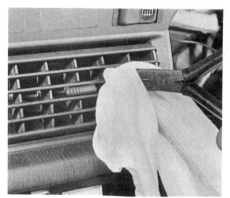

42.19 Pull out the centre vent grilles

42.20 Undo the screws in the centre vent aperture (arrowed)

42.21 Prise off the ignition switch trim surround

42.22 Undo the bolt (arrowed) through the lever slot

42.23 Pull off the centre vent air hose (arrowed)

42.24 Undo the bolt behind the glovebox cover (arrowed)

43 Heater unit – removal and refitting

1   Drain the cooling system as described in Chapter 2.
2   Remove the facia as described in Section 42.
3   Release the cable retaining tie on the left-hand side of the heater unit, and undo the screw on the wiring terminal.
4   Disconnect the wiring plug at the rear of the blower motor switch.
5   Disconnect the vacuum lines and illumination bulb wiring at the rear of the heater controls.
6   Disconnect the heater feed hose at the rear of the cylinder head.
7   Place a container beneath the engine, under the disconnected feed hose.
8   Disconnect the heater return hose at the thermostat housing. Using compressed air from a foot pump, blow the residual coolant out of the heater matrix by inserting the foot pump hose into the heater return hose. The coolant will be forced out of the feed hose into the container.
9   Undo the two bolts and separate the return flow pipe at the matrix flange joint (photo).
10 Pull off the right-hand air duct at the heater unit below the return flow pipe.
11 Undo the two bolts and separate the feed flow pipe at the matrix

flange joint on the other side of the heater.
12 Pull off the left-hand air duct at the heater unit below the feed flow pipe.
13 Force off the feed flow pipe holder at the bulkhead on the left-hand side.
14 Unscrew the mounting bracket nut below the feed flow pipe holder.
15 Unscrew the right-hand mounting bracket nut below the return flow pipe.
16 Unscrew the two mounting nuts at the top of the heater unit.
17 Disconnect the control cable at the blower motor slide switch.
18 Disconnect the control cable at the main air flap on the side of the heater unit.
19 Withdraw the heater unit from the mounting studs, lift the unit upwards and remove it from the car.
20 Refitting is the reverse sequence to removal. When connecting the blower control cable, connect and secure the cable at the slide switch, then move the switch to blower position 'MAX'. Connect the control cable end to the main air flap lever, open the main air flap up to its stop, then clip the outer cable into position.
21 On completion, refill the cooling system as described in Chapter 2.

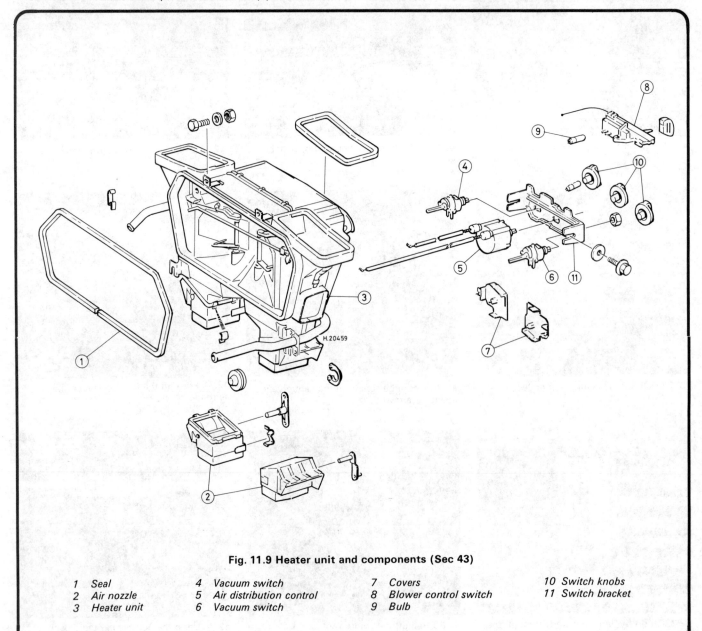

Fig. 11.9 Heater unit and components (Sec 43)

1	Seal	4	Vacuum switch	7	Covers	10	Switch knobs
2	Air nozzle	5	Air distribution control	8	Blower control switch	11	Switch bracket
3	Heater unit	6	Vacuum switch	9	Bulb		

43.9 Undo the return flow pipe bolts (arrowed)

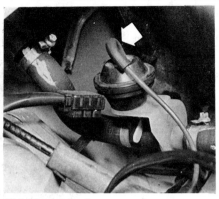

45.2 Disconnect the vacuum hose (arrowed)

45.3 Undo the blower motor cover screws (arrowed)

45.4 Inner bulkhead retaining screws (arrowed)

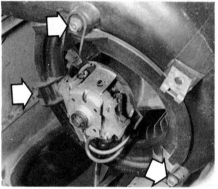

45.7 Blower motor retaining bolts (arrowed)

44 Heater matrix – removal and refitting

1   Remove the heater unit as described in Section 43.
2   Undo the screws on the heater unit air intake.
3   Carefully prise off all the retaining clips along the top, on both sides, and on the bottom of the heater unit.
4   Force the connecting linkage out of the left- and right-hand demister flap arms.
5   Push back the lock on the left-hand demister flap, while at the same time pulling off the connecting linkage lever.
6   Pull off the gaskets on the left- and right-hand demister nozzle connections.
7   Push off the connecting levers of the mixed air flaps on the left- and right-hand levers.
8   Prise the left- and right-hand mixed air flap connecting lever ball heads off the ball sockets.
9   Separate the two halves of the heater unit and remove the mixed air flaps.
10 Undo the matrix frame retaining screws, remove the frame and take out the matrix.
11 Refitting is the reverse sequence to removal.

45 Heater blower motor – removal and refitting

1   Remove the air intake cover over the plenum chamber as described in Chapter 12, Section 28, paragraphs 1 to 7 inclusive for pre-January 1985 models, or paragraphs 13 to 17 inclusive for January 1985 models onwards.
2   Disconnect the vacuum hose at the heater valve (photo).
3   Undo the two screws on the blower motor cover (photo).
4   Lift the rubber sealing strip off the inner bulkhead wall and undo the two bulkhead retaining screws each side (photo).
5   Move the bulkhead wall upwards and forwards, then remove the

blower motor cover.
6   Remove the cable ties and disconnect the blower motor wiring plug.
7   Undo the blower motor retaining bolts and remove the motor sideways out of the housing (photo).
8   Refitting is the reverse sequence to removal.

46 Heater valve – removal and refitting

1   Remove the air intake cover over the plenum chamber as described in Chapter 12, Section 28, paragraphs 1 to 7 inclusive for pre-January 1985 models, or paragraphs 13 to 17 for January 1985 models onwards.
2   Remove the expansion tank pressure cap slowly to release any residual pressure in the cooling system.
3   Disconnect the vacuum hose at the heater valve, located adjacent to the heater blower motor in the plenum chamber.
4   Disconnect the coolant hoses and remove the heater valve from its bracket.
5   Refitting is the reverse sequence to removal, but note that the side of the valve marked 'water inlet' must be towards the engine. Top up the cooling system on completion.

47 Air conditioning system – precautions and maintenance

1   Never disconnect any part of the air conditioner refrigeration circuit unless the system has been discharged by your Mercedes-Benz dealer, or a qualified refrigeration engineer.
2   Where the compressor or condenser obstruct other mechanical operations such as engine removal, then it is permissible to unbolt their mountings and move them to the limit of their flexible hose deflection, but not to disconnect the hoses. If there is still insufficient room to

carry out the required work, then the system must be discharged before disconnecting and removing the assemblies.

3   The system will, of course, have to be recharged on completion.

4   Regularly check the condenser for clogging with flies or dirt. Hose clean with water or compressed air.

5   Check the drivebelt condition and if necessary adjust the belt tension, as described in Section 48.

48 Air conditioning refrigerant compressor drivebelt – removal, refitting and adjustment

Note: *The following procedure covers models in which multiple drivebelts are used to drive the engine ancillaries (up to approximately October 1984). On later cars with a single drivebelt layout, refer to Chapter 12, Section 6.*

1   Refer to Chapter 12 and remove the alternator drivebelt.

2   Refer to Chapter 10 and remove the power steering pump drivebelt.

3   Slacken the refrigerant compressor mounting bolt, unscrew the tensioning bolt to move the compressor in towards the engine, and slip the belt off the pulleys.

4   Fit a new belt over the pulleys, and tighten the tensioning bolt until it is just possible to deflect the belt by 10.0 mm (0.4 in) under thumb pressure at a point midway between the pulleys. Tighten the mounting bolt when the tension is correct.

5   Refit the power steering pump drivebelt (Chapter 10) and the alternator drivebelt (Chapter 12).

Fig. 11.10 Air conditioning refrigerant compressor mountings (Sec 48)

1   Mounting bolt   *2   Tensioning bolt*

Chapter 12 Electrical system

Contents

Specifications

System type .... 12 volt, negative earth

Battery
Type .... 12 volt lead-acid 55 or 62 Ah

Alternator
Type .... Bosch
Rated output (14 volts at 6300 rpm alternator speed) .... 55 A
Minimum brush length .... 5.0 mm (0.20 in)

Starter motor
Type .... Bosch pre-engaged, 1.4 kW rating
Minimum brush length .... 10.0 mm (0.39 in)

Torque wrench settings

	Nm	lbf ft
Alternator pulley retaining nut:		
With V-belt pulley	40	30
With multi-ribbed pulley	65	48
Drivebelt adjustment pointer lockbolt	75	55
Wiper motor retaining bolts	5	4

1 General description

The electrical system is of the 12 volt negative earth type, and consists of a 12 volt battery, alternator, starter motor and related electrical accessories, components and wiring. The battery is charged by an alternator which is belt-driven from the crankshaft pulley. The starter motor is of the pre-engaged type incorporating an integral solenoid. On starting, the solenoid moves the drive pinion into engagement with the flywheel ring gear before the starter motor is energised. Once the engine has started, a one-way clutch prevents the motor armature being driven by the engine until the piston disengages from the flywheel.

Further details of the major electrical systems are given in the relevant Sections of this Chapter.

Caution: *Before carrying out any work on the vehicle electrical system, read through the precautions given in Safety First! at the beginning of this manual and in Section 2 of this Chapter.*

2 Electrical system – precautions

It is necessary to take extra care when working on the electrical system to avoid damage to semi-conductor devices (diodes and transistors), and to avoid the risk of personal injury. In addition to the precautions given in Safety First! at the beginning of this manual, observe the following items when working on the system.

1 *Always remove rings, watches, etc before working on the electrical system.* Even with the battery disconnected, capacitive discharge could occur if a component live terminal is earthed through a metal object. This could cause a shock or nasty burn.

2 *Do not reverse the battery connections.* Components such as the alternator or any other having semi-conductor circuitry could be irreparably damaged.

3 If the engine is being started using jump leads and a slave battery, connect the batteries, *positive to positive,* and *negative to negative.* This also applies when connecting a battery charger.

4 Never disconnect the battery terminals, or alternator wiring when the engine is running.

5 The battery leads and alternator wiring must be disconnected before carrying out any electric welding on the car.

6 Never use an ohmmeter of the type incorporating a hand cranked generator for circuit or continuity testing.

7 Always ensure that the battery negative lead is disconnected when working on the electrical system.

3 Maintenance and inspection

1 At regular intervals (see Routine Maintenance) carry out the following maintenance and inspection operations on the electrical system components.

2 Check the operation of all the electrical equipment, ie wipers, washers, lights, direction indicators, horn etc. Refer to the appropriate Sections of this Chapter if any components are found to be inoperative.

3 Visually check all accessible wiring connections, harnesses and retaining clips for security, or any signs of chafing or damage. Rectify any problems encountered.

4 Check the alternator drivebelt for cracks, fraying or damage. Renew the belt if worn or, if satisfactory, check and adjust the belt tension, as described in Section 6.

5 Check the condition of the wiper blades and if they are cracked or show signs of deterioration, renew them, as described in Section 27. Check the operation of the windscreen and headlamp washers (if fitted). Adjust the nozzles using a pin, if necessary.

6 Check the battery terminals, and if there is any sign of corrosion disconnect and clean them thoroughly. Smear the terminals and battery posts with petroleum jelly before refitting. If there is any corrosion on the battery tray, remove the battery, clean the deposits away and treat the affected metal with an anti-rust preparation. Repaint the tray in the original colour after treatment.

7 Top up the washer reservoir and check the security of the pump wires and water pipes (photo).

8 Check the electrolyte level in the battery after unscrewing the cell filler caps. Top up using distilled or de-ionized water as necessary until

the water level in the filling chamber no longer drops. Refit the filler caps after topping-up (photo).

9 It is advisable to have the headlight aim adjusted using optical beam setting equipment.

10 When carrying out a road test, check the operation of all the instruments and warning lights, and the operation of the direction indicator self-cancelling mechanism.

4 Battery – removal and refitting

1 The battery is located at the rear of the engine compartment on the left-hand side.

2 Slacken the negative terminal clamp (photo) and disconnect the lead.

3 Slacken the positive terminal clamp and disconnect the lead.

4 Unscrew the nut and remove the battery holding clamp (photo).

5 Lift the battery out of its location, taking care to keep it upright.

6 Refitting is the reverse sequence to removal, but make sure that the positive terminal is connected first and the negative (earth) terminal last.

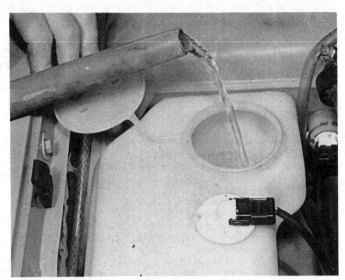

3.7 Topping-up the washer reservoir

3.8 Topping-up the battery

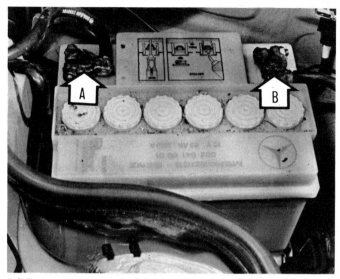

4.2 Battery positive terminal (A) and negative terminal (B)

4.4 Battery holding clamp nut (arrowed)

5 Battery – charging

1 In winter when a heavy demand is placed on the battery, such as when starting from cold and using more electrical accessories, particularly on short journeys, it may be necessary to have the battery fully charged occasionally from an external source.

2 Ideally, the battery should be charged at a rate of 10% of battery capacity (ie 6.2 amps for a 62 Ah battery) until no further increase in specific gravity or charging voltage occurs over a two hour period. The battery leads must be disconnected while the battery is being charged.

3 Alternatively a trickle charger, charging at a rate of 1.5 amps, can be safely used overnight.

4 Special rapid 'boost' chargers should not be used as they can cause serious damage to the battery plates through overheating.

6 Alternator drivebelt – removal, refitting and adjustment

Engines with multiple drivebelt layout

1 Cars manufactured up to approximately October 1984 are fitted with a number of separate drivebelts to drive the various engine ancillaries. The following procedure describes the removal, refitting and adjustment of the belt used to drive the alternator and coolant pump. Procedures relating to the other belts are described in the relevant Chapters.

2 To remove the drivebelt, slacken the alternator upper and lower mounting nuts as well as the adjustment arm bolt at its timing cover bracket attachment.

3 Turn the adjuster bolt to move the alternator in toward the engine, then slip the belt off the pulleys.

4 Refit the drivebelt over the pulleys then turn the adjuster bolt to tension the belt. The tension is correct when it is just possible to deflect the belt by approximately 12.0 mm (0.5 in) under moderate finger pressure midway along its longest run.

5 Hold the adjuster bolt in this position and tighten the upper and lower mounting nuts, then the adjustment arm bolt, in that order.

6 If the drivebelt has been renewed, recheck the belt tension after running the engine for several minutes.

Engines with single drivebelt layout

7 Cars manufactured from approximately October 1984 onwards are fitted with a single multi-ribbed poly V-belt to drive all the engine ancillaries. Removal, inspection, refitting and adjustment procedures are as follows.

8 To remove the belt, slacken the adjustment pointer lock bolt on the adjuster mechanism by 1/4 to 1/2 of a turn (photo).

9 Turn the tensioning nut, (photo) using a socket or spanner in an

Fig. 12.1 Alternator upper and lower mounting nuts (1 and 2) – early models (Sec 6)

Fig. 12.2 Alternator adjustment arm bolt (1) and adjuster bolt (2) – early models (Sec 6)

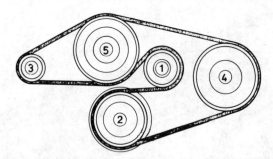

Fig. 12.3 Drivebelt run diagram for cars with power
steering – later models with single drivebelt layout (Sec 6)

1	Tensioning roller	4	Power steering pump
2	Crankshaft	5	Coolant pump
3	Alternator		

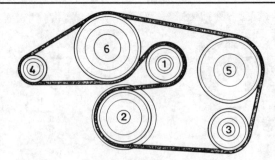

Fig. 12.4 Drivebelt run diagram for cars with power
steering and air conditioning – later models with single
drivebelt layout (Sec 6)

1	Tensioning roller	4	Alternator
2	Crankshaft	5	Power steering pump
3	Refrigerant compressor	6	Coolant pump

anti-clockwise direction until the tensioning roller has retracted
sufficiently to allow the belt to be slipped off the pulleys. Remove the
belt carefully so that the ribs are not damaged by the pulley edges.
10 With the belt removed, carefully examine its condition and check
for rubber lumps or dirt between the ribs, broken or detached ribs,
fraying or pulling out of the backing strands, or a pointed upper edge in
the ribs. If any of these conditions are evident, renew the drivebelt.
11 Before refitting the belt, move the adjustment pointer to the left and
align it with the first divisional mark on the tensioning scale (photo).
12 Refer to the accompanying illustrations according to ancillaries
fitted, and slip the drivebelt over the pulleys starting with the
tensioning roller.
13 Turn the tensioning nut clockwise until the adjustment pointer is
aligned with the appropriate divisional mark as follows:

Cars without power steering – fifth divisional mark
Cars with power steering, or with power steering and air
conditioning – seventh divisional mark (photo)

14 With the belt correctly tensioned, tighten the adjustment pointer
lockbolt to the specified torque.

7 Alternator – removal and refitting

1 Disconnect the battery negative terminal.
2 Remove the drivebelt as described in the previous Section.
3 Release the retaining wire clip and disconnect the wiring
multi-plug at the rear of the alternator (photo).
4 On pre-October 1984 models, undo the upper and lower mounting
nuts and remove the bolts, noting the arrangement of the tensioner on
the upper bolt. Withdraw the alternator from the engine.
5 On post-October 1984 models, undo the upper and lower retaining
bolts and remove the alternator from the engine (photo).
6 Refitting is the reverse sequence to removal. Refit the drivebelt as
described in Section 6.

6.8 Adjustment pointer lock bolt (arrowed)

6.9 Drivebelt tensioning nut (arrowed)

6.11 Align the adjustment pointer (A) with
the first divisional mark on the scale (B)

6.13 Adjustment pointer aligned with the
seventh divisional mark

7.3 Release the alternator multi-plug
retaining clip (arrowed)

7.5 Alternator retaining bolts (arrowed) on
later models

8 Alternator – fault tracing and rectification

Due to the specialist knowledge and equipment required to test or repair an alternator, it is recommended that, if the performance is suspect, the car be taken to an automobile electrician who will have the facilities for such work. Because of this recommendation, information is limited to the inspection and renewal of the brushes. Should the alternator not charge, or the system be suspect, the following points should be checked before seeking further assistance:

(a) *Check the drivebelt condition and tension*
(b) *Ensure that the battery is fully charged*
(c) *Check the ignition warning light bulb, and renew it if blown*

9 Alternator brushes and regulator – renewal

1   Remove the alternator as described in the previous Section.
2   Undo the two screws and withdraw the brushbox and regulator from the rear of the alternator (photos).
3   Measure the brush length and if less than the specified minimum, renew the brushbox and regulator as an assembly.
4   Refitting is the reverse sequence to removal.

10 Starter motor – removal and refitting

1   Disconnect the battery negative terminal.
2   Jack up the front of the car and support it on axle stands.
3   Remove the engine undertray on models so equipped.
4   Remove the air cleaner as described in Chapter 3.
5   Undo the two bolts and remove the inlet manifold support strut.
6   Where fitted, disconnect the electrical lead at the oil level sensor on the side of the sump.
7   On starter motors fitted with a rear support bracket, undo the bolts securing the bracket to the cylinder block, and the nuts securing it to the starter, then remove it.
8   Unscrew the bolts securing the starter motor to the bellhousing.
9   Release the wiring support bracket on the manifold, then turn the steering to provide maximum clearance between the starter motor and the steering drag link.
10 Withdraw the starter slightly, disconnect the wiring at the solenoid and remove the starter from under the car.
11 Refitting is the reverse sequence to removal.

11 Starter motor – overhaul

Note: *Two types of starter motor are used on 190 models covered by this manual. Prior to June 1985 a 1.4 kW Bosch pre-engaged unit is used, while on later models a similar Bosch starter is fitted but incorporating a reversing gear arrangement at the drive pinion end. The following procedures are applicable to both types but the accompanying photos depict the later unit.*
1   Remove the starter motor from the car as described in the previous Section.
2   Mark the housings in relation to each other as an aid to reassembly.
3   Unscrew the nut and disconnect the field wire at the solenoid (photo).
4   Undo the three screws and withdraw the solenoid body from the drive end bracket (photos).
5   Remove the spring, unhook the solenoid plunger from the actuating lever and remove the plunger (photos).
6   Undo the screws and remove the small end cover (photos). Recover the seal (where fitted).
7   Extract the armature circlip and remove the shims (photos). Note the exact number of shims as they determine the shaft endfloat.
8   Unscrew the through-bolts and remove the end cover or end plate as applicable (photo). Where fitted remove the brush holder support plate (photo).
9   Slip the grommet out of the housing and withdraw the brush holder complete with brushes (photo).
10 Withdraw the drive end bracket and armature from the housing (photo).

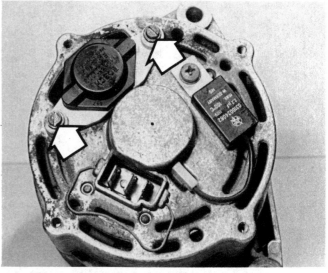

9.2A Undo the two screws (arrowed) ...

9.2B ... and withdraw the brushbox and regulator

11 On the early type starter motors, prise out the actuating lever cover pad from the drive end bracket and withdraw the armature and actuating lever.
12 On reversing gear (later) type starters, withdraw the armature (photo), lift off the reversing gear cover and take out the ring gear (photos). Prise out the actuating lever cover pad from the drive end bracket and withdraw the reversing gear assembly (photos) complete with actuating lever.
13 Using a metal tube, drive the stop ring down the armature to reveal the retaining circlip (photo).
14 Extract the circlip and remove the stop ring (photos).
15 Withdraw the drive pinion off the armature or reversing gear shaft (photo).
16 Extract the drive pinion circlip and withdraw the retaining cap, actuating lever, inner cap and spring from the drive pinion (photos).
17 On reversing gear type starters, extract the locking ring, withdraw the washer, and remove the support plate from the reversing gear shaft (photos).
18 Clean all the components in paraffin and wipe dry, then examine them for wear and damage. Check the pinion drive for damaged teeth and make sure that the one-way clutch only rotates in one direction. If the shaft bushes are worn they can be removed using a soft metal drift and new bushes installed. However, the new bushes must first be soaked in hot oil for approximately five minutes. Clean the commutator with a rag moistened with a suitable solvent. Minor scoring can be removed with fine glasspaper, but deep scoring will necessitate the

11.3 Disconnect the field wire at the solenoid

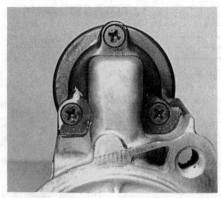

11.4A Undo the three screws ...

11.4B ... and withdraw the solenoid body

11.5A Remove the plunger spring ...

11.5B ... then unhook and remove the plunger

11.6A Undo the two screws (arrowed) ...

11.6B ... and remove the end cover

11.7A Extract the armature circlip ...

11.7B ... and remove the shims

11.8A Remove the end plate ...

11.8B ... and brush holder support plate

11.9 Remove the brush holder with brushes

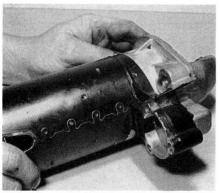

11.10 Withdraw the drive end bracket and armature

11.12A Withdraw the armature ...

11.12B ... reversing gear cover ...

11.12C ... ring gear ...

11.12D ... actuating lever cover pad ...

11.12E ... then remove the reversing gear assembly

11.13 Drive the stop ring (arrowed) down the armature

11.14A Remove the circlip ...

11.14B ... and stop ring

11.15 Withdraw the drive pinion

11.16A Extract the drive pinion circlip (arrowed) ...

11.16B ... withdraw the retaining cap ...

11.16C ... actuating lever ...

11.16D ... inner cap ...

11.16E ... and spring

11.17A Extract the locking ring ...

11.17B ... withdraw the washer ...

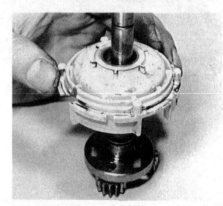

11.17C ... and remove the support plate

11.21 Fit the brushes and holder over the commutator first when assembling

12.1 Central electrics unit location in engine compartment

12.2 Lift off the central electrics unit cover

commutator being skimmed in a lathe and then being undercut. Commutator refinishing is a job which is best left to a specialist.

19 On the reversing gear type starter, check the condition of the gear teeth and their fit on the spindles. Also check the fit and condition of the ring gear. Renew the reversing gear as an assembly if wear is detected.

20 Check the condition of the brushes, and renew the brush holder as an assembly if the brushes have worn down to the specified minimum length. To do this on the early units, cut off the copper braid next to the brush holder and solder it to the new holder.

21 Reassembly is the reverse of the dismantling procedure. When refitting the brush holder, engage the brushes over the commutator with the armature slightly withdrawn from the housing, then fit this assembly to the housing and drive end bracket (photo).

12 Fuses and relays – general

Fuses

1 The fuses are situated in the central electrics unit, located at the rear of the engine compartment on the right-hand side (photo).

2 To gain access to the fuses, lift up the clips at the front and rear of the central electrics unit cover and lift the cover up at the front (photo). Squeeze the two legs of the rear clip together to disengage them from the hinge and remove the cover from its location. The fuse locations, current rating and circuits protected are shown on the cover.

3 To renew a blown fuse, withdraw it from its contacts and fit a new fuse of an identical rating. Never renew a fuse more than once without finding the cause of the trouble.

12.4 Additional relay holder location

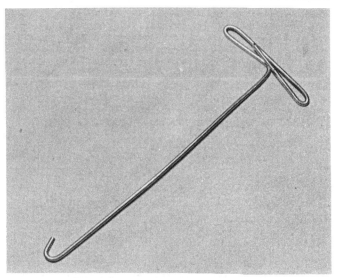

13.3 Tool for disconnnecting wiring multi-plugs

Relays

4   The relays are also located in the central electrics unit behind the fuses, and also in an additional holder situated just to the front of the main unit (photo). The layout of the relays is shown in Figs. 12.5 and 12.6.
5   To remove a relay carefully pull it upwards from its location. Refit by pushing firmly into place.

13 Central electrics unit – removal and refitting

1   Disconnect the battery negative terminal.
2   Remove the cover under the facia on the driver's side for access to the connections on the underside of the unit.
3   Disconnect all the wiring multi-plugs from the underside of the central electrics unit. Each multi-plug is a different shape so they can

only be fitted one way round into one particular socket. However it is advisable to label each plug as to its approximate location as they are removed. If a small hooked piece of wire is used to engage in the tag of each plug, this will make removal easier (photo).
4   Undo the bolts securing the main earth connections to the bulkhead behind the instrument panel. Make a note of each of the earth lead locations.
5   From within the engine compartment, undo the screws and remove the additional relay holder.
6   Remove the cover over the fuses on the central electrics unit.
7   Undo the two screws and two nuts securing the unit to the bulkhead.
8   Pull the unit forwards and upwards, then unscrew the wiring terminals and disconnect the wiring plugs. Make a note of their locations as each wire is removed.
9   Remove the central electric unit from the engine compartment.
10 Refitting is the reverse sequence to removal.

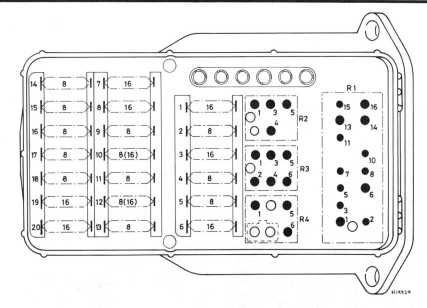

Fig. 12.5 Relay locations in the central electrics unit (Sec 12)

R1 Combination relay (direction indicators, heated rear window, wipers)
R2 Electric window regulator
R3 Air conditioning
R4 Overvoltage protection

236   Chapter 12 Electrical system

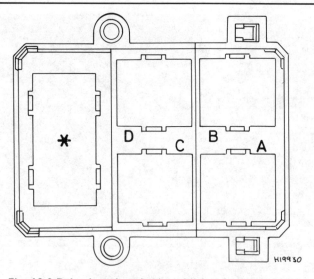

Fig. 12.6 Relay locations in the additional relay holder (Sec 12)

A Auxiliary heater fuse element
B Seat adjustment fuse element
C Inlet manifold heater (carburettor engines)
D Headlamp washers and wipers
* Fuel pump (fuel injection engines)

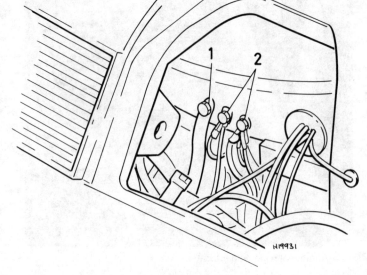

Fig. 12.7 Main earth connection (1) and additional earth connections (2) behind instrument panel (Sec 13)

14 Ignition switch – removal and refitting

1 Removal and refitting of the ignition switch is combined with the steering lock removal and refitting procedures as described in Chapter 10, Section 26.

15 Steering column combination switch – removal and refitting

1 Disconnect the battery negative terminal.
2 Remove the cover under the facia on the driver's side.
3 Remove the steering wheel as described in Chapter 10.
4 Undo the three screws securing the combination switch to the steering column (photo).
5 Disconnect the combination switch wiring multi-plug from the central electrics unit under the facia. To do this, use a small hooked

piece of wire to engage in the tag of the wiring plug, and pull the plug out using the wire (photo).
6 Withdraw the combination switch and steering column shroud from the column, then remove the switch and cable from the shroud.
7 Refitting is the reverse sequence to removal.

16 Facia and centre console switches – removal and refitting

1 Before removing any switches, disconnect the battery negative terminal, and reconnect on completion.

Facia switches

2 To remove the switches on either side of the instrument panel, carefully prise one end of the relevant switch out of its location using a knife blade or thin screwdriver. Protect the facia face as you do this.

15.4 Combination switch retaining screws (arrowed)

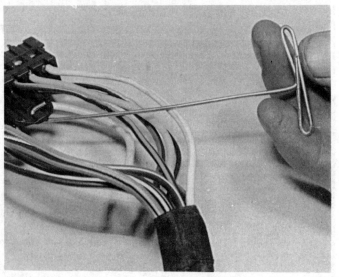

15.5 Wiring multi-plug removal tool engaged with plug tag

16.3 Prise out the switch and disconnect the wiring plug

16.6A Use pliers and a protective cloth to release the switch knob ...

16.6B ... then withdraw the knob

16.7 Headlamp beam control switch removal

16.8 Headlamp switch retaining nut (arrowed)

16.10 Centre console switch removal

3 Withdraw the complete switch and disconnect the wiring plug at the rear (photo).
4 To refit, connect the wiring plug and push the switch into position, one end at a time.

Headlamp switch

5 Remove the cover under the facia on the driver's side.
6 Using pliers and a protective cloth, carefully pull off the switch knob (photos).
7 Using a small screwdriver, prise out the beam control rotary switch (photo). Disconnect the vacuum hoses, pull out the illumination bulbholder and remove the switch.
8 Undo the main lighting switch retaining nut (photo) and withdraw the switch from behind the facia. Disconnect the wiring plug and remove the switch.
9 Refitting is the reverse sequence to removal.

Centre console switches

10 Using a small screwdriver, carefully prise the relevant switch from its location (photo).
11 Disconnect the wiring multi-plug and remove the switch.
12 Refitting is the reverse sequence to removal.

17 Door courtesy light switches – removal and refitting

1 Disconnect the battery negative terminal.
2 Carefully prise out the switch (photo), disconnect the wiring and remove the switch.
3 Refitting is the reverse sequence to removal.

18 Instrument panel – removal and refitting

1 Disconnect the battery negative terminal.

2 Remove the steering wheel as described in Chapter 10.
3 Remove the cover under the facia on the driver's side.
4 Working under the facia from below, detach the air duct to the right-hand vent for access to the rear of the instrument panel.
5 Unscrew the speedometer cable retaining nut and withdraw the cable.
6 Push out the instrument panel from the rear to release it from the five retaining spring clips.
7 Make a note of the wiring plugs and connections on the rear of the panel and disconnect them (photos).
8 Remove the panel from the car.
9 Refitting is the reverse sequence to removal.

19 Instrument panel components – removal and refitting

1 Remove the instrument panel as described in the previous Section.

Panel illumination and warning lamp bulbs

2 Turn the bulb holders anti-clockwise and remove them from the rear of the instrument panel (photo).
3 Remove the illumination bulbs by pulling them out of their holders. The warning lamp bulbs (except for the alternator warning lamp) are renewed complete with their holders.
4 Refit the bulbholders by pushing down and turning clockwise.

Speedometer

5 Remove the resistance pack adjacent to the rear of the speedometer by pulling it upwards (photo). If it is secured by two screws, undo these first.
6 Undo the four screws securing the speedometer to the rear of the instrument panel.
7 Undo the two screws, or release the two clips and pull off the lamp carrier above the speedometer.

17.2 Door courtesy light switch location

18.7A Disconnect the wiring on the left-hand side ...

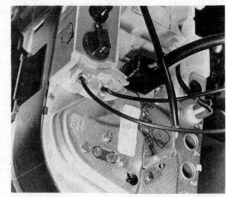

18.7B ... and right-hand side of the instrument panel

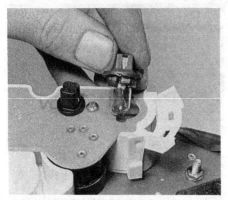

19.2 Instrument panel illumination bulb renewal

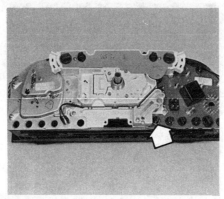

19.5 Instrument resistance pack location (arrowed)

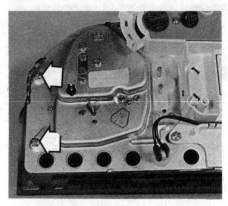

19.12 Tachometer retaining screws (arrowed)

19.15 Gauge cluster retaining screws (arrowed)

20.7 Undo the speedometer cable retaining bolt (arrowed)

20.8 Release the cable from the transmission support clips (arrowed)

8   Where fitted, remove the water level indicator bulb and release the wiring adjacent to the speedometer.
9   Withdraw the speedometer from the instrument panel.
10 Refitting is the reverse sequence to removal.

Tachometer

11 Remove the speedometer as previously described.
12 Undo the two additional screws (photo) and remove the unit.
13 Refitting is the reverse sequence to removal.

Gauge cluster

14 Remove the speedometer as previously described.
15 Undo the two additional screws (photo) and remove the gauge cluster.
16 Refitting is the reverse sequence to removal.

20 Speedometer cable – removal and refitting

1   Disconnect the battery negative terminal.
2   Remove the cover under the facia on the driver's side.
3   Working under the facia, detach the air duct to the right-hand vent for access to the rear of the instrument panel.
4   Unscrew the speedometer cable retaining nut and withdraw the cable.
5   Pull the cable into the engine compartment and releae it from any brackets or support clips.
6   Jack up the front of the car and support it on axle stands.
7   From under the car, undo the cable retaining bolt on the side of the gearbox or automatic transmission and withdraw the cable (photo).
8   Release the cable from the support clips below and to the side of the transmission (photo) then remove the cable from the car.
9   Refitting is the reverse sequence to removal.

21 Bulbs (exterior lamps) – renewal

Headlamp

1 From within the engine compartment, spring up the two lamp unit cover clips (photo), tip the cover back and lift it up to remove (photo).
2 Disconnect the wiring plug (photo) and release the bulb retaining clip by squeezing the clip arms together and swinging outward (photo).
3 Withdraw the bulb from the lamp unit (photo). Take care not to touch the glass with your fingers. If the glass is touched, wipe the bulb with a rag moistened with methylated spirit.
4 Refitting is the reverse sequence to removal, but ensure that the tags on the bulb plate engage with the recesses in the lamp unit.

Sidelamp

5 Remove the headlamp unit cover as described in paragraph 1.
6 Pull out the sidelamp bulbholder, located beneath the headlamp bulb.
7 Remove the bulb by turning it slightly anti-clockwise.
8 Refitting is the reverse sequence to removal.

Foglamp

9 Remove the headlamp unit cover as described in paragraph 1.
10 Disconnect the bulb electrical lead at the connector (photo).
11 Compress the retaining clip arms and swing the clip outwards (photo).
12 Withdraw the bulb from the lamp unit, taking care not to touch the glass. Wipe the glass with a rag moistened with methylated spirit if the glass is touched.
13 Refitting is the reverse sequence to removal.

Front direction indicator

14 If working on the right-hand bulb, disconnect the wiring on the washer reservoir level sensor, unscrew the large plastic cap nut (photo) and move the reservoir slightly to provide access to the bulb.
15 Disconnect the wiring at the bulbholder, then turn the holder slightly anti-clockwise to remove (photos).
16 Turn the bulb slightly anti-clockwise to remove it from the holder.
17 Refitting is the reverse sequence to removal.

Front direction indicator side repeater

18 Carefully prise the side repeater lens unit out of the body side panel, using a screwdriver inserted under the front edge of the unit.
19 Withdraw the bulb holder from the lens unit and remove the bulb from the holder (photo).
20 Refitting is the reverse sequence to removal.

Rear lamp cluster bulbs

21 From inside the luggage compartment, turn the two lock catches as far as they will go to the left and withdraw the bulb carrier from the lamp unit (photos).
22 Remove the relevant bulb by turning anti-clockwise slightly (photo). The bulb numbers and their wattages are shown adjacent to each bulb location.
23 Refitting is the reverse sequence to removal.

Number plate lamp

24 Undo the two retaining bolts and withdraw the lens unit (photos).
25 Spread the contacts and remove the festoon type bulb.
26 Refitting is the reverse sequence to removal.

22 Bulbs (interior lamps) – renewal

Interior courtesy lamp

1 Carefully prise out the lamp and lens unit, then fold back the reflector (photos).
2 Spread the contacts and remove the festoon type bulb.
3 Refitting is the reverse sequence to removal.

21.1A Spring up the headlamp cover clips ...

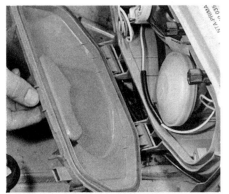
21.1B ... and remove the cover

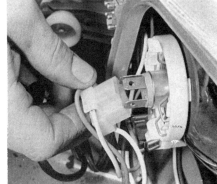
21.2A Disconnect the wiring plug ...

21.2B ... and release the headlamp bulb retaining clip ...

21.3 ... then remove the bulb

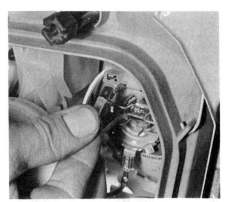
21.10 Disconnect the electrical lead at the foglamp

21.11 Release the retaining clip to remove the foglamp bulb

21.14 Washer reservoir cap nut removal

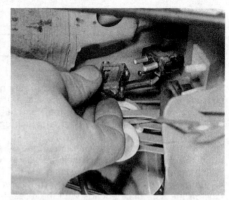
21.15A Disconnect the direction indicator bulb wiring ...

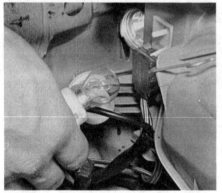
21.15B ... and remove the bulbholder

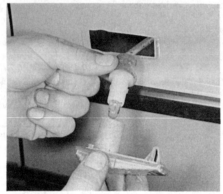
21.19 Renewing the direction indicator side repeater bulb

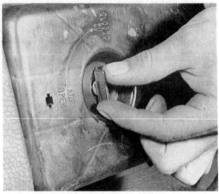
21.21A Release the lock catches ...

21.21B ... and withdraw the rear lamp bulb carrier

21.22 Remove the relevant bulb from the carrier

21.24A Undo the two screws (arrowed) ...

21.24B ... and withdraw the number plate lamp

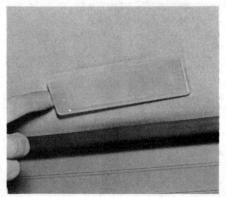
22.1A Prise out the interior lamp and lens unit ...

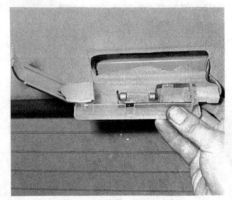
22.1B ... then fold back the lens and remove the bulb from the rear ...

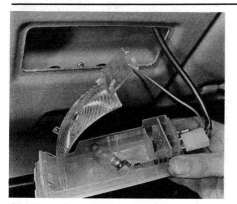

22.1C ... or from the front interior lamp

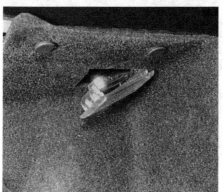

22.7 Glovebox lamp and bulb

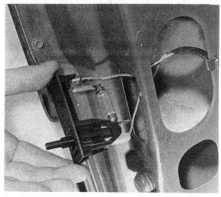

22.10 Remove the luggage compartment lamp switch and bulbholder for increased clearance

Sun visor illumination

4   Fold down the sun visor and carefully prise off the cover on the left-hand and right-hand recesses.
5   Spread the contacts and remove the festoon type bulb.
6   Refitting is the reverse sequence to removal.

Glovebox lamp

7   Prise the lamp lens unit out of its location and spread the contacts to remove the festoon type bulb (photo).
8   Refitting is the reverse sequence to removal.

Luggage compartment lamp

9   Working through the boot lid aperture, spread the contacts and remove the festoon type bulb.
10 For increased working clearance, withdraw the switch and bulbholder then remove the bulb (photo).

23 Exterior lamps – removal and refitting

Front direction indicator lamp

1   If working on the right-hand unit, disconnect the wiring on the washer reservoir level sensor, unscrew the large plastic cap nut and move the reservoir slightly to provide access.
2   Disconnect the wiring at the rear of the bulbholder.
3   Unscrew the knurled retaining nut (photo) and pull the lamp out in a forward direction.
4   Refitting is the reverse sequence to removal, but ensure that the two lugs engage with the guides in the headlamp unit (photo).

Headlamp unit

5   Remove the front direction indicator lamp as described previously.

6   Disconnect the vacuum hose and the wiring multi-plug at the rear of the lamp unit (photos).
7   Undo the inner end retaining bolt (photo) then disengage the finishing strip outer end by sliding it toward the centre of the car (photo). Remove the strip.
8   Undo the two upper retaining bolts (photo) and the single lower bolt (photo), then withdraw the unit from its location.
9   Refitting is the reverse sequence to removal, but ensure that the lower retaining lug engages with the slot in the bodywork (photo) before fitting the lower retaining screw. Tighten the mountings initially finger-tight and make any small corrections to the unit fitted position by turning the upper retaining nuts as necessary. Tighten the mountings securely after positioning.

Rear lamp cluster

10 From inside the luggage compartment, turn the two lock catches as far as they will go to the left and withdraw the bulb carrier from the lamp unit.
11 Disconnect the wiring multi-plug, then undo the six lamp cluster retaining nuts (photos).
12 Depress the two catches and remove the unit from the outside of the car (photos).
13 Refitting is the reverse sequence to removal.

24 Headlamp glass – removal and refitting

1   Remove the headlamp as described in the previous Section.
2   Using a screwdriver carefully release the eight retaining tags, four on the top and four on the bottom securing the glass to the headlamp unit (photo).
3   Remove the glass and frame as an assembly (photo) then pull off the lower rubber seal.
4   Refitting is the reverse sequence to removal.

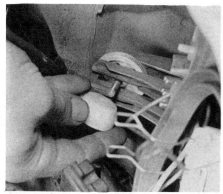

23.3 Unscrew the direction indicator lamp knurled nut

23.4 Direction indicator lamp upper retaining lug (arrowed)

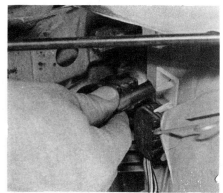

23.6A Disconnect the headlamp unit vacuum hose ...

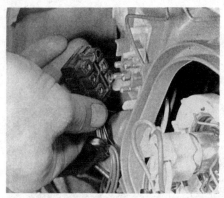

23.6B ... and multi-plug

23.7A Undo the finishing strip retaining bolt ...

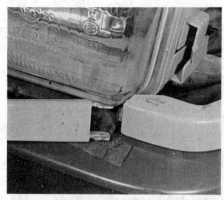

23.7B ... and disengage the outer end tags

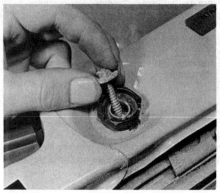

23.8A Undo the upper retaining bolts ...

23.8B ... and single lower bolt (arrowed)

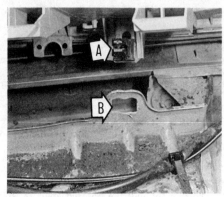

23.9 Ensure that the lower lug (A) enters the slot (B) when refitting

23.11A Disconnect the rear lamp cluster wiring multi-plug ...

23.11B ... undo the six nuts ...

23.12A ... depress the two catches ...

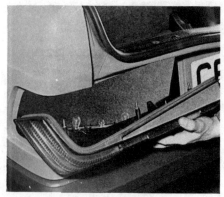

23.12B ... and remove the lamp unit

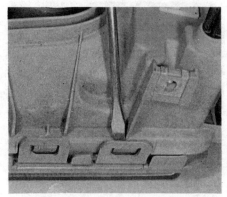

24.2 Release the retaining tags ...

24.3 ... and remove the headlamp glass

25 Headlamps – alignment

1 At periodic intervals the headlamp aim should be checked and if necessary adjusted.
2 Due to the light pattern of the lenses, optical beam setting equipment must be used to achieve satisfactory aim of the headlamps. It is recommended therefore that this work is carried out by a Mercedes-Benz dealer.

26 Headlamp height adjustment system – description

The headlamps are provided with a beam height adjustment system to enable the driver to regulate the beam height from inside the car to cater for different vehicle loading.

The system is operated by vacuum supplied by the inlet manifold and stored in a vacuum reservoir under the left-hand front wheel arch.

Control of the system is by a three position switch adjacent to the lighting switch on the facia. According to switch position, the vacuum supplied to the headlamp adjusting unit is regulated. The adjusting unit consists of a diaphragm which is connected to the movable headlamp lens by means of a pullrod having a stroke of approximately 3.0 mm (0.12 in). Vacuum applied to the diaphragm causes it to deflect which in turn moves the pullrod to raise or lower the headlamp beams.

Apart from periodically checking the condition of the vacuum hoses, the system does not require any maintenance or adjustment in service.

27 Windscreen wiper blades and arms – removal and refitting

Wiper blades (up to January 1985)
1 Lift the wiper blade and arm from the windscreen.

2 Depress the catch on the blade and withdraw the blade from the end of the arm.
3 Where an auxiliary blade is fitted at the base of the arm, extract the retaining clip and washer and remove the auxiliary blade.
4 Refitting is the reverse sequence to removal.

Wiper blades (January 1985 onwards)
5 Lift the wiper blade and arm from the windscreen.
6 Depress the plastic clip and lift the blade from the hooked part of the arm (photos).
7 Insert the blade, then move the clip up to lock. Release the wiper arm from the raised position by prising the spring catch on the underside of the arm and lower the blade onto the screen.

Wiper arm (up to January 1985)
8 Raise the bonnet to its vertical position by depressing the catch on the left-hand hinge and releasing the spring clip on the support strut.
9 Hinge back the plastic cover, then unscrew the nut securing the arm to the spindle. Remove the washer and pull off the arm.
10 Refitting is the reverse sequence to removal, but ensure that the blade rests on the windscreen in the parked position before pushing the arm onto the spindle.

Wiper arm (January 1985 onwards)
11 To remove the arm on the panoramic wiper assembly, release the wiper arm cover using a thin screwdriver and open the cover (photo).
12 Undo the wiper arm retaining bolt and withdraw the arm from the drive mechanism (photo).
13 Refit the arm onto the drive mechanism and push it up until the arm bolt hole is aligned with the machined slot in the pumping shaft (photo).
14 Refit the retaining bolt and close the cover.

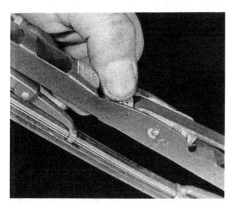
27.6A Depress the plastic clip ...

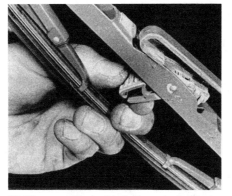
27.6B ... and lift the blade from the hooked part of the arm

27.11 Release the cover with a thin screwdriver

27.12 Undo the wiper arm retaining bolt

27.13 The bolt hole (A) must align with the slot (B) when refitting

28 Windscreen wiper motor and linkage – removal and refitting

Pre-January 1985 models

1 Disconnect the battery negative terminal.
2 Remove the wiper arm as described in the previous Section.
3 Prise off the closing cover on the top of the wiper arm spindle.
4 Push out the two clips, one each side at the front, securing the air intake cover over the plenum chamber.
5 Lift up the rubber seal to release the front part of the air intake cover.
6 Lift up the rear rubber seal on both sides then undo the two screws, one each side, securing the air intake cover to the bulkhead.
7 Withdraw the air intake cover from the plenum chamber.
8 Undo the three rear bolts and one front bolt securing the motor and linkage assembly to the bulkhead.
9 Remove the cover over the central electrics unit (fusebox) and undo the two retaining nuts and two screws.
10 Lift the central electrics unit up and forward, then disconnect the wiper motor wiring multi-plug from the unit base.

11 Manipulate the motor and linkage assembly out of its location.
12 Refitting is the reverse sequence to removal.

January 1985 models onwards

13 Remove the panoramic wiper arm as described in the previous Section.
14 Undo the two screws and clips, one each side at the front, securing the air intake cover over the plenum chamber (photo).
15 Lift up the rubber seal to release the front part of the air intake cover (photo).
16 Lift up the rear rubber seal on both sides, then undo the two screws, one each side, securing the air intake cover to the bulkhead (photo).
17 Withdraw the air intake cover from the plenum chamber (photo).
18 Undo the bolt and pull the front support bracket off the linkage stud (photos).
19 Undo the bolts securing the linkage to the bulkhead and withdraw it forward into the plenum chamber (photo).
20 Disconnect the motor wiring multi-plug and remove the assembly from the car (photos).
21 Refitting is the reverse sequence to removal.

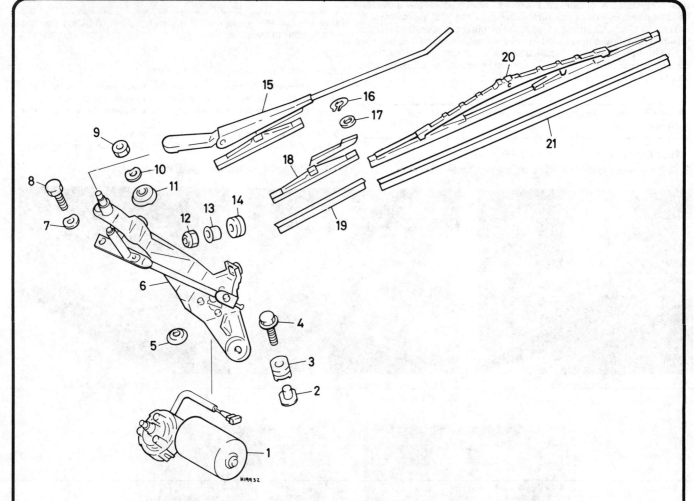

Fig. 12.8 Windscreen wiper motor and linkage – pre-January 1985 models (Sec 28)

Note: *Left-hand drive set-up shown – right-hand drive is a mirror-image*

1	Wiper motor	7	Washer	12	Nut	17	Washer
2	Cap nut	8	Bolt	13	Collar	18	Auxiliary blade
3	Spacer	9	Spindle nut	14	Spacer	19	Auxiliary blade rubber
4	Bolt	10	Washer	15	Wiper arm	20	Main blade
5	Washer	11	Closing cover	16	Auxiliary blade clip	21	Main blade rubber
6	Linkage and bracket						

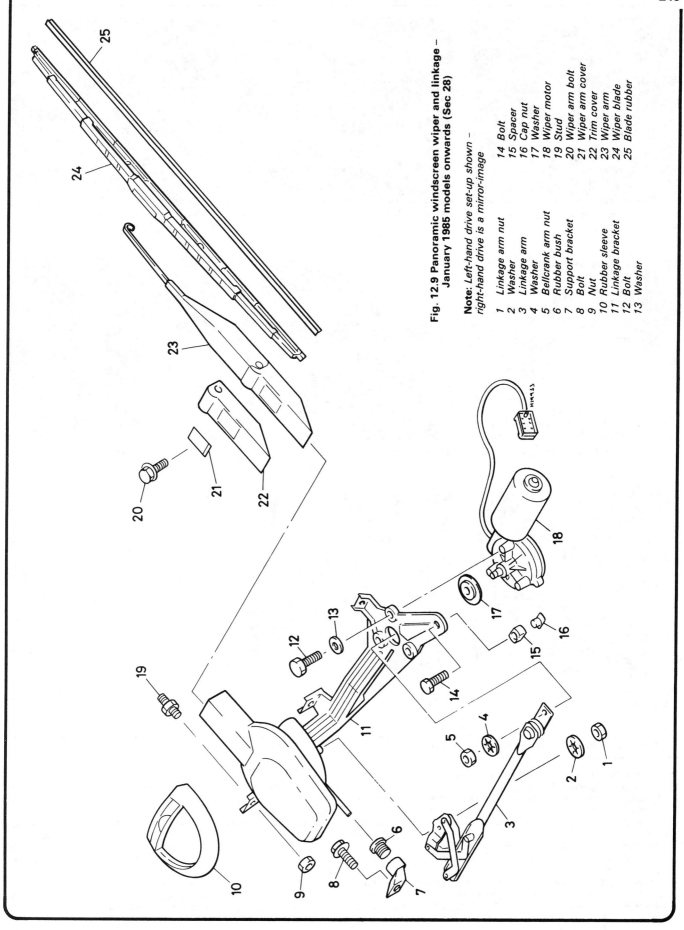

Fig. 12.9 Panoramic windscreen wiper and linkage –
January 1985 models onwards (Sec 28)

Note: *Left-hand drive set-up shown –
right-hand drive is a mirror-image*

1 Linkage arm nut	14 Bolt
2 Washer	15 Spacer
3 Linkage arm	16 Cap nut
4 Washer	17 Washer
5 Bellcrank arm nut	18 Wiper motor
6 Rubber bush	19 Stud
7 Support bracket	20 Wiper arm bolt
8 Bolt	21 Wiper arm cover
9 Nut	22 Trim cover
10 Rubber sleeve	23 Wiper arm
11 Linkage bracket	24 Wiper blade
12 Bolt	25 Blade rubber
13 Washer	

28.14 Undo the air intake cover front screws

28.15 Lift up the rubber seal

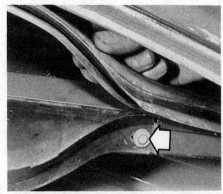

28.16 Lift up the rear rubber seal and undo the screw (arrowed) on both sides

28.17 Withdraw the air intake cover

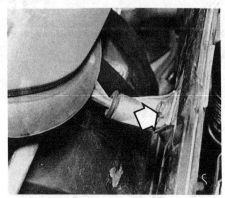

28.18A Undo the bolt (arrowed) ...

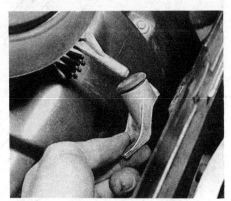

28.18B ... and remove the support bracket

28.19 Withdraw the assembly into the plenum chamber

28.20A Disconnect the motor wiring multi-plug ...

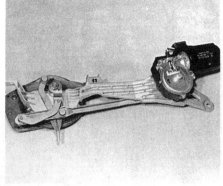

28.20B ... and remove the motor and linkage assembly

29 Windscreen wiper motor – removal and refitting

1   Remove the wiper motor and linkage assembly from the car as described in the previous Section.
2   Unscrew the retaining nut and remove the bellcrank arm from the motor spindle (photo).
3   Undo the three bolts and remove the motor from the linkage bracket.
4   Additionally, on the panoramic wiper assembly, the linkage arm can be removed from the wiper arm assembly after undoing the nut at the other end (photo).
5   Refitting is the reverse sequence to removal, but with the linkage and motor in the parked position, the bellcrank and linkage must be parallel with each other as the bellcrank is fitted to the motor spindle (photo).

30 Windscreen washer system – removal, refitting and adjustment

1   The windscreen washer system consists of a water reservoir located at the front right-hand side of the engine compartment, an electric pump attached to the reservoir and an electrically heated triple nozzle jet located in the centre of the bonnet, or two double nozzle jets located on each side of the bonnet, on cars equipped with the panoramic windscreen wiper. A water level indicator is also fitted to the reservoir on later models to inform the driver of low water supply in the reservoir.
2   To remove the reservoir, disconnect the wiring and water hoses at the pump and also the wiring plug at the water level indicator, if fitted.
3   Unscrew the large plastic cap nut, then lift the reservoir up and out of its location.

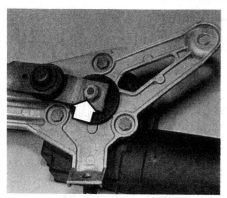

29.2 Undo the bellcrank arm retaining nut (arrowed)

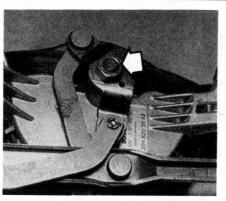

29.4 Linkage arm retaining nut (arrowed)

29.5 The bellcrank arm and linkage arm must be parallel and in line when refitting the bellcrank arm

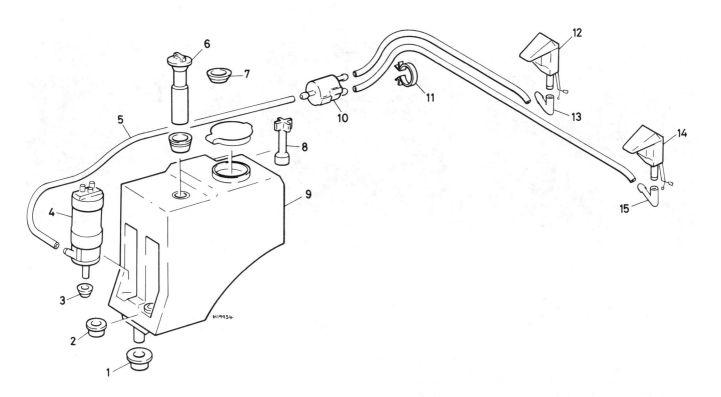

Fig. 12.10 Windscreen washer system components (Sec 30)

1 Reservoir mounting grommet	4 Washer pump	8 Cap nut	12 Right-hand jet
2 Pump grommet	5 Water hose	9 Reservoir	13 Connector
3 Pump seal	6 Water level indicator	10 Check valve	14 Left-hand jet
	7 Grommet	11 Clip	15 Connector

4   The pump is a push fit in the reservoir and can be removed by carefully prising it out. The pump is a sealed unit and cannot be repaired.

5   A check valve is located in the water hose alongside the right-hand front suspension strut turret. The valve can be removed after detaching the hoses.

6   To remove the jets, disconnect the water hose and electrical connection from within the aperture on the inside of the bonnet.

7   Push the jet upwards and withdraw it from the bonnet.

8   Refitting all the components is the reverse sequence to removal.

9   Adjust the nozzles using a pin so that the water contact areas on the windscreen are as shown in Fig. 12.11.

31 Horns – removal and refitting

1   The twin horns are attached to the support strut in front of the radiator, accessible with the bonnet open.

2   To remove the horns, disconnect the battery negative terminal, then unscrew the wiring terminal screws on each horn. Make a note of the wiring locations on each terminal (photo).

3   Undo the horn bracket attachments and remove the horns.

4   Refitting is the reverse sequence to removal.

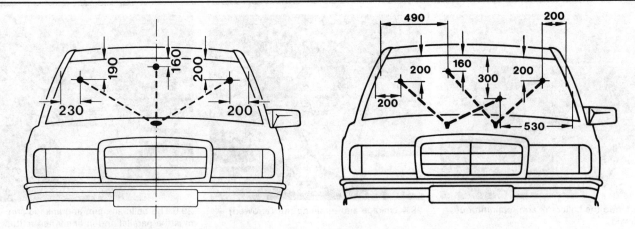

Fig. 12.11 Windscreen washer water contact areas on windscreen (Sec 30)

Left illustration – triple nozzle single jet
Right illustration – double nozzle twin jets
All dimensions in millimetres

31.2 Horn wiring terminal screws (arrowed)

32.3 Removing the radio with the removal tools

32.4 Disconnect the wiring at the rear of the radio

32 Radio/cassette player – removal and refitting

1   Disconnect the battery negative terminal.
2   According to the type of equipment fitted, the method of removal varies slightly. If there are two small holes vertically in line on each side of the radio faceplate, then the unit has a DIN standard attachment and is removed by inserting two special hooked removal tools into these holes to release the internal catches. These special tools may be purchased from radio accessory outlets, or can be made up from suitable wire rod such as welding rod (Fig. 12.12).
3   Insert the removal tools into the slots until they can be felt to engage with the catches. Now pull the unit forward out of its aperture (photo).
4   Disconnect the electrical connections and aerial lead at the rear of the radio (photo) and push the retaining clips inward to release the removal tools. Remove the unit from the car.
5   To refit, push the radio cassette player back into its aperture until the clips engage.
6   If the radio faceplate does not have holes for removal tools, then the unit is secured in position by means of the ashtray holder mountings.
7   Open the ashtray and undo the screws at the top of the ashtray holder.
8   Lower the ashtray and push the radio out of its aperture.
9   Disconnect the electrical connections and aerial lead at the rear and remove the radio from the car.
10   Refitting is the reverse sequence to removal.

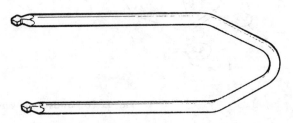

Fig. 12.12 Radio cassette player removal tool (Sec 32)

33 Front and rear speakers – removal and refitting

Front speakers

1   The front speakers are located at each side of the facia at the top.
2   Undo the two screws and remove the speaker grille (photo).
3   Using a plastic wedge, carefully ease the speaker out of its location (photo).
4   Disconnect the wiring and remove the speaker.
5   Refitting is the reverse sequence to removal. If two colour marks are visible on the speaker rim, these should point towards the rear of the car when the speaker is fitted.

33.2 Speaker grille retaining screw

33.3 Speaker removal

Rear speakers

6   The rear speakers are located on each side of the rear parcel shelf.
7   Using a short screwdriver, undo the four screws and remove the speaker grille.
8   Undo the speaker retaining screws and withdraw the speaker from the parcel shelf.
9   Disconnect the wiring and remove the speaker.
10 Refitting is the reverse sequence to removal.

34 Radio aerial – removal and refitting

1   Disconnect the battery negative terminal.
2   Remove the inner trim covering on the left-hand side of the luggage compartment.
3   Disconnect the aerial lead, wiring connections and earth strap from the aerial motor.
4   Undo the retaining bolts and withdraw the unit from inside the luggage compartment.
5   Refitting is the reverse sequence to removal.

35 Fault diagnosis – electrical system

Symptom	Reason(s)
Starter fails to turn engine	Battery discharged or defective
	Battery terminal and/or earth leads loose
	Starter motor connections loose
	Starter solenoid faulty
	Starter brushes worn or sticking
	Starter commutator dirty or worn
	Starter field coils earthed
	Starter armature faulty
Starter turns engine very slowly	Battery discharged
	Starter motor connections loose
	Starter brushes worn or sticking
Starter noisy	Pinion or ring gear teeth badly worn
	Mounting bolts loose
Battery will not hold charge	Plates defective
	Electrolyte level too low
	Alternator drivebelt slipping
	Alternator or regulator faulty
	Short in electrical circuit
Ignition light stays on	Alternator faulty
	Alternator drivebelt broken
Ignition light fails to come on	Warning bulb blown
	Warning light open circuit
	Alternator faulty
Instrument readings increase with engine speed	Voltage stabilizer faulty
Fuel or temperature gauge gives no reading	Wiring open circuit
	Sender unit faulty

35 Fault diagnosis – electrical system

Symptom	Reason(s)
Fuel or temperature gauge gives maximum reading all the time	Wiring short circuit Sender unit or gauge faulty
Lights inoperative	Bulb blown Fuse blown Switch faulty Wiring open circuit Connection corroded
Failure of component motor	Commutator dirty or burnt Armature faulty Brushes sticking or worn Armature shaft bearings seized Field coils faulty Fuse blown Wiring loose or broken
Failure of an individual component	Wiring loose or broken Fuse blown Switch faulty Component faulty

Wiring diagrams commence overleaf

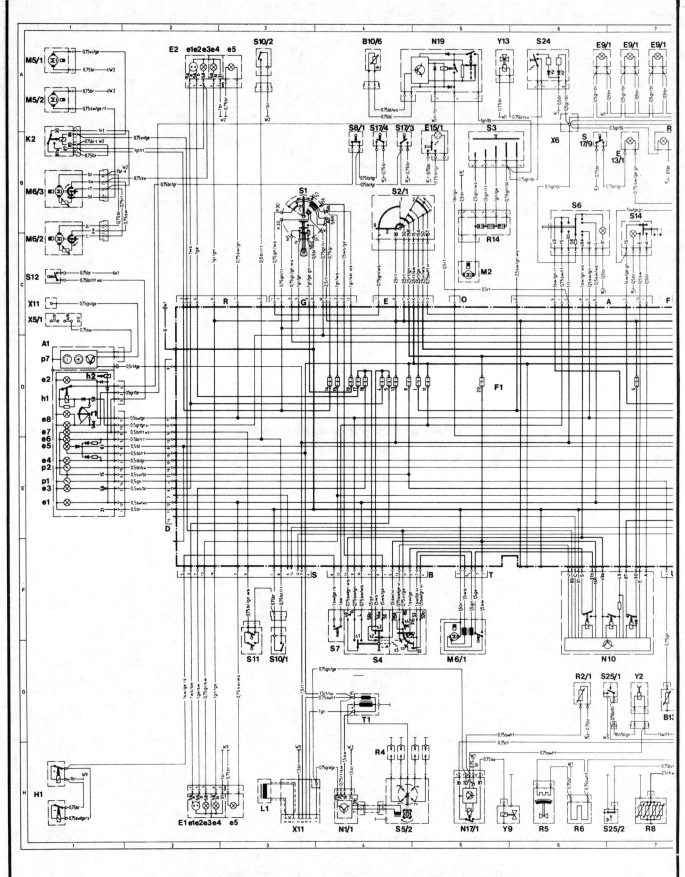

Fig. 12.13 Wiring diagram for 190 models up to chassis number 000 001-017 940

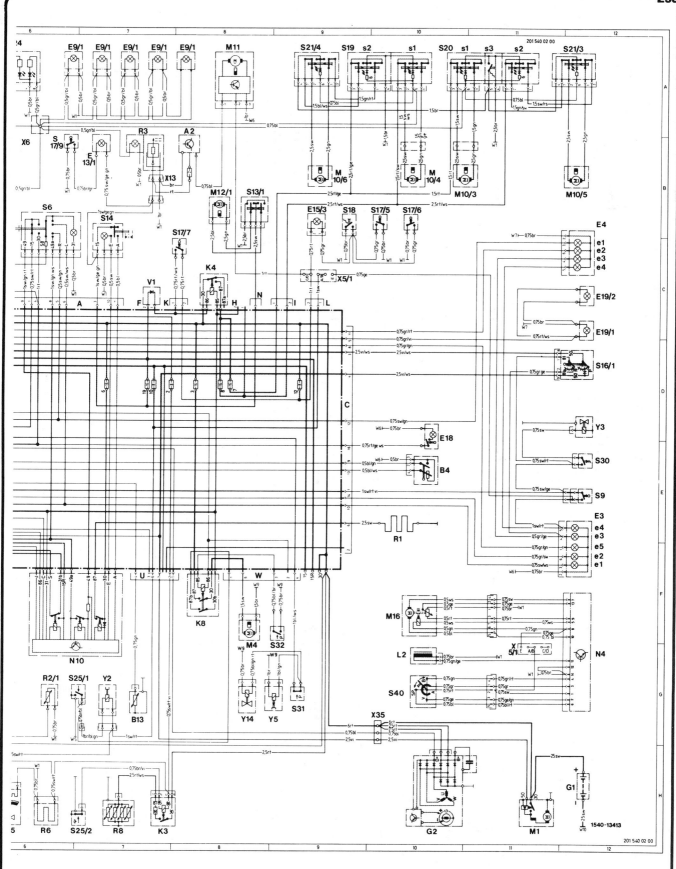

Fig. 12.13 Wiring diagram for 190 models up to chassis number 000 001-017 940 (continued)

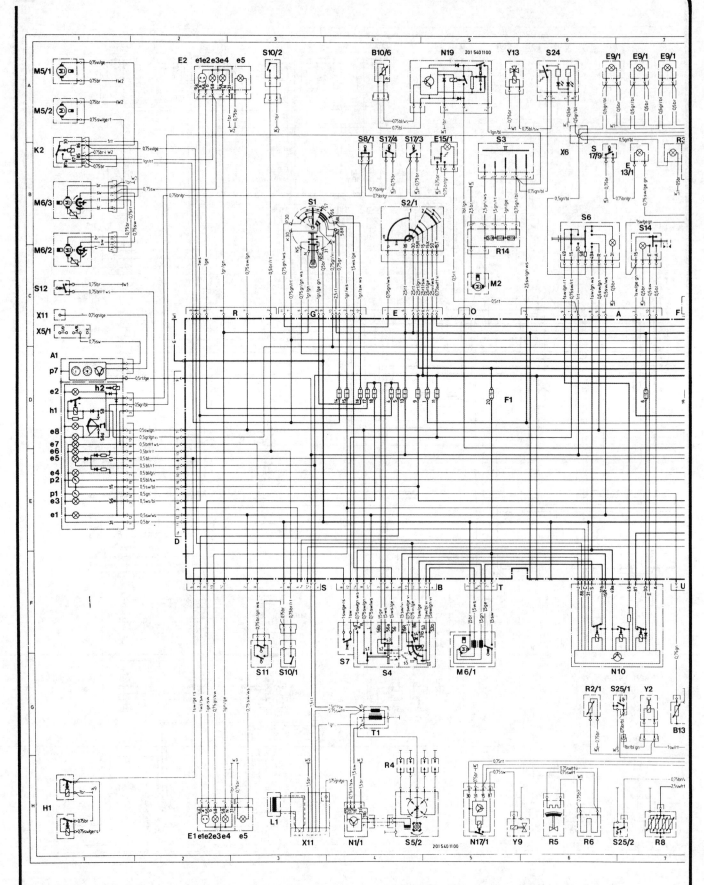

Fig. 12.14 Wiring diagram for 190 models from chassis number 1A 000 001-109 999 or 1F 000 001-023 656

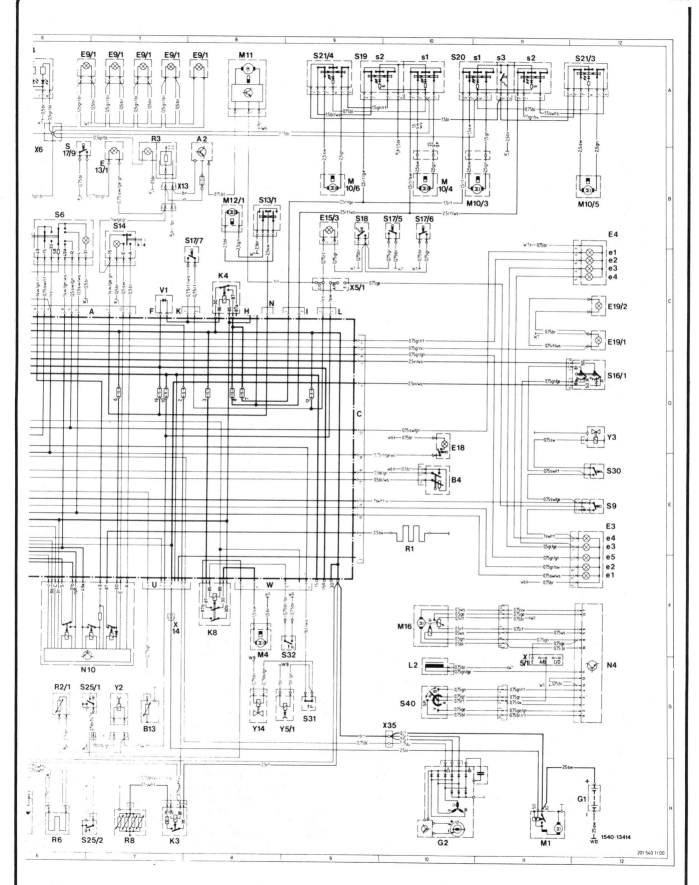

255

Fig. 12.14 Wiring diagram for 190 models from chassis number 1A 000 001-109 999 or 1F 000 001-023 656 (continued)

Key to Figs. 12.13 and 12.14

Not all items are fitted to all models

Component		Location	Component		Location
A1	Instrument cluster	1D	L2	Road speed sensor	10G
e1	Indicator warning, left	1E	M1	Starter motor	11H
e2	Indicator warning, right	1D	M2	Blower motor	5C
e3	Main beam warning	1E	M4	Auxiliary fan	8F/8G
e4	Fuel reserve warning	1E	M5/1	Washer pump	1A
e5	Charge indicator	1E	M5/2	Washer pump, headlamps	1A
e6	Brake pad wear indicator	1E	M6/1	Wiper motor	5G
e7	Brake fluid/handbrake indicator	1D	M6/2	Wiper motor, headlamp, left	1C
e8	Instrument lighting	1D	M6/3	Wiper motor, headlamp, right	1B
h1	Warning buzzer	1D	M10/3	Window lift motor, front left	10B/11B
h2	Indicator warning, acoustic	1D	M10/4	Window lift motor, front right	10B
r1	Instrument lighting rheostat	1D	M10/5	Window lift motor, rear left	12B
p1	Coolant temperature gauge	1E	M10/6	Window lift motor, rear right	9B
p2	Fuel gauge	1E	M11	Electric aerial	8A
p7	Clock/Tachometer	1D	M12/1	Sunroof motor	8B
A2	Radio	8A	M16	Actuator, 'Tempomat'	10F
B4	Fuel gauge sensor	10E	N1/1	Electronic ignition switching unit	4H
B10/6	Temperature sensor, evaporator	4A	N4	Control unit, 'Tempomat'	12G
B13	Coolant temperature sensor	7G	N10	Combination relay – indicators, heated rear window, wiper motor	6G
E1	Headlamp unit, left	2H	N17/1	Fuel cut-off valve relay	5H
e1	Main beam	2H	N19	Air conditioning control unit	5A
e2	Dipped beam	2H	R1	Heated rear window	10E
e3	Sidelamp	2H	R2/1	Washer nozzle heater	6G
e4	Foglamp	2H	R3	Cigar lighter/front ashtray lighting	7A
e5	Indicator	3H	R4	Spark plugs	4H
E2	Headlamp unit, right	2A	R5	Pull-down valve heater coil	6H
e1	Main beam	2A	R6	Automatic choke heater coil	6H
e2	Dipped beam	2A	R8	Inlet manifold heater	7H
e3	Sidelamp	2A	R14	Blower motor ballast resistor	5C
e4	Foglamp	2A	R21	Auxiliary air valve heater coil	8H
e5	Indicator	3A	S1	Rotary light switch	3B
E3	Rear lamp unit, left	12E	S2/1	Ignition starter switch	4B
e1	Indicator	12F	S3	Air volume switch	5A
e2	Tail/parking lamp	12F	S4	Combination switch	4G
e3	Reversing lamp	12E	s1	Indicator switch	4F
e4	Brake lamp	12E	s2	Headlamp flasher switch	4F
e5	Rear foglamp	12F	s3	Dimmer switch	4F
E4	Rear lamp unit, right	12B	s4	Washer switch	4F
e1	Indicator	12C	s5	Wiper speed switch	4F/4G
e2	Tail/parking lamp	12C	s5	I Intermittent wipe	4F/4G
e3	Reversing lamp	12C	s5	II Slow wipe	4G
e4	Brake lamp	12C	s5	III Fast wipe	5G
E9/1	Heater control lighting	6A to 8A	S5/2	Ignition distributor	4H
E13/1	Glovebox lamp	7B	S6	Hazard flasher switch	6B
E15/1	Interior lamp, front	5A	S7	Horn contact	4G
E15/3	Interior lamp, rear	9B	S8/1	Lights-on buzzer contact	4A
E18	Boot lamp	10D	S9	Stop-lamp switch	12E
E19/1	Number plate lamp, left	12C	S10/1	Brake pad wear contact, front left	3G
E19/2	Number plate lamp, right	12C	S10/2	Brake pad wear contact, front right	3A
F1	Central electrics unit	5D	S11	Brake fluid indicator switch	3G
G1	Battery	12H	S12	Handbrake indicator switch	1C
G2	Alternator and regulator	10H	S13/1	Electric sunroof switch	8B
H1	Dual-tone horns	1H	S14	Heated rear window switch	7B
K2	Headlamp cleaning relay	1B	S16/1	Starter interlock/reversing light switch	12D
K3	Inlet manifold heater relay	7H	S17/3	Door switch, front left	4A
K4	Electric window relay	8C	S17/4	Door switch, front right	4A
K8	Relay for auxiliary fan/engine fan	8F	S17/5	Door switch, rear left	10B
L1	TDC sensor	3H			

Key to Figs. 12.13 and 12.14 (continued)

Not all items are fitted to all models

Component		Location	Component		Location
S17/6	Door switch, rear right	10B	W1	Main earth (behind instruments)	
S17/7	Door switch, comfort circuit, left	8B	W2	Earth, front right (near lamp unit)	
S17/9	Glovebox lamp switch	6B	W3	Earth, front left wheel arch (igntion coil)	
S18	Rear interior lamp switch	9B	W4	Earth, front interior lamp	
S19	Switch group, electric windows, right	9A	W5	Earth, engine	
s1	Window switch, front right	10A	W6	Earth, boot wheel arch, left	
s2	Window switch, rear right	9A	W7	Earth, boot wheel arch, right	
S20	Switch group, electric windows, left	10A	W9	Earth, front left (near lamp unit)	
s1	Window switch, front left	10A/11A	W10	Earth, battery	
s2	Window switch, rear left	11A	X5/1	Interior cable connector	1C/9C/11G
s3	Safety switch, rear electric windows	11A	X6	Cable connector	6B
S21/3	Window switch, rear left	12A	X11	Diagnostic socket	1C/3H
S21/4	Window switch, rear right	9A	X13	Cigar lighter connection	7B
S24	Fresh/recirculated air switch	6A	X14	Plug connection	7F
S25/1	Temperature switch, 100°C	7G	X35	Cable connector, battery	10G
S25/2	Temperature switch, 40°C	7H	Y2	Engine fan solenoid	7G
S30	Kickdown switch	12E	Y3	Switchover valve, automatic transmission	12D
S31	Refrigerant compressor switch	9G	Y5/1	Refrigerant compressor solenoid	9G
S32	Auxiliary fan switch	9F/9G	Y9	Fuel cut-off valve	5H
S40	'Tempomat' switch	10G	Y13	Switchover valve, fresh/recirculated air flap	5A
T1	Ignition coil	4G	Y14	Switchover valve, idle speed stabilisation	8G
V1	Comfort circuit diode	7C			

Colour codes

bl	Blue	nf	Neutral
br	brown	rs	Pink
el	Ivory	rt	Red
ge	Yellow	sw	Black
gn	Green	vi	Purple
gr	Grey	ws	White

Wire codes

Example: Wire code 1.5 gr/rt
Basic colour – grey
Tracer colour – red
Cross-sectional area of wire = 1.5 mm²

258

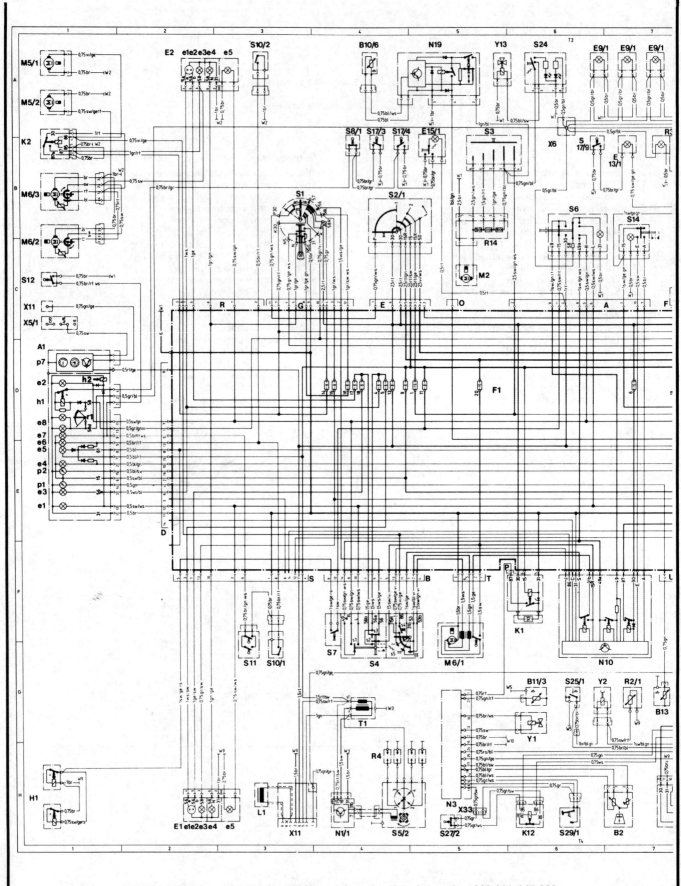

Fig. 12.15 Wiring diagram for 190 E models up to chassis number 000 001-045 803

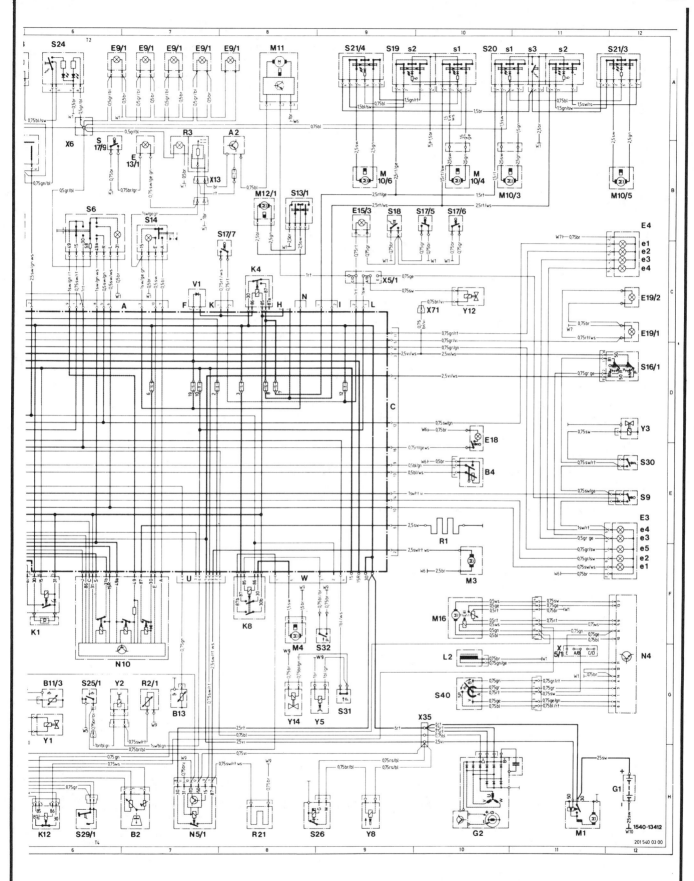

Fig. 12.15 Wiring diagram for 190 E models up to chassis number 000 001-045 803 (continued)

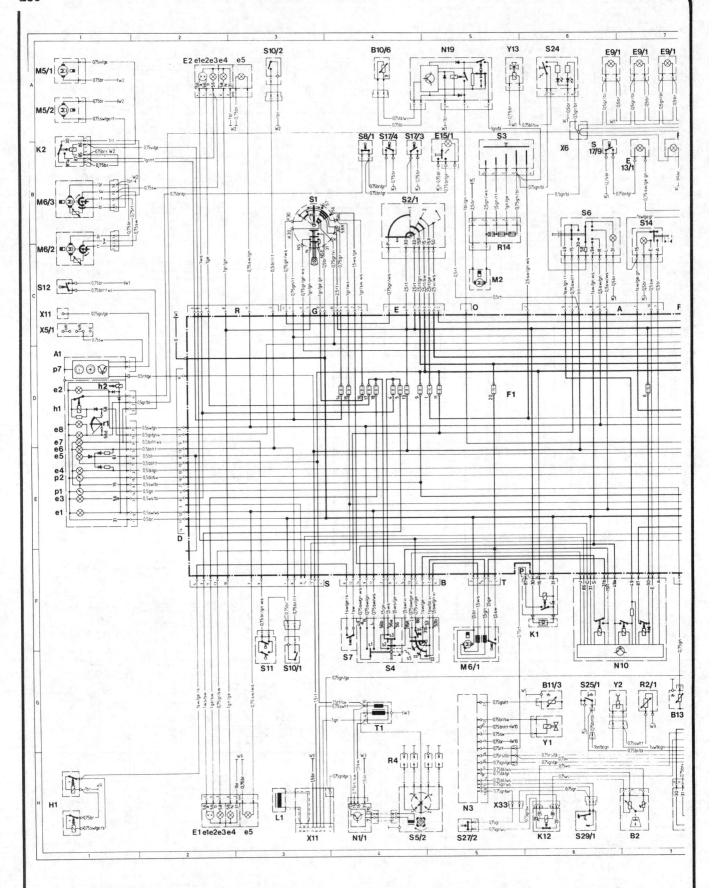

Fig. 12.16 Wiring diagram for 190 E models from chassis number 1A 000 001-153 269 or 1F 000 001-050 579

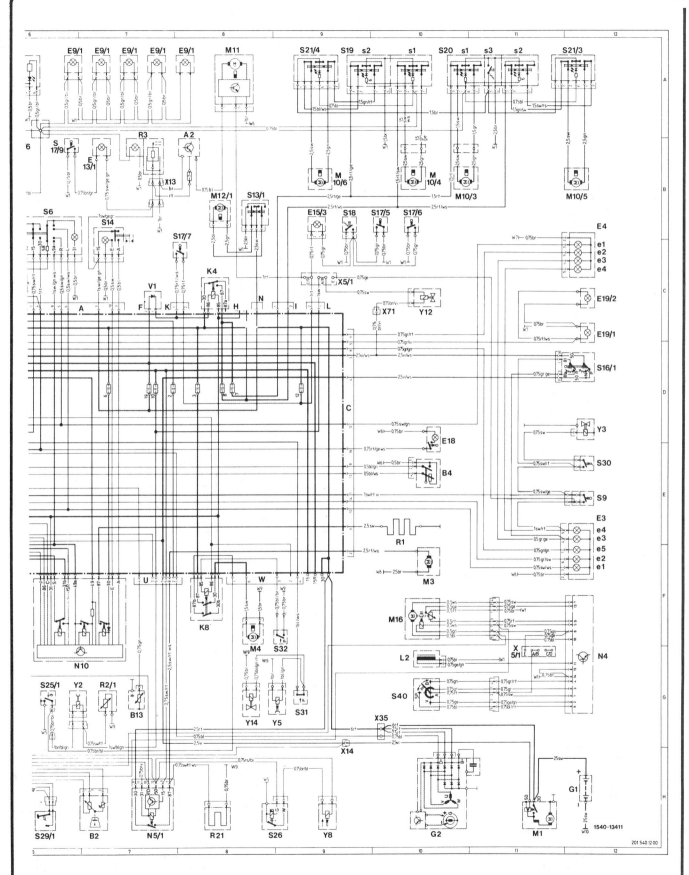

Fig. 12.16 Wiring diagram for 190 E models from chassis number 1A 000 153-269 999 or 1F 000 001-050 579 (continued)

Key to Figs. 12.15 and 12.16

Not all items are fitted to all models

Component		Location
A1	Instrument cluster	1D
e1	Indicator warning, left	1E
e2	Indicator warning, right	1D
e3	Main beam warning	1E
e4	Fuel reserve warning	1E
e5	Charge indicator	1E
e6	Brake pad wear indicator	1E
e7	Brake fluid/handbrake indicator	1D
e8	Instrument lighting	1D
h1	Warning buzzer	1D
h2	Indicator warning, acoustic	1D
r1	Instrument lighting rheostat	1D
p1	Coolant temperature gauge	1E
p2	Fuel gauge	1E
p7	Clock/Tachometer	1D
A2	Radio	8A
B2	Air volume meter sensor	7H
B4	Fuel gauge sensor	10E
B10/6	Temperature sensor, evaporator	4A
B11/3	Coolant temperature sensor, KE	6G
B13	Coolant temperature sensor, gauge	7G
E1	Headlamp unit, left	2H
e1	Main beam	2H
e2	Dipped beam	2H
e3	Sidelamp	2H
e4	Foglamp	2H
e5	Indicator	3H
E2	Headlamp unit, right	2A
e1	Main beam	2A
e2	Dipped beam	2A
e3	Sidelamp	2A
e4	Foglamp	2A/3A
e5	Indicator	3A
E3	Rear lamp unit, left	12E
e1	Indicator	12F
e2	Tail/parking lamp	12F
e3	Reversing lamp	12E/12F
e4	Brake lamp	12E
e5	Rear foglamp	12F
E4	Rear lamp unit, right	12B
e1	Indicator	12C
e2	Tail/parking lamp	12C
e3	Reversing lamp	12C
e4	Brake lamp	12C
E9/1	Heater control lighting	6A to 8A
E13/1	Glovebox lamp	7B
E15/1	Interior lamp, front	5A
E15/3	Interior lamp, rear	9B
E18	Boot lamp	10D
E19/1	Number plate lamp, left	12C
E19/2	Number plate lamp, right	12C
F1	Central electrics unit	5D
G1	Battery	12H
G2	Alternator and regulator	10H
H1	Dual-tone horns	1H
K1	Overvoltage protection relay	6F
K2	Headlamp cleaning relay	1B

Component		Location
K4	Electric window relay	8C
K8	Relay for auxiliary fan/engine fan	8F
K12	'Tempomat' deceleration relay	6H
L1	TDC sensor	3H
L2	Road speed sensor	10G
M1	Starter motor	11H
M2	Blower motor	5C
M3	Fuel pump	10F
M4	Auxiliary fan	8G
M5/1	Washer pump	1A
M5/2	Headlamp washer pump	1A
M6/1	Wiper motor	5G
M6/2	Wiper motor, headlamp, left	1C
M6/3	Wiper motor, headlamp, right	1B
M10/3	Window lift motor, front left	10B
M10/4	Window lift motor, front right	10B
M10/5	Window lift motor, rear left	12B
M10/6	Window lift motor, rear right	9B
M11	Electric aerial	8A
M12/1	Sunroof motor	8B
M16	Actuator, 'Tempomat'	10F
N1/1	Electronic ignition switching unit	4H
N4	Control unit, 'Tempomat'	12G
N5/1	Fuel pump relay	7H
N10	Combination relay – indicators, heated rear window, wiper motor	6G
N19	Air conditioning control unit	5A
R1	Heated rear window	10E
R2/1	Washer nozzle heater	7G
R3	Cigar lighter/front ashtray lighting	7A
R4	Spark plugs	4H
R14	Blower motor ballast resistor	5C
R21	Auxiliary air valve heater coil	8H
S1	Rotary light switch	3B
S2/1	Ignition starter switch	4B
S3	Air volume switch	5A
S4	Combination switch	4G
s1	Indicator switch	4F
s2	Headlamp flasher switch	4F
s3	Dimmer switch	4F
s4	Washer switch	4F
s5	Wiper speed switch	4G
s5 I	Intermittent wipe	4G
s5 II	Slow wipe	4G
s5 III	Fast wipe	5G
S5/2	Ignition distributor	4H
S6	Hazard flasher switch	6B
S7	Horn contact	4G
S8/1	Lights-on buzzer contact	4A
S9	Stop-lamp switch	12E
S10/1	Brake pad wear contact, front left	3G
S10/2	Brake pad wear contact, front right	3A
S11	Brake fluid indicator switch	3G
S12	Handbrake indicator switch	1C
S13/1	Electric sunroof switch	8B
S14	Heated rear window switch	7B
S16/1	Starter interlock/reversing light switch	12D

Key to Figs. 12.15 and 12.16 (continued)

Not all items are fitted to all models

Component		Location
S17/3	Door switch, front left	4A
S17/4	Door switch, front right	4A
S17/5	Door switch, rear left	10B
S17/6	Door switch, rear right	10B
S17/7	Door switch, comfort circuit, left	8B
S17/9	Glovebox lamp switch	6B
S18	Rear interior lamp switch	9B
S19	Switch group, electric windows, right	9A
s1	Window switch, front right	10A
s2	Window switch, rear right	9A
S20	Switch group, electric windows, left	10A
s1	Window switch, front left	10A
s2	Window switch, rear left	11A
s3	Safety switch, rear electric windows	11A
S21/3	Window switch, rear left	12A
S21/4	Window switch, rear right	9A
S24	Fresh/recirculated air switch	6A
S25/1	Temperature switch, 100°C	6G
S26	Thermotime switch	8H/9H
S27/2	Deceleration microswitch	5H
S29/1	Throttle valve switch, full load	6H
S30	Kickdown switch	12E
S31	Refrigerant compressor switch	9G
S32	Auxiliary fan switch	9G
S40	'Tempomat' switch	10G
T1	Ignition coil	4G
V1	Comfort circuit diode	7C

Component		Location
W1	Main earth (behind instruments)	
W2	Earth, front right (near lamp unit)	
W3	Earth, front left wheel arch (ignition coil)	
W4	Earth, front interior lamp	
W5	Earth, engine	
W6	Earth, boot wheel arch, left	
W7	Earth, boot wheel arch, right	
W9	Earth, front left (near lamp unit)	
W10	Earth, battery	
X5/1	Interior cable connector	1C/9C/11G
X6	Cable connector	6B
X11	Diagnostic socket	1C/3H
X13	Cigar lighter connection	7B
X14	Plug connection	9H
X33	Plug connection, KE/'Tempomat'	5H
X35	Cable connector, battery	10G
X71	Plug connection, switchover valve idle speed stabilisation	10C
Y1	Electrohydraulic actuator	6G
Y2	Engine fan solenoid	6G
Y3	Switchover valve, automatic transmission	12D
Y5	Refrigerant compressor solenoid	9G
Y8	Starting valve	9H
Y12	Switchover valve, idle speed increase	10C
Y13	Switchover valve, fresh/recirculated air flap	5A
Y14	Switchover valve, idle speed stabilisation	8G

Colour codes

bl	Blue	nf	Neutral
br	brown	rs	Pink
el	Ivory	rt	Red
ge	Yellow	sw	Black
gn	Green	vi	Purple
gr	Grey	ws	White

Wire codes

Example: Wire code 1.5 gr/rt
Basic colour – grey
Tracer colour – red
Cross-sectional area of wire = 1.5 mm²

Index